Cornelis Bennema

The Power of Saving Wisdom

An Investigation of Spirit and Wisdom in Relation
to the Soteriology of the Fourth Gospel

WIPF & STOCK · Eugene, Oregon

CORNELIS BENNEMA, born 1964; 1995 BA in Theology at London Bible College/Brunel University, London; 2001 Ph.D. in London; since 2002 Lecturer of New Testament Studies at SAIACS (South Asia Institute of Advanced Christian Studies) in Bangalore, India.

Wipf and Stock Publishers
199 W 8th Ave, Suite 3
Eugene, OR 97401

The Power of Saving Wisdom
An Investigation of Spirit and Wisdom
in Relation to the Soteriology of the Fourth Gospel
By Bennema, Cornelis
Copyright©2002 Mohr Siebeck
ISBN 13: 978-1-55635-737-4
ISBN 10: 1-55635-737-0
Publication date 12/7/2007
Previously published by Mohr Siebeck, 2002

For my Friend
who laid down his life for me
to give me life
(John 6.51; 15.13)

Preface

During my second year as an undergraduate student in theology at London Bible College, my view of the gift of the Spirit as a 'second blessing' dissolved rapidly when I was challenged by Max Turner's lectures on the teaching and ministry of Jesus. Nevertheless, my interest in the Spirit, dating prior to my undergraduate studies, only intensified. Consequently, I started to research the role of the Spirit in John's Gospel under Professor Turner's supervision, resulting in a thesis for which I was awarded with a Ph.D. by Brunel University (UK) in June 2001. This book is a slightly revised version of my doctoral thesis.

My research has inevitably been more extensive than what is included in this thesis. Attention is drawn particularly to two articles which further substantiate or develop parts of the argument contained within it. I have investigated the Jewish wisdom literature of the OT and the intertestamental period (ITP) as a whole, and the results of this have been presented in C. Bennema, 'The Strands of Wisdom Tradition in Intertestamental Judaism: Origins, Developments and Characteristics', *TynB* 52 (2001) 61-82. I have also examined the moment, nature and significance of the gift of the Spirit in the Fourth Gospel, and its findings will appear in C. Bennema, 'The Giving of the Spirit in John's Gospel — A New Proposal?', *EvQ* 74 (forthcoming, 2002).

Two studies, which came to me at a late stage, partly overlap with my chapter 3, which deals with John's overall soteriology (S. Hamid-Khani, *Revelation and Concealment of Christ: A Theological Inquiry into the Elusive Language of the Fourth Gospel* [WUNT II/120; Tübingen: Mohr Siebeck, 2000]; J.G. van der Watt, *Family of the King: Dynamics of Metaphor in the Gospel according to John* [BIS 47; Leiden: Brill, 2000]). However, I arrived at my own understanding of John's soteriology, independently — and had presented the main parts of my analysis on John's soteriology in two papers prior to the publication of their works: 'Spirit & Salvation in the Fourth Gospel' at Aberdeen University, 17 September 1999, and 'An Introduction to and a Model of Johannine Soteriology' at London Bible College, 26 June 2000.

Some further minor points deserve mention. First, due to space restrictions, the footnotes do not contain an exhaustive list of references, but 'merely' show interaction with key protagonists. Second, my spelling of the term 'judgment' is perhaps more conventional in strictly legal contexts, but since the Fourth Gospel has forensic connotations, this spelling is used throughout, whether or not the cotext has specifically 'forensic' overtones. Third, in this study I have preferred the phrase 'the Father and Son' to 'the Father and the Son' in order to emphasize the oneness and intimacy of their relationship, i.e., our formulation means 'the Father-and-Son' in an even tighter relationship than would be implied by 'the Father and the Son'. Fourth, with regard to the use of models (see ch. 3 section 7), I recognize that a model is, by its very nature, an abstraction of reality (in order to assist in understanding reality), and hence a simplification; I hope it will not prove an *over*-simplification. Finally, biblical references and quotations in English are taken from the NRSV unless specified otherwise.

I would like to express my thanks to several people and organisations that have contributed in the completion of this work.

First of all, I am greatly indebted to Professor Max Turner, who supervised this work in thesis form, for his guidance, competence, patience and support. His probing has challenged and stretched me in my understanding both of research and of John.

I am also grateful to the community of London Bible College for having provided a stimulating intellectual and spiritual environment, and for having offered the opportunity to be a tutor for two years.

I would like to thank my fellow-members of the 'Greek Club' (Annette Glaw, Desta Heliso, André Munzinger and Volker Rabens) for their friendship, support and stimulating discussions.

I want to express my deep appreciation to the Laing Trust, my homechurch 'de Ark' in Holland, Perivale Mission Church in London and to many friends for their financial generosity over the years, which enabled me to do my research.

I want to thank Dr Mohan Uddin, Mr David Wallington and Ms Helen Wright for proofreading various parts of my work.

I am also very thankful to my parents for bringing me up in a Christian home and for their unwavering support throughout my life.

I am especially grateful to Professor Dr Jörg Frey who read and accepted this work for publication in the WUNT II monograph series, and to Herr Dr Georg Siebeck and the staff of Mohr Siebeck in Tübingen for all their assistance.

Above all, I would like to thank God for his inspiration, guidance, strength and joy in my research. My greatest desire is that this work will please God and be acceptable to him.

Cornelis Bennema

December 2001

Table of Contents

Part III
Conclusions and Recommendations

Chapter 6

Appendices

Appendix 1

Appendix 2

List of Abbreviations

General abbreviations and abbreviations of periodicals, series, lexicons and publishers follow the rules of *IATG*² (S.M. Schwertner, *Internationales Abkürzungsverzeichnis für Theologie und Grenzgebiete* [Berlin-New York: Walter de Gruyter, 1992²]). The following abbreviations are used in addition to or where they differ from the *IATG*².

BCE	Before Common Era
BIS	Biblical Interpretation Series
CE	Common Era
CUP	Cambridge University Press
DSS	Dead Sea Scrolls
ITP	Intertestamental period
IVP	Inter-Varsity Press
JPT	*Journal of Pentecostal Theology*
JPT.S	*Journal of Pentecostal Theology* Supplement Series
NIV	New International Version
NRSV	New Revised Standard Version
NSBT	New Studies in Biblical Theology
OBS	Oxford Bible Series
OUP	Oxford University Press
RSV	Revised Standard Version
SAP	Sheffield Academic Press
SBL.SBS	Society of Biblical Literature Sources for Biblical Study
TDNT	G. Kittel and G. Friedrich (eds.), *Theological Dictionary of the New Testament* (10 vols.; Transl. G. Bromiley; Grand Rapids: Eerdmans, 1964-76)
TrinJ	*Trinity Journal*
UMI	University Microfilms International
WBC	Word Biblical Commentary

Chapter 1

Introduction

1. Rationale, Aim and Task

Salvation is one of the most fundamental concepts of the Christian faith. Questions, such as 'What is salvation?', 'How does one enter into salvation?' and 'How does one stay in salvation?', must be answered adequately in order to understand the Christian faith. To these important questions we add an additional one, namely, 'What is the role of the Spirit in all this?'. We will examine the Fourth Gospel to address these questions and look especially at the concept of W/wisdom because we have found this concept to be significant in explaining the relationship between Spirit and salvation.[1] Scholars have made significant contributions in the areas of John's understanding of the Spirit, of salvation and of W/wisdom, but in general these three areas have not been related or synthesized. The task of this study, therefore, is an investigation of the relationship between the pneumatology and soteriology of the Fourth Gospel along the lines of W/wisdom, i.e., an examination of the *interrelationship* between the Johannine conceptions of Spirit, salvation and W/wisdom, in order to elucidate John's Pneumatic Wisdom Soteriology. Before we can outline more precisely our strategy, however, we need to examine recent Johannine scholarship concerning the questions and issues that we have raised.

2. Overview of Contemporary Johannine Scholarship

In this section we shall examine the scholarly contribution towards: (i) the Johannine concept of salvation in general; (ii) Jesus as, and in relation to, Wisdom, and the relationship between W/wisdom and salvation; (iii) the relationship between Spirit, salvation and W/wisdom. Moreover, scholars'

---

[1] The term 'Wisdom' will be used to denote the personification of an attribute of God; in all other cases we will use 'wisdom' (e.g., to express that which God or Wisdom possesses, gives or mediates).

views will be presented in accordance with and in direct proportion to their importance and contribution to our agenda. The originality of this survey lies in its focus on how, i.e., the extent to which, scholarship has (or has not) provided an adequate synthesis.

2.1. Salvation

This subsection has three foci: John's concept of salvation in general, the role of faith in salvation, and the realized dimension of salvation in Jesus' ministry.

2.1.1. Salvation

Our agenda consists of four leading questions. How is salvation depicted in John? What or who leads to and maintains this salvation? What is the place of the cross in salvation? How is salvation mediated?

Cullmann argues that for John salvation is fellowship with the exalted Lord, which is created and maintained through the sacraments because they actualize the presence of the exalted Lord among the community of believers.[2] Dodd also interprets salvation relationally, in that eternal life is the personal (comm)union of the believer with Jesus by mutual indwelling, reproducing the archetypal mutual indwelling of Father and Son.[3]

Contrary to Cullmann's view of salvation through the sacraments stands Bultmann's concept of salvation through revelation.[4] For Bultmann, the starting-point is the human quest for self-understanding, which results in the quest for God because of the human existential inclination to God.[5] Salvation, then, is the reception of authentic self-understanding — the understanding of one's own personal existence in relation to God, namely, that a person is created by God — which results in the transition into eschatological existence.[6] This salvation, i.e., this authentic self-understanding and its consequent transference into this new mode of eschatological existence, can only be received through faith in the

---

[2] O. Cullmann, *Early Christian Worship* (Transl. A.S. Todd and J.B. Torrance; London: SCM Press, 1953) 37-38, 58, 117-19. Cf. R.E. Brown, *The Gospel according to John: Introduction, Translation, and Notes* (AncB 29; 2 vols.; London: Chapman, 1971) 1:507; R. Schnackenburg, *The Gospel according to St John* (3 vols.; London: Burns & Oates, 1968-82) 1:525.

[3] C.H. Dodd, *The Interpretation of the Fourth Gospel* (Cambridge: CUP, 1953) 194-97, 397-98. Cf. Schnackenburg, *Gospel*, 2:355-56; S.C. Barton, *The Spirituality of the Gospels* (London: SPCK, 1992) 115-18.

[4] For R. Bultmann the sacraments play no role in John, and were introduced into the text by an ecclesiastical redactor (*Theology of the New Testament* [2 vols.; Transl. K. Grobel; London: SCM Press, 1952, 1955] 2:9, 58-59).

[5] R. Bultmann, *Jesus Christ and Mythology* (New York: Scribner's, 1958) 50-53.

[6] R. Bultmann, *The Gospel of John: A Commentary* (Transl. G.R. Beasley-Murray; Philadelphia: Westminster Press, 1971) 44-60; *idem, Theology*, 2:20-21, 75-78.

revelation/Revealer.[7] The locus of salvation, according to Bultmann, is the incarnation rather than the crucifixion, since Jesus' death has no salvific role but is merely the completion of the 'work' (of revelation) that began with the incarnation. Hence, salvation is mediated by revelation and John has no concept of an atoning sacrifice for sins.[8] However, we may ask whether self-understanding as the primary salvific concept arises out of the text of the Fourth Gospel or out of Bultmann's existentialist hermeneutic. Passages such as John 3.14-16; 14.6-7; 17.3-8 seem to indicate that a saving understanding is primarily an authentic understanding of (the identity and mission of) the Father and Son rather than an authentic self-understanding. Moreover, Bultmann does not really describe how this salvation or eschatological existence can be maintained.[9]

---

[7] Bultmann, *Gospel*, 53-59.

[8] Bultmann, *Theology*, 2:48, 52-55; *idem, Gospel*, 467-68, 472, 624. For Bultmann, release from sin will not come through Jesus' death but through (the 'truth' mediated by) Jesus' word (*Theology*, 2:55). E. Käsemann also denies the centrality of the cross to salvation by reducing the cross to a mere transitional stage in Jesus' return to the Father (*The Testament of Jesus: A Study of the Gospel of John in the Light of Chapter 17* [Transl. G. Krodel; London: SCM Press, 1968] 10, 17-18). The main difference between Bultmann and Käsemann is that Bultmann, taking σάρξ in 1.14a as starting-point, interprets the cross in the light of the incarnation, and Käsemann, focusing on δόξα in 1.14b, interprets the cross in the light of Jesus' glorification and return to the Father. Both Bultmann and Käsemann have their disciples: Müller and Nicholson are disciples of Käsemann (U.B. Müller, 'Die Bedeutung des Kreuzestodes Jesu im Johannesevangelium: Erwägungen zur Kreuzestheologie im Neuen Testament', *Kerygma und Dogma* 21 [1975] 49-71; G.C. Nicholson, *Death as Departure: The Johannine Descent-Ascent Schema* [SBL.DS 63; Chico: Scholars Press, 1983] 141-44, 163-66), whereas Loader, who will be presented below, is Bultmann's disciple (cf. W.G. Kümmel, *The Theology of the New Testament: According to Its Major Witnesses Jesus — Paul — John* [Transl. J.E. Steely; London: SCM Press, 1974] 296-98). Besides Bultmann's incarnation- and Käsemann's glorification-hermeneutic, Bornkamm is the classical representative of a third hermeneutical perspective, namely to interpret the Fourth Gospel from a post-Easter perspective in which the Paraclete-sayings are the hermeneutical key (G. Bornkamm, 'Der Paraklet im Johannesevangelium' in G. Bornkamm [ed.], *Geschichte und Glaube I* [Gesammelte Aufsätze Band III; München: Kaiser, 1968] 68-89 [esp. 88-89]; *idem*, 'Zur Interpretation des Johannes-Evangeliums: Eine Auseinandersetzung mit Ernst Käsemanns Schrift "Jesu letzter Wille nach Johannes 17"' in G. Bornkamm [ed.], *Geschichte und Glaube I* [Gesammelte Aufsätze Band III; München: Kaiser, 1968] 104-21 [esp. 114, 117]). For our hermeneutic concerning the Fourth Gospel, see excursus 1, below.

[9] At the heart of Bultmann's existential approach to revelation is the *Dass/Was* distinction: the Fourth Gospel only presents the *Dass* of the revelation but not its *Was* (*Theology*, 2:66). Contra Bultmann, G.R. O'Day proposes to approach the concept of revelation by the category of *Wie*, i.e., the 'how' or mode of revelation (*Revelation in the Fourth Gospel: Narrative Mode and Theological Claim* [Philadelphia: Fortress Press, 1986] 44-46). For a critique of O'Day, see W.[R.G.] Loader, *The Christology of the Fourth Gospel: Structure and Issues* (BET 23; Frankfurt: Verlag Peter Lang, 1989) 138;

T. Müller agrees with Bultmann on the prominence of the theme of revelation in the Fourth Gospel, but he criticizes Bultmann's concept of the content of revelation being merely that Jesus is the Revealer. According to Müller, the content of revelation includes knowledge of the nature and work of the Father and Son.[10] Contra Bultmann, Müller sets out to prove that the cross is central or integral to salvation and that Jesus' death is an expiatory and vicarious sacrifice for sin.[11] However, Müller's case is not very strong: Müller admits, for example, that John does not view Jesus' death as a priestly/cultic act nor does he consider it to establish reconciliation with God; it is actually not clear, Müller says, in what sense Jesus' death is a sacrifice and hence can only be called a 'sacrifice' in a broad sense.[12]

Forestell, whose objective is to isolate the properly Johannine theology of salvation, agrees with Bultmann that salvation is mediated by revelation, but, like Müller, disagrees that Bultmann has gratuitously reduced the concept of revelation to the simple recognition by man of his status as a creature before God.[13] For Forestell, revelation has as its object the identity of the Father and Son and their mutual relationship, and as its aim the communication to people of eternal life, namely, that life which the Father has in himself, which he has given to the Son and which the Son offers to people.[14] Salvation, then, is the possession of eternal life, i.e., the entrance into a dynamic communion of mutual knowledge and love which exists between the Father and Son.[15] This salvation/communion is fostered and maintained by obedience to Jesus' words/commandments and the reception of the eucharist.[16] Forestell partly adopts Cullmann's concept of the sacraments being the locus of salvation, and essentially argues for a 'two-stage' model of salvation: faith supplemented by (the external expression of this faith in) the sacraments.[17] According to Forestell, the cross is both revelatory and salvific in that it is: (i) the exaltation and

---

J. Ashton, *Understanding the Fourth Gospel* (Oxford: Clarendon Press, 1991) 549 n.53, 552-53.

[10] T. Müller, *Das Heilsgeschehen im Johannesevangelium: Eine exegetische Studie, zugleich der Versuch einer Antwort an Rudolf Bultmann* (Zürich: Gotthelf-Verlag, 1961) 13-38, 135-36. Cf. Ashton, *Understanding*, Part III (esp. pp.515-53).

[11] Müller, *Heilsgeschehen*, esp. 38-75.

[12] Müller, *Heilsgeschehen*, 56-57, 110, 114, 124 n.402. For a more convincing defence of Jesus' death as an objective atonement for sin, see the works of Turner and Knöppler mentioned in n.27, below.

[13] J.T. Forestell, *The Word of the Cross: Salvation as Revelation in the Fourth Gospel* (Rome: Biblical Institute Press, 1974) 2, 14-18, 190.

[14] Forestell, *Word*, 17, 57, 114.

[15] Forestell, *Word*, 113, 117, 122, 196-97.

[16] Forestell, *Word*, 122.

[17] Forestell, *Word*, 139-46.

glorification of Jesus; (ii) the culmination of Jesus' revelatory work in that the cross is the supreme revelation of God's love for people; (iii) both a symbol of the gift of eternal life and the means whereby the sources of divine life are finally opened for people.[18] Forestell concludes that the cross in John is evaluated in terms of revelation rather than in terms of a vicarious and expiatory sacrifice for sin.[19] Thus, Forestell argues, with Müller, against Bultmann, that the cross is central or integral to salvation, but agrees with Bultmann, against Müller, that the cross is no objective atonement for sins.[20]

Loader, who has also been strongly influenced by Bultmann, remains much more Bultmannian than Forestell by arguing that Jesus' death is: (i) not an act of vicarious or sacrificial atonement for sin (agreed by Forestell); (ii) only revelatory but not salvific, i.e., the cross does not add anything soteriologically (contra Forestell); (iii) not only the completion of Jesus' work of revelation but also its climax. Jesus' death is not only *das Ende* but also *die Wende* (turning point); it marks the start of the 'greater event' which results in 'greater things' (see section 2.3, below) (beyond Bultmann, Käsemann et al.).[21]

Concerning the place of the cross in salvation, virtually everyone (except Bultmann, Käsemann, Loader and a few others)[22] accepts that the cross is integral or climactic to salvation.[23] However, there is some division about whether or not Jesus' death is an expiatory sacrifice for sins. At one end of the spectrum, besides Forestell, scholars such as Dodd, Barrett and Appold also deny a vicarious or expiatory interpretation of Jesus' death.[24] At the other end of the spectrum we find, besides T. Müller,

---

[18] Forestell, *Word*, 73, 101, 113, 191-92. Cf. R.T. Fortna, *The Fourth Gospel and Its Predecessor: From Narrative Source to Present Gospel* (Edinburgh: T&T Clark, 1989) 274-83.

[19] Forestell, *Word*, 165-66, 191.

[20] See Forestell (*Word*, 1-2, 75-76, 191) for a critique of Müller.

[21] Loader, *Christology*, 93-135. Nevertheless, Loader observes that John knows and makes incidental, illustrative and confessional use of traditions of vicarious atonement (*Christology*, 102, 135).

[22] E.g., Kümmel, U.B. Müller, Nicholson, M. de Jonge, *Jesus: Stranger from Heaven and Son of God: Jesus Christ and the Christians in Johannine Perspective* (SBL.SBS 11; edited and translated by J.E. Steely; Missoula: Scholars Press, 1977) 210.

[23] For additional names, see T. Knöppler, *Die theologia crucis des Johannesevangeliums: Das Verständnis des Todes Jesu im Rahmen der johanneischen Inkarnations- und Erhöhungschristologie* (WMANT 69; Neukirchen-Vluyn: Neukirchener Verlag, 1994) 8-18.

[24] Dodd, *Interpretation*, 233; C.K. Barrett, *The Gospel according to St John: An Introduction with Commentary and Notes on the Greek Text* (London: SPCK, 1978²) 81; M.L. Appold, *The Oneness Motif in the Fourth Gospel: Motif Analysis and Exegetical Probe into the Theology of John* (WUNT II/1; Tübingen: Mohr Siebeck, 1976) 273-74.

scholars such as Schnackenburg, Kohler, Carson, Beasley-Murray et al., who do believe that Jesus' death is central/integral to salvation as well as an expiatory and vicarious sacrifice.[25] In between there are various positions.[26] However, the most convincing defence of the cross as an expiatory sacrifice and objective atonement for sin has been put forward by Turner, who critically evaluates the views of Forestell (and Bultmann), and especially by Knöppler, who has written the most extensive and recent monograph on John's theology of the cross.[27] Nevertheless, even if it were not possible to decide decisively on the atoning nature of Jesus' death in the Fourth Gospel, it seems, against Bultmann, Käsemann and Loader, that the consensus of Johannine scholarship reflects at least that the cross is not

---

[25] Schnackenburg, *Gospel*, 1:157-58; H. Kohler, *Kreuz und Menschwerdung im Johannesevangelium: Ein exegetisch-hermeneutischer Versuch zur johanneischen Kreuzestheologie* (AThANT 72; Zürich: Theologischer Verlag, 1987) 144, 199-201, 271-72, *passim* (holding the concepts of σάρξ and δόξα together, Kohler creates a *via media* between Bultmann's incarnation-christology and Käsemann's glorification-christology, and argues that Jesus' death is the crucial salvific event); D.A. Carson, *The Gospel according to John* (Leicester: IVP, 1991) 97, 152-53, 295, 386-87, 422, 567; G.R. Beasley-Murray, *John* (WBC 36; Milton Keynes: Word, 1991) lxxxiv-lxxxv, 51; *idem*, *Gospel of Life: Theology in the Fourth Gospel* (Peabody: Hendrickson, 1991) 36-58; J.T. Williams, 'Cultic Elements in the Fourth Gospel' in E.A. Livingstone (ed.), *Studia Biblica 1978: II. Papers on the Gospels* (JSNT.S 2; Sheffield: JSOT Press, 1980) 339-50; G.L. Carey, 'The Lamb of God and Atonement Theories', *TynB* 32 (1981) 97-122; B.H. Grigsby, 'The Cross as an Expiatory Sacrifice in the Fourth Gospel', *JSNT* 15 (1982) 51-80; L. Morris, 'The Atonement in John's Gospel', *Criswell Theological Review* 3 (1988) 49-64; J.W. Pryor, *John: Evangelist of the Covenant People. The Narrative & Themes of the Fourth Gospel* (Downers Grove: IVP, 1992) 168-73; J.P. Heil, 'Jesus as the Unique High Priest in the Gospel of John', *CBQ* 57 (1995) 729-45.

[26] The main intermediate positions are: (i) the issue whether Jesus' death is an expiatory sacrifice for sin is not addressed (J. Riedl, *Das Heilswerk Jesu Nach Johannes* [Freiburg: Herder, 1973]; M.M. Thompson, *The Incarnate Word: Perspectives on Jesus in the Fourth Gospel* [Peabody: Hendrickson, 1988] ch. 4); (ii) agnosticism (H.K. Nielsen, 'John's Understanding of the Death of Jesus' in J. Nissen and S. Pedersen [eds.], *New Readings in John: Literary and Theological Perspectives. Essays from the Scandinavian Conference on the Fourth Gospel Århus 1997* [JSNT.S 182; Sheffield: SAP, 1999] 232-54); (iii) the concept of Jesus' death as an atoning sacrifice is only secondary (W. Thüsing, *Die Erhöhung und Verherrlichung Jesu im Johannesevangelium* [Münster: Verlag Aschendorff, 1970²] 31-33; A.J. Hultgren, *Christ and His Benefits: Christology and Redemption in the New Testament* [Philadelphia: Fortress Press, 1987] 149-50; Ashton, *Understanding*, 490-501); (iv) the idea of atonement appears only in the latest redaction of the Gospel (M.C. de Boer, *Johannine Perspectives on the Death of Jesus* [Kampen: Kok, 1996] 279-80).

[27] M.[M.B.] Turner, 'Atonement and the Death of Jesus in John — Some Questions to Bultmann and Forestell', *EvQ* 62 (1990) 99-122; *idem*, *The Holy Spirit and Spiritual Gifts — Then and Now* (Carlisle: Paternoster, 1999 [rev. edn]) 71-75; Knöppler, *Theologia*, esp. chs. 2 and 9. Knöppler (like Kohler) does not develop a theology of salvation but limits himself to formulating a theology of the cross.

merely central/integral to the Johannine concept of salvation but also climactic and constitutional.[28]

A more complete outline of Johannine soteriology is presented by Carson, in which he also highlights further responsibilities demanded by faith, such as obedience, love for one another, perseverance, witness, prayer — in short, aspects of discipleship.[29] However, Carson's model is dominated by the divine sovereignty-human responsibility tension, and does not deal with the process of coming to salvation nor with the Spirit's soteriological role.[30] Motyer also gives brief attention to the important issue of discipleship in order to answer the question of what leads to salvation. He argues that not all faith leads to life, and that the Fourth Gospel consequently presents a two-stage model of salvation: first one comes to believe that Jesus is the Christ; then, if this faith is supplemented by discipleship, it will lead to life.[31] However, we may ask whether Motyer does not virtually create a false dichotomy between faith and discipleship, as if faith and discipleship are subsequent (complementary) stages leading to life. Although other scholars have elucidated the Johannine concept of discipleship to a greater extent, they have not (adequately) related it to the soteriology of the Fourth Gospel.[32] An exception is Pazdan's study, which

---

[28] This has become evident especially through the work of Forestell (*Word*, 58-102) and Knöppler.

[29] See D.A. Carson, 'Predestination and Responsibility: Elements of Tension-Theology in the Fourth Gospel against Jewish Background' (Cambridge: Ph.D. dissertation, 1975) ch. 5; *idem, Divine Sovereignty and Human Responsibility: Biblical perspectives in tension* (London: Marshall, Morgan & Scott, 1981) ch. 12.

[30] G.R. Osborne has a similar agenda to Carson's ('Soteriology in the Gospel of John' in C.H. Pinnock [ed.], *The Grace of God, the Will of Man: A Case for Arminianism* [Michigan: Academic Books, 1989] 243-60).

[31] S. Motyer, *Your Father the Devil?: A New Approach to John and 'the Jews'* (Carlisle: Paternoster, 1997) 58-61. Cf. R.A. Culpepper, *Anatomy of the Fourth Gospel: A Study in Literary Design* (Philadelphia: Fortress Press, 1987) 116.

[32] E.g., de Jonge, *Jesus*, ch. 1; F.F. Segovia, *Love Relationships in the Johannine Tradition: Agapē/Agapan in 1 John and the Fourth Gospel* (SBL.DS 58; Missoula: Scholars Press, 1982); *idem,* '"Peace I Leave with You; My Peace I Give to You": Discipleship in the Fourth Gospel' in F.F. Segovia (ed.), *Discipleship in the New Testament* (Philadelphia: Fortress Press, 1985) 76-102; *idem, The Farewell of the Word: The Johannine Call to Abide* (Minneapolis: Fortress Press, 1991); R.F. Collins, *These Things Have Been Written: Studies on the Fourth Gospel* (Louvain: Peeters Press, 1990) ch. 2; D.F. Tolmie, *Jesus' Farewell to the Disciples: John 13:1-17:26 in Narratological Perspective* (BIS 12; Leiden: Brill, 1995); D.R. Beck, *The Discipleship Paradigm: Readers and Anonymous Characters in the Fourth Gospel* (BIS 27; Leiden: Brill, 1997); D. Kim, 'The Church in the Gospel of John' (Cambridge: Ph.D. dissertation, 1999) 107-24.

presents discipleship in the Fourth Gospel as the appropriation of salvation.[33]

Most scholars so far have allowed a relational aspect to salvation (Cullmann, Dodd, Bultmann, Forestell), but a few scholars have a more explicit *relational soteriology*. Loader's objective is to identify the central structure of Johannine christology (like Bultmann), and then, on this basis, to integrate the wider issues of the Fourth Gospel, especially soteriology.[34] Loader argues that the central structure of Johannine christology is the *revealer-envoy model*, which is essentially that Jesus is sent by the Father, to reveal the Father, to bring salvation, and consequently to return to the Father.[35] Besides Bultmann's influence on Loader's formulation of John's christology, Loader is also strongly influenced by him in the formulation of John's soteriology. Agreeing with Bultmann's insight that the content of Jesus' revelation is not the giving of information (*kein Was, nur ein bloßes Dass*), Loader argues that the revealer-envoy model is *modified* by John and used as a means of epiphany, encounter and invitation to a relationship with the Son and the Father.[36] The saving event then is the Son's coming to reveal the Father, not by imparting information but, on the basis of his intimacy with the Father, by calling people into a saving relationship with himself and the Father, and so salvation comes in response to this revelation-encounter-invitation.[37] Thus, the primary focus in the modified revealer-envoy model is life-giving encounter; the primary focus in John's soteriology is life in relationship with the Son and the Father.[38] Loader's soteriology also includes a *cognitive* element: a saving relationship includes right understanding (=belief) of who Jesus is, namely, that the Son is the sent one, has a unique relationship of oneness with the Father, and speaks and acts for him (cf. Bultmann's 'knowing' faith).[39] However, the question of *how* this right understanding will come about remains untouched (also by Bultmann).

---

[33] M.M. Pazdan, *Discipleship as the Appropriation of Eschatological Salvation in the Fourth Gospel* (University of St. Michael's College: Ph.D. dissertation, 1982; Ann Arbor: UMI, 1998). She argues that: (i) the *basis* for discipleship is belief in Jesus; (ii) the *heart* of discipleship is formed by the mutual relationships of knowing, loving and abiding between Jesus and the disciples; (iii) the *tasks* of discipleship, which foster these developing relationships, are to hear and keep Jesus' word, and to seek and find him (see *Discipleship*, chs. 2-4). Pazdan only investigates the πιστεύω εἰς-construction.

[34] Loader, *Christology*, 19.

[35] Loader, *Christology*, 20-92.

[36] Loader, *Christology*, 136-41, 206, 228.

[37] Loader, *Christology*, 135-41, 147, 228.

[38] Loader, *Christology*, 206.

[39] Loader, *Christology*, 141-43.

Thompson argues that (eternal) life or salvation is a share in God's own life and received in a continuous and dynamic relationship with God, through the mediation of God's life by Jesus.[40] Thompson draws attention to John's stress on the necessity of *faithfulness* (as expressed by μένω): if eternal life/salvation is knowing God, namely, fellowship with God, then it demands a continual, ongoing, mutual relationship. Eternal life is not something that one has as a gift apart from connection with the Giver.[41] Although Thompson rightly draws attention to the issue of how salvation can be maintained, the issues of *how* people enter into this saving relationship with God, and *how* God's life is mediated through Jesus to people are not raised.

For Harner, eternal life is to 'know' God and Christ; not simply to have an intellectual understanding of them but actually to be in a living relationship with them.[42] Faith, then, is a response to divine revelation, and allows believers to enter a new relationship of heightened spiritual perception and ongoing life.[43]

Ford approaches salvation from the angle of friendship with God: from a feminist perspective, she looks at the *pathos* of friendship and investigates whether redemption can be expressed in terms of restoration of friendship with God.[44] Ford sees a Greek and Hebraic idea of friendship woven into the fabric of the Prologue, which sets the tone for the entire Gospel; it is the friendship of the Father and Son who seek a symbiosis with humanity.[45] This symbiosis, which results in a new mode of relationship/existence, is accomplished through the concept of the incarnation and of rebirth. The Logos, functioning as friend and embodiment of covenantal חסד, mediates this *saving* חסד to his special friends so that they attain, by way of a new birth, an intimate and filial relationship with (and in) the Godhead.[46] However, Ford does not work out either *how* people enter into this saving relationship with God, or *how* this saving חסד is mediated by Jesus to people. Neither does she hint at how this friendship with God is maintained, unless she might use her image of Jesus as a breast-feeding mother for the growing child as the solution to

---

[40] M.M. Thompson, 'Eternal Life In The Gospel Of John', *Ex Auditu* 5 (1989) 40-42.

[41] Thompson, 'Life', 41, 46-47.

[42] P.B. Harner, *Relation Analysis of the Fourth Gospel: A Study in Reader-Response Criticism* (New York: Edwin Mellen Press, 1993) 61-62.

[43] Harner, *Relation*, 46.

[44] J.M. Ford, *Redeemer — Friend and Mother: Salvation in Antiquity and in the Gospel of John* (Minneapolis: Fortress Press, 1997).

[45] See Ford, *Redeemer*, ch. 7.

[46] Ford, *Redeemer*, 113.

this;[47] but then, growing children surely do not need breast-feeding forever.

Examining the metaphorical language of the Fourth Gospel, van der Watt argues that John's metaphors are best understood within the macro family metaphor; the metaphors of birth and life, for example, denote respectively how one becomes a member of the family of God, and how one exists within the divine family.[48]

2.1.2. Faith

Virtually everyone agrees that faith is the primary (if not sole) means of attaining eternal life/salvation, but there is no consensus about what leads to full salvific faith (i.e., is faith staged or progressive?) nor about the relationship between faith and signs.

For Cullmann, a faith which is based exclusively on physical seeing (and hearing) is not true faith, but must be followed by a deeper, spiritual understanding.[49] Bultmann follows a similar line, and argues that faith, as the only way to salvation, proceeds from 'hearing' and 'seeing' and calls for decision, but is genuine only insofar as it is a *knowing* faith; signs-faith is just a first tentative step toward Jesus which has yet to prove itself as genuine faith.[50] For Bultmann, the cognitive element of salvation/eternal life — knowing faith — is nothing more than the (ac)knowledge(ment) that God is revealed/known through the Son.[51] Bultmann briefly mentions further that genuine faith needs to be continuous and needs to illustrate discipleship.[52]

Some scholars develop a more explicitly staged model of faith. Fortna presents two stages of faith: (i) signs-faith is genuine faith, although Jesus' miracles as a basis for faith are ambiguous; (ii) faith-without-seeing, i.e., faith not dependent on signs, is a superior form of faith and can be reached

---

[47] Ford, *Redeemer*, 124-35.

[48] J.G. van der Watt, *Family of the King: Dynamics of Metaphor in the Gospel according to John* (BIS 47; Leiden: Brill, 2000) ch. 3.

[49] Cullmann, *Worship*, 40-47.

[50] Bultmann, *Gospel*, 69 n.4; 131, 434-35; *idem, Theology*, 2:71-78. Cf. W. Nicol, *The Sēmeia in the Fourth Gospel: Tradition and Redaction* (NT.S 32; Leiden: Brill, 1972) 99-106; Appold, *Motif*, 98-99; Loader, *Christology*, 141-42; J. Painter, *The Quest for the Messiah: The History, Literature and Theology of the Johannine Community* (Edinburgh: T&T Clark, 1993²) 411; Pazdan, *Discipleship*, 117.

[51] Bultmann, *Gospel*, 494-95.

[52] Bultmann, *Gospel*, 434, 698-99; *idem, Theology*, 2:73, 79; *idem*, 'Γινώσκω, κτλ.' in *TDNT*, I:712. Cf. Schnackenburg, *Gospel*, 1:566.

in progressive stages.[53] Forestell and Kysar present independently a similar staged model in the genesis of faith: (i) an openness to God as a disposition to faith (Forestell) or as an embryonic faith (Kysar);[54] (ii) signs-faith — faith which requires signs to keep it going — which should lead to (iii) true or mature faith about the person of Jesus and his relationship with the Father on the basis of Jesus' word, and which does not require signs any more.[55] Although these scholars in general agree that John does not depreciate signs-faith, they do not (adequately) explain whether John thinks signs-faith is partially salvific, nor how one can move from one level to the next.

Koester's case, on the other hand, is that signs-faith cannot be understood as a first step towards genuine faith; those whose initial perception of Jesus was based on seeing regularly failed to come to true faith, but those who manifested a genuine faith, did so after an initial experience of hearing.[56] Rather, the signs confirmed and were perceived by a faith that had been engendered through hearing.[57]

Contrary to all these positions, Twelftree provides the most substantial defence for the view that Jesus' words and signs are an equally valid basis for faith. Twelftree entirely rejects any view of progressive stages of faith,

---

[53] R.T. Fortna, 'Source and Redaction in the Fourth Gospel's Portrayal of Jesus' Signs', *JBL* 89 (1970) 156-66; *idem, Gospel,* 240-50. Cf. Brown, *Gospel,* 1:530-31; Schnackenburg, *Gospel,* 1:523-24, 570-72; Collins, *Things,* ch. 10; Carson, *Gospel,* 99-100. G. Ziener finds this view of faith, namely, a faith that is based only on God's word as that which is really expected from disciples, already in Wis. ('Weisheitsbuch und Johannesevangelium [II]', *Bib* 39 [1958] 55-57).

[54] Forestell calls this disposition the gift or the drawing of God (*Word,* 111). Bultmann, however, argues against a deterministic view by stating that the Father's drawing of a person and the believer's decision of faith are simultaneous events (*Theology,* 2:23). R. Kysar defines embryonic faith as the openness to the possibility of God's reality and activity (*John The Maverick Gospel* [Louisville: Westminster John Knox Press, 1993 (rev. edn)] 84).

[55] Forestell, *Word,* 70-71, 106-11; R. Kysar, *The Fourth Evangelist and His Gospel: An examination of contemporary scholarship* (Minneapolis: Augsburg, 1975) 69-73; *idem, John,* 79-86. Kysar's model is most explicit, and, like Bultmann, he argues that the basic experiences of sensory perception are a prerequisite for faith perception (*John,* 86-90). Kysar goes even further by arguing that John appeared to be partly responsible for the beginning of a gradual shift in the early church from a relational understanding of faith towards a creedal understanding of faith (*John,* 92-95). However, this is perhaps somewhat anachronistic and too speculative. Moreover, Kysar's model seems to rest on a false dichotomy of the Johannine usage of πιστεύω (πιστεύω with a ὅτι-clause over against, e.g., πιστεύω εἰς with the accusative [*John,* 93-94]).

[56] C.[R.] Koester, 'Hearing, Seeing, and Believing in the Gospel of John', *Bib* 70 (1989) 327-48. Cf. G.E. Ladd, *A Theology of the New Testament* (Cambridge: Lutterworth Press, 1993 [rev. edn]) 310.

[57] Koester, 'Hearing', 332, 348.

and his thesis is that authentic faith can be based on either Jesus' words or on his signs.[58] Faith that recognizes the true identity of Jesus, whatever the basis of that faith — seeing the signs, hearing the words, or witnessing the risen Lord — is sufficient for salvation.[59] The signs alone are adequate for salvation and a full understanding of Jesus.[60] Nevertheless, although signs-faith may be authentic, would it be adequate? Can people really perceive the true identity of Jesus and penetrate his revelation on the basis of signs only, or do people obtain only partial or fractured images of Jesus?

Other scholars have concentrated more on the responses of people to Jesus and his revelation rather than on the concept of faith itself, and proposed various taxonomies or typologies of faith-responses.[61]

2.1.3. Salvation and Realized Eschatology

Virtually everyone agrees that John's soteriology has a realized dimension, i.e., for John eternal life/salvation is a present reality (without denying a possible future consummation),[62] but there is disagreement about *when* this

---

[58] See G.H. Twelftree, *Jesus The Miracle Worker: A Historical & Theological Study* (Downers Grove: IVP, 1999) chs. 7-8. Cf. de Jonge, *Jesus*, ch. 5; Y. Ibuki, 'Viele glaubten an ihn — Auseinandersetzung mit dem Glauben im Johannesevangelium —', *Annual of the Japanese Biblical Institute* 9 (1983) 128-83 (esp. 142); W.J. Bittner, *Jesu Zeichen im Johannesevangelium: Die Messias-Erkenntnis im Johannesevangelium vor ihrem jüdischen Hintergrund* (WUNT II/26; Tübingen: Mohr Siebeck, 1987) 259-90; Thompson, *Word*, ch. 3 (esp. pp.75, 80, 86); Motyer, *Father*, 58-59. Ibuki is actually very sceptical about the possibility of genuine faith: he concludes, e.g., that πιστεύω has from the outset by no means a positive meaning, but denotes frequently a *Scheinglaube* or even *Unglaube* ('Viele', 140-41, 144). See also F.L. Crouch, who understands signs (miraculous and non-miraculous) as public acts that lead to, maintain or deepen belief (*Everyone Who Sees the Son: Signs, Faith, Peirce's Semeiothics, and the Gospel of John* [Duke University: Ph.D. dissertation, 1996; Ann Arbor: UMI, 1997]).

[59] Twelftree, *Jesus*, 232. Nevertheless, Twelftree admits that faith based on Jesus' words is the ultimate form of faith-response to Jesus (*Jesus*, 231-32, 342-43).

[60] Twelftree, *Jesus*, 233.

[61] Brown, *Gospel*, 1:530-31; F.J. Moloney, 'From Cana to Cana (John 2:1-4:54) and the Fourth Evangelist's Concept of Correct (and Incorrect) Faith' in E.A. Livingstone (ed.), *Studia Biblica 1978: II. Papers on the Gospels* (JSNT.S 2; Sheffield: JSOT Press, 1980) 185-213; *idem*, *Belief in the Word — Reading the Fourth Gospel: John 1-4* (Minneapolis: Fortress Press, 1993); Culpepper, *Anatomy*, 146-48; Barton, *Spirituality*, 128-30; M.W.G. Stibbe, *John's Gospel* (London: Routledge, 1994) 124. Nonetheless, Culpepper could also arrange the faith-responses into a hierarchy of various stages ('The Theology of the Gospel of John', *Review and Expositor* 85 [1988] 426-27).

[62] Only Bultmann (*Theology*, 2:37-39, 57-58, 79), Käsemann (*Testament*, 16-17) and Fortna (*Gospel*, 289-91) defend an exclusively present eschatology. Due to his existential worldview, Bultmann historizes or demythologizes eschatology and rules out future eschatology; the incarnation is *the* eschatological event, and Easter, Pentecost and the parousia are not separate but one single (chronological) event. Many scholars, however, have reacted against, e.g., Bultmann's exclusively present eschatology and defended the

eternal life/salvation became available. That is, was eternal life/salvation already available *during* Jesus' ministry (and if so, *how*) or only *after* Jesus' death and resurrection?[63]

The vast majority of scholars and commentators hold that eternal life/salvation only became available after the cross (and resurrection).[64] To the question whether salvation was possible during Jesus' earthly ministry, Bultmann, for example, would answer that the believer's eschatological existence can only be facilitated by a genuine faith-relationship with the *exalted* Jesus (through the Spirit), which would only be possible after Jesus' death and resurrection.[65] Forestell also believes that (the goods of) salvation, namely, the communion of life with the Father and Son, was not available to people prior to Jesus' death on the cross.[66] However, if, according to Forestell, the cross is merely a revelation of God's love, why is it that salvation can only be bestowed after the cross?[67] Nevertheless, some scholars do recognize and account for the apparent (partial) presence of the availability of life/salvation within Jesus' ministry. They interpret those statements in the Fourth Gospel that suggest such a reality either proleptically/symbolically (of what would become available only after the

---

presence of future eschatology in the Fourth Gospel (e.g., D.E. Holwerda, *The Holy Spirit and Eschatology in the Gospel of John: A Critique of Rudolf Bultmann's Present Eschatology* [Kampen: Kok, 1959] 126-33; O. Cullmann, *Salvation in History* [London: SCM Press, 1967] 268-91; Forestell, *Word*, 119, 126-34; cf. Schnackenburg, *Gospel*, 1:159-60; Beasley-Murray, *Gospel*, 5-6).

[63] Although J.C. Davis' article ('The Johannine Concept of Eternal Life as a Present Possession', *Restoration Quarterly* 27 [1984] 161-69) sounds promising, he does not address the issue whether eternal life could already be experienced during Jesus' ministry. Neither do Thompson and Ford discuss whether a saving relationship with God was already possible during Jesus' ministry. Thüsing finds the question of whether salvation was already available in Jesus' ministry irrelevant (although he thinks salvation is only available after the cross) (*Erhöhung*, 161-64).

[64] Cullmann, *Worship*, 40, 47; Dodd, *Interpretation*, 372, 383, 386, 398, 437-38; Brown, *Gospel*, 1:cxviii, 507, 531; Riedl, *Heilswerk*, 35-36, 408, 419, 425-426 n.44, 428; Barrett, *Gospel*, 68, 80, 229, 233-34, 237; Schnackenburg, *Gospel*, 1:523-24; 2:353; G.M. Burge, *The Anointed Community: The Holy Spirit in the Johannine Tradition* (Grand Rapids: Eerdmans, 1987) 116, 149; Kohler, *Kreuz*, 146; Carson, *Gospel*, 202 (cf. *idem*, *Sovereignty*, 178-79); Beasley-Murray, *John*, 50-51; *idem*, *Gospel*, 4, 11, 50-56; Painter, *Quest*, 387-88, 411-15; Knöppler, *Theologia*, 107-10, 159-60.

[65] Bultmann, *Theology*, 2:42, 85; *idem*, *Gospel*, 467, 619-20, 691. Loader wrongly gives the impression that Bultmann thought eternal life was already available before Easter (*Christology*, 13-16).

[66] Forestell, *Word*, 19, 98, 100, 119, 191-92.

[67] Turner, 'Atonement', 115-16.

cross) or from a post-Easter perspective (to indicate the reality in the post-Easter situation).[68]

Only a few scholars argue that salvation was a reality already possible during Jesus' earthly ministry.[69] T. Müller distinguishes between the time before and after Easter: after Easter, salvation comes on the basis of Jesus' atoning death; before Easter, there was a unique and unrepeatable situation in which eternal life was given in encounter and fellowship with Jesus.[70] Fortna holds that salvation was already available during Jesus' ministry because salvation came with the arrival of the Messiah; salvation is inaugurated in Jesus' public ministry.[71] However, both Müller and Fortna fail to explain *how* salvation could be available during Jesus' ministry when they maintain that the cross was the soteriological focal point and the climax of Jesus' mission.[72] Twelftree, stating that the signs are the centre or heart of Jesus' life-giving ministry and adequate for salvation,[73] seems to imply that salvation was already fully available during Jesus' ministry, and hence, that the cross does not add anything soteriologically.[74]

Porsch, whose main interest is Johannine pneumatology, nevertheless developed a two-stage model of salvation, in which (i) during Jesus' ministry partial salvation or beginning faith is offered to people in the form of Jesus' revelatory word, but (ii) only after Jesus' glorification would this faith be perfected/completed.[75] Loader argues that the gift of life, salvation, is centred not in events but in the person of Jesus, and hence fully available already before the cross.[76] The revealer-envoy model has,

---

[68] Dodd, *Interpretation*, 372; Brown, *Gospel*, 1:cxviii; Riedl, *Heilswerk*, 17-23; Barrett, *Gospel*, 68, 80, 229, 233-34, 237; cf. Painter, *Quest*, 412-15; de Jonge, *Jesus*, 16.

[69] J.C. Thomas probably also implies the presence of salvation in Jesus' ministry (*Footwashing in John 13 and the Johannine Community* [JSNT.S 61; Sheffield: JSOT Press, 1991] 105).

[70] Müller, *Heilsgeschehen*, 24-25, 32-33, 132, 138-39.

[71] R.T. Fortna, 'From Christology to Soteriology: A Redaction-Critical Study of Salvation in the Fourth Gospel', *Interp* 27 (1973) 33-34, 37, 44-45; *idem*, *Gospel*, 252-57, 286.

[72] Müller, *Heilsgeschehen*, 38-75; Fortna, 'Christology', 45; *idem*, *Gospel*, 282.

[73] Twelftree, *Jesus*, 199, 235-36.

[74] Although Twelftree interprets Jesus' death and resurrection as life-giving, he does not seem to attribute any objective salvific significance to the cross. Jesus' death and resurrection, reduced to a mere (although the largest and clearest) 'sign', are effectively put on the same footing as the other life-giving miracles in Jesus' ministry (*Jesus*, 203, 224, 227, 339-43). Consequently, Twelftree seems to imply that salvation before and after Jesus' glorification was equally available and of the same qualitative calibre.

[75] F. Porsch, *Pneuma und Wort: Ein exegetischer Beitrag zur Pneumatologie des Johannesevangeliums* (FTS 16; Frankfurt: Knecht, 1974) 66-72, 144. Porsch's two-stage model of salvation is essentially derived from his two-stage model of the gift of the Spirit (see section 2.3).

[76] Loader, *Christology*, 129.

by its very structure, little place for a soteriological significance to be attributed to Jesus' death and no need of a vicarious and sacrificial atonement, because life is in the person of the Son and in relationship with him, and nothing more needs to be done.[77] Koottumkal's objective is to discover the life-giving dimension of Jesus' word in the Fourth Gospel.[78] Although Koottumkal acknowledges the availability of eternal life already during Jesus' ministry because Jesus is the source of life and his word is salvific,[79] he is not clear about how this could be possible. Turner has a similar model to Porsch's. During Jesus' ministry partial faith was possible, but authentic Christian faith became a reality only after Jesus' glorification through death, resurrection and the gift of the Spirit. In Jesus' ministry people could already have *'foretastes'/experiences* of the life which was only fully available after Jesus' glorification.[80] Turner describes the disciples' coming to salvation as a *process*, which started in Jesus' earthly ministry and which reached its climax in the gift of the Spirit.[81]

How salvation can be (partially) available during Jesus' ministry and in the time after, is explained by Porsch, Loader, Koottumkal and Turner in their understanding of the role of the Spirit in salvation, which also constitutes the main difference between them (see section 2.3, below).

Excursus 1: A Post-Easter Hermeneutic and a Pre-Easter Reality?

If Bornkamm is right that the Fourth Gospel should be interpreted from a post-Easter pneumatological perspective (see n.8, above), then the question could be raised whether an investigation into the availability of life/salvation and the work of the Spirit prior to the cross (as this study endeavours to do) is at all relevant. If the pre-Easter reality can only be perceived through post-Easter spectacles, then to make a differentiation between pre- and post-Easter realities with regard to the Spirit and salvation may seem irrelevant (if not impossible). Hence, we will make some preliminary remarks and observations in order to clarify our hermeneutical perspective on the Fourth Gospel.

We agree, with Bornkamm et al., that the Fourth Gospel (including Jesus' earthly ministry and the work of the Spirit prior to the cross) is written from a post-Easter perspective (as are the Synoptics). John's post-Easter perspective was provided by the Paraclete, especially through the Paraclete's anamnesis and guidance into all truth (see

---

[77] Loader, *Christology*, 206-207.

[78] S. Koottumkal, *Words of Eternal Life: An Exegetical-Theological Study on the Life-giving Dimension of the Word of Jesus in the Fourth Gospel* (Rome: Pontificia Universitas Gregoriana, 1995). Koottumkal's thesis is hardly obtainable and I was able to gain access only to ch. 2, the most important chapter of his thesis for our study.

[79] Koottumkal, *Words*, 133-37.

[80] Turner, *Spirit*, 60-75.

[81] Turner, *Spirit*, 98-99. Brown had already briefly hinted that the disciples' coming to full salvific faith was a process which started during Jesus' ministry and reached its climax after the resurrection (*Gospel*, 1:531). See also E. Liebert, 'That You May Believe: The Fourth Gospel and Structural Developmental Theory', *BTB* 14 (1984) 67-73.

ch. 5). Nevertheless, the Fourth Gospel seems to indicate a difference between the work of the Spirit before and after the cross (hence the comments in Jn 7.39 and 16.7), and between the quality and availability of salvation before and after Easter. The Fourth Gospel seems to have differentiated between what was possible before and after the cross, i.e., the Gospel retains the difference that Jesus' hour (namely, the cross-resurrection-ascension) had made.[82] The issue we shall examine in our study (from the post-Easter stance of John and his readers) is how (and to what extent) life was already available before the cross, and what role the Spirit had in this. It seems unlikely to us, for example, that life only became available after the cross and that John had read this back into the time before the cross; rather, from a post-Easter, Spirit-provided perspective John understood much more clearly what actually had happened during Jesus' earthly ministry. Our observation after the brief overview of Johannine scholarship so far is that the realized dimension of salvation and the Spirit's work prior to the cross need more investigation.

While we will investigate the work of the Spirit and the availability of life before the cross, we will not attempt to reconstruct a 'historical' account in a strict sense. In our view, the Fourth Gospel is a theological narration from a post-Easter perspective (as are indeed the other Gospels) (cf. the brief treatment of the genre of the Fourth Gospel in ch. 3 section 2).[83] John's aim in retelling the dialogue between Jesus and, for example, Nicodemus or the Samaritan woman, was to persuade and convince his readers not of certain historical facts but of their significance and theological truths. However, our presupposition is that theological truth needs a historical anchor — the existence of the historical Jesus, the crucifixion and resurrection are necessary historical facts for theological truth. Whether it is necessary (in order to accept the truth claim of John 3) that Nicodemus existed, or whether it is necessary that his conversation with Jesus took place exactly as has been recorded is perhaps more ambivalent. Nevertheless, even if historical facts cannot be reconstructed any more, we still require a kind of narrative plausibility: for example, we prefer to see some historical reality behind the Nicodemus story, in that it must be plausible that such a conversation could have taken place. In our understanding, the Fourth Gospel moves along a spectrum of a mixture of (what we would call) 'history' and 'fiction', in which the stories about Nicodemus and the Samaritan woman, for example, perhaps contain more fiction than the passion narrative in John 18-19.

Looking at some scholars who have adopted Bornkamm's hermeneutical perspective on the Fourth Gospel, it seems that such a post-Easter perspective virtually neglects (and probably finds irrelevant), or remains (deliberately?) agnostic (so in general Frey),[84] or even (implicitly) denies (so Hoegen-Rohls)[85] the work of the Spirit and the availability of

---

[82] Cf. J. Frey, *Die johanneische Eschatologie II: Das johanneische Zeitverständnis* (WUNT 110; Tübingen: Mohr Siebeck, 1998) 250-51, 262-63, 290-92.

[83] Cf. the designation of John's Gospel as 'fictionalized history' (M.W.G. Stibbe, *John as Storyteller: Narrative criticism and the fourth gospel* [SNTS.MS 73; Cambridge: CUP, 1992] ch. 4), 'theologized history' (D. Tovey, *Narrative Art and Act in the Fourth Gospel* [JSNT.S 151; Sheffield: SAP, 1997] 226-27, 255), or 'history-like narrative' (A.T. Lincoln, *Truth on Trial: The Lawsuit Motif in the Fourth Gospel* [Peabody: Hendrickson, 2000] 389-90).

[84] See Frey, *Eschatologie II, passim.*

[85] C. Hoegen-Rohls, *Der nachösterliche Johannes: Die Abschiedsreden als hermeneutischer Schlüssel zum vierten Evangelium* (WUNT II/84; Tübingen: Mohr Siebeck, 1996) 294-95, cf. 310-11). Cf. those in n.68, above.

life in Jesus' earthly ministry prior to the cross. For such a perspective essentially interprets all the Spirit-passages in the Fourth Gospel as post-Easter activity, i.e., the Fourth Gospel explains the post-Easter experience of the Spirit in the believer. This could lead to a view that the post-Easter reality is integrated into (or read back into) the pre-Easter events.[86]

If this perspective were true, our question regarding the work of the Spirit and the availability of salvation prior to the cross would indeed be irrelevant. However, there are reasons to assume that the work of the Spirit did not merely start after the cross, but is a continuation (though in a fuller way) of those activities the Spirit was already performing during Jesus' earthly ministry. First, the reason that Jesus can say to his disciples in John 14.16-17 that the future Paraclete would not be a stranger to them is precisely that they already knew the Paraclete as the Spirit being active in and through Jesus (cf. ch. 5 section 3.2). Second, rather than reading a post-Easter reality back into pre-Easter events, we suggest that John draws out the reality of the pre-Easter events from a post-Easter Spirit-informed perspective, which was not possible before the cross.[87] In our understanding, the Fourth Gospel evidences the apparent reality of Jesus' pointing the way into the kingdom of God to Nicodemus, and of Jesus' offering life-giving water and bread to people (unless these acts were mere symbolic gestures or proleptic promises for later). Moreover, if Jesus performed healings and other miraculous signs during his earthly ministry, it would be reasonable to assume that people could also have had pre-Easter experiences of the life and Spirit that were present in Jesus and his words. Hence, rather than reading a post-Easter Spirit-experience back into the pre-Easter story in which the Spirit was not really/yet active (so, e.g., Hoegen-Rohls), we shall argue that the Spirit was already active before the cross in lives of people (see ch. 4) but that John only 'saw' this reality retrospectively through the work of the Paraclete. Third, a hermeneutical post-Easter perspective on John as held by Bornkamm, Hoegen-Rohls, Frey et al. seems to necessitate an interpretation of John 20.22 as the so called 'Johannine Pentecost' since 20.22 describes the post-Easter experience of the disciples and relates to the post-Easter work of the Spirit-Paraclete (as promised, e.g., in the farewell discourse).[88] However, we have argued elsewhere against a 'Johannine Pentecost' and proposed that 20.22 secures the life-giving work of the Spirit in the disciples that had already started during Jesus' ministry.[89]

In conclusion, the pre-Easter reality, as presented in the Fourth Gospel, is indeed reconstructed from a post-Easter perspective, but the Fourth Gospel also upholds a difference between what was possible before and after the cross, and we shall merely attempt to reconstruct what, according to the Evangelist, 'happened' during Jesus' earthly ministry.

---

[86] So Hoegen-Rohls, *Johannes*, 295, but see also Frey, *Eschatologie II*, 266, 287, 298; *idem, Die johanneische Eschatologie III: Die eschatologische Verkündigung in den johanneischen Texten* (WUNT 117; Tübingen: Mohr Siebeck, 2000) 486.

[87] Cf. G.N. Stanton, who contends that it is often possible to show that the central post-Easter concerns of Christian communitites have *not* been read back into the gospel traditions (*The Gospels and Jesus* [OBS; Oxford: OUP, 1989] 157).

[88] Hoegen-Rohls, *Johannes*, 293-95 and Frey, *Eschatologie III*, 176 indeed hold a view that Jn 20.22 is the 'Johannine Pentecost'.

[89] C. Bennema, 'The Giving of the Spirit in John's Gospel — A New Proposal?', *EvQ* 74 (forthcoming, 2002).

2.2. W/wisdom and Salvation

The major players in scholarly discussion of Johannine soteriology —
Bultmann, Forestell, Loader — all emphasize the importance of knowledge
and understanding, i.e., they attribute a cognitive aspect to salvation.[90] To
explore this dimension further, we examine the study of the concept of
W/wisdom by Johannine scholars, and how they relate it to salvation, in
order to discover to what extent this may contribute to a deeper
understanding of the precise nature of Johannine soteriology.

2.2.1. Jesus as, and in Relation to, Wisdom

Our aim is not to produce an overview of Johannine christology in general,
but to survey the concept of Jesus as, and in relation to, Wisdom. Hence,
we will focus on John's *Wisdom* christology, because we merely want to
explore to what extent Jesus' soteriological functions can be explained in
categories of W/wisdom.[91] Although the concept of Wisdom in the Jewish
sapiential traditions may not be *the* or the *only* conceptual background to
John's christology, many scholars have shown that the Jewish figure of
Wisdom is at least *a* possible and plausible background to John's
presentation of Jesus.[92] Moreover, our interest is synchronic rather than

---

[90] Other scholars we have presented so far have also looked in the direction of
W/wisdom, as this section will reveal.

[91] For surveys on the general christology of the Fourth Gospel, see, e.g., Kysar,
Evangelist, 107-19; Loader, *Christology*, 1-19; M. Scott, *Sophia and the Johannine Jesus*
(JSNT.S 71; Sheffield: JSOT Press, 1992) 25-30; M.J.J. Menken, 'The Christology of the
Fourth Gospel: A Survey of Recent Research' in M.C. de Boer (ed.), *From Jesus to John:
Essays on Jesus and New Testament Christology in Honour of Marinus de Jonge*
(JSNT.S 84; Sheffield: JSOT Press, 1993) 292-320; P.N. Anderson, *The Christology of
the Fourth Gospel: Its Unity and Disunity in the Light of John 6* (WUNT II/78;
Tübingen: Mohr Siebeck, 1996) ch. 1. Both Anderson and Loader do not have a Wisdom
christology. Although Loader briefly mentions the influence of wisdom on the Johannine
Prologue, he is quick in pointing out the assumed departure of Johannine christology
from the wisdom tradition (*Christology*, 158, 168-69).

[92] R. Harris, *The Origin of the Prologue to St John's Gospel* (Cambridge: CUP, 1917);
F.-M. Braun, 'Saint Jean, la Sagesse et l'histoire' in W.C. van Unnik (ed.),
*Neotestamentica et Patristica: Eine Freundesgabe, Herrn Professor Dr. Oscar Cullmann
zu seinem 60. Geburtstag überreicht* (NT.S 6; Leiden: Brill, 1962) 123-28; *idem*, *Jean le
Théologien* (4 vols.; Paris: Gabalda, 1959-72) 4:121-42; H.R. Moeller, 'Wisdom Motifs
and John's Gospel', *BETS* 6 (1963) 92-100; A. Feuillet, 'The Principal Biblical Themes
in the Discourse on the Bread of Life', in A. Feuillet (ed.), *Johannine Studies* (Transl.
T.E. Crane; New York: Alba House, 1964) 53-128; *idem*, *Le Prologue du quatrième
évangile: Étude de théologie johannique* (Paris: Desclée De Brouwer, 1968) 239-44;
Brown, *Gospel*, 1:cxxii-cxxv, 519-24; R.G. Hamerton-Kelly, *Pre-existence, Wisdom, and
the Son of Man: A Study of the Idea of Pre-existence in the New Testament* (SNTS.MS
21; Cambridge: CUP, 1973) 197-215; E.J. Epp, 'Wisdom, Torah, Word: The Johannine
Prologue and the Purpose of the Fourth Gospel' in G.F. Hawthorne (ed.), *Current Issues*

diachronic, i.e., our aim is to discover *how* John's Wisdom christology
functions rather than to provide further proof for (the history of) its
conceptual background.

Our emphasis on the *concept* of Wisdom — rather than on דָּבָר or
Memra — and on the *functionality* of John's Wisdom christology also

---

in *Biblical and Patristic Interpretation: Studies in Honor of Merrill C. Tenney Presented
by His Former Students* (Grand Rapids: Eerdmans, 1975) 130-41; C.H. Talbert, 'The
Myth of a Descending-Ascending Redeemer in Mediterranean Antiquity', *NTS* 22 (1976)
421-22, 438-39; W. Grundmann, *Der Zeuge der Wahrheit: Grundzüge der Christologie
des Johannesevangeliums* (Berlin: Evangelische Verlagsanstalt, 1985) (the manuscript,
however, dates from before 1976); E.D. Freed, 'Theological Prelude to the Prologue of
John's Gospel', *SJTh* 32 (1979) 257-69; H. Gese, 'The Prologue to John's Gospel' in H.
Gese (ed.), *Essays on Biblical Theology* (Minneapolis: Augsburg, 1981) 167-222, esp.
197-222; Culpepper, 'Theology', 421-22; J. Painter, 'Christology and the History of the
Johannine Community in the Prologue of the Fourth Gospel', *NTS* 30 (1984) 465-68;
idem, *Quest*, 145-52; J. Ashton, 'The Transformation of Wisdom: A Study of the
Prologue of John's Gospel', *NTS* 32 (1986) 161-86; J.D.G. Dunn, *Christology in the
Making: A New Testament Inquiry into the Origins of the Doctrine of the Incarnation*
(London: SCM Press, 1989[2]) 164-65, 239-45; *idem*, 'Let John be John: A Gospel for Its
Time' in P. Stuhlmacher (ed.), *The Gospel and the Gospels* (Grand Rapids: Eerdmans,
1991) 313-20; M.E. Willett, *Wisdom Christology in the Fourth Gospel* (San Francisco:
Mellen Research University Press, 1992); Scott, *Sophia*, ch. 3; C.A. Evans, *Word and
Glory: On the Exegetical and Theological Background of John's Prologue* (JSNT.S 89;
Sheffield: JSOT Press, 1993); M.W.G. Stibbe, *John* (Sheffield: JSOT Press, 1993) 23-24;
B. Witherington III, *Jesus the Sage: The Pilgrimage of Wisdom* (Minneapolis: Augsburg
Fortress, 1994) 282-89, 368-80; *idem*, *John's Wisdom: A Commentary on the Fourth
Gospel* (Cambridge: Lutterworth Press, 1995); P. Borgen, 'The Gospel of John and
Hellenism: Some Observations' in R.A. Culpepper and C.C. Black (eds.), *Exploring the
Gospel of John: In Honor of D. Moody Smith* (Louisville: Westminster John Knox Press,
1996) 107-109; J.E. McKinlay, *Gendering Wisdom the Host: Biblical Invitations to Eat
and Drink* (JSOT.S 216; Sheffield: SAP, 1996) esp. ch. 10; M. Coloe, 'The Structure of
the Johannine Prologue and Genesis 1', *Australian Biblical Review* 45 (1997) 40-55;
Ford, *Redeemer*, 115-17; S.H. Ringe, *Wisdom's Friends: Community and Christology in
the Fourth Gospel* (Louisville: Westminster John Knox Press, 1999). Others admit the
presence or influence of Jewish wisdom motifs, without necessarily or explicitly arguing
for a Jewish sapiential background: Dodd, *Interpretation*, 274-78 (Dodd prefers the
Hermetic literature, Philo and Rabbinic Judaism as the background of Johannine
thought); Schnackenburg, *Gospel*, 1:493; Forestell, *Word*, 30, 49, 105-106, 116, 125-26,
142, 196, 204; Kysar, *Evangelist*, 118-19; T.H. Tobin, 'The Prologue of John and
Hellenistic Jewish Speculation', *CBQ* 52 (1990) 252-69. Before Bultmann came up with
his Gnostic Redeemer myth, he defended a wisdom background ('The History of
Religions Background of the Prologue to the Gospel of John' in J. Ashton [ed.], *The
Interpretation of John* [Edinburgh: T&T Clark 1997[2]] 27-46), and even later Bultmann
admitted that '[t]here can be no doubt...that a connection exists between the Judaic
Wisdom myth and the Johannine Prologue' (*Gospel*, 22). Most of these scholars also
offer, although with variations, an explanation for why Logos is used in the Prologue,
and not Sophia. Part of the rationale may be that Sophia and Logos became closely
related in Wis. and were used interchangeably in Philo (cf. Grundmann, *Zeuge*, 17-18).

seems justified by Brown's observation that the *title* ὁ λόγος may be closer
to the prophetic יהוה דְּבַר, but the description of the *activity* of ὁ λόγος is
very much like that of Wisdom.[93] Hence, our survey will be dominated by
the following questions. To what extent is Jesus presented as Wisdom —
in the Prologue *and* in the rest of the Fourth Gospel? What is Jesus'
functional relation to Wisdom, i.e., how does Jesus act as, or similar to,
Wisdom, especially in relation to salvation?[94]

Many scholars who propose the figure of Wisdom as a conceptual
background to the Johannine Jesus have limited themselves to an
investigation of the Logos hymn, but this could result in too limited a view
of John's Wisdom christology.[95] However, a few scholars, such as Ziener,
Braun, Moeller, Feuillet, Brown, Clark and Grundmann, have also
elucidated the presence of Wisdom christology in the rest of the Fourth
Gospel, and accentuated its functional features.[96] However, what these
scholars have done is primarily to draw out the (functional) parallels
between Wisdom and Jesus, but they have not really done much more than
that.[97] They have not, for example, asked *why* John used the figure of

---

[93] Brown, *Gospel*, 1:522; cf. E. Harris, *Prologue and Gospel: The Theology of the
Fourth Evangelist* (JSNT.S 107; Sheffield: SAP, 1994) 197-98. Nevertheless, the Hebraic
conception of Word and the Targumic use of Memra might still be a possible part of the
complex conceptual background of the Logos (see, e.g., B. de Pinto, 'Word and Wisdom
in St John', *Scripture* 19 [1967] 19-27).

[94] To what extent the Johannine Jesus understood himself as Wisdom incarnate, see,
e.g., Brown, *Gospel*, 1:537-38; Witherington, *Jesus*, 374-75.

[95] Those who merely highlight the Prologue for their understanding of Jesus as
Wisdom are, among others, R. Harris, Hamerton-Kelly, Epp, Freed, Gese, Culpepper,
Painter, Ashton, Evans, Coloe. According to Witherington, '[t]his is a mistake, especially
if the Logos Hymn strongly shapes the way the story of Jesus is told thereafter' (*Jesus*,
370; cf. Dodd, *Interpretation*, 285).

[96] G. Ziener, 'Weisheitsbuch und Johannesevangelium (I)', *Bib* 38 (1957) 396-418;
Braun, 'Jean', 124-28; *idem*, *Jean*, 4:121-27; Moeller, 'Wisdom', 92-97; Feuillet,
'Themes', 53-128; Brown, *Gospel*, 1:cxxiii-cxxiv; D.K. Clark, 'Signs in Wisdom and
John', *CBQ* 45 (1983) 201-209; Grundmann, *Zeuge*, ch. 1. Surprisingly, Clark, who
makes a similar case as Ziener, does not interact with him. Grundmann finds some
additional parallels to Brown between Wisdom and the Johannine Jesus in the area of
soteriology (both are portrayed as givers of life, to know Wisdom/Jesus results in
immortality/eternal life, and to keep Wisdom's/Jesus' commandments is a necessity) and
pneumatology (both Wisdom and Jesus are empowered by the Spirit, and the reception of
the Spirit provides insight in heavenly things) (*Zeuge*, 18-27). McKinlay, who focuses on
the intertextual relationships of the invitations of Sophia/Jesus to eat and drink in Prov.
9, Sir. 24 and Jn 4, has a totally different agenda from ours; her interest is in the role of
gender within these texts and its implications (*Wisdom*, see esp. ch. 10).

[97] Grundmann's work, e.g., shows a serious discontinuity between ch. 1, where he
argues that Jewish wisdom literature (esp. Wis.) is the most important factor that
influenced the christology of the Fourth Gospel, and the rest of the chapters, where there
is merely one reference to the sapiential corpus. Although both Ziener and Clark discover

personified Wisdom to present Jesus, or shown where the presentation of the Johannine Jesus *differs* from that of Wisdom.

Other scholars go further than merely pointing to some parallels. Scott, for example, demonstrates the great extent to which Jesus acts as Wisdom in the whole of John's Gospel.[98] Scott is also able to explain why Sophia is used for John's christology, namely that the concept of the Logos is used as a vehicle to accommodate the gender switch between the female Sophia and the male Jesus, i.e., Jesus is the incarnation of both the female and male principles of God.[99] However, although Scott notices a soteriological parallel between Sophia and Jesus — they both impart eternal life/salvation — he does not develop it, nor does he integrate John's Wisdom christology with his soteriology (or pneumatology).[100] Moreover, it seems that Scott's gender-driven agenda, giving prominence to the role of women in the Fourth Gospel (and the Johannine community), is accomplished through a 'forced' feminine christology.[101] Witherington recognizes that John's Gospel is greatly indebted to the (Hellenistic) Jewish wisdom tradition, and the originality of his commentary is the attempt to read the whole of the Fourth Gospel in the light of this wisdom tradition.[102] However, although Witherington interacts with Ziener, Moeller, Brown, Clark and Scott, he frequently does not go beyond them. Ringe, after identifying the Prologue as a 'Wisdom hymn', also demonstrates that the Jewish wisdom traditions have permeated the whole of the Fourth Gospel.[103] Ringe explores the christological and ecclesiological aspects of friendship in John against a Jewish wisdom background, but she does not link it with John's soteriology; only Ford sees friendship as a soteriological category (see below).

---

some soteriological connotations in the way Jesus' signs correspond to Wisdom's signs in Wis. 11-19, they do not actually draw out the significance of their observations. Willett, however, who interacts with Ziener and Clark, observes that John's Wisdom christology is linked to the Exodus motif; the signs become acts of liberation (*Wisdom*, 116-18).

[98] Scott, *Sophia*, 115-68.

[99] Scott, *Sophia*, 170-73, 244-45.

[100] Scott, *Sophia*, 134-39.

[101] For Scott's agenda, see *Sophia*, 13-14. In his investigation of the Jewish wisdom literature, Scott argues that Sophia is depicted as the female expression of the one God (just as Yahweh is the traditional male expression of the one God elsewhere), and claims that the zenith of Sophia's development is reached in Wis., where she is not pictured as dependent upon or subordinate to but as coterminous with Yahweh (*Sophia*, 49-62, 81). However, Wis. 3.10-11 (people despising Yahweh's Sophia) and Wis. 9.1-4 (Yahweh created humanity by his Sophia, who sits by Yahweh's throne) seem to indicate otherwise. Cf. Witherington for a critique on Scott (*Jesus*, 370 n.102).

[102] Witherington, *Wisdom*, vii, *passim*; see also *idem*, *Jesus*, 368-80.

[103] See Ringe, *Friends*, ch. 4.

Thus, only very few scholars have observed that there are wider implications of the many parallels between John's Gospel and the Jewish wisdom literature.[104] Nonetheless, some scholars have tried to integrate John's Wisdom christology with his soteriology. Talbert made a good, though brief, start; he sees two important parallels between Wisdom and Jesus — a *pattern* of κατάβασις-ἀνάβασις and a soteriological *function* — and is able to put these together under the concept of a descending-ascending redeemer.[105] Based on John 6, Thompson is able to link John's Wisdom christology with his soteriology via the concept of agency: (i) Wisdom is a category of agency that allows for the closest possible unity between the agent (Jesus as Wisdom incarnate) and sender (God); (ii) Wisdom is envisioned as a life-giving agent; (iii) Jesus, as God's agent, embodies God's wisdom, and hence, Jesus mediates God's life.[106] Ford connects the Wisdom christology of the Fourth Gospel with its soteriology, in that she perceives (i) the concept of 'friendship with God' as the soteriological category, and (ii) Jesus as Wisdom incarnate, who came to make people 'friends of God' through a renewal of the covenant חסד.[107] Important as this observation may be, this is virtually the only study Ford makes of how Jesus functions as Wisdom, and then only briefly.

Willett, like Scott, notices almost the same parallels between the figure of Wisdom and the Johannine Jesus, but is able, unlike Scott, to integrate them with John's concept of salvation. Willett arranges the parallels between Wisdom and Jesus under six themes — pre-existence, descent-ascent, revelation-hiddenness, acceptance-rejection, intimacy with disciples, glory and life — and uses the last four of these themes to sketch John's soteriology:

> Out of his intimacy with the Father, Jesus reveals the Father, just as Wisdom reveals God out of her intimacy with God, though both are depicted as "hidden revealers".

---

[104] Witherington, e.g., remarks that John's pneumatology, christology and soteriology owe something to the sapiential corpus, but he does not pursue this (*Jesus*, 378-79; *Wisdom*, 25-26). Cf. the conclusion of M.E. Isaacs, that John's christology and pneumatology owe something to the (Hellenistic Jewish) wisdom literature (*The Concept of Spirit: A Study of Pneuma in Hellenistic Judaism and its Bearing on the New Testament* [Heythrop Monographs 1; Huddersfield: Charlesworth, 1976] 135-38).

[105] Talbert, 'Myth', 421-22, 438-39. Talbert's aim is to prove that the Hellenistic-Jewish mythology of a descending-ascending redeemer, as found in the wisdom tradition and in Jewish angelology, served as the conceptual background for the NT presentation of Jesus.

[106] M.M. Thompson, 'Thinking about God: Wisdom and Theology in John 6' in R.A. Culpepper (ed.), *Critical Readings of John 6* (BIS 22; Leiden: Brill, 1997) 221-46.

[107] Ford, *Redeemer*, 115-18. Cf. Gese ('Prologue', 205-209), who also mentions the soteriological concept of חסד in the Prologue but who does not connect it with the concept of friendship.

The soteriological dualism of the Gospel, which divides people into two camps based on their response to the revealer, resembles the soteriological dualism of the Wisdom material. Those who accept Jesus form a community in which they experience intimacy with her. Glory and life, the primary benefits which the disciples receive from Jesus, are also the benefits which Wisdom gives to her disciples.[108]

Although Willett is the one who contributes most significantly towards an integration of John's Wisdom christology and his soteriology, his model is not complete; it may be expanded if it incorporates the Spirit and if it explains how this intimacy with Jesus is maintained.[109]

Turner is most able to integrate John's Wisdom christology with his soteriology. He argues that Jesus, as Wisdom incarnate, provides revelatory wisdom teaching which brings life/salvation because it contains saving wisdom.[110] How the content of Jesus' teaching can be salvific is explained by Turner in terms of the Spirit being the source of this saving revelatory wisdom (see section 2.3, below).

2.2.2. Knowledge/Wisdom

The leading issue of this section is the relationship between the concept of knowledge/wisdom and salvation. Bultmann's conception of genuine faith is that it contains/possesses knowledge (or 'truth') of the Revealer/revelation (γινώσκειν is a *constitutive* element in πιστεύειν), and that it results in life.[111] For Bultmann, γινώσκω refers to the divine mode of being, i.e., the relationship between the Father and Son, and has primarily the sense of recognizing/understanding this unity and of accepting the divine act of love in Jesus.[112] However, Bultmann does not explicitly mention the locus of this knowledge nor how it can be accessed/obtained. Moreover, Bultmann's concept of knowledge seems to be as empty as his concept of revelation: if Jesus' revelation/word has 'no definable content at all', except that Jesus is the Revealer,[113] then the (content of) knowledge possessed by genuine faith is necessarily also reduced to this fact.[114] However, Johannine passages such as 14.26, 16.13

---

[108] See Willett, *Wisdom*, ch. 2 (quotation from p.125).

[109] However, see Willett's recommendation for further research (*Wisdom*, 153).

[110] See Turner, *Spirit*, ch. 4.

[111] Bultmann, 'Γινώσκω', 1:713; *idem, Gospel*, 434-35; *idem, Theology*, 2:73-74, 78. Although Bultmann has a relational concept of 'knowledge', he argues that it is built on the γινώσκειν of Hellenistic Gnosticism rather than derived from the Hebrew ידע, but, unlike Gnosticism, faith and knowledge are not two distinct stages ('Γινώσκω', I:711-13; cf. *Theology*, 2:74; *Gospel*, 367-68, 380-82).

[112] Bultmann, 'Γινώσκω', I:711-12.

[113] Bultmann, *Theology*, 2:63, 66.

[114] This seems confirmed by Bultmann's understanding of γινώσκω primarily in terms of perception, reception and recognition (*Gospel*, 55, 435, 495). A related problem is that

and 17.3 indicate a more comprehensive understanding of the identity and mission of the Father and Son.

Other scholars could also describe salvation in terms of knowledge. For Dodd, eternal life is or consists in the knowledge of God, which is an apprehension of divine reality manifested in Jesus, and the awareness of a relation of mutual indwelling of God and people.[115] Forestell recognizes that true faith is a grasp of and an access to heavenly knowledge of the Father and Son, and that eternal life, as the very life of God himself, is realized in a communion of knowledge and of love communicated by Jesus to the believer.[116] Barrett follows Bultmann by saying that the bestowal or communication of knowledge (of God) results in life/salvation.[117] However, in contrast to Bultmann's gnostic view of knowledge, Barrett argues that John creates a unique fusion of the Greek understanding of knowledge (with its emphasis on observation, objectivity and intellect) and the Hebrew understanding of knowledge — where it is more a relational term, in which saving knowledge is rooted in the knowledge of God in the historical Jesus; it is therefore objective and at the same time relational.[118]

Nevertheless, questions of how and where this saving knowledge is rooted in Jesus, and how this saving knowledge is mediated to people are not addressed. A very few scholars have attempted to address these issues. Barton, for example, believes that the locus of saving knowledge is the revelation of the Father by the Son, but he does not expand upon his view.[119] Turner also identifies Jesus' revelatory teaching as the locus of this saving wisdom, and he interprets saving wisdom in terms of the authentic insight into or understanding of Jesus' revelation, especially of

---

Bultmann does not really explain *how* one acquires or comes to this perception/reception/recognition; Bultmann does not explain his statement that γινώσκειν 'certainly refers to an act of cognition' (*Gospel*, 55 n.5), and an answer in terms of πιστεύω (possibly *Gospel*, 435 n.4) would only create a vicious circle (γινώσκω through πιστεύω and πιστεύω through γινώσκω).

[115] Dodd, *Interpretation*, 169, 177-78. Cf. Schnackenburg, *Gospel*, 2:360. Although Dodd's understanding of 'knowledge' is based on Bultmann's, he allows, contra Bultmann, an interweaving of the Greek and Hebrew conceptions (*Interpretation*, 151-69). Moreover, *pace* Bultmann, Dodd mentions that faith is the *equivalent* of the knowledge of God, by virtue of equating faith with spiritual sight and knowledge of God with vision of God (*Interpretation*, 165-68, 185-86; cf. Kysar, *John*, 91).

[116] Forestell, *Word*, 42-43, 108, 116-17. Forestell's understanding of 'knowledge' seems to be derived from the Jewish wisdom and apocalyptic traditions.

[117] Barrett, *Gospel*, 79-82, 157-58, 503.

[118] Barrett, *Gospel*, 162, 504. Brown (*Gospel*, 1:508) and Schnackenburg (*Gospel*, 1:565-66) also emphasize the relational aspect of γινώσκω. Kysar argues that γινώσκω is used exclusively in the Hebraic sense of ידע (*John*, 91-92; cf. Ladd, *Theology*, 298-99).

[119] Barton, *Spirituality*, 124.

his death on the cross.[120] According to Turner, this saving wisdom is provided by the Spirit (see section 2.3, below).

Ford perceives Jesus as incarnate Wisdom who mediates salvation, i.e., restoration of friendship with God, but she uses the concept of *saving* חֶסֶד instead of saving wisdom/knowledge.[121] Moreover, Ford does not seem to elaborate this concept; when she goes on to present Jesus/Wisdom incarnate as a breast-feeding mother, nourishing her children,[122] we might not easily link Wisdom's nourishment with חֶסֶד.

2.3. Spirit, Salvation, W/wisdom

As indicated at the end of section 2.1.3, the main difference between Porsch, Loader, Koottumkal and Turner lies in their understanding of the Spirit's role in salvation. Moreover, both in the Jewish wisdom traditions and in the Fourth Gospel, there is a close connection between the Spirit, Wisdom (see ch. 2) and Jesus. Hence, it seems not merely legitimate but also necessary to incorporate the concept of Spirit into our investigation. Our agenda for this section, then, is twofold. What are the *soteriological* functions of the Spirit? Has the Spirit a realized dimension, i.e., *how* and to what extent was the Spirit already soteriologically active *during* Jesus' earthly ministry?

Concerning the relationship between Spirit and salvation, scholars and commentators in general do recognize that the Spirit has a salvific role in John, but they hardly spell out this function. Moreover, on Johannine pneumatology only five major works have been produced in the last thirty years: those by Porsch, Ferraro, Burge, Chevallier and Keener.[123] Ferraro, not referred to by Keener and Burge, deals with all the Spirit-passages sequentially, i.e., in order of appearance in John (more like a commentary), rather than thematically, and does not really integrate John's pneumatology with his (Wisdom) christology and soteriology. Burge's aim is to elucidate

---

[120] Turner, *Spirit*, 57, 64-66, 69-70, 98-99.

[121] Ford, *Redeemer*, 113, 118.

[122] Ford, *Redeemer*, 124-35.

[123] Porsch, *Pneuma*; G. Ferraro, *Lo Spirito e Cristo nel vangelo di Giovanni* (Studi Biblici 70; Brescia: Paideia Editrice, 1984); Burge, *Community*; M.-A. Chevallier, *Souffle de Dieu: Le Saint-Esprit dans le Nouveau Testament* (2 vols.; Paris: Beauchesne, 1978, 1990); C.S. Keener, 'The Function of Johannine Pneumatology in the Context of Late First Century Judaism' (Duke University: Ph.D. dissertation, 1991; Ann Arbor: UMI, 1992). Although the work of G. Johnston (*The Spirit-Paraclete in the Gospel of John* [SNTS.MS 12; Cambridge: CUP, 1970]) seems to deal with John's pneumatology as a whole, his treatment of the Spirit in Jn 1-12, 19-20 is far from adequate (cf. Burge [*Community*, 4] for an assessment of Johnston's monograph). Other dissertations on Johannine pneumatology merely focus on one aspect of John's concept of the Spirit and do not contribute significantly towards our objective (e.g., Holwerda, *Spirit*; E. Franck, *Revelation Taught: The Paraclete in the Gospel of John* [Lund: Gleerup, 1985]).

the role of the Spirit in the Johannine community according to its view both of Jesus and of Christian experience, but he does not focus on soteriology. One quarter of Chevallier's impressive two-volume work on the Spirit in the NT is devoted to the Johannine literature, but Chevallier emphasizes more the ecclesiological and missiological aspects of the role of the Spirit-Paraclete rather than the soteriological.[124] Keener focuses on the water motif and the purification function of the Spirit, but he does not really explain even the content of the purifying work of the Spirit, nor what the effects and implications are for people. If he had, he would have discovered that the purifying function of the Spirit could be explained in terms of salvation and wisdom. Thus, the studies of Ferraro, Burge, Chevallier and Keener do not contribute significantly to our questions. Before we investigate Porsch's contribution, however, we need to look first at the work of Thüsing because its influence can be seen, for example, in the works of Porsch and Loader.

Thüsing's objective is to investigate the Johannine concepts of lifting up (*Erhöhung*) and glorification (*Verherrlichung*) in relation to John's soteriology,[125] and he has also been able to integrate the Spirit into it. Thüsing presents a *two-stage model of John's pneumatic soteriology*: (i) the earthly work of Jesus which culminated in his salvific death on the cross (*Erhöhung*); (ii) subsequently, the outworking or unfolding of *die Erhöhung* in the community of believers, which is identical with the revelatory work of the Paraclete.[126] Hence, the first stage focuses on *die Aufrichtung des Heilzeichens* by Jesus, and the second stage on *die Auswirkung des Heilzeichens* by the Paraclete.[127] According to Thüsing, salvation is only available after the cross and the coming of the Spirit-Paraclete, and John was not interested in what might have been available before Easter; all references to the gift of life in Jesus' ministry are proleptic and only realized after the coming of the Spirit-Paraclete.[128] Furthermore, the references to the Spirit in Jesus' ministry are also merely proleptic and point to the work of the Spirit as Paraclete in the second stage of salvation.[129] Thus, besides the practical denial of salvation during Jesus' earthly ministry,[130] Thüsing also virtually denies any work of the Spirit in Jesus' ministry. Moreover, although Thüsing mentions that the revelatory work of Jesus' earthly life and of the Paraclete are not two

---

[124] Chevallier, *Souffle*, 2:409-564.

[125] Thüsing, *Erhöhung*, iii.

[126] Thüsing, *Erhöhung*, 45-48, 201-204. For a description of the Paraclete's work, see *Erhöhung*, 141-74.

[127] Thüsing, *Erhöhung*, 292-93.

[128] Thüsing, *Erhöhung*, 161, 164, 321-25.

[129] Thüsing, *Erhöhung*, 324-25.

[130] This is Loader's main problem with Thüsing (*Christology*, 127-29).

different works but a unity, in that the object of revelation is in both stages the same (namely, the Father),[131] it still seems that Thüsing distinguishes too strongly between the earthly work of Jesus and the subsequent work of the Paraclete.

The main task of Porsch is to investigate Johannine pneumatology in regard to its unity, i.e., whether John presents two views of the Spirit — an impersonal Spirit and a personal Paraclete — or a single view. He concludes that there is a unified concept behind the Pneuma-sayings, which emphasizes the christological focus of Johannine pneumatology.[132] The basis for Porsch's two-stage model of salvation (see section 2.1.3, above) is essentially his *two-stage model of the gift of the Spirit*: (i) during Jesus' ministry, the Spirit is 'given', i.e., proleptically present, in Jesus' revelatory words but not yet really active; (ii) only after Jesus' glorification, the Spirit becomes active in its life-giving effectiveness and can be (fully) experienced as such, in that the Spirit interprets and opens up Jesus' revelation.[133] Thus, Porsch closely relates Jesus' revelatory word and the Spirit, and argues that there must hence also be a relationship between Johannine soteriology and pneumatology, which Porsch understands as follows: the 'not yet' of true faith/salvation during Jesus' ministry corresponds with the 'not yet' of (the work of) the Spirit during Jesus' ministry.[134] Although Porsch does not explicitly integrate John's pneumatology with his soteriology, it is possible to deduce from his work a *two-stage model of John's pneumatic soteriology*: (i) during Jesus' ministry, partial salvation or beginning faith is offered to people in the form of Jesus' revelatory word in which the Spirit is proleptically/actively present, but (ii) only after Jesus' glorification will this faith be perfected/completed through the Spirit-Paraclete who interprets and opens up Jesus' revelation.[135] Although Porsch points in the right direction and

---

[131] Thüsing, *Erhöhung*, 203.

[132] Porsch, *Pneuma*, 3, 405.

[133] Porsch, *Pneuma*, 65-72, 139-45, 200-12.

[134] Porsch, *Pneuma*, 3, 66-67.

[135] Porsch's two-stage model is influenced by de la Potterie, who was first to distinguish between two stages in the economy of revelation — the time of Jesus and the time of the Spirit (Porsch refers to de la Potterie's unpublished thesis from 1965 [*Pneuma*, 144]; cf. I. de la Potterie, 'Parole et Esprit dans S. Jean' in M. de Jonge [ed.], *L'Évangile de Jean: Sources, rédaction, théologie* [BEThL 44; Leuven: Leuven University Press, 1977] 187-92; idem, *La Vérité dans Saint Jean* [2 vols.; Rome: Biblical Institute Press, 1977] 2:684-96). However, de la Potterie in turn is strongly influenced by Porsch again (in de la Potterie's article 'Parole', e.g., Porsch is referred to in fifteen out of eighty-six footnotes). Porsch is also influenced by Thüsing, although not always agreeing with him. Ferraro is influenced by both de la Potterie and Porsch (*Spirito*, 82, 93, 118, 121, 301-302). The influence of de la Potterie and Porsch can also be seen in Chevallier (*Souffle*, 2:427-30, 450-54, 502, 510-14).

influenced scholars like Loader, Koottumkal and Turner, he leaves two critical questions unanswered. *What* exactly is unlocked by the opening up of Jesus' revelation? *How* is the opening up of Jesus' revelation soteriologically significant? Moreover, Porsch does not seem to be very clear about the role of the Spirit during Jesus' ministry: how can the Spirit already be actively present in Jesus' words during Jesus' ministry but only become active, functionally or in its life-giving effectiveness, after Jesus' glorification?

Loader's christological and soteriological model is more nuanced than we have presented so far. Loader's model of Johannine christology is essentially a synthesis of two significant streams of christological thought: the *revealer-envoy model*, which is the dominating one in that it is central and foundational, and the *Son of Man cluster*, which is the 'greater' one in that it bridges the hermeneutical distance between the ministry of Jesus and the time of the author of the Fourth Gospel.[136] Based on his twofold model of Johannine christology, Loader develops, through integration with John's soteriology and pneumatology, a *two-stage model of Johannine pneumatic soteriology*: (i) according to the revealer-envoy christology, salvation was already fully available prior to the cross in the person of and in relationship with Jesus; (ii) according to the Son of Man christology, which focuses on the climax of Jesus' ministry (his death and return to the Father), this life of Jesus is available after the cross through the work of the Spirit-Paraclete mediating a deeper understanding of and access to Jesus' revelation.[137] According to Loader, John holds together two christological traditions which reflect different salvific foci. On the one hand, the revealer-envoy model points to the saving presence of Jesus in his ministry and the offer of life as present in his person. On the other hand, the Son of Man cluster points forward to the coming of the Spirit-

---

[136] Loader, *Christology*, 204-14, 230-31. Loader calls the nexus of Jesus' death-resurrection-exaltation-glorification-ascension-return to the Father as the Son of Man, the 'Son of Man cluster' or 'greater event', and this 'greater event' results in 'greater things' — greater/deeper understanding of (the significance of) Jesus' revelation, empowerment for mission, building up of the community of faith — through the sending of the Spirit-Paraclete (and of the disciples). The 'greater event' thus has a hermeneutical function — it makes available for all the true significance of the event of revelation — and the Spirit-Paraclete is the primary agent in this hermeneutical function in that the Spirit-Paraclete deepens the knowledge of faith already in existence (*Christology*, 105, 126-35, 208).

[137] Loader, *Christology*, 78, 84-88, 105-107, 126-32, 204-14. Loader interacts substantially with Thüsing, and his model is similar to that of Thüsing, in that the cross is the turning-point after which the coming of the Spirit-Paraclete is possible and which in turn results in the release of the soteriological functions of the Spirit-Paraclete. Loader's main difference from Thüsing, however, is that of the availability of salvation already during Jesus' ministry.

Paraclete who will secure and assure the ongoing availability and abundance of this gift of life in the community of believers after Easter.[138]

Loader's two-stage model of John's pneumatic soteriology seems to be influenced by, and a variant on, the model of Porsch.[139] Moreover, concerning the cognitive aspect of salvation Loader's views seem to be confusing: on the one hand, Jesus (and his revelation) does not impart 'information'; yet, on the other hand, Loader mentions that the work of the Spirit-Paraclete includes the giving of 'information'.[140] Does Loader imply that the cognitive aspect of salvation only comes into being after Easter? Although he indicates *what* the information-giving task of the Spirit-Paraclete entails — calling to remembrance Jesus' words, interpreting them in the light of scripture, mediating the words of the exalted Lord to the community, and leading the disciples into all truth concerning who Jesus is and the meaning of his death and return to the Father[141] — Loader does not explain *how* the Spirit-Paraclete imparts this information. Finally, Loader's model has some serious implications that need to be tested. First, Loader does not indicate a necessity for the Spirit in the revealer-envoy model; although the Spirit was 'present and active' through Jesus in the earthly ministry, the Spirit seems to have no (significant) soteriological role.[142] Second, because the soteriological work of the Spirit as Paraclete only starts after Jesus' glorification, Loader creates a dichotomy between the (soteriological) work of the Spirit during and after Jesus' ministry. Third, although the Spirit-Paraclete is soteriologically necessary for people after Easter, for the disciples the gift of the Spirit-Paraclete seems to have been virtually a *donum superadditum* for empowerment for mission; they had already received life in relationship with Jesus.

Koottumkal investigates the life-giving dimension of Jesus' word and defines it in terms of the Spirit, using John 6.63, 68 as the paradigmatic foundation for his model. Jesus' word is life-giving *because* in it the life-giving Spirit is active, i.e., in Jesus' revelatory word one can experience

---

[138] Loader, *Christology*, 208-14, 227. Independently of Loader, Hultgren presents a model that also integrates John's (redemptive) christology and soteriology, and has some similarities with Loader's model (see *Christ*, 41-44, ch. 8 [esp. pp.146-47]). However, Hultgren does not integrate John's redemptive christology with John's pneumatology. Moreover, Hultgren differs from Loader in that Hultgren argues that the cross is salvific and atoning (although the latter is presupposed more) (*Christ*, 148-49). Finally, Hultgren does not emphasize, as Loader does, the relational aspect of salvation but merely how one will respond to Jesus (*Christ*, 153).

[139] See, e.g., *Christology*, 128-31, where Loader develops an important part of his soteriological model and interacts intensively with Porsch.

[140] Loader, *Christology*, cf. 136-41 over against 212.

[141] Loader, *Christology*, 227. Cf. Loader's description of the Spirit-Paraclete's hermeneutical function in n.136, above.

[142] Loader, *Christology*, 129-32.

the life-giving Spirit; without the action of the Spirit Jesus' words cannot give life but remain offensive and scandalous.[143] However, although Koottumkal is strongly influenced by de la Potterie and Porsch, he does not go beyond them. Like Porsch, he merely answers the question of how Jesus' words can give life, but still leaves the most important questions unanswered, namely, *why* Jesus' words cannot give life and remain unacceptable without the Spirit, and *how* the life-giving Spirit is active in Jesus' word. Moreover, on the one hand, Koottumkal says that Jesus can give life because he is the source of life and has life in himself. On the other hand, he argues that the Spirit has the power to give life, that life is the result of the Spirit's work, that Jesus can give life because in his word the life-giving Spirit is active, and that there is no life-giving power without the Spirit.[144] Now who, for Koottumkal, is the source of life: the Spirit or Jesus? Is Jesus the source of life because he is the Son or because he has the Spirit? Finally, Koottumkal does not seem to have preserved any eschatological tension because he does not consider the significance of the cross or the gift of the Spirit. Is, for Koottumkal, salvation and the Spirit's life-giving activity already available (partially or in all its fullness) before the cross?

To the questions raised by the models of Porsch, Loader and Koottumkal, Turner's model provides a possible answer: it is the concept of *saving wisdom*, which is then mediated to people by the Spirit.[145] Turner's model of *John's pneumatic W/wisdom soteriology* can then be described as follows. The Spirit upon Jesus enables Jesus, as Wisdom incarnate, to give revelatory wisdom teaching. The Spirit upon Jesus also affects people (already in Jesus' ministry), in that the Spirit is actively reaching out to people through Jesus' teaching. The Spirit has to unfold or illumine to people the revelation that Jesus brings by imparting spiritual wisdom, for only then does it bring life. The two-stage experience of the Spirit the disciples had — during Jesus' ministry, the process of life-giving experiences of the Spirit-and-word (through Jesus) reaching its climax in the gift of the Spirit in 20.22, and, after Jesus' departure, the coming of the Spirit as Paraclete — is not paradigmatic for later generations because the reception of the Spirit-Paraclete is the necessary and sufficient condition of salvation.[146] Thus, Turner argues that already during Jesus' ministry the Spirit was soteriologically active (with probably Koottumkal, but contra Thüsing, Loader and, in essence, also Porsch), but that this salvation was only partial (with Porsch, but contra Thüsing, Loader and probably

---

[143] Koottumkal, *Words*, 104-20.
[144] Koottumkal, *Words*, 110, 112, 118-20, 126, 131-33.
[145] See Turner, *Spirit*, chs. 4-5.
[146] See Turner, *Spirit*, chs. 4-6.

Koottumkal).[147] However, Turner seems to focus more on the cognitive aspect of salvation at the expense of its relational aspect.[148] Moreover, although Turner is the only scholar who describes the interrelation between Spirit, W/wisdom and salvation in John, his material on John is merely preparatory because the main purpose of his book is to explore the significance of the gift of the Spirit in the whole of the NT and for today.[149]

Hamid-Khani's comprehensive study examines the enigmatic language of the Fourth Gospel within John's theological framework, especially in the context of Jesus as the Christ according to Israel's Scriptures (the OT).[150] From Hamid-Khani's investigation, a model of *John's pneumatic soteriology* can be derived. Jesus, as the Christ, is the embodiment of God's self-manifestation and the climax of God's salvific revelation.[151] However, the perception of this reality is beyond the capacity of natural people to comprehend; spiritual perception of Jesus' identity and comprehension of God's salvific revelation in Jesus is *only* available for those who are born of God by faith. To believers who have 'abiding faith' the Spirit illuminates the truth, i.e., the Spirit reveals to those who have entered into a relationship with God the true significance of the revelation given in Christ.[152] Hamid-Khani's study is an excellent introduction into the function of John's elusive language, but concerning his soteriological model some questions can be raised. First, if spiritual perception and understanding is exclusively for believers, then the faith needed to enter into a relationship with God seems to have been robbed largely of its cognitive dimension. The implication of this is also that the Spirit seems to have no illuminative role in bringing unbelievers to salvation. According to Hamid-Khani, faith should include the belief in Jesus' divine origin and

---

[147] In Turner's most recent work on the Spirit (*Spirit*, 1999), Porsch is hardly mentioned, but Turner interacts much more with Porsch in one of his earliest articles ('The Concept of Receiving the Spirit in John's Gospel', *VoxEv* 10 [1977] 24-42), although he does not explicitly show awareness of Porsch's two-stage model.

[148] Only twice Turner mentions explicitly the relational aspect of salvation and the Spirit (*Spirit*, 88, 154). Although Turner does more justice to the relational aspect of the Spirit and salvation in a forthcoming article, its main thrust is the *spirituality* of the Johannine community, i.e., the experience of the Father and Son by the Spirit in the Johannine community (M.[M.B.] Turner, 'The Churches of the Johannine Letters as Communities of "Trinitarian" *Koinōnia*' in W. Ma and R.P. Menzies [eds.], *Spirit and Spirituality: Essays in Honor of Russell P. Spittler* [forthcoming, 2002]).

[149] Cf. Turner, *Spirit*, xi-xiii.

[150] S. Hamid-Khani, *Revelation and Concealment of Christ: A Theological Inquiry into the Elusive Language of the Fourth Gospel* (WUNT II/120; Tübingen: Mohr Siebeck, 2000).

[151] See Hamid-Khani, *Revelation*, ch. 4.

[152] See Hamid-Khani, *Revelation*, ch. 6.

in his death as salvifically efficacious.[153] However, if people naturally are unable to comprehend this reality, will it then not be natural to assume that people need to be aided by the Spirit's illumination in order to come to this faith? Second, Hamid-Khani does not explain precisely *how* the Spirit illuminates the truth to the believer, except in terms of unveiling the truth and true significance of Jesus' revelation. Third, Hamid-Khani seems to attribute the illuminative role of the Spirit only to the period after Easter, and hence diminishes the work of the Spirit during Jesus' earthly ministry.[154]

2.4. Conclusion

Concerning the Johannine concept of salvation in general, the question of what or who leads to and maintains salvation has been answered unsatisfactorily so far and needs further research. Moreover, we have not been able to find a satisfactory answer to the issue of the development of faith — staged, progressive? — and its relation to the signs. Finally, concerning the realized dimension of salvation, virtually everyone agrees that salvation is available after the cross, but what is neglected in general is the *possibility* of salvation during Jesus' ministry, and *how* this might have been possible.[155] Porsch, Loader and Turner have attempted to do more justice to the note of realized eschatology, even within Jesus' earthly ministry, although Porsch and Turner, *pace* Loader, yet maintain that the centre of gravity lies beyond Jesus' glorification. Interestingly, Porsch and Turner try to solve the tension between salvation before and after the cross via John's pneumatology, whereas Loader attempts to solve it via John's christology. In conclusion, what is missing is a more coherent and complete model of Johannine soteriology that integrates the various activities/aspects of coming into and remaining in salvation. Only then will

---

[153] Hamid-Khani, *Revelation*, 373.

[154] Hamid-Khani, *Revelation*, 333-37, 360. This is of course also implied by Hamid-Khani: if the disciples are only born of God in 20.22, and if the Spirit's illumination is only for these kind of people, then this illumination of the truth is only available after Easter.

[155] For our rationale behind the investigation of a realized dimension of salvation during Jesus' earthly ministry, see excursus 1, above. Moreover, if the soteriological functions of the Spirit came into being only after the cross (so Thüsing, Loader and, essentially, also Porsch), then we need to account for the discontinuity between the work of the Spirit before (if any) and after the cross. Furthermore, there is also then a discontinuity between the functions of the Spirit in relation to Jesus before the cross in John's Gospel and the soteriological function of the Spirit in relation to Wisdom in Judaism (see ch. 2). However, if during Jesus' ministry salvation was already available and if the Spirit was already performing a soteriological function, then this might deepen our understanding of John's soteriology and the Spirit's role in it.

we be able to identify, and consequently examine, those activities in which the Spirit is involved.

A related problem is the relative neglect of the cognitive element of salvation; most scholars either tend to emphasize only the relational aspect of John's soteriology (e.g., Thompson, Willett, Ford), or they do not seem to give much place to the cognitive aspect. Only a few try to combine the relational and cognitive aspects of Johannine soteriology. Bultmann is the first who offers a 'model' of Johannine soteriology that combines relational and cognitive aspects; for him salvation is authentic human existence in relationship with the Son and the Father through 'knowing' faith. Loader's soteriology, based on his christological model and integrated with John's pneumatology, is strongly influenced by Bultmann and Porsch. Nevertheless, for both Bultmann and Loader the cognitive aspect of salvation seems rather vacuous, being defined primarily as re-cognition/identification (of Jesus as the Revealer sent by God). Although some others (e.g., Dodd, Barrett and Forestell) also recognize, besides the relational aspect, the concept of saving knowledge, they do not shed more light on it. Turner gives the most complete and coherent model of the cognitive aspect of John's soteriology, but he pays lesser attention to the relational aspect. Thus, we observe that although some scholars have identified a cognitive element of salvation, they have, with the exception of Turner, not fully explored it, and even Turner has not sufficiently shown how the cognitive aspect relates to the relational aspect and how they can be integrated into a model of Johannine soteriology.

We make two further comments about this cognitive aspect. First, although Bultmann and Dodd touched on the significant issue of saving knowledge, their interests were etymological whereas ours is primarily conceptual; rather than studying the etymology of γινώσκω, our strategy will be to investigate the *concept* of salvific knowledge, which lies, we think, in the concept of wisdom in sapiential Judaism. Second, when we investigate the cognitive aspect of salvation, the focus will be on the 'objective' element, i.e., on the concept of saving knowledge/wisdom as the content of salvation, rather than on the 'subjective' response or psychological dimension of the human mind.

Another general problem is that scholars have studied aspects of Johannine theology — soteriology, christology and pneumatology — too much in isolation. None who wrote theses on John's soteriology — T. Müller, Riedl, Forestell, Kohler and Knöppler — attributes any significant soteriological function to the Spirit.[156] Of those who focused on John's

---

[156] Although Forestell, e.g., says that 'the Spirit is that divine power…which produces faith in the believer, and by which the gift of eternal life is bestowed' (*Word*, 135), he does not explain this at all.

Wisdom christology, the two most significant contributors — Scott and Willett — have not looked at John's pneumatology and insufficiently at John's soteriology. Moreover, most of those who concentrate on John's pneumatology — Ferraro, Burge, Chevallier and Keener — do not shed much light on the Spirit's soteriological function. The main exceptions are Porsch, Loader, Turner and Hamid-Khani, who are the main contributors to the issue of the soteriological functions of the Spirit in the Fourth Gospel.[157]

Both Porsch and Loader present a two-stage model of John's pneumatic soteriology — Porsch on pneumatological grounds, Loader on christological. The seminal work of Porsch (but also that of Loader) has been seriously neglected. Although Porsch's thesis was published in 1974, no-one has sufficiently and satisfactorily dealt with his work. Keener does not interact with Porsch, and although Burge, for example, does engage with Porsch, he has totally missed Porsch's two-stage model, which forms not only the backbone of his thesis but also the foundation for his innovative interpretation of 20.22.[158] Neither has anyone seriously engaged with Loader, who is profoundly influenced by both Bultmann and Porsch.

Nevertheless, the questions raised by Porsch's and Loader's models of John's pneumatic soteriology are possibly answered by Turner's concept of W/wisdom. Turner has not only recognized the centrality of W/wisdom to the Johannine concept of salvation but has also been able to integrate the Spirit into it. However, he did not attempt to research the background for this Johannine constellation of ideas, and hence one of the tasks of this study will be to investigate whether, and to what extent, Judaism prepared for such a view. Moreover, Turner's nexus of salvation-W/wisdom-Spirit is merely presented as a sketch, and needs to be elucidated more substantially. Turner was not aware, for example, of all the contributions Johannine scholarship has made (such as those of Loader and Koottumkal), and has, in our view, interacted insufficiently with Porsch. Finally, Turner does not show how his theory fits into the larger picture of John's understanding of salvation, i.e., how the cognitive and relational aspects of Johannine soteriology are held together.

Hamid-Khani's recent work is impressive and since an entire chapter is devoted to the soteriological role of the Spirit, this study needs to be taken seriously into consideration. However, Hamid-Khani has not interacted

---

[157] Another exception is van der Watt, who demonstrates how the family imagery integrates traditional loci like christology, soteriology, pneumatology, ethics (*Family*, see esp. p.411 figure 45). The contributions of Thüsing and Koottumkal are essentially subsumed within the works of Porsch and Loader.

[158] For an assessment of Porsch's interpretation of 20.22, see Bennema, 'Giving', section IV.5.

with the soteriological models put forward by Porsch, Loader and Turner, and shows minimal or no engagement with the works of Ferraro, Burge, Chevallier and Keener. Neither has he explored a possible wisdom background to John, which could have assisted him to be more specific about the Spirit's soteriological role in relation to Jesus.

In conclusion, Johannine scholarship has not adequately explored the soteriological functions of the Spirit (in relation to W/wisdom) in the Fourth Gospel. Hence, a fuller investigation of how faith, signs, saving knowledge/wisdom, salvation, Spirit and Jesus as Wisdom, are co-ordinated, both before and after the glorification of Jesus, is needed. Only Turner has put forward a coherent and potentially inviting theory about this nexus of Spirit-salvation-W/wisdom. However, because of its limited scope, we need to test its strengths and weaknesses. Moreover, there is also a need to engage much more thoroughly with the significant contributions of the other major players — especially with those of Bultmann, Porsch and Loader.

3. Thesis

Scope of the study. We shall limit our study of the Johannine and Jewish sapiential literature to the extent that we are able to formulate an adequate synthesis of the Johannine concepts of Spirit, salvation and W/wisdom. Although the centre of gravity of our study is the Fourth Gospel, we will also take the Johannine letters (esp. 1 John) into account, since they are in continuity with the Fourth Gospel (at least in their theology), but we shall not attempt a critical account of these letters. We shall not engage either in formulating a hypothesis of a possible *Sitz im Leben* of a possible Johannine community or in giving information about its spirituality.[159]

Aim, objectives, task. The main aim of this study is to investigate the soteriological role of the Spirit in the Fourth Gospel. The more specific objectives are to elucidate John's understanding about: (i) the nature of salvation; (ii) how salvation is mediated to and appropriated by people; (iii) how salvation is sustained; (iv) how the Spirit performs soteriological functions; (v) how the concept of W/wisdom relates to Jesus, the Spirit and salvation. Moreover, we shall also examine to what extent sapiential

---

[159] We agree with Hamid-Khani that there is no compelling reason to make a sharp distinction between the time of Jesus' ministry and that of a Johannine community, between the pre-70 CE and the post-70 CE situation, from the perspective of being receptive to revelation and from the perspective of opposition (whether the latter from the religious leaders in Jesus' time or from a post-70 CE priestly religious party) (*Revelation*, 160).

Judaism prepared for such an understanding. Our task, then, is to investigate the nexus of Spirit-salvation-W/wisdom, both in Judaism and in John. We are primarily interested how the readers of the text (rather than the original disciples) are expected to enter into and remain in salvation (although the portrayal of the original disciples in the Gospel is of utmost importance). The envisaged intended reader is a first-century reader of the Fourth Gospel with knowledge of Judaism (cf. ch. 3 section 2).[160]

Strategy. The strategy for achieving the objectives of this study is threefold. First, we shall investigate the interrelationship between the concepts of Spirit, 'salvation' and W/wisdom in sapiential Judaism (ch. 2).[161] Second, we will develop a model of John's Pneumatic Wisdom Soteriology (i) that incorporates all the activities of bringing people into and keeping them in salvation, and (ii) that holds together both relational and cognitive aspects (ch. 3). We will also attempt to provide a plausible rationale for *why* John used the Jewish concept of W/wisdom to present his pneumatic soteriology. Third, we will elucidate those activities of this model that involve the Spirit and W/wisdom (chs. 4-5).[162]

Some scholars favour Jewish apocalypticism or mysticism as a background to the Fourth Gospel.[163] On the one hand, we must avoid setting up the Jewish apocalyptic tradition over against the wisdom tradition; they are both offshoots of the prophetic tradition and have mutually influenced one another.[164] On the other hand, the Fourth Gospel

---

[160] This formulation of the Gospel's intended reader does not exhaust its readership; any reader today with knowledge of Judaism can fit into this category.

[161] I had already done much of the work on John before turning to the question of wisdom background. I then revised aspects of the Johannine material. Thus, the study of John and of sapiential Judaism were virtually parallel studies, and hence the chapter on John's possible conceptual background could have been either before or after the Johannine chapters. However, we chose this order because John was a 'child of his time' and his Gospel was not written in a vacuum, but reflects and criticizes the worldview of his contemporaries.

[162] An additional objective — the elucidation of John's understanding of the moment, nature and soteriological significance of the giving of the Spirit(-Paraclete) as depicted in Jn 19-20 — is realized elsewhere (see Bennema, 'Giving').

[163] E.g., W.A. Meeks, *The Prophet-King: Moses Traditions and the Johannine Christology* (NT.S 14; Leiden: Brill, 1967); Ashton, *Understanding*, ch. 10 (although see *idem*, 'Transformation'); C. Rowland, 'Apocalyptic, Mysticism, and the New Testament' in H. Cancik, H. Lichtenberger and P. Schäfer (eds.), *Geschichte — Tradition — Reflexion: Festschrift für Martin Hengel zum 70. Geburtstag. Band I Judentum* (Tübingen: Mohr Siebeck, 1996) 422-28; J.J. Kanagaraj, *'Mysticism' in the Gospel of John: An Inquiry into its Background* (JSNT.S 158; Sheffield: SAP, 1998); cf. Motyer, *Father*, 45-46.

[164] See C. Bennema, 'The Strands of Wisdom Tradition in Intertestamental Judaism: Origins, Developments and Characteristics', *TynB* 52 (2001) 65-66, *passim*; cf. J.G. Gammie, 'Spatial and Ethical Dualism in Jewish Wisdom and Apocalyptic Literature',

does not really describe people undertaking heavenly ascents or receiving apocalyptic visions (which are then interpreted by an *angelus interpres* [or the Spirit]). Thus, although Jewish apocalypticism/mysticism may be another possible background to the Fourth Gospel, we contend that the Jewish wisdom traditions are more suitable for elucidating the relationship between John's pneumatology and soteriology.[165]

Definitions. Within this study, we shall sometimes use terminology in slightly specialized ways in order to make appropriate distinctions. 'Sensory perception' describes the activity of becoming aware of something through the senses. 'Cognitive perception' is the conscious mental activity or process of acquiring knowledge/information and understanding through thought, experience and sensory perception in order to determine the meaning and significance of what is perceived. 'Understanding' is the processed information as the net result of cognitive perception. Hence, without distinguishing too sharply between the two, cognitive perception is the activity that precedes and results in understanding.[166] Although we do not differentiate in meaning between the verbs 'to have faith' and 'to believe' and between their respective nouns 'faith' and 'belief' — both verbs and both nouns have cognitive (in terms of intellectual assent) and relational (in terms of personal allegiance) aspects — we prefer the category 'to believe' and 'belief' since John himself prefers the verb πιστεύω, whereas the noun πίστις never occurs in the Johannine literature (except for 1 Jn 5.4). With the phrase 'the Spirit as the power of W/wisdom' we denote a *function* of the Spirit, namely the Spirit's ability to do something or to act in a particular way in relation to W/wisdom to affect people, but the phrase carries no connotations of ontology or control. Finally, we use the term 'agent' to refer to someone who produces or causes an effect, and the word 'affective' to relate to moods, feelings, will, attitudes and motivations.

Formulation of the thesis. Our focal theory concerning the soteriological function of the Spirit is twofold. First, the Spirit *creates* a saving relationship between the believer and God, i.e., brings a person into such a relationship with the Father and Son, through the mediation of saving wisdom which is itself present in Jesus' revelatory teaching. Second, the Spirit *sustains* this saving relationship between the believer, Father and Son, through further mediation of wisdom that enables the believer to manifest discipleship (as an ongoing belief-response).

JBL 93 (1974) 356-85; J.J. Collins, 'Wisdom, Apocalypticism, and Generic Compatibility' in L.G. Perdue et al. (eds.), *In Search of Wisdom: Essays in Memory of John G. Gammie* (Louisville: Westminster John Knox Press, 1993) 165-85.

[165] We will further account for having selected this background in ch. 2 section 1.

[166] In ch. 3 we will demonstrate that these definitions are based on Johannine words.

The interrelationship between Spirit, W/wisdom and salvation can be defined as follows: Jesus, as Wisdom incarnate, is the *source* of salvation, in that Jesus' revelatory teaching contains saving wisdom/truth that leads to eternal life, and the Spirit is the *agent* of salvation, in that the Spirit functions as the disclosing or interpretative power of saving W/wisdom. The Spirit opens up Jesus' revelatory teaching, unlocks its saving wisdom, and mediates it to people, in order to give them a new or deeper understanding of God/Jesus, which both creates and sustains a life-giving relationship with God in Jesus.

Thus, according to the Fourth Gospel the Spirit accomplishes his soteriological role precisely in his function as a *life-giving cognitive agent*, i.e., through the mediation of saving wisdom the Spirit facilitates and provides cognitive perception, understanding, and hence life. Moreover, the Spirit functions also as an *affective agent* with soteriological consequences, in that (i) a continuous demonstration of discipleship is linked with proper attitudes and motivations; (ii) a Spirit-imbued understanding of God (and his will, demands, etc.) will influence people's moods, feelings, will, attitudes and motivations. These soteriological functions of the Spirit in the Fourth Gospel are best understood against the background of the concept of the Spirit in Jewish wisdom literature as the revelatory and interpretative power of saving W/wisdom.

Method. We shall be eclectic in our methodological approach because we will primarily elucidate theological concepts in discourses, for which no one method will suffice. The thesis follows a thematic approach, drawing on insights from literary-historical criticism, i.e., a literary approach to John (synchronic dimension) with historical inquiries where necessary (diachronic dimension). On the one hand, this study will work with the final form of the text and apply a combination (of elements) of literary methods, such as narrative criticism,[167] speech act theory, modern

---

[167] According to narrative criticism, the text can be divided into two levels. At the level of story, the narrator interacts with the narratee through the explicit commentary by using settings, characters, events and plot. At the level of narrative, the implied author interacts with the implied reader through implicature (the implicit commentary) by using literary devices such as irony, misunderstanding, symbolism, double entendre, metaphor, dualism. Irony is a 'two-story' phenomenon: underneath is the appearance or apparent meaning, above is a meaning, perspective or belief that is contradictory, incongruous or incompatible with the lower level (Culpepper, *Anatomy*, 167). The speech-act principle involved in irony is the principle of flouting the maxim of quality ('be sincere'); the truth is exactly the opposite to what is being said and this is, in essence, ironical (J.E. Botha, *Jesus and the Samaritan Woman: A Speech Act Reading of John 4:1-42* [NT.S 65; Leiden: Brill, 1991] 132-33). Symbols are connecting links between two levels of meaning in a story, between two spheres (the sphere of the symbol itself and the sphere which the symbol represents) (Stibbe, *Storyteller*, 19, 27). Double entendre refers to the fact that a word can have two meanings, both of which may be applicable (Stibbe,

linguistics, discourse analysis and structuralism. On the other hand, concerning historical-critical inquiry, we shall elucidate those aspects of the Fourth Gospel's context which are assumed by the narrative — the presupposition pool — and which will assist us in uncovering the meaning of the text. Our emphasis falls on the Jewish sapiential intertexts, i.e., those Jewish sapiential writings that are either evoked by the text or contribute to the understanding of the text.[168] However, our historical-critical task will not include the reconstruction of a socio-historical setting of a Johannine community, the historical Jesus or the literary sources or history of the Fourth Gospel.

Storyteller, 18-19). Metaphor is a device which speaks of one thing (tenor) in terms which are appropriate to another (vehicle), with the vehicle serving as the source of traits to be transferred to the tenor (N. Friedman, *Form and Meaning in Fiction* [Athens: University of Gregoria Press, 1975], 289).

[168] In contrast to *sources*, which contribute to the *making* of a text and hence direct the author's way of writing, *intertexts* contribute to the *reading* of the text. Intertexts direct the manner in which the text is intended to be received by the audience, and hence are located *between* the reader and the text.

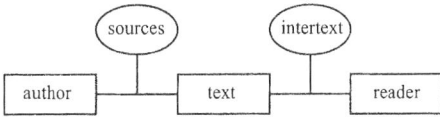

The hermeneutical implication of choosing Jewish sapiential writings as intertexts rather than possible sources is that, instead of focusing on the question whether or not the author of the Fourth Gospel was literary dependent on these writings, the emphasis now falls on *our* understanding of John's thought milieu and of a particular nexus of Johannine ideas.

Part I

The Conceptual Background to
John's Pneumatic Wisdom Soteriology

Chapter 2

Spirit, Wisdom and Salvation in Sapiential Judaism

1. Introduction

The objective of this chapter is to define the *interrelation* between Spirit, W/wisdom and 'salvation' in sapiential Judaism. The reason for this investigation is to discover the extent to which the Jewish wisdom traditions prepare for and possibly explain a particular constellation of Johannine concepts that will be more fully explored later. We expect the soteriological functions of the Spirit in the Fourth Gospel to be best understood against the background of the concept of the Spirit in Jewish wisdom literature as the revelatory and interpretative power of Wisdom.

Regarding our choice for sapiential Judaism, we do not claim this is or can be the only background to understand John. We have said in chapter 1 section 3, for example, that the Jewish apocalyptic literature (which cannot be clearly separated from the wisdom literature) can be another possible background to John. However, we have chosen a *wisdom* background (not as an exclusive but as one possible way) to understand John because we contend that the apocalyptic tradition does not shed further significant light on the nexus Spirit-W/wisdom-salvation, and that the wisdom traditions are most suitable for explaining the relationship between John's pneumatology and soteriology. We will see that Wisdom and Spirit in sapiential Judaism are not only closely related (like John's christology and pneumatology) but are also soteriological categories, which might assist us in elucidating the relationship Jesus-Spirit-salvation in John.

In addition, we have selected a *Jewish* background over against, for example, a Hellenistic (wisdom) background because the thought world of John and his intended audience was most probably primarily Jewish (although it should not be forgotten that Hellenism had affected Jewish thinking to some extent).[1] The explanations of certain Jewish terms and

---

[1] Concerning the relationship between Judaism and Hellenism, we believe that M. Hengel has cogently demonstrated that Hellenistic influence may have (in various degrees) permeated the whole of first-century Judaism (*Judaism and Hellenism: Studies*

customs (1.38, 41; 4.9; 20.16), and the display of accurate topographical and geographical knowledge (3.23; 5.2; 11.18), suggests that the author of the Fourth Gospel was himself a Palestinian Jew (or at least was very familiar with and had detailed knowledge of Judaism). These explanations of aspects of Judaism do, however, not necessarily hint at a complete non-Jewish audience; certainly the topographical and geographical information can readily be explained if the Jewish part of John's readership were Diaspora Jews. However, whether Jewish or non-Jewish, John wants his readers to be acquainted with Judaism. Moreover, John especially seems to assume knowledge of Judaism: (i) frequent allusions to the Hebrew Scriptures (e.g. 1.29, 51; 3.5, 14; 6.31-33; 7.38; 19.37) and Jewish literature (4.10-14 alludes to Sir. 15.3; 24.21); (ii) notable emphasis on Jewish festivals, Moses and the Law; (iii) use of symbolism (e.g., Jesus as the true Light, Shepherd, Bread, Vine alludes to OT imagery). Hence, since the author of the Fourth Gospel himself appears to be immersed in Jewish thought, and since the envisaged intended reader is expected to have knowledge of Judaism, it seems reasonable (if not essential) to examine a Jewish background.[2]

Our strategy is to limit our research to the representative writings of the various sapiential strands in Judaism, which are essentially Proverbs, Sirach, Wisdom of Solomon, Philo and some of the Qumran writings.[3] Our leading questions for each of these writings are as follows. How does the book understand 'salvation'? What is the role of W/wisdom in salvation?

---

in their Encounter in Palestine during the Early Hellenistic Period [2 vols.; Transl. J. Bowden; London: SCM Press, 1974]).

[2] It would still be worthwhile to examine the wisdom motif in Hellenistic literature (especially if one considers that John's readers probably lived in Asia Minor). J. Breck has even done a comparative study of religion and found many parallels in Egyptian, Babylonian and Iranian religion (*Spirit of Truth — The Holy Spirit In Johannine Tradition: Volume 1. The Origins of Johannine Pneumatology* [Crestwood: St Vladimir's Seminary Press, 1991]). Hamid-Khani defends an almost exclusive use of Israel's Scriptures (the OT) as the conceptual background to the Fourth Gospel (see esp. *Revelation*, ch. 3). We are not denying of course the importance of the OT — every Jewish intertestamental writing is conceptually dependent on the OT, and the OT formed the presupposition pool for both Jewish and NT authors — but the intertestamental literature discloses the intellectual milieu of John and his contemporaries, including their understanding of the OT and the influence of 400 years of Hellenistic thought. Hamid-Khani's approach may be appropriate for his case — to demonstrate how John establishes that Jesus is the Christ according to the OT — but to explain the precise role of the Spirit in salvation in relation to Jesus, we probably need more than that. Hence, Hamid-Khani is right in what he asserts — John's conceptual dependence on the OT — but wrong in what he denies/discourages — the use of Jewish intertestamental literature to elucidate John's thought world.

[3] For an elucidation of the various wisdom strands and their main representatives, see Bennema, 'Strands'.

What is the role of the Spirit in salvation? What is the relationship between Spirit and W/wisdom (in relation to salvation)? After a brief overview of the relevant contributions of contemporary scholarship (section 2), we will elucidate the concepts of Spirit, W/wisdom and salvation for each of the chosen writings (sections 3-7). Methodologically, we examine the related concepts for each of the sapiential writings on their own. The originality of this chapter is twofold: (i) a synthesis of the concepts of Spirit, W/wisdom and salvation as they are represented by the main Jewish sapiential writings; (ii) the development of a model of salvation that is defined in degrees of intensity and quality of Spirit and W/wisdom, and that holds together cognitive and relational aspects.

2. Overview of Scholarship

The objective of this section is briefly to review the contribution of contemporary scholarship on our subject. We shall proceed according to theme/concept rather than chronology. Within the concept of the covenant as the principal soteriological category (Sanders),[4] we initially suggest a broad or 'core' working definition of 'salvation' in Judaism in terms of *the restoration and spiritual transformation of 'Israel' in history* (Wright, Turner).[5]

---

[4] E.P. Sanders, 'The Covenant as a Soteriological Category and the Nature of Salvation in Palestinian and Hellenistic Judaism' in R. Hamerton-Kelly and R. Scroggs (eds.), *Jews, Greeks and Christians: Religious Cultures in Late Antiquity. Essays in Honor of William David Davies* (Leiden: Brill, 1976) 11-44; *idem, Judaism: Practice and Belief, 63 BCE-66 CE* (London: SCM Press, 1992) 262-78. Contra Sanders's 'covenantal nomism', which reflects a Jewish nationalistic soteriology and envisaged more or less the salvation of *all* Israel, M.A. Elliott argues that intertestamental Judaism did *not* anticipate the salvation of all Jews but only of a faithful remnant within Israel, and he calls this pattern of salvation 'destruction-preservation soteriology' (see *The Survivors of Israel: A Reconsideration of the Theology of Pre-Christian Judaism* [Grand Rapids: Eerdmans, 2000] esp. 52-56, chs. 3-4, 12). However, at least the early Sanders acknowledged that 'Israel' was variously defined ('Covenant', 40).

[5] N.T. Wright interprets 'salvation' primarily as the *historical restoration* of 'Israel', i.e., the liberation from enemies, the restoration of the national symbols and a state of *shalom* (*The New Testament and the People of God. Christian Origins and the Question of God Volume One* [London: SPCK, 1992] 300, 334-36). M.[M.B.] Turner understands 'salvation' chiefly as the *spiritual transformation* of 'Israel', in terms of Ezekiel's new creation — the inner/moral renewal of people in order to be faithful to God and his covenant — and Joel's outpouring of the Spirit upon all 'Israel' (*Power from on High: The Spirit in Israel's Restoration and Witness in Luke-Acts* [JPT.S 9; Sheffield: SAP, 1996] 133-37). However, Wright's and Turner's emphases are not mutually exclusive and they both allow for each other's category. 'Israel' may refer to the whole nation or to a remnant, dependent on the theology of a particular group.

Wisdom and Salvation. With regard to wisdom and 'salvation', Murphy proposes a broad understanding of wisdom that allows for a soteriological dimension: from wisdom giving life in the present, in terms of blessing, prosperity, well-being, longevity and deliverance from the evils that afflict human beings (in short, *shalom* or salvation), to providing eternal life/immortality in Wisdom of Solomon.[6] Wisdom is a means to salvation, in that wisdom has the power to transform human existence and determines the way life is lived.[7] In his significant study, Schnabel argues that the identification of wisdom and Torah is found throughout Judaism, and concludes that law and wisdom are repeatedly linked with the concept of life, in that they contain and promulgate the norms and criteria of moral conduct and lead to a pious, holistic way of life.[8]

Spirit and Salvation. Despite the many contributions towards the understanding of the concept of the Spirit in Judaism, only a few have briefly mentioned its role in 'salvation'.[9] For Neve et al., the Spirit in the OT is Yahweh's power which creates and maintains the life of all creatures (Gen. 1.2; Job 33.4; 34.14-15; Pss. 33.6; 104.29-30),[10] which will also renew and transform Yahweh's people in the future (Isa. 32.15; 44.3; Ezek.

---

[6] R.E. Murphy, 'Wisdom and Salvation' in D. Durken (ed.), *Sin, Salvation, and the Spirit: Commemorating the Fiftieth Year of The Liturgical Press* (Collegeville: The Liturgical Press, 1979) 177-83. Cf. L.G. Perdue, *Wisdom & Creation: The Theology of Wisdom Literature* (Nashville: Abingdon Press, 1994) ch. 7.

[7] Murphy, 'Wisdom', 177-80.

[8] E.J. Schnabel, *Law and Wisdom from Ben Sira to Paul: A Tradition Historical Enquiry into the Relation of Law, Wisdom, and Ethics* (WUNT II/16; Tübingen: Mohr Siebeck, 1985) chs. 1-3; 344-45. Cf. also C.M. Pate, *The Reverse of the Curse: Paul, Wisdom, and the Law* (WUNT II/114; Tübingen: Mohr Siebeck, 2000) chs. 1-4. However, the Torah is not *the* locus of Wisdom in Wis. and Philo (Bennema, 'Strands', 71-73).

[9] D. Lys, *Rûach: Le Souffle dans l'Ancien Testament* (Paris: Presses Universitaires de France, 1962); L. Neve, *The Spirit of God in the Old Testament* (Tokyo: Seibunsha, 1972); Isaacs, *Concept*; G.T. Montague, *The Holy Spirit: Growth of a Biblical Tradition* (Peabody: Hendrickson, 1976) chs. 1-11; Chevallier, *Souffle*, 1:19-80; A.I.C. Heron, *The Holy Spirit: The Holy Spirit in the Bible in the History of Christian Thought and in recent Theology* (London: Marshall Morgan & Scott, 1983) chs. 1-2; W. Hildebrandt, *An Old Testament Theology of the Spirit of God* (Peabody: Hendrickson, 1995); J.R. Levison, *The Spirit in First Century Judaism* (Leiden: Brill, 1997). The primary concern of our study is the *functionality* rather than the ontology of the Spirit, but even if the latter would want to be examined, one needs to be careful about the method (see, e.g., V. Rabens, 'The Development of Pauline Pneumatology: A Response to F.W. Horn', *BZ* 43 [1999] 169-72).

[10] Although רוּחַ is presented as the life-breath/life-principle, it is ambiguous whether every occurrence refers to the divine Spirit, which is due to its broad semantic domain (cf. Turner, *Spirit*, 4-5; Montague, *Spirit*, 5-7, 64-66). Nevertheless, most scholars — e.g., Neve, Baumgärtel, Chevallier, Heron, Hildebrandt — prefer a reference to the divine Spirit. See also excursus 2, below.

36.26-27; 37.14; Joel 2.28-29), and which will bring about Yahweh's continuous abiding presence with his people (Ezek. 39.29).[11] Other scholars, such as Isaacs, Bieder and Levison, confirm a similar concept widespread in intertestamental literature (e.g., in Wis., Philo, Qumran).[12] Chevallier argues that the majority of Palestinian literature (rabbinic, targumic and some apocalyptic writings) presents the Spirit as being largely absent in their own day and as an element of moral renewal only in the future, whereas heterodox Palestinian literature (e.g., Qumran, *Jub.*, *Test. XII Patr.*) and Diaspora literature manifest more (soteriological) activity of the Spirit, due to their partly realized eschatology.[13]

Those who have made major contributions towards the understanding of the relationship between Spirit and 'salvation' in Judaism include Menzies, Keener and the new-found 'school' of Turner. Menzies believes that the majority of the literature of intertestamental Judaism presents the Spirit as the 'Spirit of prophecy', i.e., largely as the source of prophetic inspiration, and that the gift of the Spirit is generally regarded as a *donum superadditum*, a charismatic endowment for service rather than a soteriological necessity.[14] According to Menzies, the only exceptions are Wisdom of Solomon and the hymns of 1QH, which, as the culmination of a process of development within the wisdom tradition, attribute soteriological significance to the gift of the Spirit.[15]

Keener argues that the material about the Spirit in early Judaism can be divided in two categories: (i) the Spirit of purification (the ethical aspect); (ii) the Spirit of prophecy, in which prophecy is defined as inspired or oracular speech.[16] Keener concludes that the rabbinic understanding of the

---

[11] Neve, *Spirit*, ch. 4. Cf. Lys, *Rûach*, chs. 1-2, 4-5. F. Baumgärtel, 'Πνεῦμα, πνευματικός' in *TDNT*, VI:363-66; Montague, *Spirit*, chs. 1, 3-4; Chevallier, *Souffle*, 1:19-32; Heron, *Spirit*, 10-12, 17-22; Hildebrandt, *Theology*, chs. 1-3. Neve does not strictly distinguish between the Spirit being the source of 'physical' life and spiritual life (*Spirit*, 76).

[12] Isaacs, *Concept*, 35-36, 43-44; W. Bieder, 'Πνεῦμα, πνευματικός' in *TDNT*, VI:368-73; Levison, *Spirit*, 1-3, 57-65, 74, 218-19.

[13] Chevallier, *Souffle*, 1:44-73. Cf. Montague, *Spirit*, 100-103, 116-24. Concerning the supposed withdrawal of the Spirit in intertestamental Judaism, see esp. J.R. Levison, 'Did the Spirit Withdraw from Israel? An Evaluation of the Earliest Jewish Data', *NTS* 43 (1997) 35-57; cf. J. Neusner, 'What "The Rabbis" Thought: A Method and a Result. One Statement on Prophecy in Rabbinic Judaism' in J.C. Reeves and J. Kampen (eds.), *Pursuing the Text: Studies in Honor of Ben Zion Wacholder on the Occasion of his Seventieth Birthday* (JSOT.S 184; Sheffield: SAP, 1994) 303-20; Turner, *Spirit*, 14-15, 187-92.

[14] See R.P. Menzies, *Empowered for Witness: The Spirit in Luke-Acts* (JPT.S 6; Sheffield: SAP, 1994) 49-102.

[15] Menzies, *Witness*, 80, 102.

[16] See Keener, 'Function', 58-114.

Spirit of prophecy prevailed over rival understandings of the Spirit in early Judaism (such as the purifying-ethical dimension of the Spirit).[17] Due to this bifurcation of the concept of the Spirit in Judaism, Keener's 'Spirit of prophecy' is, as Menzies', essentially a *donum superadditum* with no soteriological consequences.

Turner, who disagrees with Menzies' 'rigidly fixed concept' of the 'Spirit of prophecy', argues for a broader semantic concept, and concludes that the Spirit of prophecy has also potential for spiritual/ethical renewal.[18] Moreover, the combination of the gift of the Spirit to the Messiah and the fulfilment of Joel's promise to the rest of Israel would provide the major means of the eschatological 'salvation' Jews awaited.[19] Furthermore, whereas Keener bifurcates the concept of the Spirit in Judaism, Turner argues that the purifying-ethical function of the Spirit is often included in the concept of the 'Spirit of prophecy'. Levison independently makes similar observations to Turner's (in terms of the Spirit's activities), but arrives at a slightly different conclusion: the identification of the Spirit in first-century Judaism as the 'Spirit of prophecy' can be made only with the awareness of the broad spectrum of possible effects of the Spirit across Judaism, and also, that no first-century author seemed to have one dominant conception of the Spirit.[20] Turner, however, essentially contends that the concept of the Spirit of prophecy was the predominant understanding within first-century Judaism.

Wenk focuses on and extends one aspect of Turner's challenge to Menzies' position, namely, the Spirit's role in the anticipated ethical renewal/transformation of God's people.[21] With regard to the Spirit as a positive ethical influence upon God's people in intertestamental Judaism, Wenk concludes that the dominant motive is that of Spirit-endowed leadership, in that the Spirit (i) influences an individual charismatic leader — for example, an anointed judge, a Spirit-endowed sage or ruler, the coming Davidic ruler — towards the ethical qualities he is to restore among God's people, and consequently (ii) restores, through the charismatic leader, covenant-faithfulness among God's people.[22]

---

[17] Keener, 'Function', 113.

[18] Turner, *Power*, 89-92, ch. 5. Fatehi and Wenk, former students of Turner, follow in his footsteps (see M. Fatehi, *The Spirit's Relation to the Risen Lord in Paul: An Examination of Its Christological Implications* [WUNT II/128; Tübingen: Mohr Siebeck, 2000] chs. 4-8; M. Wenk, *Community-Forming Power: The Socio-Ethical Role of the Spirit in Luke-Acts* [JPT.S 19; Sheffield: SAP, 2000] chs. 3-5).

[19] Turner, *Power*, 137.

[20] Levison, *Spirit*, 242-53. In this Levison criticizes Menzies' (and Keener's) too narrow concept of the Spirit of prophecy.

[21] See Wenk, *Power*, chs. 3-5.

[22] Wenk, *Power*, 117-18, 309-10.

Spirit, Wisdom, Salvation. Concerning the relationship between Spirit, W/wisdom and 'salvation', Breck essentially seems to deny the existence of such a relationship in pre-Christian Judaism. Breck, who sets out to discover the origins of Johannine pneumatology by a study of comparative religion, argues that in the later post-exilic period the Spirit disappeared and Wisdom emerged, gradually appropriating or 'absorbing' the characteristics and functions of Spirit and 'replacing' Spirit.[23] Nevertheless, Breck admits that in these writings Wisdom never assumes the *eschatological* role of the Spirit; Wisdom is never depicted, for example, as the *agent* of moral regeneration as is the Spirit.[24] Menzies believes that the author of Wisdom of Solomon uses the terms πνεῦμα and σοφία interchangeably — functions normally reserved for the Spirit are transferred to wisdom — but they are not completely identified; rather, wisdom is *experienced* through the Spirit.[25] Menzies, following Verbeke, then eventually arrives at a dualism of πνεῦμα as the source of physical life and πνεῦμα as the source of wisdom. Moreover, as this Spirit of wisdom is essentially the source of moral and religious life, it is a soteriological necessity.[26]

Only van Imschoot, Davis and the Turner 'school' have contributed significantly to an understanding of the interrelationship between Spirit, W/wisdom and 'salvation'. Van Imschoot wrote extensively (in the 1930s) on the concept of the Spirit in relation to 'salvation' and W/wisdom,[27] but in general scholars have neglected him or not adequately interacted with his work. In our view, van Imschoot — especially in his article 'Sagesse et

---

[23] Breck, *Spirit*, 82, 86, 92.

[24] Breck, *Spirit*, 82, 93.

[25] Menzies, *Witness*, 57-58.

[26] Menzies, *Witness*, 57-59; G. Verbeke, *L'Évolution de la Doctrine du Pneuma du Stoicisme à S. Augustin* (Paris: Desclée De Brouwer, 1945) 228-30. J. Rea virtually bifurcates the role of Spirit and wisdom in salvation: on the one hand, he argues that regeneration by the Spirit of God, resulting in a living relationship with God, was already a present reality in the OT; on the other hand, the OT believer's daily spiritual life and fellowship with God were primarily sustained not by the Spirit but by the word and wisdom of God ('The Personal Relationship of Old Testament Believers to the Holy Spirit' in P. Elbert [ed.], *Essays on Apostolic Themes: Studies in Honor of Howard M. Ervin Presented to him by Colleagues and Friends on his Sixty-Fifth Birthday* [Peabody: Hendrickson, 1985] 92-103).

[27] P. van Imschoot, 'L'action de l'Esprit de Jahvé dans l'Ancien Testament', *RSPhTh* 23 (1934) 553-87; *idem*, 'L'Esprit de Jahvé, source de vie dans l'Ancien Testament', *RB* 44 (1935) 481-501; *idem*, 'L'Esprit de Jahvé et l'alliance nouvelle dans l'Ancien Testament', *EThL* 13 (1936) 201-20; *idem*, 'Sagesse et Esprit dans l'Ancien Testament', *RB* 47 (1938) 23-49; *idem*, 'L'Esprit de Jahvé, principe de la vie morale dans l'Ancien Testament', *EThL* 16 (1939) 457-67; *idem*, *Theology of the Old Testament. Volume I: God* (Transl. K. Sullivan and F. Buck; New York: Desclée & Co., 1954) 172-88.

Esprit dans l'Ancien Testament' — produced the most significant contribution on the subject. Van Imschoot detects two strands of wisdom tradition — rational/practical wisdom and popular/prophetic wisdom. After the exile these merged, with the result that Wisdom became identified with Torah and with the Spirit.[28] Van Imschoot defines divine Torah as 'le code de la sagesse'.[29] The culmination of the relationship between Wisdom and Spirit is found in Wisdom of Solomon, which pushes the assimilation of Wisdom and Spirit almost to (the point of) complete identification, and which makes both Wisdom and Spirit the internal principle of the physical and moral life.[30]

In order not to blur completely the concept of Wisdom and Spirit, van Imschoot makes two qualifying remarks. First, concerning Wisdom as the source of the *physical* life, the analogy with the Spirit is entirely verbal, and all references to Wisdom as 'the source of life' (Prov. 4.23; 10.11; 13.14; 16.22; Sir. 21.13), 'the way of life' (Prov. 2.19; 5.6; 6.23; 10.17; 15.24) and 'the tree of life' (Prov. 3.18; 11.30), are only metaphors affirming that she *assures* a long and blessed life. Wisdom is not the vital force, like the Spirit, by which Yahweh communicates or maintains the physical life; rather, she remains the educator, teaching and showing people the means of acquiring and preserving a long, fortunate and gratifying life.[31] The only exception is Wisdom of Solomon, where both Wisdom and Spirit are designated as the vital principle of the physical life.[32] Second, concerning Wisdom as the source of the *moral* life, she is the moral and religious educator. Unlike the Spirit, the divine force which creates and renews the moral and religious life of the people, Wisdom exhorts and instructs people, and communicates the truth, but she does not give people the ability to accomplish the divine will and thereby to avoid sin, as the Spirit does.[33] Although van Imschoot admits that in Wisdom of Solomon Wisdom is depicted as a divine moral force, this force only

---

[28] Van Imschoot, 'Sagesse', 23-26, 35-37, 43-46. We have criticized elsewhere van Imschoot's view that these two wisdom strands merged into one (Bennema, 'Strands', 80).

[29] Van Imschoot, 'Sagesse', 26, 35, 47.

[30] Van Imschoot, 'Sagesse', 37, 43, 44, 46.

[31] Van Imschoot, 'Sagesse', 28, 46-47. For the Spirit as the principle of the physical life, see van Imschoot, 'Source', 481-92, *idem*, 'Action', 554-56.

[32] Van Imschoot, 'Sagesse', 46.

[33] Van Imschoot, 'Sagesse', 48-49. Cf. Y.M.J. Congar, *I Believe in the Holy Spirit. Volume 1: The Holy Spirit in the 'Economy'* (Transl. D. Smith; London: Chapman, 1983) 10. For the Spirit as the principle of the moral life, see van Imschoot, 'Alliance', 201-20; *idem*, 'Principe', 457-67; *idem*, *Theology*, 176-82. According to van Imschoot, the idea of the Spirit as the principle/power of the moral life was developed after the Spirit as the principle/power of the physical life; the former concept started in Isa. and culminated in Ezek.

resides with the righteous (Wis. 1.4-5; 7.27).[34] Wisdom is more a reward than a free gift of God, and does not create the moral and religious life, but only *maintains* it in the righteous: '[e]lle ne transforme pas le pécheur en saint, comme l'esprit de Jahvé.'[35]

Davis, who investigates the relationship between W/wisdom and Spirit, argues that Sirach, the Qumran literature and Philo (and Wisdom of Solomon), present a model of several levels or stages of sapiential achievement of which the achievement of the highest level of wisdom is attributed to (the gift of) the Spirit, and is reserved for a select group.[36] Davis virtually implies that the gift of the Spirit might be understood as a *donum superadditum*, which is exactly the point that Menzies, who accepts Davis' theory, makes explicitly.[37]

Turner, on the other hand, contends that the gift of the Spirit is sometimes also soteriologically necessary. Turner argues that the charismatic revelation and wisdom provided by the Spirit of prophecy had transforming ethical influences, revealing God's presence, wisdom and will to the human heart in such a way as thereby to motivate (and so enable) the life of filial righteousness.[38] Turner concludes that

> It would appear various sectors of Judaism expected the 'Spirit of prophecy' to give such important and/or transforming revelation, and such ethically *renewing* wisdom, that these activities would almost inevitably be regarded as *virtually essential* for fully authentic human existence before God, and so also for that future state of it which writers mean by 'salvation'.

> Nor was the 'Spirit of prophecy' merely a *donum superadditum* of little ethical consequence. The Spirit's revelatory and wisdom-granting roles were understood (in many quarters) as transformative, and thus as potentially soteriological.[39]

Wenk, whose main interest is the ethical renewal of God's people through a Spirit-endowed leader, agrees that in some instances this ethical

---

[34] Van Imschoot, 'Sagesse', 44-45, 49.

[35] Van Imschoot, 'Sagesse', 49.

[36] See J.A. Davis, *Wisdom and Spirit: An Investigation of 1 Corinthians 1.18-3.20 Against the Background of Jewish Sapiential Traditions in the Greco-Roman Period* (Lanham: University Press of America, 1984) chs. 1-3.

[37] Davis, *Wisdom*, 19-24, 39, 52, 60-62; Menzies, *Witness*, 60-65, 69-70. Cf. G. Maier, *Mensch und freier Wille: Nach den jüdischen Religionsparteien zwischen Ben Sira und Paulus* (WUNT 12; Tübingen: Mohr Siebeck, 1971) 37; Schnabel, *Law*, 53.

[38] Turner, *Power*, ch. 5 §2; *idem*, *Spirit*, 16-19. Charismatic revelation and wisdom are the two most frequent prototypical gifts of the Spirit of prophecy (*Power*, 92-97; *Spirit*, 8-12).

[39] Turner, *Spirit*, 16-17, 20 (author's emphasis). Cf. Fatehi, who confirms the soteriological effects of Spirit and W/wisdom in Wis. and the Qumran literature (*Relation*, 68-79, 103-108).

transformation (resulting in obedience to the Torah) occurs through Spirit-inspired wisdom.[40]

Conclusion. The Jewish understanding was that God would bring about 'salvation' by means of his Spirit, in that the Spirit is depicted as the power of Israel's eschatological transformation.[41] The רוּחַ/πνεῦμα could be understood as: (i) the source of (physical) life of all creatures, in that God gives and sustains life by means of his רוּחַ/πνεῦμα (upheld by all scholars);[42] (ii) a soteriological necessity, in that the Spirit is depicted as the power of Israel's eschatological salvation, and as potentially soteriological through the mediation of revelation and wisdom (advocated by, e.g., the Turner 'school'). However, scholarship has not adequately elucidated the concept of 'salvation' and the salvific function of the Spirit in the Jewish wisdom traditions. Our study will concentrate primarily on this second (but not in isolation from the first) aspect of the role of the רוּחַ/πνεῦμα — the soteriological role of the divine Spirit in relation to people — which is, so to speak, the added dimension of the Spirit to (the physical) life, in terms of quantity and quality. We will address the following questions. How does each sapiential writing envisage 'salvation'? Is the author's concept of 'salvation' entirely eschatological, or is there a realized dimension to it? What is the role of the Spirit and W/wisdom in 'salvation', and in relation to one another?

3. Proverbs[43]

The Nature of Wisdom. In Proverbs, Wisdom has become a personified (or even a hypostatized) figure (1.20-33; 3.13-18; 8.1-36; 9.1-12).[44] She is

---

[40] Wenk, *Power*, 66-69, 79-80, 87-88, 93-94, 106-108.

[41] It would also be natural to expect Israel's *restoration* to happen by means of the Spirit: if Yahweh delivered Israel from her enemies in the past by means of Spirit-empowered judges and kings, then the Spirit-endowed Messiah would be expected to liberate the Jews from the Romans.

[42] Some scholars take the term רוּחַ/πνεῦμα as referring to God's (life-)breath, the majority, however, prefers a reference to God's Spirit (see n.10, above).

[43] Prov., or at least Prov. 1-9 (in which we are mainly interested), can be dated as (post-)exilic (cf. Prov. 25.1; Hengel, *Judaism*, 1:153; 2:97 n.289; R.E. Murphy, *Proverbs* [WBC 22; Nashville: Nelson, 1998] xx). For other views, see R.N. Whybray, *Proverbs* (NCeB; Grand Rapids: Eerdmans, 1994) 28-30; C.H. Bullock, 'The Book of Proverbs' in R.B. Zuck (ed.), *Learning from the Sages: Selected Studies on the Book of Proverbs* (Grand Rapids: Baker Books, 1995) 27-30.

[44] We adopt a broad definition of the term 'hypostasis': 'the quasi-personification of certain attributes proper to God. They occupy an intermediate position between personalities and abstract beings' (W.O.E. Oesterley and G.H. Box, *The Religion and Worship of The Synagogue: An Introduction to the Study of Judaism from the New*

characterized by or as possessing life (3.16, 18; 8.35; 9.11; 16.22), love (8.17), peace (3.17), truth (8.6-9), wisdom/knowledge/understanding (8.10-14, 33), glory (8.18) and joy (8.30-31). Wisdom is associated with Yahweh, in the sense that she is attributed and belongs to Yahweh; Yahweh is the source of Wisdom (2.6; 8.22).

The relationship between Yahweh and Wisdom is one of intimacy (8.22-31), wisdom/knowledge/understanding (2.5-6; 8.10-14), life (3.16-18; 10.27; 14.27; 22.4), love (3.12; 8.17; 15.9) and glory (8.18; 25.2). Solomon, the implied author, encourages people to be in relationship with Wisdom (7.4; cf. 3.18; 4.5-9). Moreover, Wisdom herself invites people to enter into a life-giving relationship with her: in 9.1-6 she invites people to come to her banquet and to eat her food and drink her wine, whereby the references to 'eat' and 'drink' in v.5 are metaphors for 'consuming', i.e., accepting, her life-giving revelatory words. Finally, in 8.32 Wisdom is addressing people as 'sons'. The benefits of adhering to and being in relationship with Wisdom are essentially (a share in) the qualities/virtues which characterize Wisdom: love (8.17), life (3.18; 8.35; 9.11), wisdom/knowledge/understanding (1.23; 8.10-14), glory/honour (3.16; 4.8-9), peace (3.17) and truth (23.23). Further benefits of adhering to Wisdom and her teaching are prosperity (3.2, 16; 8.18, 21), blessing (3.18) and protection from evil and evil people (1.33; 2.1-19; 4.6; 28.26). In short, the concept of 'salvation' in Proverbs is entirely played out in the present, and has a quantitative (long life) and a qualitative (blessing, prosperity, well-being, protection) dimension; there is no place for an afterlife, either in terms of immortality or resurrection (cf. 11.31).[45]

Although the content of Wisdom's teaching is basically ethical, in order to shape the moral and religious life (Wisdom is the source of right ethical behaviour [see esp. Prov. 1-9]),[46] it has also soteriological implications. Acceptance or rejection of Wisdom and her revelatory teaching/instruction leads respectively to long life/peace/blessing or death/disaster (1.24-33;

Testament Period [London: Pitman, 1911[2]] 195). However, our use of 'hypostasis' does not include the sense of a divine person or entity distinct from Yahweh (contra H. Ringgren, *Word and Wisdom: Studies in the Hypostatization of Divine Qualities and Functions in the Ancient Near East* [Lund: Gleerup, 1947]). See Fatehi (*Relation*, 86-92) for a more informed discussion of an understanding of the figure of Wisdom in Prov. 1-9. We will not pursue whether the personification of Wisdom is merely a literary/poetical device or whether non-Israelite mythological notions lie behind it (see Whybray [*Proverbs*, 27-28] for a brief discussion). It will suffice to interpret Lady Wisdom primarily as being set up in contrast with the prostitute Lady Folly.

[45] Although 12.28 and 14.32 may possibly hint at life beyond death, it is too ambiguous to pursue further.

[46] Cf. Breck, *Spirit*, 84; R.C. van Leeuwen, 'Liminality and Worldview in Proverbs 1-9', *Semeia* 50 (1990) 113-15.

2.21-22; 3.2, 16-18; 4.13; 8.35-36; 9.11, 18 [Lady Wisdom versus Lady Folly]).[47] Moreover, Wisdom is called a tree of life (3.18), which alludes to the tree in the Garden of Eden (Gen. 2.9), and implies that Wisdom is the source of (moral) life (cf. 16.22).[48] Van Imschoot argues that Wisdom is only a source of the physical life in a *metaphorical* sense (see section 2). However, the point of portraying Wisdom metaphorically, for example, as a 'tree of life' (3.18) and a 'fountain of life' (16.22) is precisely that Wisdom is a *real* source of life; the only question being in what *sense* Wisdom is a source of life. Although we agree with van Imschoot that Wisdom is not depicted as the source of the physical life, she is nevertheless portrayed as the source of the *moral/ethical* life. Moreover, we have to be careful not to create two mutually exclusive categories of life (physical and moral); if W/wisdom, as the source of the moral life, is the means of acquiring and preserving a long and blessed physical life, then W/wisdom maintains or adds a quantitative and qualitative dimension to the physical life.[49] The reason *why* Wisdom is the source of life is her intimate relationship with Yahweh. If we were to ask *how* Wisdom can be the source of life, we would suggest that the *content* of Wisdom's revelatory teaching/words is moral wisdom, knowledge or truth (8.6-14). Thus, *truth is the moral wisdom/knowledge contained in Wisdom's revelatory teaching* (ἀλήθεια, παιδεία, γνῶσις and φρόνησις [LXX] are partially synonymous).[50]

The Quest for Wisdom. In Proverbs, it is possible to discern a pattern in the interplay between Wisdom and people, which essentially consists of Wisdom's encounter and invitation, people's perception and response, and the subsequent consequences. First, Wisdom takes initiative and confronts people; she calls out to people to listen to her, and encourages them to accept her and her teaching (1.20-33; 8.1-9.12). She invites people to her banquet and have fellowship with her (9.1-6). People perceive Wisdom and her teaching at a sensory and cognitive level. The first step is people's

---

[47] Wisdom's teaching is revelatory because people do not possess wisdom intrinsically; it is Yahweh/Wisdom who teaches, discloses and gives wisdom (1.23; 2.6; 8.6-8).

[48] Solomon (the implied author and prototypical wisdom-imbued ruler) and the wise sage, along with their teaching, are also depicted as sources of life/wisdom (4.10, 22; 6.20-23; 8.15-16; 10.11; 13.14). This is possible because Wisdom empowers kings/rulers to reign and govern (8.15-16).

[49] 'Death', in contrast to 'life', then denotes either the loss of physical life or the loss of blessing and well-being in life (cf. R.B. Zuck, 'A Theology of Proverbs' in R.B. Zuck [ed.], *Learning from the Sages: Selected Studies on the Book of Proverbs* [Grand Rapids: Baker Books, 1995] 100 n.1).

[50] The teaching of the sages also contains truth (22.17-21), and one is exhorted to purchase, i.e., obtain, truth/wisdom (23.23).

'sensory perception' of Wisdom's speech; people are exhorted to listen to what Wisdom has to say (8.6, 32-33).[51] The following step is people's 'cognitive perception' of what is perceived at a sensory level.[52]

Further, the purpose of Proverbs is that people will *know* (יָדַע/γινώσκω [LXX]) and *understand* (בִּין/νοέω [LXX]) wisdom in order to live ethically right (1.2).[53] Proverbs 2.1-10 is essentially an exhortation to listen to and search for wisdom, and to acquire wisdom through cognitive perception and subsequent understanding: wisdom (חָכְמָה/σοφία [LXX]) will come into your mind (לֵב/διάνοια [LXX]) (v.10a; cf. v.10b). According to the standard lexicons, the Hebrew לֵב (mostly translated by καρδία in the LXX) denotes the inner part of man — the 'heart' — and includes the mind, will, thought, emotions, etc. In the context of Proverbs, where cognitive functions are frequently attributed to the 'heart' (e.g. 2.2, 10; 3.1; 4.4; 14.10; 15.14; 16.21; 18.15), לֵב can be interpreted as 'mind', i.e., the faculty of understanding, reasoning, thinking, deciding, etc. (hence the translation of לֵב by διάνοια in 2.10 in the LXX). Thus, the לֵב is the locus of cognitive perception. The same concept is expressed in 22.17: 'incline your ear and listen to my words (sensory perception), and set your mind (לֵב) on knowledge (דַּעַת) (cognitive perception)' (cf. 23.12). Proverbs 14.33 even depicts the concept of W/wisdom indwelling the wise: 'W/wisdom rests/settles down in the mind of the one who has understanding.'[54]

Finally, based on sensory and cognitive perception, people then make a response to Wisdom and her teaching — acceptance or rejection — which results either in long life and well-being or in disaster and death.[55] Moreover, people are exhorted to love and stay with Wisdom (4.6; 8.17, 21), which is essentially an allusion to the concept of being a disciple of Wisdom (cf. 3.18; 4.5-9; 8.32-34).[56] Wisdom saves and gives life to her disciples, to those who remain faithful to her (8.32-35), but those who cease to follow her and follow Lady Folly instead will perish (8.36; 9.13-18).

---

[51] People are also encouraged to listen to the teaching of the wise (e.g. 1.5, 8; 4.1, 10; 5.1; 19.27; 22.17; 23.19).

[52] See ch. 1 section 3 for our definitions of sensory and cognitive perception.

[53] Cf. J.J. Collins, *Jewish Wisdom in the Hellenistic Age* (Edinburgh: T&T Clark, 1998) 9.

[54] The translations of Prov. 14.33 and 22.17 are my own.

[55] Cf. the concept of two paths in Prov. 1-9 set out before the reader: the path of W/wisdom, leading to life, and the path of F/folly, leading to death.

[56] Cf. the imperative to keep the teachings/commandments of the wise and to write them on the tablet of one's heart (3.1, 3; 6.21; 7.3), which possibly reflects the new covenantal language of Jer. 31.33.

Is there any indication for a role of the Spirit in Proverbs? We think the answer may be yes, although it will be very tentative. Proverbs 1.23 says that Wisdom pours out her רוּחַ and makes known her דְּבָר to people. We suggest that רוּחַ could refer to the divine Spirit and דְּבָר to Wisdom's teaching/words, so that this text might suggest that the Spirit reveals Wisdom's words to people.[57]

4. Sirach[58]

The Nature of Wisdom. In Sirach, Wisdom is also personified/hypostatized (1.1-20; 4.11-19; 6.18-31; 14.20-15.10; 24.1-22; 51.13-26).[59] God is the source of Wisdom; she is created by God and comes forth from God (1.1, 9; 24.3, 9). Sirach 24 describes Wisdom's search for a dwelling place, which culminates in her indwelling and being identified with the Torah (v.23; cf. 15.1; 17.11; 19.20; 21.11; 34.8; 45.5).[60] Sirach 24.25-29 even goes on to say that the Torah overflows with wisdom, denoting the abundance of wisdom available in the Torah. Hence, the Torah is the locus or embodiment of W/wisdom.[61] Because W/wisdom is identified with Torah, the acquisition of W/wisdom is necessarily linked to the study of the Torah: study, meditation and observance of the Torah leads to

---

[57] Cf. W. McKane, *Proverbs: A New Approach* (London: SCM Press, 1970) 274; Montague, *Spirit*, 94-95; Hildebrandt, *Theology*, 43. Most scholars, however, translate רוּחַ by 'heart/thoughts' (e.g., van Imschoot, 'Sagesse', 27; R.B.Y. Scott, *Proverbs-Ecclesiastes: Introduction, Translation, and Notes* [AncB 18; New York: Doubleday, 1979²] 40; Whybray, *Proverbs*, 47). The Targum on 1.23 agrees with our view, but the LXX takes 1.23 as 'thoughts'. The concept of the Spirit mediating wisdom to people is well attested in the OT, and occasionally also occurs in wisdom writings (Ps. 51.6, 10-11; Job 32.8) (see Bennema, 'Strands', 63-67).

[58] The book of Sirach probably functions as the best representative of (the continuation of) the Torah-centred wisdom tradition, although it may also be influenced by the OT Spirit-centred wisdom tradition (Bennema, 'Strands', 68). Cf. P.W. Skehan and A.A. Di Lella, *The Wisdom of Ben Sira: A New Translation with Notes, Introduction and Commentary* (AncB 39; New York: Doubleday, 1987) 75; J.G. Gammie, 'The Sage in Sirach' in J.G. Gammie and L.G. Perdue (eds.), *The Sage in Israel and the Ancient Near East* (Winona Lake: Eisenbrauns, 1990) 361-64; Collins, *Wisdom*, 44-45.

[59] Sir. 24.1-22 seems to owe much to Prov. 8.22-31. Hengel sees a parallel between Wisdom in Sirach and the Stoic Logos (*Judaism*, 159-60).

[60] *1 En.* 42.1-2 tells a contrasting story.

[61] For a more complete investigation of the identification of Wisdom and Torah in Sirach, see Schnabel, *Law*, 69-79. Cf. Davis, *Wisdom*, 10-16; Skehan/Di Lella, *Wisdom*, 75-79; Pate, *Reverse*, 24-33. Breck mentions that Sirach's identification of Wisdom with Torah marked a bifurcation within the one sapiential tradition (*Spirit*, 88, 92), but see Bennema ('Strands', 68 n.31) for a critique.

W/wisdom (1.26; 6.37; 15.1; 21.11).[62] Wisdom is not given to fools and sinners, but to those who trust God, who are upright, determined, disciplined and persevering. Wisdom is given to those who are prepared to seek her, to those who are prepared to work for the acquisition of W/wisdom and to those who observe the Torah, because she will test those who want to follow her (2.1-17; 4.16-19; 6.18-27; 15.1-10).

Although the quest for Wisdom is laborious, her testing is severe and only a few perceive her (6.21-22), the fruits of Wisdom are sweet: the acquisition of Wisdom leads to long life, blessing, peace/*shalom*, glory, joy, prosperity, protection and right ethical conduct (1.11-20; 4.11-15; 14.20-15.6; 51.15). In fact, life and death are a matter of choice, the consequences of accepting or rejecting Wisdom and the commandments of Torah (4.16-19; 15.15-17; cf. 48.22-23 with 49.4; cf. the doctrine of retribution in Deut. 28).[63] Life is attributed both to Torah (17.11; 45.5) and to Wisdom (1.20; 4.12), because the latter are identified. We suggest that Wisdom is depicted as the source of life, and because Wisdom indwells Torah, Torah became a derivative source of life/wisdom (cf. 24.25-27).[64] Moreover, the sage will also become a derivative source of wisdom (24.30-33; cf. 21.13; 39.6-11).[65] As in Proverbs, Sirach does not envisage an afterlife — in terms of either resurrection or immortality[66] — and 'salvation' is defined in terms of long life, blessing and well-being in the present.

The Quest for Wisdom. We can also find in Sirach a pattern, as in Proverbs, concerning the relationship between Wisdom, people and 'salvation'. The main difference between Proverbs and Sirach is that, whereas in Proverbs Wisdom takes initiative and confronts people (she calls out in the streets and stands at the most important places to meet

---

[62] Ben Sira is not merely transmitting what he found in the Torah but also drawing from it (and from other sources of wisdom) to create his new work of wisdom (Collins, *Wisdom*, 56-57; cf. Gammie, 'Sage', 360-61).

[63] In Sirach, βίος seems to denote daily existence, i.e., life in its daily functions (29.22; 31.4; 38.19; 40.29), whereas ζωή denotes the life that Wisdom possesses and mediates to people.

[64] Cf. Schnabel, who concludes that '[r]ight ethical conduct is prescribed and described in the law and outlined and concretized in wisdom' (*Law*, 89; cf. 46-49).

[65] The hymn honouring Israel's ancestors also includes wisdom-endowed leaders (44.3-4, 15; 45.5 [Moses]; 47.12-17 [Solomon, the prototypical wise king]).

[66] Cf. E. Sjöberg, 'Πνεῦμα, πνευματικός' in *TDNT*, VI:377; Montague, *Spirit*, 98-99; Collins, *Wisdom*, 92-96; J. Liesen, *Full of Praise: An Exegetical Study of Sir 39,12-35* (JSJ.S 64; Leiden: Brill, 2000) 282. Passages such as 8.7; 17.1-2, 30; 37.25; 41.13 merely express that human beings are not immortal and that death (eternal sleep [30.17]) will come to all. Cf. also the references to Hades, the world of the dead (17.27; 48.5; 51.6). Sirach possibly demonstrates some Platonic influence: the body returns to the earth, and the 'spirit' returns to heaven (38.23; 40.11).

people), in Sirach Wisdom is a more elusive/evasive figure. On the one hand, Wisdom is encountered in Torah, and Wisdom invites people to 'eat' and 'drink' of her (metaphors for accepting her teaching/instruction), so that they will desire her even more (24.19-21). On the other hand, Wisdom is not revealed (φανερά) to many people (6.22); only the diligent seekers receive from her (6.18-27; cf. 4.11-19; 14.22), only to them will Wisdom give ἄρτος συνέσεως καὶ ὕδωρ σοφίας (15.3), teaching and help (4.11). The wise sage virtually functions as an intermediary between Wisdom and people; the sage encourages and exhorts people to love, seek, serve, obey, listen to, hold on to and remain faithful to Wisdom (4.11-16). Moreover, people are exhorted to cultivate Wisdom (6.19), to live with her (14.23-27; 51.23) and to be yoked with her, i.e., to be in a relationship with Wisdom (6.24-31; 51.26).[67]

As we have mentioned before, the acquisition of W/wisdom is necessarily linked to the study of the Torah, which implies that Wisdom is obtained through 'sensory perception'. People are encouraged to listen to Wisdom (4.15), and W/wisdom is revealed through speech/words (and so perceived by hearing) (4.24). Moreover, people are advised to listen to the wisdom teaching of the sage (3.1; 6.23; 23.7; 31.22; 39.13; 51.28), because listening leads to wisdom and knowledge (6.33; 16.24).[68] This information perceived at a sensory level then needs to be processed cognitively in order to produce understanding.[69] Wisdom pours forth ἐπιστήμην καὶ γνῶσιν συνέσεως (1.19) — through Torah and the teaching of the sages — which can be acquired through reflection, thinking, meditation, learning, etc., in order to bring about understanding (6.37; 8.9; 14.20-21). The 'mind' (καρδία) is the locus of cognitive perception (3.29; 6.37; 16.20; 17.6; 22.17).[70] The instruction of wisdom (παιδεία σοφίας) takes place in the 'mind' (23.2; cf. σοφία ἐν καρδίᾳ in 45.26), and it is Sirach's 'mind' that pours forth wisdom (50.27).

On the basis of sensory and cognitive perception people then need to make a choice: whether or not to keep the commandments (of Torah/Wisdom), which results respectively in long life and well-being or in ruin and death (15.15-17). However, besides cognitive perception and understanding, Wisdom's disciples also need perseverance in order to

---

[67] It is even a love-relationship (E. Jacob, 'Wisdom and Religion in Sirach' in J.G. Gammie et al. [eds.], *Israelite Wisdom: Theological and Literary Essays in Honor of Samuel Terrien* [Missoula: Scholars Press, 1978] 254-55).

[68] Sinners, on the contrary, will not 'see', i.e. perceive, Wisdom (15.7).

[69] Cf. the Prologue, where Ben Sira reveals that the purpose of the book of Sirach is to mediate instruction and wisdom to those living outside Palestine who wish to gain *learning* so that they might make progress in living according to Torah (cf. 50.27).

[70] The justification for translating καρδία as 'mind' is the attribution of cognitive functions to καρδία (cf. the use of לֵב in Prov.).

remain faithful to Wisdom; if they defect, i.e., go astray or cast her aside, she will forsake them and hand them over to disaster (4.19; 6.21).

Spirit, Wisdom, Salvation. Besides the identification of Wisdom and Torah, Sirach also makes a close association between Wisdom and Spirit. Marböck thinks that 1.9-10, through the allusion to Joel 2.28, already suggests this connection between Wisdom and Spirit.[71] However, the cotext has no reference to the Spirit, and it is much more likely that 1.9-10 refers to the pouring out of Wisdom like *water* rather than to the pouring out of Wisdom like Spirit (cf. 1.19; 15.3; 24.21, 25-29). More important, if we have to compare 1.9-10 and Joel 2.28, the intended point of comparison is not in each case the *referent* of the outpouring metaphor but the *mode*. The purpose of the metaphor 'to pour out' in both cases is that what is given is given/experienced abundantly. Other scholars have seen an association between Wisdom and Spirit in 24.3, in the light of a possible allusion to Genesis 1.2.[72] However, this is debatable because רוח in Genesis 1.2 may refer to 'Spirit' or to 'wind', and also, 'to cover the earth like a mist' is not exactly the same as 'to hover over the waters'.

Nonetheless, the correlation between Wisdom and Spirit is made clear in Sirach 39.6, where the sage, if God is willing, will be filled with the Spirit of understanding (πνεῦμα συνέσεως).[73] In order to understand the exact nature of the correlation we have to look at the cotext of 39.6, which is the literary unit 38.24-39.11. The pericope starts by implying that only those who have enough time to study the Torah (the scribes), will have the opportunity to become sages. In 38.25-34a, Ben Sira describes several people with secular professions, and explains that although they do have wisdom associated with their skill, they are preoccupied with their profession and have no time left to acquire more wisdom.[74] The ideal scribe, however, who devotes himself to study and observance of the Torah (cf. Ezra 7.10), to extensive travel, and to discipline and prayer, in other words, he who devotes himself to the pursuit of Wisdom, is already wiser than the skilled worker (38.34b-39.5). After that, if God is willing, he will receive the Spirit of wisdom, i.e., the Spirit that will fill him with wisdom, so that he will become himself a (derivative) source of wisdom (39.6; cf.

---

[71] J. Marböck, 'Sir., 38,24 - 39,11: Der schriftgelehrte Weise. Ein Beitrag zu Gestalt und Werk Ben Siras' in M. Gilbert (ed.), *La Sagesse de l'Ancien Testament* (BEThL 51; Leuven: Leuven University Press, 1979) 308.

[72] Van Imschoot, 'Sagesse', 38; R.E. Murphy, *The Tree of Life: An Exploration of Biblical Wisdom Literature* (Grand Rapids: Eerdmans, 1996²) 139.

[73] Skehan and Di Lella, in their important commentary on Sirach, surprisingly do not refer at all to the Spirit in 39.6 (*Wisdom*, 447-53).

[74] This coincides with 17.7, 11, which depicts the concept that 'all' human beings (i.e., probably all of Israel [17.12; 43.33]) have received a certain measure of wisdom by virtue of their creation (cf. 1.9-10).

21.13; 24.30-33), and, consequently, a blessing to other people (39.7-11).[75] Hence, Sirach reveals a type of epistemological hierarchy.[76]

This interpretation seems to dovetail nicely with Davis' thesis. Davis, based on Stadelmann's threefold stratification of people in relation to W/wisdom, argues that in 38.24-39.11 three levels or stages of sapiential achievement are delineated: (i) those who are engaged in traditional vocations attain the lowest level of wisdom; (ii) a higher degree of wisdom is realized by the scribe who devotes himself to the study and practice of the Torah, to prayer and to the maintenance of covenantal righteousness; and (iii) the highest level, and culmination, of sapiential achievement is obtained only by the sage, to whom God freely and willingly gives the Spirit.[77] Hence, for Davis, the gift of the Spirit in Sirach is depicted virtually as a *donum superadditum* in order to reach the highest level of sapiential achievement rather than as a soteriological necessity.[78]

Liesen, however, disputes Stadelmann's interpretation of the gift of the Spirit being a *donum superadditum* restricted to merely *some* of the scribes, and argues that the subject of 39.5 and 39.6 remains unchanged and that no mention is made of a special category within the profession of the scribe.[79] Liesen, recognizing an allusion to 17.7, contends that the scribe in general is the person in whom the creational endowment of W/wisdom comes to full fruition, whereas others attain only a limited degree of wisdom.[80] Moreover, the Spirit-filled scribe now in turn produces wisdom, and guides and instructs people.[81]

Whether there are two or three categories of people in relation to wisdom is perhaps not the most important issue; what is crucial, however,

---

[75] J.L. Crenshaw even sees in 39.6 an allusion to the Davidic ruler of Isa. 11.2, who would be filled with the Spirit of understanding ('The Book of Sirach: Introduction, Commentary, and Reflections' in L.E. Keck et al. [eds.], *The New Interpreter's Bible: Volume V* [Nashville: Abingdon Press, 1997] 813).

[76] A.R. Brown, *The Cross and Human Transformation: Paul's Apocalyptic Word in 1 Corinthians* (Minneapolis: Fortress, 1995) 38-39.

[77] Davis, *Wisdom*, 16-24; cf. H. Stadelmann, *Ben Sira als Schriftgelehrter. Eine Untersuchung zum Berufsbild des vor-makkabäischen Sōfēr unter Berücksichtigung seines Verhältnisses zu Priester-, Propheten- und Weisheitslehrertum* (WUNT II/6; Tübingen: Mohr Siebeck, 1980) 232-35.

[78] So also Maier, *Mensch*, 37; Stadelmann, *Ben Sira*, 232-34; Schnabel, *Law*, 53. However, Maier merely states it rather than arguing it through, and Schnabel just quotes Maier. Based on Davis' study, Menzies then argues explicitly that the Spirit in Sirach is a *donum superadditum* and not a soteriological necessity (*Witness*, 63-65, 69-70).

[79] Liesen, *Praise*, 64. Cf. Skehan/Di Lella, *Wisdom*, 449-50.

[80] Liesen, *Praise*, 64-65. Cf. van Imschoot, who sees two sources of wisdom: one which is accessible to all intelligent and free men (38.24-34), and another which is available to those who are called by God to be religious educators (39.6) ('Sagesse', 35).

[81] Liesen, *Praise*, 66-89.

is the question whether the gift of the Spirit of wisdom is portrayed merely as a *donum superadditum* or as a soteriological necessity. We suggest that the latter option is nearer the truth for several reasons. The Spirit is portrayed as an agent of wisdom, which brings the scribe to a higher level of cognitive perception and understanding of Torah (39.7-8).[82] Consequently, this Spirit-imbued wisdom which results in a new/deeper understanding of Torah should enable the scribe to experience a higher level of covenantal faithfulness, i.e., of life. Moreover, the nature of the gift of the Spirit to the scribe was to enable the scribe himself to become a source of wisdom (39.6). The Spirit-imbued scribe as a (derivative) source of wisdom has considerable soteriological consequences. He will disclose his wisdom to others and instruct people (to live ethically right lives in adherence to Torah, which will bring life) (39.7-11); his knowledge and counsel is like a πηγὴ ζωῆς (21.13); he becomes an increasing (life-giving) river of wisdom pouring forth teaching of the law of life (24.30-33; cf. 17.11). Hence, the Spirit given to the wise scribe, which enables him to progress cognitively in understanding Torah, to be a derivative source of wisdom and to be an intermediary between Wisdom and people, is depicted as an agent of wisdom having soteriological consequences.[83]

Although the Spirit of wisdom and Wisdom are gifts from God (1.9-10; 17.7; 39.6), they are not automatically given to all people. One still needs to merit these gifts through devotion to the pursuit of Wisdom, which implies study and observance of the Torah, discipline, prayer, perseverance, zeal, determination, testing, etc. Even if one has fulfilled all necessary conditions/requirements, special grace is still needed to acquire the highest level of wisdom and to receive the Spirit of wisdom. Thus, the gift of the Spirit and Wisdom seems to be a combination of divine grace and human works, namely, a reward for human endeavour.[84]

---

[82] Cf. Levison, *Spirit*, 198-99.

[83] Cf. Liesen (*Praise*, 66-89), although he does not really draw out the soteriological consequences of the Spirit-endowed scribe. Wenk only briefly mentions the ethical consequences of Ben Sira's being filled with the Spirit (*Power*, 67-68). According to Menzies, one need not possess the gift of the Spirit in order to live in a right relationship with God and attain 'salvation' (*Witness*, 64, 70). Menzies may be right, when he says that Ben Sira thought that not everyone personally needed the Spirit, but one could only live in a right relationship with God if one adhered to Torah. And this required a proper understanding of and instruction in Torah, which was exactly the responsibility of the Spirit-filled scribe.

[84] Cf. Marböck, 'Weise', 305-307; Davis, *Wisdom*, 19. Although 48.24 probably also contains a reference to the divine Spirit (in providing charismatic revelation to Isaiah), it does not shed more light on the Spirit's soteriological role (48.12 is even more ambiguous).

5. Wisdom of Solomon[85]

The Nature of Wisdom. We find in this book also the personification/hypostatization of Wisdom (6.12-11.1), and she is characterized primarily by life (6.18; 8.13, 17), wisdom/knowledge/understanding (8.4, 8, 18; 9.9, 11) and glory (7.25; 9.11).[86] She originates from and lives with God, and her relationship with God is one of intimacy, love, knowledge, glory and life (6.18; 7.25-27; 8.3-4; 9.4, 9-10; 16.13). Wisdom of Solomon also portrays people being in relationship with Wisdom (7.28; 8.16-18). We have argued elsewhere that in Wisdom of Solomon, the locus of wisdom is probably not the Torah but rather Wisdom herself, i.e., Wisdom's teaching is the locus/source of wisdom (cf. 6.17-18).[87] Following and accepting Wisdom and her teaching leads to blessing, peace, joy, glory, protection, ethical guidance, renewal and immortality/(eternal) life (6.18; 7.27; 8.9-18; 9.11; cf. 3.1-9; 5.15-16). By implication, rejection of Wisdom and her words leads to death and 'damnation' (cf. chs. 3-5 for the judgment and destination of the wicked).[88]

Wisdom of Solomon is the first wisdom book that expands the concept of 'life' to immortality: God created humankind for immortality (2.23),

---

[85] For the influence of Prov. on Wis., see P.W. Skehan, *Studies in Israelite Poetry and Wisdom* (CBQ Monograph Series 1; Worcester, MA: Heffernan Press, 1971) 173-91. For the confluence of wisdom and apocalyptic traditions in Wis., see Pate, *Reverse*, 45-46. Collins elucidates the socio-historical context of Wis. (*Wisdom*, ch. 8), and the genre of Wis. is briefly discussed in L.L. Grabbe, *Wisdom of Solomon* (Sheffield: SAP, 1997) 25-28; Collins, *Wisdom*, 181-82; M. McGlynn, *Divine Judgement and Divine Benevolence in the Book of Wisdom* (WUNT II/139; Tübingen: Mohr Siebeck, 2001) 3-9.

[86] Although the term ζωή is not directly used in connection with Wisdom, the concept of Wisdom providing life is evoked by the use of ἀθανασία and ἀφθαρσία. For the meaning of δόξα, see F. Raurell, 'The Religious Meaning of "Doxa" in the Book of Wisdom' in M. Gilbert (ed.), *La Sagesse de l'Ancien Testament* (BEThL 51; Leuven: Leuven University Press, 1979) 370-83. D.K. Berry certainly goes too far by stating that Wisdom is a member of the Godhead (*An Introduction to Wisdom and Poetry of the Old Testament* [Nashville: Broadman & Holman Publishers, 1995] 47-48). See Fatehi (*Relation*, 105-108) for a corrective view.

[87] Bennema, 'Strands', 71. Cf. Isaacs, *Concept*, 53; D. Winston, *The Wisdom of Solomon: A New Translation with Introduction and Commentary* (AncB 43; New York: Doubleday, 1979) 42-43; Schnabel, *Law*, 131-34; Breck, *Spirit*, 90; Collins, *Wisdom*, 196; Pate, *Reverse*, 46-47. Contra Davis, *Wisdom*, 178 n.11; N.T. Wright, *Jesus and the Victory of God. Christian Origins and the Question of God Volume Two* (London: SPCK, 1996) 213. We are not setting up Torah over against Wisdom's teaching, since Wisdom's commands are essentially God's commands (as expressed also in Torah), but Wis. seems to have a broader, more universalistic outlook than, e.g., Sirach.

[88] For the concept of death in Wis., see Grabbe, *Wisdom*, 52-53; Collins, *Wisdom*, 187-90. See also McGlynn, *Judgement*, *passim*, since the central theme of her book is God's treatment of the 'righteous' and the 'wicked'.

which is guaranteed by righteousness (1.15; 3.1-4; 5.15) and adherence to Wisdom's laws (6.18-19).[89] 'Salvation' can then be defined in terms of the immortality of the souls of the righteous (cf. 3.1).[90] However, this 'salvation', provided by Wisdom, is not merely eschatological; it also has a realized dimension. First, in 10.1-11.1 Wisdom is depicted as a soteriological figure in Israel's history (before the Torah was even given); Wisdom is a way of describing God's salvific acts in history.[91] Second, Wisdom provides Solomon with wisdom (8.18) and ethical guidance (9.11) in order to govern God's people justly (9.12) and to teach them what is pleasing to God (9.18), i.e., Wisdom 'saves' God's people through the wisdom-imbued king.[92] Hence, Wisdom is depicted as the source of 'salvation', namely, of moral wisdom/knowledge (8.18; 10.10) and (or leading to) immortality.

Nevertheless, the benefits of (adherence to) Wisdom are not an end in themselves; the ultimate goal of the pursuit of Wisdom is friendship/fellowship/union with God (6.18-19; 7.14, 27; cf. 2.13-18 where the righteous person calls God his father and claims to be his child). Thus, the final aim of humankind is to have an intimate relationship with God, which is only possible by having an intimate relationship with Wisdom; union with God is only achieved/mediated through union with Wisdom.[93] The reason for this is that Wisdom herself has an intimate relationship with God, and hence if one sees/experiences Wisdom, one sees/experiences God himself (7.25-26; 8.3-4; 9.4, 9-10). As an initiate in the knowledge of God (8.3), understanding what is pleasing to God and right according to his

---

[89] We suggest that the author of Wis., drawing on the Platonic concept of the immortal soul (without accepting its idea of pre-existence), saw immortality as the wages of righteousness rather than as an innate quality of the soul (cf. J. Geyer, *The Wisdom of Solomon: Introduction and Commentary* [London: SCM Press, 1963] 42-45; Winston, *Wisdom*, 29-30; R.J. Miller, 'Immortality and Religious Identity in Wisdom 2-5' in E.A. Castelli and H. Taussig [eds.], *Reimagining Christian Origins: A Colloquium Honoring Burton L. Mack* [Valley Forge: Trinity Press Int., 1996] 199-213; Collins, *Wisdom*, 183-87; R.J. Clifford, *The Wisdom Literature* [Nashville: Abingdon Press, 1998] 145). The unrighteous mistakenly believes there is no afterlife (2.1-5) — hence their strategy for life is *carpe diem* — but they will receive punishment (3.10-19; 5.1-23). According to Collins, the author of Wis. never describes everlasting punishments of the unrighteous; the immortality that interests him is the blessed afterlife of the righteous (*Wisdom*, 186).

[90] Collins contends that Wis. only envisages the immortality of the soul, but not a resurrection of the body (*Wisdom*, 186; cf. Miller, 'Immortality', 211 n.2), whereas Wright believes that this immortality refers to a temporary state in heaven, which will be followed by a bodily resurrection (*Testament*, 330).

[91] See also P. Enns, *Exodus Retold: Ancient Exegesis of the Departure from Egypt in Wis 10:15-21 and 19:1-9* (Atlanta: Scholars Press, 1997) *passim*.

[92] Cf. Winston, who believes that the author of Wis. already enjoys this prize of immortality in his present existence (*Wisdom*, 31-32).

[93] Cf. Winston, *Wisdom*, 41; U. Wilckens, 'Σοφία κτλ.' in *TDNT*, VI:499.

commandments (9.9), she mediates this revelatory knowledge of God to people (8.18; cf. Wisdom's teaching and guiding function in 7.21 and 9.11). Moreover, the possession of this knowledge of God leads to eternal life and intimacy with God (cf. 15.3); to know God implies having a relationship with God (through Wisdom). Knowledge of God does not primarily come through study of Torah but essentially through union with Wisdom; one should primarily meditate on Wisdom (6.15) because Wisdom will explicate Torah.

In sum, Wisdom, as the mediator of revelatory saving knowledge of God, is soteriologically necessary. Wisdom's teaching/word contains saving wisdom that leads to knowledge of God, which in turn leads to eternal life and fellowship with God. Wisdom can actually be seen as a circumlocution to describe God in action, especially his communication of revelatory saving knowledge to people. Wisdom's salvific role is summed up nicely in 7.27: Wisdom *renews* all things, she *indwells* holy people (cf. Moses in 10.16) and brings them into an *intimate relationship with God*.[94]

The Quest for Wisdom. We now turn to the question of *how* one can achieve this salvific union with Wisdom, i.e., the question of the nature of the quest for Wisdom. Chapter 6, which depicts the quest for Wisdom essentially as a two-way process, may serve as an answer to our question. On the one hand, people are exhorted to desire and listen to Solomon's wise teaching (6.1-2, 11). Implicitly, the exhortation of the implied author to desire his wisdom is an exhortation to desire Wisdom herself (ἐπιθυμέω in 6.11 is repeated in 6.13). Moreover, one needs to perceive W/wisdom cognitively — taking in Solomon's wise teaching is meant to produce wisdom (ἵνα μάθητε σοφίαν [6.9]), and one is exhorted to think about Wisdom (6.15; cf. the emphasis on learning and understanding in 6.1, 9 as a result of sensory perception). The mind is again identified as the locus of cognitive activity (νοῦς πολυφρόντιδα [9.15]; cf. 2.2; 8.17).[95] Hence, Wisdom of Solomon also portrays the concept of sensory perception leading to cognitive perception and understanding (cf. 11.13; 12.27; 16.18).[96] On the other hand, Wisdom also takes initiative — Wisdom quickly makes herself known to those who desire her (6.13), Wisdom seeks for those worthy of her and graciously meets them (6.16) — and she

---

[94] The use of the present tense may indicate the realized dimension of Wisdom's saving activity.

[95] The mind of the unrighteous person is blinded by his wickedness, which prevents knowledge and discernment (2.21-22). Hence, the νοῦς is the locus of Wisdom's activities as well as of evil/wickedness (cf. 4.11-12).

[96] Cf. 16.5-7, which explains that it was not the physical sight of the bronze serpent that was salvific but the cognitive perception of the *significance* of the serpent (as a salvific symbol of the God who saves). However, sensory perception does not guarantee cognitive perception and understanding (4.15; 13.1).

will easily be discerned/understood and found by those who love and seek her (6.12).[97]

Thus, people's pursuit of Wisdom is a mutual search in which Wisdom meets people who seek and desire her half-way.[98] The beginning of the pursuit of Wisdom is to truly desire and love her (6.12, 17). There is no reference to preparatory works (such as study, discipline, perseverance), which people have to perform, nor is there any mention of struggle or stages of sapiential achievement, which people have to go through in order to obtain Wisdom (*pace* Davis[99]).[100] Wisdom of Solomon 6.17-19, for example, cannot be used to develop a model of several levels or stages of sapiential achievement, which people have to pass in order to reach the highest level of wisdom (as in Sirach). The point of 6.17-19 is to show that the quest for Wisdom is like a chain made up of individual links which are logically connected.

It starts with the desire to learn, the desire to learn implies love for Wisdom, love for Wisdom means or is expressed in following her teaching, adherence to her teaching leads to immortality and fellowship with God. Hence, 6.17-19 depicts essentially the quest for union with God, which is achieved and mediated through the union with Wisdom, i.e., Wisdom is the means by which one knows God. In the light of 6.12-16, then, it is Wisdom herself who is depicted as one's travel companion; it is Wisdom herself who goes out to meet those who have started their journey for her and for God. Hence, on one's sapiential journey to God Wisdom comes alongside as a travel companion to give divine guidance and assistance. Moreover, the journey with Wisdom is the way of the Lord (5.7), and Wisdom functions as a guide on this way that is, leads to, or contains, truth (5.6-7), because Wisdom's teaching contains truth (6.22; cf. 3.9). The sapiential journey to God with Wisdom stands in contrast to the journey of the ungodly, who journey through trackless deserts and who take the paths of lawlessness and destruction (5.7).

Spirit, Wisdom, Salvation. We now come to the issue concerning the relationship between Wisdom and Spirit in relation to 'salvation'. In 1.4-5

---

[97] This picture of Wisdom is much more in continuity with that in Prov. than with Ben Sira's portrayal.

[98] Cf. E.G. Clarke, *The Wisdom of Solomon* (Cambridge: CUP, 1973) 46-47.

[99] Although Davis only investigates Philo, where he finds a model of stages of sapiential achievement, he argues that Philo and Wis. have so much in common that a similar model may be assumed for Wis. (*Wisdom*, 49-50, 177-78 n.7).

[100] Cf. McGlynn, *Judgement*, 107. 'Those worthy of her' (6.16) should probably not be interpreted in terms of human works/achievement, but rather as parallel expressions to 'those who love her', 'those who seek her' and 'those who desire her' (6.12-13). Winston offers an explanation in the context of (the tension between) human freedom and divine determinism (*Wisdom*, 58).

Wisdom and Spirit are already closely associated (they both flee from unrighteousness), but in 1.6 the association is made explicit: Wisdom is (or is represented by) a/the benevolent Spirit. This concept is elaborated in 7.22-23, where it says that the Spirit in Wisdom is intellectual, holy, etc.[101] In other words, Wisdom is depicted as being indwelled and being empowered by the Spirit; the Spirit indwells Wisdom and endows her with intellectual and moral qualities as well as power.[102]

This Spirit-indwelled Wisdom is the object of Solomon's desire for two main reasons. First, God had chosen Solomon to be king of his people, and Solomon's concern was how to govern God's people justly (7.15; 9.7). Second, and related to this, Solomon is concerned to know what is pleasing to God (9.13; cf. the use of ἀρεστός in 9.9-10, 18). Solomon realizes that the answer to his concerns is the figure of Wisdom. Wisdom will give him understanding (7.7), Wisdom will enable Solomon to govern and judge justly (7.15; 8.11, 14; 9.12), and Wisdom will give him ethical guidance and teach him what is pleasing to God (9.10-11; cf. 7.21, which mentions that Solomon could come to a certain understanding/wisdom through cognitive perception of what Wisdom taught him). Wisdom will empower Solomon and enable him to be a just king because Wisdom knows God's intention and what is pleasing to him (8.4; 9.9-11). Moreover, Solomon also realized that Wisdom lives with God and that he would not possess Wisdom unless God gave her to him (8.21). Hence, Solomon deeply desires Wisdom (7.8-14; 8.2, 9, 18) and appeals to God for the gift of Wisdom (9.1-18; cf. 7.7). The result of Solomon's prayer is the gift of Wisdom (7.7; 9.17),[103] and the gift of the Spirit of Wisdom (7.7; cf. 9.17). Solomon received Wisdom and the accompanying Spirit, which would mediate or communicate to Solomon wisdom and understanding (7.7; 9.17). Thus, the Spirit functions as the revelatory power of Wisdom in that the Spirit discloses W/wisdom to Solomon.[104]

---

[101] That πνεῦμα in 1.6; 7.22 refers to the divine Spirit is clear by virtue of its association with divine Wisdom. If the Spirit is God's own life and vitality (so, e.g., Turner, *Spirit*, 5), and if Wisdom is a circumlocution to describe God in his wise action, then the πνεῦμα of Wisdom is most likely God's Spirit (contra Willett, *Wisdom*, 17, 43). Moreover, if the πνεῦμα of Wisdom is Wisdom's 'personality', then 7.22-23 essentially describes the character of Wisdom (and thus of God).

[102] This concept of πνεῦμα indwelling Wisdom (7.22) and holding everything together (1.7) probably reflects Stoic influence.

[103] Indeed, chs. 7-9 make it clear that Solomon did receive Wisdom.

[104] With the concept of πνεῦμα as the power of Wisdom, we denote a *function* of the divine Spirit, i.e., the Spirit that functions as the disclosing power of Wisdom, rather than πνεῦμα as a sort of impersonal power. Contra Bieder, who defines this πνεῦμα merely as intellectual and ethical suprahuman power that permeates rational and morally pure men ('Πνεῦμα', VI:371). Isaacs (*Concept*, 46) may be in the same danger.

How exactly do Wisdom and Spirit then relate to salvation? First, through Wisdom, Solomon receives understanding, enters into an intimate relationship with God, and inherits immortality (7.14, 27; 8.13, 17-18). Moreover, knowledge/understanding of God leads to righteousness and immortality (15.3; cf. 1.15; 2.13; 5.15). The key to this salvific knowledge is Wisdom, who is the source of all knowledge and wisdom (7.21; 8.4, 8, 18; 9.9-11).[105] Second, Wisdom 'saves' God's people through the Spirit-endowed wisdom-imbued ruler in that Wisdom facilitates right ethical conduct, i.e., a behaviour that pleases God (9.10-12, 18). In fact, Solomon presents himself as a (derivative) source of W/wisdom. How can this be? First, because Solomon received the gift of the Spirit of Wisdom. Second, because Wisdom herself taught Solomon and provides him with wisdom and understanding. Thus, Wisdom and the accompanying Spirit cause such ethical transformation (directly and indirectly) that people are enabled to live righteous lives.[106]

We can conclude, then, that both Wisdom and the accompanying Spirit of Wisdom are depicted as a soteriological necessity, in which Wisdom functions as the *source* (or locus) and the Spirit as the *agent* (or effective cause) of 'salvation'.[107] The Spirit provides the wisdom that is available in or through Wisdom; Wisdom, or what Wisdom has to offer, is mediated to people by the Spirit. This is why we have introduced the concept 'the Spirit as the power of (saving) Wisdom', because the Spirit is the agent of that which Wisdom offers, i.e., the Spirit functions as the power which brings into effect that which is available in or by Wisdom. Finally, the gift of (the Spirit of) Wisdom seems to be a free gift from God, which cannot be acquired by any human achievement, and therefore, has to be implored of God (7.7; 8.21; 9.17).

---

[105] Cf. Grabbe, *Wisdom*, 53.

[106] Cf. Winston, *Wisdom*, 208; Wenk, *Power*, 86-88.

[107] We should be careful not to bifurcate the gift of Wisdom and the gift of the Spirit as if they are two distinct gifts — for with the gift of Wisdom also comes the accompanying Spirit of Wisdom — nor to identify Wisdom completely with the Spirit (contra van Imschoot, 'Sagesse', 37, 43, 44, 46; Chevallier, *Souffle*, 1:67-68; Collins, *Wisdom*, 198; McGlynn, *Judgement*, 115, 132). Although Wis. goes furthest in the association of Wisdom with Spirit, the distinctions between them are still clear enough not to blur the two concepts. First, the Spirit functions as the power of Wisdom, i.e., the Spirit is the agent of wisdom whereas Wisdom is its source/locus. Second, the Spirit is never personified or hypostatized to the extent that Wisdom is. Neither in the OT nor in Judaism is the Spirit hypostatized (with van Imschoot, 'Action', 563-65, 586). And although the Spirit is sometimes personified (e.g., in Isa. 63.10), this personification never goes as far as what is said about Wisdom (e.g., Wisdom lives with God, sits by his throne, is an initiate in the knowledge of God and is depicted as a female figure who has her own speeches) (contra van Imschoot, 'Sagesse', 37-43).

We are now in a position to assess the positions of Breck, van Imschoot and Menzies (see section 2, above). According to Breck, Wisdom 'replaced' the Spirit, although she never assumed the Spirit's eschatological role. However, Breck's argument is based, in our view, on an incorrectly presupposed withdrawal of the Spirit in the intertestamental period (ITP) (see n.13, above), and Breck fails to see that the Spirit is the power and accomplice of Wisdom. Moreover, there are reasons to believe that Wisdom has an eschatological dimension: 5.1-23 describes the eschatological judgment, dependent on whether people have followed the way of the Lord/truth (which is the way of Wisdom) or the way of lawlessness and destruction (5.6-7).[108]

Van Imschoot in general maintains the correct distinction between Wisdom (as the source of life) and Spirit (as the agent of life). The only exception, according to van Imschoot, is Wisdom of Solomon, which depicts the complete identification of Wisdom and Spirit and portrays both as the internal principle of the physical and moral life. Nevertheless, van Imschoot still argues that although Wisdom is depicted in 1.4-5 and 7.27 as a divine moral force, unlike the Spirit she does not *create* the moral and religious life but only reside with the righteous to *maintain* it. However, besides the question as to whether van Imschoot's categories of physical and moral life are always helpful (see section 3, above), we have argued that the important distinction between the Spirit being the agent and Wisdom being the source of life is also upheld in Wisdom of Solomon (cf. n.107, above). Moreover, 7.27 seems to indicate that it is Wisdom who *renews* all things and who *makes* people friends of God, suggesting that Wisdom is making people righteous.[109]

Notably, even Menzies, who vigorously defends the theory that the gift of the Spirit for Judaism is usually a *donum superadditum*, admits that the Spirit in Wisdom of Solomon (and 1QH) is a soteriological necessity, although this is an exception and the culmination of a process of development within the sapiential tradition. However, we have argued elsewhere that there were several strands of wisdom tradition and that, in

---

[108] Wis. does not merely describe the future destinies of the righteous and the ungodly but also their eschatological destinies (Gammie, 'Dualism', 376). Cf. Isaacs, *Concept*, 24; Wright, *Jesus*, 211-13, 313.

[109] Although 1.4-5 and 7.27 seem paradoxical, the point of both passages may simply be that the presence of Wisdom is an *identifying mark* of the righteous (J.J. Collins, *Between Athens and Jerusalem: Jewish Identity in the Hellenistic Diaspora* [New York: Crossroad, 1983] 183; D. Winston, 'Wisdom in the Wisdom of Solomon' in L.G. Perdue et al. [eds.], *In Search of Wisdom: Essays in Memory of John G. Gammie* [Louisville: Westminster John Knox Press, 1993] 162-63).

some, the Spirit was perceived as a soteriological necessity, whereas the Spirit in other strands played a lesser role or none at all.[110]

Two Categories of Πνεῦμα. It seems that the author of Wisdom of Solomon uses two concepts of πνεῦμα — the Stoic idea of πνεῦμα that permeated everything (1.7; 7.22; 12.1) and the charismatic gift of πνεῦμα (7.7; 9.17) — and thus raises the question as to what extent these are compatible. We suggest that the author used a language with Stoic overtones to confirm the OT concept of the πνεῦμα as the life-principle, and also perceived πνεῦμα in a different sense to be the principle of 'salvation'.[111]

First, the author can speak about Wisdom indwelled by πνεῦμα (7.22-23; cf. 1.6), in that the πνεῦμα in Wisdom represents her life and character. Second, every human being has received πνεῦμα by virtue of her/his creation, which constitutes and sustains life — God ἐμφυσήσαντα πνεῦμα ζωτικόν (15.11; cf. Gen. 2.7 [LXX]). In fact, the πνεῦμα given to people (15.11) — 'their spirit' — is nothing other than God's immortal Spirit (12.1) that they have on loan (15.16) (cf. excursus 2, below). Moreover, it seems plausible that this universal endowment of πνεῦμα also provides the ability to reason by providing some measure of knowledge/wisdom to the mind, which is the locus of cognitive activity (cf. 1.5). This may be confirmed by 12.1-2, which reveals that God can address people rationally concerning their moral conduct and correct them *because* people have received πνεῦμα (cf. the cognate verbs ἐλέγχω, ὑπομιμνήσκω and νουθετέω in 12.2).[112]

In 13.1-9 it becomes clear that 'all' people have the ability/power to know, and that hence by looking at creation they should be able (at least according to the author's expectation) to perceive the Creator (esp. vv.5 and 9). Nevertheless, they were unable or failed to know God (13.1; 15.11).[113] People lacked the knowledge of God that leads to righteousness, immortality and intimacy with God (15.1; 6.18-19). Thus, 13.1-9 essentially says that sensory perception should lead to cognitive perception, yet some people get stuck at the level of sensory perception or do not acquire adequate knowledge. However, this salvific knowledge is available in the figure of Wisdom and provided by the Spirit of Wisdom; hence, Solomon's request for the gift of Wisdom and the accompanying Spirit (7.7; 9.17).

---

[110] See Bennema, 'Strands', *passim*.

[111] The use of Stoic terminology need not imply an interpretation of these terms according to Stoic philosophy (see Isaacs, *Concept*, 23).

[112] The πνεῦμα also functions as the means of judgment: (i) the Spirit of the Lord will flee from immorality and cause judgment for the unrighteous (1.5-9); (ii) God will judge his enemies by the Spirit of power (5.23; 11.20). Cf. Montague, *Spirit*, 105.

[113] Cf. Perdue, *Wisdom*, 314.

In conclusion, according to Wisdom of Solomon, all human beings are endowed with πνεῦμα to provide life and reason, but in order to know God and thus ensure 'salvation' a further endowment of πνεῦμα is needed: the πνεῦμα that comes with Wisdom.[114] Thus, both concepts of πνεῦμα are in continuity with one another, namely through that which they provide — life and wisdom; the only difference is in *intensity* and *quality*, i.e., in the concentration, measure and calibre of endowment.[115] These two concepts of πνεῦμα are theologically *one* concept or two closely related overlapping concepts.

The Recipients of (the Spirit of) Wisdom. The final issue which needs to be addressed is the *identity* of the potential recipients of this gift of (the Spirit of) Wisdom. At one end of the spectrum, Wenk believes that the gift of the Spirit of Wisdom is only for the rulers.[116] At the other end of the spectrum, Clarke contends that the author's appeal to rulers (1.1; 6.1-2) is, in the light of Genesis 1.26, an appeal to everyone.[117] Wenk's perspective seems too narrow, which is probably due to the fact that he focuses only on Spirit-endowed leaders who have a positive ethical influence on God's people; neither can we justify reading Genesis 1.26 into 1.1; 6.1-2.

It is difficult to determine the right balance. On the one hand, there is evidence that points to the fact that the author addresses the rulers (1.1; 6.1-2, 9, 21, 24; 7.1-6; 9.18). In this case, the ruler is the recipient of the gift (of the Spirit) of Wisdom, and it is Wisdom who teaches and saves people through the Wisdom-imbued ruler (8.10-15; 9.18; 10.1-11.1). That is, the wise king functions as the channel or medium through which Wisdom is available and passed on to people. On the other hand, there is also evidence that the author widens the scope for the recipients of the gift (of the Spirit) of Wisdom. First, 1.6-5.23 addresses the wise and unwise in general, and not just the ruler/king. Second, it is unlikely that texts such as 1.4, 7.14, 27-28 merely address rulers/kings. Third, at least 8.7-8 ('if anyone...') seems to widen the scope of those who have access to Wisdom.

---

[114] Cf. Turner, who contends that Wis. contains a tension (similar to Philo) between the universal gift of a 'rational spirit' (with Stoic overtones), which reflects God's wisdom and is implanted in creation, and the special gift of the Spirit to Solomon through which Israel is instructed in the way of salvation (*Power*, 126). However, Turner has not attempted to explain or solve this tension.

[115] Most scholars, however, distinguish more sharply between the two concepts of πνεῦμα — the πνεῦμα as source of life and as source of wisdom (e.g., Bieder, 'Πνεῦμα', VI:370-71; Isaacs, *Concept*, 46; Menzies, *Witness*, 57-59) — whereas we attribute both life and wisdom to both concepts.

[116] Wenk, *Power*, 85-87, 97.

[117] Clarke, *Wisdom*, 4-5, 14-15, 45. Cf. Menzies, who essentially argues that *each individual* needs to possess the gift of the Spirit in order to attain salvation (*Witness*, 58, 62). However, we will argue that salvific wisdom could also be made widely available to people through a Spirit-endowed ruler.

Fourth, although the king is directly addressed in 6.1-11 and in 6.21-25, 6.12-20 seems to be general truth for everyone, which the author uses to make his point to the king. Fifth, 7.1-6 portrays Solomon as sharing the common existence of all human beings, which might imply that what Solomon received is also within reach for everyone.

Weighing the evidence, we suggest that although in 1.1 and 6.1-2 the author primarily points to the rulers and kings of this world, the gift (of the Spirit) of Wisdom is perhaps not exclusively for them. Solomon functions as the ideal wise man, and his prayer for Wisdom functions as the paradigmatic pattern for everyone who wants to acquire Wisdom. Thus, the gift (of the Spirit) of Wisdom seems to be available for everyone who asks God for it in prayer.[118]

Still, we need to define further the term 'everyone'. In favour of interpreting 'everyone' in terms of any person, one could argue that in chapters 2-5 the 'wicked' and the 'righteous' are not clearly identified and so refer to any person. However, a few things speak against this interpretation. First, chapters 10-19 clearly focus on Israel, by retelling her basic story from the perspective of Wisdom.[119] Second, in chapters 10-19 the 'righteous' are clearly identified with faithful Israelites (e.g. 10.20; 15.1-3; 16.2, 6-7, 20; 18.1, 7) and the 'wicked' with Gentiles (e.g. 12.20, 22-24; 14.22-31; 15.14-15, 18). Third, Wisdom of Solomon twice refers explicitly to the covenants with Israel (12.21; 18.22), and throughout Wisdom of Solomon there are references to Torah (2.12; 6.4; 9.9; 16.6; 18.4, 9). Thus, the concept of the covenant as the principal soteriological category is also present in Wisdom of Solomon, and it seems correct to interpret 'everyone' then in terms of faithful Jews.[120]

It seems, then, that we cannot be completely conclusive about the identity of the potential recipients of the gift (of the Spirit) of Wisdom. Perhaps it is wiser to conclude that the gift (of the Spirit) of Wisdom seems to be available for every (faithful) Jew; either directly through the

---

[118] The majority of scholars include a wider scope for the recipients of (the Spirit of) Wisdom than just the rulers: e.g., Geyer, *Wisdom*, 78-79; Isaacs, *Concept*, 46; Davis, *Wisdom*, 177 n.5; M. Gilbert, 'Wisdom Literature' in M.E. Stone (ed.), *Jewish Writings of the Second Temple Period: Apocrypha, Pseudepigrapha, Qumran Sectarian Writings, Philo, Josephus* (Assen: Van Gorcum, 1984) 310; D. Winston, 'The Sage as Mystic in the Wisdom of Solomon' in J.G. Gammie and L.G. Perdue (eds.), *The Sage in Israel and the Ancient Near East* (Winona Lake: Eisenbrauns, 1990) 384-85; Perdue, *Wisdom*, 321; Enns, *Exodus*, 140 n.4; Grabbe, *Wisdom*, 63; Clifford, *Wisdom*, 148.

[119] In fact, the focus has already been narrowed down to Israel in chs. 7-9 by virtue of Solomon as implied author.

[120] It would not be impossible to include proselytes as well.

gift (of the Spirit) of Wisdom in prayer or indirectly through the Wisdom-imbued Spirit-filled ruler/king.[121]

6. Philo[122]

Philo's Categories of Πνεῦμα. There are basically four types of reference to divine πνεῦμα in Philo,[123] which we will elucidate in relation to 'salvation'. Although we will focus on two types — the rational πνεῦμα and the charismatic πνεῦμα — we will also suggest how all the four types might be interrelated.

(1) Πνεῦμα as one of the four elements (air) or cohesive force. In a number of references, πνεῦμα, as a synonym for ἀήρ, appears to be one of the four fundamental elements, along with fire, water and earth, of which the world consists (*Aet.* 111; *Cher.* 111; *Sac.* 97; *Gig.* 22; *Ebr.* 106; *Leg. All.* 1.91; *Op.* 29).[124] Moreover, πνεῦμα also appears to be the cohesive force which holds things together (*Aet.* 125; *Her.* 242; *Deus* 35; *Op.* 131).

(2) Πνεῦμα as the vital life-principle. God is the author of life, and πνεῦμα, as the 'breath' of God, is most life-giving (*Op.* 30). All creatures of land and water live by air and πνεῦμα (*Gig.* 10), including human beings (*Det.*

---

[121] Despite that McGlynn only discusses the acquisition of wisdom (and not of Spirit), she strikes a good balance: in Wis. 6-9 the kings are designated as the recipients of Wisdom and as an initial location for Wisdom's actions, but in Wis. 1-5 and 10 her actions are extended to the experience of humankind in general (to activate God's creation plan for the immortality of humans) (*Judgement*, ch. 4 [esp. pp.90, 105-10, 130]). Although M.[M.B.] Turner does not allow the character of Solomon to function as an archetype of the spiritual man, he does suggest that the author could envisage Spirit as widely given in his own generation to the pious reader of Torah, because Torah contains Spirit as revelation ('The Spirit of Prophecy and the Power of Authoritative Preaching in Luke-Acts: A Question of Origins', *NTS* 38 [1992] 84-85 n.36). Although we believe that in Wis. Torah is not *the* locus of Wisdom nor linked with the Spirit, we nonetheless welcome Turner's view of a wider audience as potentially capable of receiving the Spirit.

[122] The references to Philo's works are taken from the Loeb Classical Library. For the strong similarity between Philo and Wis., see Winston, *Wisdom*, 59-63. Although Philo was influenced by Platonism (which asserted God's transcendence) and Stoicism (which asserted God's immanence), he remained within mainstream Judaism (Isaacs, *Concept*, 28-29, 50; contra Breck, *Spirit*, 100-101).

[123] Similar classifications have been made by Verbeke, *Évolution*, 236-60; A. Laurentin, 'Le Pneuma dans la Doctrine de Philon', *EThL* 27 (1951) 390-437, esp. 391-424; Isaacs, *Concept*, 150-52; Menzies, *Witness*, 59; M.[M.B.] Turner, 'Spirit in Philo' (unpublished notes), 1-6.

[124] Contra Laurentin, 'Pneuma', 391-404.

80; *Leg.* 63; *Quaest. in Gn.* 2.8; 3.3).[125] Hence, Philo confirms the Jewish belief of the divine πνεῦμα creating and sustaining life.

(3) Πνεῦμα as the rational aspect of the human soul. In order to understand this meaning of divine πνεῦμα we need first to elucidate the creation story. According to Philo, God is transcendent and so nothing mortal or corporeal can be made in the likeness of God, but only in that of the second God, who is his Logos (*Quaest. in Gn.* 2.62; *Prov.* 1). The Logos appears to be the realm in which, as well as the instrument by which, God designs and creates; the Logos is the divine sphere in and through which God expresses himself (cf. *Op.* 20-25, 29-31). Thus, the Logos is not only the archetypal model or idea on which everything is patterned, but also a mediator between the transcendent God and the material world.[126]

Philo reasons that there are two types of man: the heavenly man of Genesis 1.26 (incorporeal, invisible, incorruptible, immortal), who was created in the image and likeness of God, and the earthly man of Genesis 2.7, called Adam, a composition of earthly substance (dust and clay) and divine πνεῦμα (*Leg. All.* 1.31-33; *Op.* 25, 69, 134-135).[127] The resemblance between the heavenly man and God in 'image' and 'likeness' was not in looks or form, but in *mind,* the most important part of the soul (*Op.* 69). Moreover, the heavenly man was an idea perceptible only to the intellect, immaterial, and consisted, so to speak, only of mind (*Op.* 134). The body of the earthly man was made of earthly substance and mortal, but his soul proceeded from God and was immortal (*Op.* 135). The soul of the earthly man consisted of two parts: the rational soul or mind (also called the soul of the soul or the dominant part of the soul), made by and through God, in which God breathed the divine πνεῦμα, and the irrational soul, made by God through the mind (*Leg. All.* 1.36-42; *Her.* 55).[128] The rational soul or mind of Adam was patterned after the Logos and participated in God's πνεῦμα (*Quaest. in Gn.* 2.62; *Leg. All.* 1.42); it received the impress of

---

[125] Even the soil itself contains the life-creating πνεῦμα to produce vegetation (*Spec.* 4.217).

[126] Philo's concept of the Logos seems similar to the concept of Wisdom in Wis.: both have a mediatory role in creation and both are in union with God. For a fuller elucidation of Philo's creation story and the Logos doctrine, see R. Williamson, *Jews in the Hellenistic World: Philo* (Cambridge: CUP, 1989) 103-36.

[127] Dodd argues that whatever belongs to the world of Ideas *is* Logos, including the heavenly and earthly man (*Interpretation*, 70-71). However, it seems more correct to say that man is *an expression of* the Logos.

[128] E.R. Goodenough prefers to explain Philo's concept of mind in Aristotelian categories of 'higher' and 'lower' mind (*An Introduction to Philo Judaeus* [Oxford: Basil Blackwell, 1962²] 113-14, 117).

divine power (πνεῦμα) (*Det.* 83).[129] The essence of the irrational soul is the blood, but the essence (οὐσία) of the mind is the divine πνεῦμα to animate (*Spec.* 4.123; *Det.* 83; *Her.* 55).

Thus, it is this participation in the divine πνεῦμα that gives the human being rational and living existence (cf. *Leg. All.* 1.32; *Det.* 80). The divine πνεῦμα is the *principle of correspondence/communication*, since it is the presence of divine πνεῦμα in man that makes contact possible with God.[130] The mind or divine πνεῦμα constitutes a *union* between man and God (*Leg. All.* 1.37) and provides the *basis* of knowing God, the *means* of a relationship with God (*Plant.* 18; *Leg. All.* 1.33-34, 37-38).[131] Moreover, this mind/divine πνεῦμα is a universal gift, given to every human being by virtue of creation (*Op.* 69; *Leg. All.* 1.34-35).[132]

The earthly man was placed in Paradise to cultivate it, i.e., to cultivate wisdom, (*Quaest. in Gn.* 1.56; *Leg. All.* 1.43-45, 47), but since all mortal things are liable to inevitable changes and alterations, it was unavoidable that Adam should also undergo some disaster (the Fall) (*Op.* 149-151). The Fall introduced a twofold death (*Leg. All.* 1.105-107), but the expulsion from Paradise, the place of wisdom, also resulted in a far lesser level of wisdom (*Quaest. in Gn.* 1.56). Adam before the Fall was at the height of perfection of what the entire human race could have become, but subsequent generations have never reached an equal state of perfection and have been constantly degenerating because imitations always fall short of the original models (*Op.* 136, 140-141). Nevertheless, Adam's descendants still partake of his original form and have preserved some traces of their relationship to him, though they are faint (*Op.* 145).

In sum, God is the archetypal Mind, whose essence is πνεῦμα (cf. *Spec.* 4.123), and both the heavenly and the earthly man partake in this divine πνεῦμα; however, the difference is that the earthly man is an inferior expression of the divine πνεῦμα than the heavenly man is.[133] In turn, the

---

[129] Fatehi argues that the in-breathed πνεῦμα does not abide in humankind in a permanent way, but rather that the mind receives only the capacity to be empowered and enabled by the divine πνεῦμα so far as it continues to abide in people, and if people loose their contact with the divine πνεῦμα this innate capacity cannot be actualized (*Relation*, 109-10).

[130] Isaacs, *Concept*, 37, 44. Verbeke argues that πνεῦμα should be understood as part of Philo's physical rather than metaphysical order (*Évolution*, 242), but Isaacs criticizes this view (*Concept*, 44-45).

[131] Turner, 'Philo', 3.

[132] Our categories (2) and (3) of Philo's thought — πνεῦμα as the principle of life and of reason — correspond with the concept in Wis. that all human beings at creation are endowed with πνεῦμα to provide life and reason.

[133] The difference between them is the different measure of endowment of, or participation in, the divine πνεῦμα (cf. Bieder, 'Πνεῦμα', VI:373). This is exactly why Moses, according to *Leg. All.* 1.42, deliberately used πνοή and not πνεῦμα in Gen. 2.7,

earthly man after the Fall has much less participation in the divine πνεῦμα and is a lesser representation of true humanity than Adam before the Fall. Thus, there is a decrease or degeneration in quantity/intensity and quality of endowment with divine πνεῦμα, causing necessarily a decrease in representation of true humanity and a lesser potential level of knowing God, because the divine πνεῦμα is the basis for and means of knowing God.[134] The question is now whether this is the end of the story for Philo or whether he allows for some sort of restoration.

(4) Πνεῦμα as charisma. The hope for any restoration lies in the fact that humankind still has a relationship with God by virtue of his mind being connected to the Logos (*Op.* 145-146); although a degeneration in endowment with the divine πνεῦμα has taken place, humankind still partakes in the divine πνεῦμα. The problem of humankind is, according to Philo, a problem of intensity and quality, and therefore, the solution lies in *a restoration of the intensity and quantity of one's relationship with God,* which is what we can call Philo's concept of 'salvation'. We suggest that the key to intensify one's relationship with God is found in an additional endowment of divine πνεῦμα, i.e., Philo's concept of the charismatic πνεῦμα: *the divine πνεῦμα provides heavenly wisdom in a charismatic event which endows a person with a fuller measure of participation in the true humanity.*[135] The following paragraphs shall further elucidate Philo's concepts of 'salvation' and the charismatic πνεῦμα.

The Quest for God. We will first look at *how* one can know God, because the ultimate goal in life is the *visio Dei,* viz., to envision God, to know and understand God, which leads to immortality (*Quaest. in Ex.* 2.39; *Deus* 142-143). Upholding both the transcendence and immanence of God, Philo asserts that whilst God cannot be known in himself, he can be known through the lower levels of his Being, principally through the λόγος, πνεῦμα and σοφία.[136]

---

namely to indicate the contrast in endowment with divine πνεῦμα between the heavenly and earthly man.

[134] Cf. Fatehi (*Relation*, 111-13). However, Fatehi does not elucidate how, in Philo's understanding, humankind could be restored.

[135] Cf. Turner, 'Philo', 5.

[136] Cf. Isaacs, *Concept,* 30. Philo can use these terms interchangeably and does not always maintain a systematic distinction between these three concepts: e.g. *Quaest. in Gn.* 1.90; *Gig.* 23; *Leg. All.* 1.65; cf. *Her.* 79 with *Leg. All.* 3.161; cf. *Deus* 142-143 with *Mig.* 174-175; in *Ebr.* 30 Wisdom's mediatory role in creation is similar to that of the Logos (cf. *Fug.* 109). Isaacs claims that πνεῦμα, in contrast to the Logos, is not so much the agency by which something is given but rather the content of what is imparted; πνεῦμα does not impart but *is* wisdom, understanding, mind and soul. Isaacs concludes

Having defined λόγος as the divine realm in and through which God reveals himself, the implication is that one can only know God in and by means of the Logos (cf. *Quaest. in Ex.* 2.39).[137] We have also seen that the divine πνεῦμα, being the essence of the mind, functions as the union or principle of communication between God and man; πνεῦμα provides the basis and the means for knowing God. Σοφία is also needed because human reason alone is unable to comprehend God (*Virt.* 212-213). The cultivation of wisdom was necessary for Adam to reach his full potential, in that it provided immortality, pleasure and the constant enjoyment of the rational soul (*Quaest. in Gn.* 1.56; cf. 1.6). Wisdom is heavenly food/manna, spiritual nourishment for the soul (*Leg. All.* 3.161-162; *Quaest. in Gn.* 4.102), which cleanses/purifies the mind (*Spec.* 1.269). Further, wisdom leads to friendship with God, in that freedom leads to friendship with God and true freedom is found in wisdom (*Prob.* 40-44, 59). Wisdom has its source in God (*Her.* 127; *Prov.* 1) and is called a 'spiritual light'; it illuminates the soul of the person to whom God has appeared (*Quaest. in Ex.* 2.7). Wisdom, like light, is not only instrumental in envisioning God, but also contains knowledge of God, i.e., knowledge of God is enclosed or locked up in wisdom (*Mig.* 39-40). Wisdom is the way to (the knowledge and understanding of) God and also functions as the guide on this way (*Deus* 142-143). In *Quod Omnis Probus Liber sit* 13 Wisdom is personified and takes up a role as teacher, who constantly receives those who thirst after her, and to whom she pours forth the inexhaustible stream of pure instruction and wisdom. *Quaestiones et Solutiones in Genesin* 4.105-106 also depicts personified Wisdom, symbolized by Rebecca, as a good teacher, who gives her pupils to drink *until* they cease drinking, continuing at length to instruct them.[138]

Philo argues that people can only know God's existence but not his essence (*Post.* 167-169); neither sensory perception nor mind can apprehend the essence of God (*Mut.* 7-10; *Post.* 15; *Abr.* 76; *Deus* 62; *Leg. All.* 3.206). However, how can one, according to Philo, acquire knowledge of God's existence? On the one hand, Philo says that knowledge of God's

---

that the lower levels of God's Being seem to be personified divine attributes rather than intermediaries having an existence independent of God (*Concept*, 55-58). However, as we will see, the (charismatic) πνεῦμα is said on numerous occasions to impart wisdom. Moreover, Philo's concepts of πνεῦμα, wisdom, understanding, mind and soul merely depict *partial* synonymy. Finally, we suggest that λόγος, σοφία and πνεῦμα are divine attributes that are personified or hypostatized in the sense we defined in n. 44, above, and we would also ascribe intermediary agencies to each one of them.

[137] See Williamson (*Jews*, 113-15) for the relationship between the Logos and man.

[138] In *Quaest. in Gn.* 4.97-107, which describes the event of Abraham's servant meeting Rebecca at the well, it becomes clear that Rebecca is a symbol for Wisdom, and the correlation between wisdom and water is described in numerous ways.

existence can be perceived only by the mind (*Post.* 167-169; *Decal.* 59; *Mut.* 3, 6). On the other hand, Philo seems to have the concept that sensory perception leads to cognitive perception and hence to knowledge that God exists (*Quaest. in Gn.* 2.34; cf. *Leg. All.* 3.57). The solution may be found in *De Opificio Mundi* 70-71, where Philo says that sensory perception can only lead the mind to a certain level of reality; higher realms of reality are perceptible only by the mind (through contemplation), although access to the vision of God himself, namely, to the perception of the essence of God, is denied. Thus, knowledge of God's existence is only perceptible by the mind, but sensory perception may be a first stage towards this cognitive perception (cf. *Spec.* 1.46).

In conclusion, the *visio Dei* is the major soteriological concept for Philo, but 'seeing God' occurs primarily through the eye of the soul rather than through the eyes of the body (cf. *Spec.* 1.50; *Cher.* 97; *Post.* 18). Yet, how is it possible that the mind can perceive knowledge of (the existence of) God? The answer to this can be found in *Legum Allegoriae* 1.36-38 and *Quod Deterius Potiori insidiari solet* 86: the mind can only perceive God, have knowledge of God's existence, because God breathed into the mind the divine πνεῦμα.[139] Thus, *the divine πνεῦμα is the facilitator of cognitive perception and understanding.* Moreover, Philo did not perceive the relationship between God and people merely as a cognitive one; Philo could also express a person's relationship with God in relational terms, namely, via the soul being God's dwelling place (*Som.* 1.149, 215).[140]

Spirit, Wisdom, Salvation. The previous conclusion subsequently leads to the question of how exactly the divine πνεῦμα facilitates cognitive perception and understanding. As we have seen, through the Fall man had a lesser participation in the divine πνεῦμα and a lesser level of wisdom, and the question is whether there is any interrelation between divine πνεῦμα and wisdom, and, if so, how this interrelation helps a person to know God. The correlation between divine πνεῦμα and wisdom would appear to be this: the divine πνεῦμα as charisma provides wisdom that is nourishment for the mind (*Leg. All.* 3.161; cf. *Gig.* 22).[141] Philo even calls the divine πνεῦμα 'the spirit of wisdom', denoting that the πνεῦμα gives/communicates/mediates wisdom (*Gig.* 24, 27, 47). Thus, *the divine πνεῦμα is the mediator of revelatory wisdom which leads to (knowledge of) God.* Philo also mentions many examples from the OT where he

---

[139] Cf. Williamson, *Jews*, 62. See also Levison's concept of the πνεῦμα as the source of the vision of God (*Gig.* 19-55) and its function in the mind's ascent (*Plant.* 18-26) (*Spirit*, 137-42, 151-59).

[140] Williamson, *Jews*, 68-69.

[141] Besides charismatic wisdom, the divine πνεῦμα as charisma also provides charismatic revelation (*Quaest. in Gn.* 3.9; *Spec.* 4.49; *Mos.* 2.265, 291) and invasive inspired prophetic speech (*Her.* 265; *Spec.* 4.49; *Mos.* 1.175, 277-278).

understands the divine πνεῦμα as responsible for providing charismatic wisdom, for example, to Abraham (*Virt.* 217), Joseph (*Jos.* 116-117), Bezaleel (*Gig.* 23), and to Moses and the seventy elders (*Gig.* 24-27; *Decal.* 175; cf. *Mos.* 2.264-265).[142] The effect of the divine πνεῦμα bestowing wisdom on a person in a charismatic event is that the person partakes more of the divine πνεῦμα, resulting in a fuller measure of participation in the original, true humanity.[143]

Philo could also describe the restoration of a person's relationship with God by the metaphorical concept of spiritual (re-)birth. Through the union of God with his Wisdom the world came into being (*Ebr.* 30), but this union between God and Wisdom not only produces offspring at a cosmic level; it also regenerates at an anthropological level. One example is the High Priest, who is born out of the union between God and Wisdom, who is completely righteous and undefiled in mind, which is illuminated with a brilliant light (*Fug.* 108-110). If we remember that wisdom is called a 'spiritual light' which illuminates the soul (*Quaest. in Ex.* 2.7), and if, for example, Caleb's mind was changed through the baths and purifications of wisdom (*Mut.* 124), then it may be that the mind of the High Priest would also have been understood to be cleansed and purified by wisdom. Another example is Philo's allegorical explanation of the birth of Jacob, which can be taken as a paradigm for spiritual birth. Rebecca, a symbol for virtue or Wisdom (*Quaest. in Gn.* 4.97-107), became pregnant through the power or divine seed from God (*Cher.* 46-47), and so Jacob, the 'practiser of virtue', was born (*Fug.* 4, 52). *De Cherubim* 49 explains that God, being the husband of Wisdom, drops the seed of happiness into good and virgin soil. *De Cherubim* 50-52 then continues to explain that when a person clings/cleaves to wisdom, God begins to associate with the soul, plants unpolluted virtues and thus an unpolluted offspring comes forth.[144] In other words, the union of God with his Wisdom producing an unpolluted child denotes the process of God's cleansing work by Wisdom in a God-seeking person, resulting in a purified mind.

---

[142] Philo himself also claims to have had charismatic experiences (*Mig.* 34-35; *Cher.* 27; *Som.* 2.1-4), although he does not attribute these charismata explicitly to the divine πνεῦμα. Hence, Isaacs asserts that Philo restricts the charismatic πνεῦμα to the time of the OT (*Concept*, 49; cf. Menzies, *Witness*, 61). However, it seems that the only concept Philo knew for the mind to be divinely inspired is by the divine πνεῦμα, and in *Som.* 2.251-252 Philo does actually claim to have received charismatic revelation from the divine πνεῦμα.

[143] Cf. Turner, who also mentions that this wisdom is principally wisdom for righteous living ('Philo', 5).

[144] If *Cher.* 52 presents polluted offspring as the negative consequence of a soul that should have clung to wisdom but instead embraced the pleasures of the flesh, then, by implication, a soul that does cleave to wisdom will produce unpolluted offspring.

Davis, followed by Menzies, seems to detect several stages in one's sapiential journey: (i) wisdom is present within and revealed by creation, and attained by disciplines such as science, mathematics and logic; (ii) a more complete wisdom is acquired through the study of philosophy; (iii) a higher level of wisdom is achieved through the study of Torah; (iv) the highest level of wisdom ('pure knowledge') is insight into the deeper meaning of Torah by means of allegorical exegesis.[145]

A few observations can be made. First, the study and (allegorical) interpretation of Torah is an important means for the acquisition of wisdom, but wisdom is not identified with Torah. Moreover, the Torah is not *the* locus of wisdom but *a* locus; besides the Torah there are also other sources of wisdom (creation, philosophy).[146] Second, according to Davis and Menzies, the highest level of (allegorical) wisdom can only be achieved by inspiration of the charismatic πνεῦμα.[147] Moreover, this gift of the charismatic πνεῦμα is reserved for only a select group and is temporary in nature.[148] Virtue, purity and the renunciation of physical desire are not only preliminary but also the continuing conditions necessary to receive the gift of the charismatic πνεῦμα.[149]

If Davis' and Menzies' theory were right, then the charismatic πνεῦμα would be portrayed virtually as a *donum superadditum*.[150] However, several arguments suggest this view is probably incorrect. First, if the divine πνεῦμα is given to every human being at creation, and if this πνεῦμα is necessary to know God and to obtain immortality, then the divine πνεῦμα in Philo is soteriologically necessary, and the gift of allegorical wisdom may be a further endowment of that same divine πνεῦμα. The fact that the divine πνεῦμα is given at creation at least as a potential soteriological necessity does not necessarily exhaust its activities; it may well be that the divine πνεῦμα starts at a particular, later point in one's sapiential journey a

---

[145] Davis, *Wisdom*, 52; Menzies, *Witness*, 60. Menzies calls prophecy/prophetic inspiration the highest form of wisdom (*Witness*, 60; cf. Bieder, 'Πνεῦμα', VI:374). For Philo as an exegete, see P. Borgen, *Philo of Alexandria — An Exegete for his Time* (NT.S 86; Leiden: Brill, 1997).

[146] Cf. Davis, *Wisdom*, 52-53. Nevertheless, the Torah remains the most important locus of wisdom.

[147] Davis, *Wisdom*, 54; Menzies, *Witness*, 60; cf. Levison, *Spirit*, 175, 192-94. Levison says that ascent requires a finely tuned philosophical mind, but which is lifted only by the divine πνεῦμα (*Spirit*, 156-58).

[148] Menzies, *Witness*, 60.

[149] Davis, *Wisdom*, 56-57.

[150] In fact, the point Davis would like to make from his investigation of Sir., Philo (and Wis.) and Qumran literature is that there are several levels/stages of sapiential achievement, and the attainment of the highest level of wisdom is attributed to the gift of the Spirit (*Wisdom*, 9-62). We agree with Davis' theory on Sirach, but it seems that he has read this pattern too rigidly into the other writings.

new nexus of activities, such as the gift of allegorical wisdom and prophetic inspiration. There is probably no reason to consider a bifurcation between the divine πνεῦμα and the charismatic πνεῦμα.[151] On the contrary, the charismatic πνεῦμα is a manifestation of the divine πνεῦμα who bestows charismatic wisdom on a person, or, to put it differently, the gift of the charismatic πνεῦμα is a fuller measure of participation in the divine πνεῦμα. Second, Philo is not as systematic as we would like him to be. Notably Davis himself gives an example where the rational and charismatic uses of πνεῦμα are associated/overlapping (*Leg. All.* 1.36-38; *Plant.* 23-24), and he concludes that 'Philo may be seen to assert that the spirit breathed into each person at creation provides the individual with a cognitive, spiritual capacity, a capacity that is actualized in the experience and encounter with the Spirit of God.'[152] Third, Turner argues concerning the divine rational πνεῦμα and the charismatic prophetic πνεῦμα that *'both gifts share the important characteristic that they enable the (ethically and spiritually orientated) wisdom which facilitates knowledge of — and fellowship with — God.'*[153] Fourth, Levison concludes that Philo thinks the divine πνεῦμα is the source of many forms of inspiration, including the poetic ecstasy

---

[151] Contra Verbeke, who contends that the charismatic πνεῦμα is not divine but merely an intermediary between God and people (*Évolution*, 256). Even Wenk seems to see a contrast within the gift of the divine πνεῦμα that Philo never hinted at. Wenk argues that, on the one hand, the divine πνεῦμα is given as a result of a virtuous life (*Gig.* 47), while, on the other hand, the divine πνεῦμα functions as the guide on the way to perfection (*Gig.* 55; cf. *Op.* 144) (*Power*, 93). However, *Gig.* 47 does not depict the divine πνεῦμα as a reward for a virtuous life. Rather, the divine πνεῦμα seems to come to every God-seeking person, guiding her/his spiritual journey, and even when that person has 'seen' God, s/he will still need the (endowment of the) divine πνεῦμα to *continue* on the way of virtue. Nevertheless, *Gig.* 26-27 indicates a difference between Moses' 'own' πνεῦμα and the charismatic/divine πνεῦμα on Moses which is distributed to the seventy elders. However, Moses' 'own' πνεῦμα is probably the measure of divine πνεῦμα given to him as a human being, and the charismatic πνεῦμα might be a fuller or different measure of this divine πνεῦμα. Hence, it may not be a difference in kind of πνεῦμα but merely a difference in kind of *quality of endowment* of the divine πνεῦμα (e.g., life/reason vs. charismatic wisdom). Otherwise the implication is that Moses' own πνεῦμα is not divine in origin, which brings up the question about what kind of πνεῦμα it is.

[152] Davis, *Wisdom*, 54-56 (quotation from p.56). Although Bieder also puts too great an antithesis between the divine and charismatic πνεῦμα, he nevertheless observes that the πνεῦμα which represents the rational soul is an impress of the divine power but that the πνεῦμα which man receives as a morally striving rational being is also an emanation of the divine nature; and Bieder wonders wherein the difference lies between the two πνεύματα if they both come from God ('Πνεῦμα', VI:374-75).

[153] Turner, *Power*, 125 (author's emphasis).

which enables Philo's own writing, the philosophical ascent of his mind and his insight as an exegete.[154]

The Recipients of the Divine Πνεῦμα. The question now concerns *who* can experience this charismatic πνεῦμα. This transformation by the divine πνεῦμα can be best seen in what is said about Abraham in *De Virtutibus* 217-218:

> (217) Indeed, they continued to treat him [Abraham] with a respect which subjects pay to a ruler, being awe-struck at the all-embracing greatness of his nature and its more than human perfection. For the society also which he sought was not the same as they sought, but oftener under inspiration another more august. Thus whenever he was possessed, everything in him changed to something better...For the divine spirit which was breathed upon him from on high made its lodging in his soul, and invested his body with singular beauty, his voice with persuasiveness, and his hearers with understanding. (218) Would you not say that this lone wanderer without relatives or friends was of the highest nobility, he who craved for kinship with God and strove by every means to live in familiarity with Him...?[155]

Abraham's quest for God, as described in *De Virtutibus* 212-219, can be seen as paradigmatic (*Virt.* 219 speaks about Abraham being the 'standard') for all proselytes who want to know God. Moreover, it would probably not be too far off the mark to suggest that it was the divine πνεῦμα which provided the necessary wisdom during Abraham's spiritual journey, which made him arrive at his destination. The reason for this assumption is fourfold: (i) it was divine inspiration that (partly) induced Abraham to leave his polytheistic environment (*Virt.* 214); (ii) a divine warning imparted to Abraham (partly) guided his steps on his journey (*Virt.* 215); (iii) Abraham succeeded in obtaining a comprehension of God (*Virt.* 215-216); (iv) Abraham was changed by the divine πνεῦμα (*Virt.* 217). If the divine πνεῦμα functions as the principle of communication between God and people, if one can only know God on the basis of the divine πνεῦμα, and if the divine πνεῦμα transforms a person more into the likeness of the original man by an endowment of charismatic wisdom, then it is plausible to argue that it was the divine πνεῦμα which, through charismatic revelation, made Abraham leave, and that it was the same divine πνεῦμα which guided him along the way through the provision of charismatic wisdom.

---

[154] J.R. Levison, 'Inspiration and the Divine Spirit in the Writings of Philo Judaeus', *JSJ* 26 (1995) 280-308.

[155] According to Levison, however, Abraham's transformation is primarily into an ideal orator with extraordinary rhetorical skill (*Spirit*, 90-97). Although Levison discovers a wide variety of effects of the divine πνεῦμα in Philo (*Spirit*, 238), he does not draw out the ethical and 'salvific' consequences. For the moral transformation of people (esp. Abraham), see also Wenk, *Power*, 88-92.

Moses is also depicted as a model of true humanity. Moses did not experience the charismatic πνεῦμα giving wisdom only occasionally; rather, the 'spirit of (perfect) wisdom' upon Moses was a *continuous* endowment of the divine πνεῦμα providing wisdom (*Gig.* 24-27, 47).[156] Moreover, about this example of Moses Philo can say in *De Gigantibus* 53-55:

> (53) Thus it is that in the many...who have set before them many ends in life, the divine spirit does not abide, even though it sojourn there for a while. One sort of men only does it [the divine πνεῦμα] aid with its presence, even those who, having disrobed themselves of all created things and of the innermost veil and wrapping of mere opinion, with mind unhampered and naked will come to God...(55) He then has ever the divine spirit at his side, taking the lead in every journey of righteousness, but from those others...it quickly separates itself.[157]

A final example is found in the description of the total change Caleb underwent in *De Mutatione Nominum* 123. The phrase 'there was another πνεῦμα in him' probably refers to a fresh endowment of divine πνεῦμα, because how else could his mind be changed into 'supreme perfection' but by a fuller participation in the divine πνεῦμα? *De Mutatione Nominum* 124 also points in this direction because it clearly indicates that Caleb's mind was changed through the baths and purifications of wisdom, and it would probably not go too far to assume that this (charismatic) wisdom is bestowed by the charismatic πνεῦμα.

Thus, it seems that every person in search of God can experience this endowment of wisdom by the charismatic πνεῦμα, which allows him to possess a closer resemblance to the true humanity as seen in Adam, and also, though weaker, in Moses and Abraham (and Caleb).[158] Moreover, this

---

[156] D. Winston even calls Moses a 'super-sage' because Moses is Philo's supreme paradigm of the sage and is described as superior even to the patriarchs ('Sage and Super-sage in Philo of Alexandria' in D.P. Wright et al. [eds.], *Pomegranates and Golden Bells: Studies in Biblical, Jewish, and Near Eastern Ritual, Law, and Literature in Honor of Jacob Milgrom* [Winona Lake: Eisenbrauns, 1995] 822-23).

[157] *Her.* 57 also speaks of two kinds of people — those who live by reason, by the divine πνεῦμα, and those who live by blood and the pleasure of the flesh. Cf. *Gig.* 47, which says that the divine πνεῦμα may be inclined to depart if one does not desist from doing wrong.

[158] Wenk also recognizes the transforming effect of the divine πνεῦμα in Abraham, Adam and Moses, but he seems to portray these moral transformations as of the same order (*Power*, 90). However, the *creation* of the paradigmatic true man (Adam) cannot be put on the same level as the *restoration* of Abraham and Moses towards this true man, even when the same divine πνεῦμα is involved. Contra Menzies (*Witness*, 60-61), the transformations in Abraham and Moses and Caleb, as described above, surely involved more than just divinely inspired speech (cf. A.J.M. Wedderburn, *Baptism and Resurrection: Studies in Pauline Theology against Its Graeco-Roman Background*

charismatic wisdom, mediated by the divine πνεῦμα, empowers and guides a God-seeking person for righteous living throughout his sapiential journey so that he may successfully arrive at his destination (cf. *Mos.* 2.265; *Fug.* 186-188). Thus, as in Wisdom of Solomon, also in Philo the quest for wisdom is depicted as a sapiential journey, which goes from earthly existence via the way of wisdom to knowledge of and union with God (cf. *Deus* 143, 160; *Post.* 18; *Quaest. in Gn.* 4.140; *Quaest. in Ex.* 4.47).[159] Nevertheless, this charismatic πνεῦμα is transient and occasional because people are flesh/corruptible: inasmuch as a person focuses on the flesh and lives by its pleasures the danger arises that the divine πνεῦμα will depart or decrease its presence in the person; however, there is no danger for the person who lives by the divine πνεῦμα and reason (*Quaest. in Gn.* 1.90; *Gig.* 19-20, 28-29, 47; *Her.* 57). Nor is this wisdom of the charismatic πνεῦμα, which seems to be necessary on one's sapiential journey to God, easily attainable, as *De Posteritate Caini* 18 clearly expresses:

> The wise man is ever longing to discern the Ruler of the Universe. As he journeys along the path that takes him through knowledge and wisdom, he comes into contact first with divine words, and with these he makes a preliminary stay...For the eyes of his understanding have been opened, and he sees perfectly clearly that he has engaged in the chase of a quarry hard to capture.

Conclusion. For Philo, 'salvation' is the restoration of the intensity and quality of one's relationship with God. It is given through a fuller measure of participation in the divine πνεῦμα enabling the mind to ascend and attain the *visio Dei*, which leads to immortality. Moreover, the divine πνεῦμα in Philo is depicted as a soteriological necessity, which is, as the giver of charismatic wisdom (and revelation), needed at every level/stage of one's sapiential journey to God in order to bring the person to a fuller measure of participation in the true humanity, i.e., the divine πνεῦμα. Thus, the divine πνεῦμα functions as the facilitator of cognitive perception and understanding in order to restore a person's relationship with God.

The interrelation between Philo's λόγος, σοφία and πνεῦμα corresponds with our concept of 'the Spirit as the power of Wisdom': *Philo's πνεῦμα might be understood as the power of the Logos in that the divine πνεῦμα imparts wisdom, which is the divine knowledge being available in and through the Logos.* In other words, the knowledge or vision of God is enclosed/locked up in wisdom (*Mig.* 39-40), and it is the divine πνεῦμα that

---

[WUNT 44; Tübingen: Mohr Siebeck, 1987] 284). Levison concludes his analysis of *Gig.* 19-55 by saying that a vision of God offered by the divine πνεῦμα in the present comes infrequently to the majority of humankind (*Spirit*, 139-44).

[159] Cf. Davis, *Wisdom*, 49, 52; Wilckens, 'Σοφία', VI:501.

discloses/opens up this divine knowledge to the mind of the person. The concept of Wisdom coming along as a guide on one's spiritual journey, and the bestowal of charismatic wisdom on God-seekers by the divine πνεῦμα, seem to indicate that both wisdom and πνεῦμα are divine gifts of grace rather than rewards for merit or *doni superadditi* with no soteriological consequences. Nonetheless, it seems, as in Sirach, that human works are co-essential in order to (continue to) receive this charismatic πνεῦμα and wisdom.

How, then, can Philo's uses of πνεῦμα possibly be reconciled? First, we suggest that all occurrences of πνεῦμα refer to its divine origin; Philo's usage of πνεῦμα has probably only one referent — God. Second, there also seems to be coherence between the various ways the divine πνεῦμα functions. By virtue of his creation, a person participates in the divine πνεῦμα, which is for him the principle of life as well as reason (categories [2] and [3]). The πνεῦμα in a different sense can endow man further with charismatic wisdom in order to participate more fully in the divine πνεῦμα (category [4]). There may also be a resemblance between category (1) and category (2), namely, in being a cohesive force; the divine πνεῦμα that holds together the cosmos is similar to the πνεῦμα that 'holds together' human beings, i.e., sustains their lives. We suggest then that Philo's concepts of divine πνεῦμα are essentially one theological concept or at least closely related overlapping concepts, in that the various senses of πνεῦμα share common traits of meaning (cf. excursus 2, below).[160]

7. Qumran[161]

The Nature of Wisdom. God is depicted as the source of all wisdom, knowledge and truth (1QS 3.15; 4.18; 1QH 7.27-29; 8.24; 9.7-26; CD 2.3-4; cf. the wisdom poems 4Q185, 4Q413, 4Q416, 4Q418, 4Q525). Wisdom is associated with Torah in that the Torah is the source of wisdom, and study and observance of the Torah leads to wisdom, right ethical conduct

---

[160] Cf. Laurentin, 'Pneuma', 395; Isaacs, *Concept*, 62-64; Fatehi, *Relation*, 116. Contra Verbeke (see n.151, above) and Levison. Levison sees such a broad diversity of effects and natures of the πνεῦμα that he essentially refrains from finding a common denominator in Philo's concept of the πνεῦμα (*Spirit*, 238-42).

[161] The references to Qumran literature are taken from F. García Martínez, *The Dead Sea Scrolls Translated: The Qumran Texts in English* (Leiden: Brill, 1996²). The Qumranian wisdom texts are also edited in DJD 20 and 34 (T. Elgvin [ed.] et al., *Qumran Cave 4: Sapiential Texts, Part 1* [DJD 20; Oxford: Clarendon Press, 1997]; J. Strugnell, D.J. Harrington and T. Elgvin [eds.], *Qumran Cave 4: Sapiential Texts, Part 2* [DJD 34; Oxford: Clarendon Press, 1999]). However, regarding the wisdom texts we have referred to, there are no major differences in translation between García Martínez and DJD 20/34.

and eternal life (1QS 1.2-3; 9.17; 4Q504 f1 2.13-15; 1Q22 2.1-9; CD 3.15-16, 20; 6.2-5; 7.4-6; 19.1-2; 1QM 10.9-11; 1QH 4.13; 12.9-11).[162] This close relationship of W/wisdom with Torah is probably best summed up in 4Q525 f2 2.3-7, which is an exhortation to adhere to Wisdom-Torah:

> Blessed is the man who attains Wisdom, and walks in the law of the Most High, and dedicates his heart to her ways...For he always thinks of her, and in his distress he meditates on [the law,] [and throughout] his [whole] life [he thinks] of her, [and places her] in front of his eyes in order not to walk on paths [of evil...][163]

According to 4Q185 2.10-13, personified Wisdom is the source of (eschatological) 'salvation':[164]

> [God has given her] to Israel, and like a good gift, gives her. He has saved all his people...Whoever glories in her will say: he shall take possession of her and she will find him...With her there are long days...Her youth [increases] favours and salvation.

The Quest for Wisdom. As in Proverbs, personified Wisdom takes the initiative and reveals herself to people (11Q5 18.12), and 11Q5 21 (=Sir. 51.13-19) describes the quest for Wisdom, expressing a deep desire for intimacy with Wisdom. The Qumran literature also expresses the concept of the acquisition of wisdom and understanding through sensory and cognitive perception. The instructor exhorts people to perceive wisdom at a sensory ('listen') and at a cognitive ('understand') level so that one may find life (4Q298 1.1-3; cf. 4Q185 1.13-14; 2.3). Cognitive perception ('meditation', 'study' and 'investigation') leads to wisdom and truth (4Q416 f2 3.14-15; 4Q417 f1 1.6;[165] 4Q418 f43 4), which is the basis for understanding (4Q418 f81 15). This wisdom of the Qumran community is the revelatory knowledge of the hidden meaning of the Torah and the

---

[162] For the concept of W/wisdom in the Qumran literature (including a history of research), see J.I. Kampen, 'The Diverse Aspects of Wisdom in the Qumran Texts' in P.W. Flint and J.C. Vanderkam (eds.), *The Dead Sea Scrolls after Fifty Years: A Comprehensive Assessment: Volume One* (Leiden: Brill, 1998) 211-43. Professor Dr Jörg Frey also drew my attention to recent developments in Qumran research, which claim that the majority of the Qumranian wisdom material, on which the 'Essenes' depended, is taken over from or reflects the theology of Jewish Palestinian wisdom circles. We have indeed asserted elsewhere that the Qumranian wisdom tradition did not occur in a vacuum but was rooted in the various OT wisdom traditions (Bennema, 'Strands', 77-79).

[163] For the correlation between Wisdom and Torah, see esp. Schnabel, *Law*, 206-26, but cf. also Pate, *Reverse*, 104-25.

[164] 4Q184 and 4Q185 express the contrast between Lady Folly and Lady Wisdom that we know from Prov.

[165] Regarding 4Q417, the reference is taken from DJD 34, since fragment 1 almost certainly preceded fragment 2 (Strugnell et al., *Qumran*, 152), whereas García Martínez has the two fragments in different order.

result of divine revelation (1QS 11.15, 18; 1QH 9.21; 15.26-27). Moreover, this divine revelatory wisdom is communicated by teaching, and the exclusive possession of the community (1QS 3.13-14; 4.22; 5.11-12; 11.5-6; CD 3.12-16). The Teacher of Righteousness *par excellence* received revelatory wisdom from God and passed it on to the community in order to direct people according to God's ways (1QpHab 2.2-3; 7.4-5; 1QH 10.8-18; 12.27-29; 20.11-13; CD 1.10-12).

In fact, this revelatory (esoteric) wisdom or knowledge of God is salvific (1QS 2.3; 4.2-8, 22; cf. 1QH 11.20-23; 19.12-13, 28; 20.11-13; 11Q5 18.3-5[166]), and enables right ethical conduct, in that it provides discernment between good and evil (4Q418 f2 6-7; f43 4-6).[167] Moreover, 'truth', as the content of God's mystery/revelation/teaching, has also a salvific dimension (1QH 13.25-26; 14.9-14; 15.26-27; 18.4; 19.4, 9; 1QS 1.11-13; 3.7; 4.20-21; cf. 1QH 12.14; 14.25; 15.14).[168] This salvific nexus of knowledge-wisdom-truth[169] is mediated by the Spirit (1QH 6.12-13, 25; 8.14-15; 20.11-13; 1QS 4.3-4). In 11Q5 19.14 the author requests God for a 'knowing spirit', and David's wisdom (as well as his songs) are attributed to the Spirit (of prophecy) (11Q5 27.2-4, 9-11).

Spirit, Wisdom, Salvation. There is an ongoing debate about the coherence of the pneumatology in the Qumran literature. The main question that has been raised, because of the different terminology used, is whether or not the *Community Rule*, on the one hand, and the *Hodayot*, on the other hand, describe different pneumatologies.

Foerster argues that the pneumatologies of 1QS and 1QH are coherent — the spirit of truth in 1QS is identical to the Holy Spirit of 1QH — and explains their different aspects in terms of different eschatological perspectives: 1QH expresses a present eschatology, in which the time of salvation has started, whereas 1QS refers to future eschatology.[170] The thesis of Wernberg-Møller is that in 1QS 3.13-4.26 the two spirits are merely human dispositions or impulses planted into every person's heart

---

[166] D.J. Harrington remarks that 11Q5 18.3-5 expresses the idea that the wisdom given by God has the power to bring the 'simple' and those without understanding to God (*Wisdom Texts from Qumran* [London: Routledge, 1996] 27).

[167] The salvific dimension of knowledge was already pointed out by M. Mansoor, *The Thanksgiving Hymns: Translated and Annotated with an Introduction* (Leiden: Brill, 1961) 67-70. Cf. Breck, *Spirit*, 132.

[168] Cf. Breck, *Spirit*, 144.

[169] These terms are often used (partially) synonymously, forming an intertwined thread running, e.g., through 1QH, and referring to a single predominant soteriological concept.

[170] W. Foerster, 'Der Heilige Geist im Spätjudentum', *NTS* 8 (1961-62) 128-32.

by God at birth.[171] Sekki seems to go along with Wernberg-Møller's position, and virtually argues, like Foerster, for one homogenous pneumatology.[172] Sekki believes that the two spirits of 1QS 3.13-4.26 are impersonal dispositions within a person given to him at birth, and concludes that those expressions which, for example, include a reference to the divine Spirit (1QS 4.6, 21) are 'part of an attempt to integrate its relatively novel two-spirit teaching into the traditional pneumatology of the sect.'[173] Hence, Sekki's theory presupposes a pneumatological 'development' within the Qumran community in which 1QS reflects a later stage than 1QH. Menzies disagrees with Foerster and, also building upon Wernberg-Møller's thesis, concludes that the spirit of truth in 1QS 3-4 is not to be equated with the Holy Spirit of 1QH, and hence the pneumatological perspectives of 1QS and 1QH are decidedly different (*pace* Sekki).[174] Menzies, as Sekki, contends that the pneumatology of Qumran underwent a process of development, but, contra Sekki, argues that 1QH represents a late stage.[175] In the light of 1QS 4.21-23, Turner contends that 1QS and 1QH are conceptually closer than Menzies maintains, and concludes that '[t]he sharpest difference between the two would then be that 1QS is framed eschatologically, while 1QH speaks (proleptically?) from the perspective of one who already enjoys the benefits of the Spirit.'[176] In a recent article Kvalvaag discusses the pneumatology of Qumran, and concludes, against Sekki, that the Qumran literature does not reflect one consistent pneumatology; rather, 1QS and 1QH must be treated separately and interpreted independently of each other.[177]

After having set out the main positions and their defenders, it seems that besides the issue of the coherence of the pneumatology in Qumran, we need to address two other issues as well. First, whether the two spirits in

---

[171] P. Wernberg-Møller, 'A Reconsideration of the two Spirits in the Rule of the Community (1Qserek III,13-IV,26)', *RdQ* 3 (1961) 413-41; cf. M. Treves, 'The two Spirits of the Rule of the Community', *RdQ* 3 (1961) 449-52; Davis, *Wisdom*, 173 n.32.

[172] See A.E. Sekki, *The Meaning of Ruaḥ at Qumran* (SBL.DS 110; Atlanta: Scholars Press, 1989).

[173] See Sekki, *Meaning*, chs. 8-9 (quotation from p.223).

[174] Menzies, *Witness*, 72-76.

[175] Menzies, *Witness*, 79-80. Interestingly, both Sekki and Menzies (who does not interact with Sekki) accept Wernberg-Møller's thesis but argue for a different pneumatological position and development.

[176] Turner, *Power*, 128-29 (quotation from p.129). This had already been argued by Foerster, although Turner has not interacted with him. Wenk also argues against Menzies' position, and essentially elaborates Turner's position (*Power*, ch. 5).

[177] R.W. Kvalvaag, 'The Spirit in Human Beings in Some Qumran Non-Biblical Texts' in F.H. Cryer and T.L. Thompson (eds.), *Qumran between the Old and New Testaments* (JSOT.S 290; Sheffield: SAP, 1998) 159-80.

1QS can be reduced to denote merely psychological forces within a person, and related to this, whether 1QS portrays solely an anthropological pneumatology (over against a divine pneumatology in 1QH). Second, whether there is any significant pneumatological development in Qumran. Our strategy will be to elucidate the pneumatologies of 1QS and 1QH each on their own terms, and then we will investigate to what extent they might be coherent.

The pneumatology of the Community Rule (1QS).[178] At creation, God placed within each human being two spirits — the spirit of truth or light and of error or darkness — which influence, wage war and determine a person's behaviour until the moment of God's visitation, i.e., the end of this age (3.17-19, 25; 4.16-17, 23-24).[179] However, to reduce the sense of the two spirits to mere psychological forces within a person (so Wernberg-Møller, Menzies et al.) seems too narrow a view, because at the same time human beings are influenced or led by cosmic forces — the Prince of Lights or Angel of Truth, and the Angel of Darkness — which thereby causes a bifurcation within humanity into the sons of light and the sons of darkness (3.20-25; 4.15-17). Thus, people are under the influence of conflicting cosmic or metaphysical forces, which is reflected at the same time in the human heart as a psychological and ethical dualism.[180] This view is best articulated by Dimant, who argues that each spirit stands for an entire domain, in exterior reality as well as in the heart, and the struggle between the two spirits takes place at a cosmic level as well as within a person.[181] His conclusion is worth quoting in length:

> Yet there is no need to distinguish between a cosmic and a psychological dualism as distinct and different types. They may be understood as aspects of the same basic cosmic dualism, which have a necessary counterpart on the moral and psychological level. This is not only possible but logically appropriate and consistent...the term 'Spirit'...which designates the two domains, at the same time denotes a cosmic entity, an angel, a manner of behaviour and a human quality. Thus the fundamental opposition between the two forces takes place on all levels, in the world at large and 'in man's heart'.[182]

---

[178] Harrington prefers to read the Community Rule as an instruction manual for the community's spiritual director, the *maśkil* (*Texts*, 76).

[179] Cf. M.A. Knibb, *The Qumran Community* (Cambridge: CUP, 1987) 94-98.

[180] Cf. A.A. Anderson, 'The Use of "Ruaḥ" in 1QS, 1QH and 1QM', *JSSt* 7 (1962) 299-300; Montague, *Spirit*, 117-18; Knibb, *Qumran*, 94-96; Turner, *Power*, 128-29; Harrington, *Texts*, 77; Kvalvaag, 'Spirit', 162; Collins, *Wisdom*, 130; Wenk, *Power*, 101-102; Elliott, *Survivors*, 403.

[181] D. Dimant, 'Qumran Sectarian Literature' in M.E. Stone (ed.), *Jewish Writings of the Second Temple Period: Apocrypha, Pseudepigrapha, Qumran Sectarian Writings, Philo, Josephus* (Assen: Van Gorcum, 1984) 534-35.

[182] Dimant, 'Qumran', 535.

The eschatological fate of each human being at the time of God's visitation is determined by whichever S/spirit is predominant in him (4.24-26). God has given people the cognitive ability to know good and evil, and the decisive issue for one's destiny is which of the two S/spirits in a person is the strongest.[183] The inauguration of the new age and God's eschatological salvation for the elect is accompanied by and consists of a refinement of the elect by God's truth. That is, a cleansing and purification by the Spirit of truth/holiness (from the S/spirit of error) occurs, along the lines of Ezekiel 36.25-27, so that they will understand the wisdom/knowledge of God and be enabled to live righteous lives (4.20-22). Thus, Qumran also knows the concept of the Spirit as facilitating cognitive perception and understanding.

This eschatological salvation, however, has a realized dimension; people can already experience this eschatological spiritual cleansing and purification in the present through entrance into the community (3.6-8).[184] In fact, this cleansing and purification by the divine Spirit at entrance into the community and covenant is an intensification by or of the S/spirit. Hence, 3.6-8 is a foretaste of what is to come (as described in 4.20-22).[185] At entrance into the community, the S/spirit(s) upon or within a person are tested/examined in respect to his insight and practice of Torah, and the person is ranked according to his insight and deeds, i.e., according to the intensity and quality of S/spirit(s) (5.20-23).[186] Moreover, this evaluation of (intensity and quality of) S/spirits happens annually, in order that the candidate may be upgraded or demoted (5.24).[187] Hence, the degree of

---

[183] Kvalvaag, 'Spirit', 162-63.

[184] There is no reason to assume that the S/spirit in 3.6-8 is different from the one in 4.20-22. First, in 3.6-8 the reference is to one S/spirit: the atonement and cleansing of sin occurs by means of the one S/spirit of true counsel, holiness and uprightness. Second, 4.21 also mentions cleansing of sin by means of the one S/spirit of truth and holiness. Third, the language of both 3.6-8 and 4.20-22 is coined in the categories of Ezek. 36. While Kvalvaag is in no doubt that the spirit of holiness in 3.7 is the Holy Spirit, he surprisingly takes 3.6, 8 as referring to the human spirit ('Spirit', 171-72). Knibb thinks that the term 'spirit' used in 3.6-8 refers to the disposition of a person (*Qumran*, 92-93). In fact, Knibb never allows 'spirit' (or even 'holy spirit') to refer to the divine Spirit. It must also be noted that after 3.13-4.26 — the treatise of the two S/spirits — regular reference to a single S/spirit in or upon a person is mentioned (e.g. 5.21, 24; 6.17; 7.20, 25; 8.3).

[185] Cf. Kvalvaag, 'Spirit', 171-72. Based on CD 20.13-15, Knibb argues that the new era of salvation was expected by the community within a relatively short time (*Qumran*, 73-74). It is also clear that salvation can only be found within the Qumran community (2.25-3.6).

[186] Cf. Kvalvaag, who also notes the correspondence with the Qumran horoscope 4Q186 ('Spirit', 168-70).

[187] Hierarchy (according to the intensity of S/spirits) in the Qumran community seemed to have been very important (2.19-23; 3.13-14; 6.8-10; cf. 1QH 17.15-16).

intensity and quality of the S/spirit of truth during a person's life may increase or decrease depending on his spiritual progress.[188] There is thus a direct link between an increase in the intensity and quality of H/holy S/spirit and an increase in cognitive perception and understanding.

In conclusion, according to 1QS, *'salvation' is a matter of and dependent on the degree of intensity and quality of the S/spirit of truth within or upon a person.* If at the time of God's visitation the intensity of the S/spirit of truth in or upon a person, which could increase or decrease during his lifetime, is higher than the intensity of the S/Spirit of error, then the intensity of the S/spirit of truth will be increased to the level of total purification.[189]

The pneumatology of the Hodayot (1QH).[190] 1QH 9.15 seems to imply that God at creation placed within human beings merely one spirit. Nevertheless, the author can also talk about spirits (plural) placed or operating within humans in a similar way as we have seen in 1QS (4.17; 6.11). Moreover, similar to the two conflicting spirits in 1QS, we also find in 1QH a spiritual dualism — the spirit of flesh/error versus the holy spirit (4.25-26). The spirit of flesh/error is a corrupt spirit whose effects need forgiveness and purification, and which are associated with a lack of knowledge and understanding (of God) (5.4, 19; 9.22, 32; 11.21). On entrance into the community, however, as described in 11.20-23, the novice (and his corrupt spirit) is purified from sin, i.e., a purification by means of God's Holy Spirit (8.20). Moreover, this Holy Spirit is 'given' by God to the sectarian (8.19), and the divine Spirit mediates to the sectarian wisdom or knowledge of God, in order to enable and sustain the living of a righteous life pleasing to God (6.25-27; 8.15; 20.11-13).[191]

Thus, in 1QH the Spirit is also depicted as the agent/source of wisdom and knowledge of God, facilitating cognitive perception and understanding

---

[188] Cf. the exhortation in 4Q416 f2 2.6 not to demean your (holy) spirit with any wealth, i.e., not to let the intensity of the spirit of truth decrease. Even defection was possible, but also restoration, although within limits (7.20-27).

[189] Cf. 4.2-14, which describes the two ways and destinations: the rewards given by the S/spirit of truth to those who walk in the paths of light/truth are long and eternal life, peace, blessing, joy and glory, whereas eternal damnation and destruction awaits those who walk in the paths of darkness. In this way we can partly agree with Elliott, who argues that the dualism is essentially not between two spirits but between *two groups of people* (*Survivors*, 404-408).

[190] Although some parts of 1QH reflect the experience of the Teacher of Righteousness, other parts also perceive every sectarian to experience the Spirit (and wisdom) (e.g. 6.11-16; 11.21-23). Moreover, the psalmist probably also expected the sectarian to sing the hymn for himself. Hence, the 'I' in 1QH may be the corporate voice of the community.

[191] Cf. Wenk, *Power*, 102-108.

of God.[192] The concept of degree of intensity and quality of S/spirit is also present in 1QH: corresponding to the spirits in people God allots them between good and evil (6.11), and God can enlarge a person's share with the Holy Spirit, which also increases the person's knowledge of God and his aversion to evil (6.12-16). Hence, knowledge and understanding of God depends on the intensity of the measure of Spirit upon/in a person.

Synthesis. Can we now conclude that the pneumatologies of 1QS and 1QH are coherent? We think the answer is affirmative. First, both documents depict an anthropological and a divine pneumatology.[193] Second, both documents portray a spiritual dualism in which the divine Spirit plays a role. Third, the main difference between the two documents is one of genre and eschatological emphasis. 1QS provides a set of regulations to govern the life of the community living in a time of eschatological tension (the 'already-not yet'), whereas the hymns of 1QH express the gratefulness and joy of the future eschatological salvation already partly experienced in the present (cf. Foerster and Turner). That this difference in genre and eschatological emphasis causes a different pneumatological terminology should not come as a surprise, but there is no need to treat and interpret 1QS and 1QH independently of each other (contra Kvalvaag). Nor is there any need to attempt to resolve the 'differences' by means of a developmental pneumatological model; besides, a theory of pneumatological development is very speculative and leads apparently to contrasting results (see, e.g., Sekki and Menzies).

Davis argues that the DSS also portray several levels/stages of sapiential achievement: (i) limited wisdom and a defiled spirit for those outside the community; (ii) advanced wisdom and a spirit of holiness for members of the community; (iii) perfect wisdom and holiness for the teachers/leaders of the community; (iv) all wisdom of all mysteries for the Teacher of Righteousness.[194] Davis contends that the acquisition of wisdom at level (iii) and (iv) is aided by the divine Spirit.[195] This partly

---

[192] Cf. Kvalvaag, who argues that 1QH 9.27-29 seems to reflect an interpretation of Gen. 2.7 which emphasizes the breath or spirit in humans as that faculty which enables human beings to speak and communicate verbally. Then, in 1QH 9.31 the underlying idea of the author's request is that human beings know God according to the quality of their creaturely-given understanding/spirit ('Spirit', 165-66; cf. 177-78).

[193] Although we use the term anthropological pneumatology to speak about a 'human spirit' or 'human spirits', what we mean are spiritual forces, beings or entities working upon or within a person. The human spirits are probably not separate entities from Belial, the Angel of Darkness, the Prince of Lights, the Angel of Truth, God's Holy Spirit, etc. Rather, these latter are spiritual entities working upon, in, and influencing a human being in such a way that the Qumran scribes could express this reality anthropologically as 'the spirits in man' (contra Kvalvaag, 'Spirit', 177-78; Davis, *Wisdom*, 42).

[194] Davis, *Wisdom*, 39-43.

[195] Davis, *Wisdom*, 42-44, 61.

contradicts our findings. As we have argued, entrance into the community coincides with the reception of the Spirit who cleanses the person and mediates revelatory knowledge, which is the means to salvation. Moreover, the Spirit also sustains the sectarian by leading the person in 'the way of truth' towards sanctification and perfection (1QH 4.26; 6.12-13, 25; 7.6-7; 8.15-20; 15.6-7; 17.32-33; 23.(f2)12-15; 4Q504 5.15-16; 1Q28b 2.24; 5.25).[196] Thus, it seems that the Spirit is required at every level/stage of sapiential achievement (contra Sirach, where the Spirit is only needed for the highest level of sapiential achievement). Consequently, the Spirit, as the mediator of revelatory saving wisdom/knowledge, is depicted as a soteriological necessity. The attribution of soteriological significance to the gift of the Spirit is confirmed by texts like 1QS 3.7; 4.21; 1QH 5.25; 8.19-20; 12.10; 4Q504 5.10, which evoke the picture of the new creation in Ezekiel 36.25-27.[197]

Conclusion. In the Qumran literature we also seem to detect a model of salvation in terms of intensity and quality of the divine Spirit upon or in a person.[198] The Spirit, as a soteriological necessity, mediates esoteric saving wisdom (of God) to the community through revelation in order to reveal the true meaning of the Torah, i.e., in order to disclose the saving wisdom hidden in the Torah, so that one can live a righteous life.[199] 'Salvation' within the Qumran community also requires, as in Sirach, human effort: one needs to study and observe the Torah (1QS 5.7-10; 6.18), and to observe the strict disciplines of the community (1QS 5-7).

---

[196] Cf. Breck, *Spirit*, 136-37.

[197] Cf. Sekki, *Meaning*, 79-82. Based on 1QH, even Menzies attributes soteriological significance to the gift of the Spirit, although he argues that this is due to the fact that 1QH probably represents a later stage in the development of the community's pneumatology (*Witness*, 79-80). However, the suggestion that 1QH is a late document may not be well-founded, and the hymns attributed to the Teacher of Righteousness, or those in which he speaks, may well belong to the earlier strands of Qumran material.

[198] Although the Qumran literature nowhere explicitly confirms the concept of the Spirit as creating and sustaining life, this was probably assumed. Perhaps the (life-giving) 'breath' in 11Q5 19.4 is a possible reference to the Spirit (cf. 11Q6 fa 4), and 4Q418 f126 2.8 does mention the Spirit of life. For Elliott's understanding of Qumran's soteriology, served by its pneumatology, see *Survivors*, 400-19 and the relevant parts of chs. 7 and 12.

[199] Insight into the true meaning of the Torah was not based on a single revelation but rather on progressive revelation, i.e., a continuing series of revelatory insights by authoritative teachers (cf. 1QS 8.15; 9.13), which resulted in an ongoing renewal of revelation that produced the DSS (M. Fishbane, *The Garments of Torah: Essays in Biblical Hermeneutics* [Bloomington: Indiana University Press, 1989] 73; D.E. Aune, 'Charismatic Exegesis in Early Judaism and Early Christianity' in J.H. Charlesworth and C.A. Evans [eds.], *The Pseudepigrapha and Early Biblical Interpretation* [JSPE.S 14; Sheffield: JSOT Press, 1993] 137).

We are now also in a position to assess Keener's bifurcation of the Spirit in Judaism — the Spirit of purification and the Spirit of prophecy (cf. section 2, above). First, Keener has concentrated on the *term* 'Spirit of prophecy' without recognizing its broader semantic concept; the Spirit of prophecy *includes* the purifying and ethical function of the Spirit (so Turner). Second, Keener's justification for his category 'Spirit of purification' is based on *Jubilees* 1.21, 23 and evidence from Qumran.[200] However, *Jubilees* 1.21, 23 does not speak explicitly about the divine Spirit, which implies that Keener's evidence is based solely on Qumran material, which can hardly be called representative of Judaism. Thus, Keener proposes a bifurcation in the concept of the Spirit that Judaism never hinted at, and there neither seems to be a substantial basis for defending a category 'Spirit of purification' across Judaism.

8. Conclusion

The most important similarities and distinctions between the various sapiential writings that we have examined can be presented in the following table:

---

[200] Keener, 'Function', 65-69.

		Prov.	Sir.	Wis.	Philo	Qumran
Salvation	Degree of intensity and quality of Spirit and W/wisdom	W/wisdom only	W/wisdom only	Yes	Yes	Yes
	Nature	Long and blessed life in present	Long and blessed life in present	Immortality of the righteous	Immortality (of the soul)	Cleansing and purification (Ezek.)
	Realized dimension[201]	—	—	Yes	Yes	Yes
	Human effort[202]	—	Yes	—	Yes	Yes
	Relational aspect	Yes	Yes	Yes	Yes	Yes
	Cognitive aspect	Yes	Yes	Yes	Yes	Yes
Spirit	Soteriological necessary[203]	—	Yes	Yes	Yes	Yes
	Life-principle	—	Possibly[204]	Yes	Yes	Probably
	Mediating W/wisdom	Possibly	Yes, but not at every level[205]	Yes	Yes	Yes
	Recipient	—	Sage	Everyone or ruler/king	Everyone	Sectarian
	Facilitator of cognitive perception and understanding	Possibly	Yes	Yes	Yes	Yes
	Power of Wisdom	Possibly	Yes	Yes	Yes	Yes
W/wisdom[206]	Soteriologically necessary	Yes	Yes	Yes	Yes	Yes
	Final aim	Long and blessed life in present	Long and blessed life in present	Union/relationship with God	Union/relationship with God	(Eschatological) salvation

We have elucidated the concept of 'saving wisdom/knowledge/truth', which can be defined either as the saving content of Wisdom's

---

[201] Yet, salvation still awaited its full consummation in the age to come.

[202] In Sir., Philo and Qumran divine grace and human effort are co-essential for the acquisition of W/wisdom and Spirit. Wis. does not mention explicitly the need for (preparatory) works, but merely the desire to obtain W/wisdom.

[203] Although it is probably incorrect to draw too sharp a line, in Sir. the Spirit seems more a reward/result of righteous life, whereas in Wis., Philo and Qumran the Spirit is more the means/basis of a righteous life. This may be because in the latter writings the Spirit is presented as necessary in every stage of one's sapiential journey.

[204] Sir. 34.13; 38.23 may imply the assumption of the Spirit being the principle of life.

[205] The Spirit in Sir. is only necessary to reach the highest level of sapiential achievement; wisdom at lower levels can be achieved by human endeavour.

[206] For a more nuanced overview of W/wisdom in Judaism at large, see the table in Bennema, 'Strands', 80.

teaching/instruction that is cognitively retrieved through sensory perception, or perhaps even as the saving understanding (of God and Wisdom) resulting from cognitive perception.[207] It has become clear that 'salvation' in sapiential Judaism has both relational and cognitive aspects, in that saving wisdom is acquired cognitively in relation to Wisdom and Spirit, and leads to a relationship with Wisdom/God.[208] Wisdom is a circumlocution for God's 'wise' actions in his dealings with his people, especially his salvific acts, i.e., his communication of revelatory saving wisdom to people.[209] The Spirit, as the channel of communication between God and people, is also a way to describe God in action, especially the communication of his presence in revelation and wisdom.[210]

Thus, both Wisdom and Spirit have a soteriological dimension and are interrelated with each other: Wisdom is the *source* of life/salvation, in that Wisdom's revelatory teaching contains saving wisdom-knowledge-truth that leads to (eternal) life/salvation, and the Spirit is the *agent* of salvation, in that the Spirit mediates this life to people. In fact, the Spirit functions as the revelatory or interpretative power of saving Wisdom, in that the Spirit mediates to people the saving content present in Wisdom's revelatory teaching, and so facilitates cognitive perception and understanding. Therefore, the Spirit enables people to 'absorb' or take in the saving content of Wisdom's teaching. As such, the Spirit provides the basis for people's epistemology with respect to God. In other words, the Spirit functions as the power that mediates to people that which is available in or by Wisdom; hence, the concept 'the Spirit as the power of (saving) Wisdom'.

It follows from this that both Wisdom and Spirit are manifestations of the one God, both function as channels of communication between God and people, and both convey similar ideas, namely to indicate the presence and activity of God in this world, especially in relation to salvation.[211] Our

---

[207] The concept of 'saving wisdom' is represented by the words σοφία, φρόνησις, γνῶσις, ἐπιστήμη and σύνεσις, which are frequently used partially synonymously.

[208] All the sapiential writings we investigated depict the possibility of people having a relationship with Wisdom, but especially Wis. and Philo emphasize that the ultimate aim is a relationship with God through his Wisdom (although this is probably implied by Prov., Sir. and the Qumran writings).

[209] Cf. R. Bauckham, who places Wisdom unequivocally within the unique self-identity of God, although the author of Wis., e.g., envisaged some form of real distinction within the unique identity of the one God (*God Crucified: Monotheism and Christology in the New Testament* [Carlisle: Paternoster, 1998] 21-22).

[210] Cf. Neve, *Spirit*, 2-3; Breck, *Spirit*, 11, 18; Hildebrandt, *Theology*, 18; Turner, *Spirit*, 5-6.

[211] Nonetheless, there are also fundamental differences between Wisdom and Spirit: (i) the Spirit is never personified or hypostatized to the extent that Wisdom is; (ii)

findings also fit our initial definition of salvation in Judaism (see section 2, above): both Spirit and Wisdom are the primary means by which sapiential Judaism envisaged her transformation/restoration.

The Spirit is not only depicted as a cognitive agent. The wisdom provided by the Spirit enables people to know God's will and demands, and is naturally expected to affect people's will, attitudes, motivations, etc. For example, in Sirach 39.6-7 the Spirit-filled scribe will gratefully acknowledge God and he will be directed in his intention (βουλή). In Wisdom of Solomon, the Spirit of Wisdom enables Solomon to reflect on what God desires and thus to rule justly (9.10-17; cf. Prov. 8.15-16), Wisdom teaches him self-control and right behaviour, and provides encouragement in concerns and grief (8.7-9). In Qumran, the Spirit-provided wisdom enables the psalmist to live a righteous life pleasing to God (1QH 6.25-27; 8.15). The Spirit causes or enables the psalmist to love God with his whole heart and to praise God (1QH 6.25-26; 11.22-23). God even delighted the psalmist with his Holy Spirit (1QH 17.32). Thus, sapiential Judaism conceives the Spirit as an *affective* agent too, who, through the mediation of wisdom, influences and transforms people's behaviour.[212]

A Model of Salvation in Sapiential Judaism. We suggest that the possession of πνεῦμα be understood in terms of various degrees of intensity and quality rather than absolute categories of 'having' it or not. Virtually all wisdom literature that we investigated confirms or assumes that every human being has πνεῦμα as the principle of life (and often of reason/wisdom) by virtue of his creation, but this measure of πνεῦμα can be increased by further infusion (the πνεῦμα of W/wisdom), which brings or leads to 'salvation'.[213] If the (divine) πνεῦμα in (relation to) humankind is an extension of God's own life and personality, then the measure of endowment of πνεῦμα human beings have will determine the quality and intensity of their lives and their knowledge of God.[214] Both concepts of πνεῦμα — the universal gift to all of humanity by virtue of creation and the charismatic gift — are in continuity with one another through that which they provide — life and wisdom. The distinction between these two

---

Wisdom is the source of salvation, whereas the Spirit is its agent; (iii) the Spirit functions as the power of Wisdom.

[212] Cf. the many references to store wisdom in one's 'heart' (e.g. Prov. 2.2, 10; 3.3; 14.33; Sir. 14.21), and if 'heart' denotes the mind, will, thought, emotions, etc., then wisdom has not merely a cognitive but also an affective influence.

[213] Sir., Wis., Philo and Qumran all affirm that people are endowed with a rational faculty and a certain endowment of wisdom at creation, but only the latter three attribute this to the divine πνεῦμα.

[214] Cf. Collins's observation based on Wis.: '[p]eople are transformed to the *degree* that the spirit of God is in them' (*Wisdom*, 198 [my emphasis]).

concepts is one of intensity and quality, i.e., one of strength, amount and calibre of endowment of πνεῦμα, and hence of life and wisdom. Human beings have or are in 'relationship' with the divine Spirit by virtue of being alive, and 'salvation', then, is a matter of intensity and quality — the degree or kind of relationship people have with God through his Spirit. Moreover, if the Spirit functions as the revealing power of Wisdom, in that the Spirit mediates 'saving wisdom' to people, then 'salvation' can also be described in terms of degree of W/wisdom.

Thus, based on our examination of the representative writings of the various wisdom strands, we propose a model of salvation in terms of *various degrees of intensity and/or quality of divine Spirit and W/wisdom.* By virtue of their creation, people have πνεῦμα, a certain measure of wisdom, and the cognitive ability to process wisdom (the 'mind'). 'Salvation', then, is a *sufficient* increase in measure and difference in *quality* of endowment of πνεῦμα and W/wisdom. In other words, 'salvation' can be understood as an intensification of that work of the Spirit that is already immanent to a person, namely, the mediation of life and wisdom, and this saving work of the Spirit was sometimes/often experienced as bringing new qualities of understanding, life and relationship with God. This 'panentheistic' model of salvation is explicitly present in Wisdom of Solomon and Philo, and to a lesser extent in Qumran and Sirach.[215]

The strength of our model is the strong coherence or continuity between the interrelated role of Spirit and Wisdom in both creation and salvation; the same Spirit and Wisdom that are at work together in creation are also co-operating with one another in salvation.[216] We have also interpreted 'salvation' within a relational framework. At creation, a person is alive and in 'relationship' with God through his Spirit, and the strength and quality of this relationship may be increased through fuller endowment of divine

---

[215] In Sir., humanity is endowed with wisdom by creation, and salvation consists of further endowment of wisdom and the gift of the Spirit. Wis. and Philo depict the endowment of humanity with πνεῦμα and wisdom at creation, and salvation entails a further endowment of πνεῦμα and wisdom. In Qumran two S/spirits are at work in or upon humankind since creation (of which the S/spirit of truth mediates wisdom), and salvation depends on whichever S/spirit is predominant. All sapiential writings we investigated confirm the 'mind' as the locus of cognitive activity. Although not every wisdom writing will confirm every single detail of our model, none of them speaks against any detail of our model either. It is beyond the scope of this thesis to test our salvific model of sapiential Judaism against every single wisdom writing.

[216] Wisdom's dual role in creation and salvation has been recognized by virtually all scholars, and hence has not been elaborated in this chapter.

Spirit, to the extent that we can speak of a 'saving' relationship.[217] Our model differs from that of Davis (and Menzies) in three ways. First, Davis has a model of various levels/stages of sapiential achievement, whereas we propose a model of various degrees of intensity and quality in Spirit and W/wisdom. Second, according to Davis, only the highest level of wisdom is attributed to the Spirit, which is then depicted virtually as a *donum superadditum* with no soteriological consequences, whereas in our model both Spirit and W/wisdom are soteriologically necessary and needed at every 'stage'. Three, we seem to allow for a broader group of potential recipients of the Spirit (in Wis., Philo and Qumran) than Davis.

Excursus 2: Πνεῦμα — A Conceptual Relation of Some of Its Senses in the LXX

The word πνεῦμα is used polysemously in the LXX, in that it has multiple senses — 'wind', 'breath (of life)', '(principle of) life', 'inner being', 'human spirit', 'divine spirit', etc.[218] We want to raise the question, to what extent there may be shared traits of meaning in those senses of πνεῦμα that are linked to the main focus of our thesis — the concept of πνεῦμα as far as it describes the activities of the divine Spirit in relation to people and 'salvation'.[219] Hence, to what extent are the senses 'breath/principle of life', 'human spirit' and 'divine spirit' of πνεῦμα related, and how?

We suggest that behind the senses 'breath/principle of life', 'human spirit' and 'divine spirit' is one shared meaning — the divine Spirit of God as the principle of life — since these three senses are linked linguistically, conceptually and theologically. The link between 'breath/principle of life' and 'divine spirit' is most easily established. First, πνεῦμα, as the divine Spirit of God, is depicted as the life-principle (of humankind and animals) (Gen. 6.3, 17; 7.15; Job 7.7; 12.10; Wis. 15.11; cf. Sir. 34.13; 38.23). Second, πνοὴ ζωῆς (the breath of life) is also depicted as the principle of the physical life (Gen. 2.7; 7.22; Sir. 33.21), and πνεῦμα frequently overlaps with πνοή in this sense of 'life' (Job 27.3; 33.4; Isa. 42.5; Wis. 2.2-3). Hence, it seems that the senses 'breath/principle of life' and 'divine spirit' of πνεῦμα are related in that God's πνεῦμα-πνοή is transferred to human beings in order to give them (physical) life. It is also possible to link 'breath/principle of life' and 'human spirit', in that the person's πνεῦμα is his life/vitality

---

[217] That a person is in 'relationship' with God through his Spirit by virtue of being alive may not necessarily be perceived by the person at a conscious level, but a person can only be in a 'saving relationship' with God through his Spirit at a conscious level; a person can only 'enter' into such a relationship through a cognitive act. In excursus 2, below, we take matters even further, although this should remain tentative.

[218] Cf. the standard lexicons; Hildebrandt, *Theology*, 1-27.

[219] Hence, we are not arguing for one single 'basic or 'core' meaning of πνεῦμα, that holds *all* its senses together (see the warning against this in [F.]P. Cotterell and M.[M.B.] Turner, *Linguistics & Biblical Interpretation* [London: SPCK, 1989] 137-39). We expect that the use of πνεῦμα in the LXX presupposes some synchrony, although further research needs to demonstrate to what extent our suggestion will work across the LXX. We have limited ourselves to Gen., Job, Isa., Wis. and Sir. because wisdom material has always made links to creation, and also, Gen. and Isa. highlight the role of the πνεῦμα in creation and the new creation respectively.

(Job 7.7; 10.12). Finally, it could be argued that the 'human spirit' is the divine Spirit on loan to man (Job 34.14-15; Wis. 15.11, 16), so that the senses 'human spirit' and 'divine spirit' are linked.

Although our suggestions are based on merely occasional references and need further testing, perhaps a case could be made to suggest that behind some senses of πνεῦμα — 'breath/principle of life', 'human spirit' and 'divine spirit' — lies a shared meaning or concept: *the divine Spirit of God, given on loan to human beings, is the 'spirit' in human beings and the principle of (physical) life.* That is, God creates and sustains human life by means of the divine Spirit, the breath of life. Hence, πνεῦμα is the main principle of correspondence between God and humanity.

This conceptual relation of some of the senses of πνεῦμα could have various implications. It might indicate that the human and divine 'spirit' are possibly not two separate entities in a person. 'Our' anthropological πνεῦμα (being our life/vitality) should perhaps not be (sharply) distinguished from the divine πνεῦμα (the extension of God's life in humankind); only at a linguistic level a distinction can be made between the anthropological and the divine πνεῦμα, and even then, these two senses of πνεῦμα probably have a shared meaning.[220] Consequently, the 'spirit' breathed into or given to a person at creation — denoting the 'human spirit' or his 'life' — should perhaps not be (sharply) distinguished from the divine Spirit 'saving' that person; it is more likely to be a matter of degree of intensity and quality of divine Spirit upon or in a person, from creation to salvation.[221] In conclusion, we tentatively suggest that the concept of πνεῦμα is essentially one theological concept with regard to some of its senses ('breath/principle of life', 'human spirit' and 'divine spirit').[222]

The major contribution of the development of our model of Spirit and W/wisdom in sapiential Judaism is that it provides a possible conceptual background for aspects of Johannine pneumatology already noted but not explained by some scholars. The model will be used alongside and in comparison with the Johannine concept of the Spirit, in order to illustrate and explicate the latter concept. Although the Jewish wisdom tradition is never a completely homogeneous entity, the different strands/varieties

---

[220] Cf. C.F.D. Moule, who states: 'the word "spirit" sometimes denotes some aspect of man; but seldom without some indication that it is really the Spirit of God, on loan, as it were, to man' ('The Holy Spirit in the Scriptures', *Church Quarterly* 3 [1970-71] 281). Cf. C. Westermann, who says that what is meant is not the natural phenomena of, e.g., 'wind' and 'breath' as such, but 'die im Wind und im Atem begegnende Kraft' ('Geist im Alten Testament', *Evangelische Theologie* 41 [1981] 224). To what extent we can speak of one (metaphysical) reality behind the anthropological and divine πνεῦμα goes beyond the scope of this investigation.

[221] The vast majority of scholars either assume or (implicitly) maintain a bifurcation between the divine Spirit and the human spirit as two separate, distinct (metaphysical) entities. However, this distinction between divine and human 'spirit' probably only exists at a linguistic level, and even then, these two senses of 'spirit' have a shared meaning. Alexandra Brown, e.g., finds in the wisdom tradition both functions of πνεῦμα — the principle of physical life and the principle of facilitating knowledge — but she formally distinguishes between this human spirit and the divine Spirit (*Cross*, 60-63).

[222] Cf. Isaacs, *Concept*, 59-64.

within the sapiential movement do have analogous themes and underlying concepts.[223] Our elucidation of Spirit and W/wisdom, especially in their interrelation with salvation, has resulted in a coherent conceptual model of salvation in terms of degrees of intensity and quality of Spirit and W/wisdom. This conceptual background of Spirit and W/wisdom has possibly given us the key to unlock the mechanism of the relation between the pneumatology and soteriology of the Fourth Gospel. Thus, it is against this background that we now turn to the Fourth Gospel to investigate its portrayal of Spirit and W/wisdom in relation to soteriology.

---

[223] This is also the point we have been trying to make in our article 'Strands'.

Part II

John's Pneumatic Wisdom Soteriology

Chapter 3

An Introduction to and a Model
of Johannine Soteriology

1. Introduction

The objective of this chapter is to develop an introductory, overall model of the soteriology of the Fourth Gospel that: (i) depicts the various activities of coming into and remaining within salvation; (ii) holds together the relational and cognitive aspects; (iii) identifies the activities in which the Spirit is involved; and (iv) indicates the parallels with the Jewish sapiential traditions. In this way, we hope to give more substance and scope to the soteriological models of (especially) Bultmann, Forestell, Loader and Willett, as well as testing Turner's theory in a broader soteriological framework. Based on this new model, we will then elucidate in chapters 4-5 the soteriological functions of the Spirit in the Fourth Gospel.

At the outset, we will work with a preliminary definition of salvation as 'being in a saving relationship with God and Jesus', and our agenda is formulated by three leading questions. How does one *enter* into this salvation/saving relationship, and related to this, what is adequate belief? How does one *stay* in this salvation/saving relationship? What are the benefits of being in this saving relationship? We make an important distinction between 'authentic' and 'adequate': 'authentic' means true, valid, genuine, and 'adequate' denotes authentic and sufficiently salvific. After a short introduction to the Fourth Gospel (section 2), most of this chapter will be dedicated to the examination of John's soteriological themes (section 3). Then, we will attempt to clarify the role of belief in relation to the cross and the signs because of the paradoxical issues involved (section 4), Jesus' role as Wisdom in relation to salvation (section 5), and the soteriological activities of the Spirit (section 6). Finally, we will present a model of John's Pneumatic Wisdom Soteriology (section 7). Methodologically, we will adopt a thematic and conceptual approach combined with the literary-historical criticism outlined in chapter 1. The originality of this chapter lies in the development of a new and more complete way of presenting important aspects of the Johannine concept of salvation.

We will also employ our findings of Spirit and Wisdom in relation to 'salvation' in sapiential Judaism (see ch. 2) to illuminate our understanding of John's soteriology. The rationale for utilizing such a possible background is as follows. First, all the Johannine soteriological themes we will elucidate in chapter 3 find a parallel in the Jewish wisdom literature (except for one less relevant theme). Second, the Spirit plays a significant part in the soteriology of the Jewish wisdom literature, and hence, it seems advantageous (if not essential) to attempt to understand the Johannine concept of Spirit against such a possible sapiential background. Moreover, in sapiential Judaism Wisdom and Spirit are closely related soteriological categories, which might assist us to elucidate the interrelations between Jesus, Spirit and salvation in the Fourth Gospel. Third, we have selected a Jewish (wisdom) background over against, for example, a Hellenistic (wisdom) background because the author of the Fourth Gospel himself appears to be immersed in Jewish thought, and because he expects his intended readership to have knowledge of Judaism (see ch. 2 section 1).

2. The Fourth Gospel — Some Pertinent Introductory Issues

We may briefly introduce John's Gospel by elucidating the issues of author, reader, genre, plot and purpose of the Fourth Gospel.[1] Concerning the real author, it will suffice to work with the concept of 'John' or 'the Evangelist',[2] but the question of the identity of the *reader* needs more

---

[1] With regard to the date of the Fourth Gospel, traditionally, the Gospel has been dated at the end of the first century, but this position has been challenged by J.A.T. Robinson, who believes that the Gospel should be dated before the destruction of Jerusalem at 70 CE (*Redating the New Testament* [London: SCM Press, 1976], ch. IX; cf. L. Morris, *The Gospel according to John* [NIC; Grand Rapids: Eerdmans, 1995 (rev. edn)] 25-30). Although most scholars have not been persuaded by Robinson's arguments, he reopened the question of the date of the Gospel, and it now seems plausible to give the origin of the traditions of the Fourth Gospel an early date and the final form a date around 80-85 CE (e.g., Beasley-Murray, *John*, lxxv-lxxviii; Carson, *Gospel*, 82-86). At present, the majority of scholars express their preference for the dating of John's Gospel tentatively somewhere within the spectrum of 80-100 CE.

[2] Concerning the issue of and relationship between the real author, implied author and narrator, see Culpepper, *Anatomy*, 43; J.L. Staley, *The Print's First Kiss: A Rhetorical Investigation of the Implied Reader in the Fourth Gospel* (SBL.DS 82; Atlanta: Scholars Press, 1988); Tovey, *Art*, 50-51; Hamid-Khani, *Revelation*, 22-28. The explicit evocation of the narratee by the 'you' in 20.31 (cf. 19.35) functions as a direct address to either the implied reader (so, e.g., Motyer, *Father*, 114) or real reader (so, e.g., Tolmie, *Farewell*, 38-39). The narrator probably identifies the eyewitness (the authority behind the Gospel)

attention. The original contribution of Martyn's seminal thesis is that he put the real reader of the Fourth Gospel in a specific social-historical context. He believes that the original readers were members of the so called Johannine community, i.e., a community of Jewish Christians who had become alienated from Judaism as a result of the *birkath ha-minim*, the curse against the Christian heretics formulated in Jamnia probably in the late first century.[3] There have always been critics of Martyn's thesis,[4] but the vast majority of Johannine scholars have accepted Martyn's basic concept that the Fourth Gospel reflects a particular *Sitz im Leben* of the Johannine community — in controversy with Judaism — through a 'two-level' reading of the text.[5] However, the recent work of Bauckham (and his colleagues) challenges the view that a Gospel was written for a specific community — instead the Gospels were written for general circulation around the churches — and thus seriously undermines the present consensus of a 'Johannine community'.[6] Esler, however, criticizes Bauckham's position and proposes a *via media*: each Gospel was primarily written for a specific local community, although each evangelist may have

---

in 19.35 and 21.24 as the Beloved Disciple (BD) (contra Staley, *Kiss*, 39-41, who thinks that the BD is the narrator [for a critique of Staley, see Culpepper, *Anatomy*, x; Tolmie, *Farewell*, 53-54]). However, there is debate whether the BD is the implied author (Culpepper, *Anatomy*, 47; Beasley-Murray, *John*, lxx-lxxv; Stibbe, *Storyteller*, 77-78; *idem*, *John*, 198, 215) or the real author (Tolmie, *Farewell*, 52-56; Witherington, *Wisdom*, 16). Carson argues that the BD is both the implied and real author (*Gospel*, 684-85), but narratologically the implied author is always distinct from the real author (cf. Culpepper, *Anatomy*, 15-16). Suffice it to say that the illocution of using the character of the BD is to assert the truthfulness of what has been narrated in the Fourth Gospel. That is, the eyewitness language adds to the plausibility of the Gospel's truth claim (cf. esp. A.T. Lincoln, 'The Fourth Gospel as Witness and the Beloved Disciple as Eyewitness', [unpublished paper given at London Bible College, December 2000] 1-17).

[3] See J.L. Martyn, *History & Theology in the Fourth Gospel* (Nashville: Abingdon, 1979[2]).

[4] E.g., W. Horbury, 'The Benediction of the *Minim* and Early Jewish-Christian Controversy', *JThS* 33 (1982) 19-61; M. Hengel, *The Johannine Question* (Transl. J Bowden; London: SCM Press, 1989) 114-15; Carson, *Gospel*, 371; Beasley-Murray, *John*, 153-54; Pryor, *John*, 42-43; Wright, *Testament*, 161-66, 451-52; Morris, *Gospel*, 41-42; Witherington, *Wisdom*, 38-39; Motyer, *Father*, 25-30, 211-18; Hamid-Khani, *Revelation*, 181-90.

[5] E.g., Brown, Barrett, Schnackenburg, Kysar, Fortna, Culpepper, Stibbe, Ashton, de Boer, Painter, Koester and Tolmie. See Motyer (*Father*, 13 n.21) for a more extensive list. Cf. X. Léon-Dufour, 'Towards a Symbolic Reading of the Fourth Gospel', *NTS* 27 (1981) 439-56.

[6] R. Bauckham, 'For Whom Were Gospels Written?' and other essays in R. Bauckham (ed.), *The Gospels for All Christians: Rethinking the Gospel Audiences* (Grand Rapids: Eerdmans, 1998). Cf. Hamid-Khani, *Revelation*, 18, 157-58, 171-72. See also Witherington, *Wisdom*, 32-35.

considered the possibility that it might be circulated beyond a local community.[7]

Motyer takes a different approach; rather than attempting to identify the real reader, he gives the implied reader specific historical features — the post-70 traumatic Jew — instead of purely literary ones. This creates the advantage that John's implied readership consists of life-like Jews across the wide spectrum of types of Judaism, but who can nevertheless not be identified with any particular group because this readership exists only in theory.[8] On the one hand, we tend to agree with Esler's position, especially bearing in mind that the Johannine letters were probably addressed to a 'Johannine community', and that there is a considerable theological overlap between the Gospel and the letters. On the other hand, because of John's explanatory comments (e.g. 1.38, 41; 4.9) the intended audience was probably wider than merely Jews or a particular community. Hence, we suggest that the envisaged intended reader is a first-century reader of the Fourth Gospel with knowledge of Judaism.[9]

The *genre* of the Fourth Gospel is probably that of the Graeco-Roman βίος.[10] The importance of recognizing βίος as the genre of the Fourth Gospel is that the subject matter of the Gospel is not primarily the contemporary experience, or even the history, of a 'Johannine community', but the story of Jesus Christ, as interpreted by the author.[11] Moreover, the

---

[7] P.F. Esler, 'Community and Gospel in Early Christianity: A Response to Richard Bauckham's *Gospels for All Christians*', *SJTh* 51 (1998) 235-48. Cf. Kim, 'Church', 174-79. See, however, Bauckham's reply to Esler ('Response to Philip Esler', *SJTh* 51 [1998] 249-53).

[8] Motyer, *Father*, 6-7, 113-14. The weakness of Motyer's approach is that he merely focuses on a *possible subset* of the whole group of possible readers. Motyer's idea is not entirely new; Culpepper had already given historical features to the implied reader (*Anatomy*, 211-27).

[9] Cf. Moloney's distinction between implied and intended reader: the implied reader *in* the narrative is a literary construct, whereas the intended reader *of* the narrative is the reader envisaged by the real author (*Belief*, 9-17).

[10] F.F. Segovia, 'The Journey(s) of the Word of God: A Reading of the Plot of the Fourth Gospel', *Semeia* 53 (1991) 32-33; R.A. Burridge, *What are the Gospels?: A Comparison with Graeco-Roman Biography* (SNTS.MS 70; Cambridge: CUP, 1992) 220-39; Witherington, *Wisdom*, 2-4; R.A. Culpepper, *The Gospel and Letters of John* (Nashville: Abingdon Press, 1998) 65-66. Although Stibbe agrees that the form of the Fourth Gospel is that of the βίος, he suggests a more comprehensive account of its genre (*Gospel*, ch. 3). The Fourth Gospel is also a 'Gospel', i.e., a *written* proclamation of what was in the first place *spoken*, the 'gospel' (εὐαγγέλιον) of Jesus Christ (cf. Stanton, *Gospels*, ch. 2). Hence, the Fourth Gospel is essentially a theological narration or interpretation of Jesus to promote belief.

[11] Burridge, *Gospels*, 256; *idem*, 'About People, by People, for People: Gospel Genre and Audiences' in R. Bauckham (ed.), *The Gospels for All Christians: Rethinking the Gospel Audiences* (Grand Rapids: Eerdmans, 1998) 113-45; Witherington, *Wisdom*, 3-4.

purpose of the βίος is to draw out the significance and interpretation of historical events, and hence it does not necessarily need to be historically accurate in all its detail; it may be a mixture of historical accuracy and fictional imagination in its witness to the T/truth.[12] This is not to deny a historical substratum to the Fourth Gospel, but the question of how much is historical need not dominate the debate concerning to what extent the Fourth Gospel is true.[13] Hence, the author wants to persuade and convince his readers not primarily of the 'basic' historical facts, such as the existence of the historical Jesus, the crucifixion and resurrection (for these were already known), but of their *significance*.

The *plot*[14] of the Fourth Gospel is the revelation of the Father and of the identity and mission of the Son, and people's response to this revelation (cf. e.g. 1.10-12, 18; 3.16-18; 20.31).[15] A structural analysis of John's plot can be visualized with Greimas's diagram to represent the way in which the implied author organized the characters in the narrated world of the Fourth Gospel:[16]

Cf. G.N. Stanton, 'The Communities of Matthew', *Interp* 46 (1992) 388. Esler, however, criticizes Burridge's view ('Community', 243-44).

[12] Cf. Lincoln, *Truth*, 369-97; *idem*, 'Gospel', 12-17.

[13] Cf. Lincoln, *Truth*, 369-78. Contra M. Casey, who argues that the Fourth Gospel is profoundly untrue in that it is historically inaccurate and anti-Jewish (*Is John's Gospel True?* [London: Routledge, 1996]).

[14] Plot is the organization of events into a coherent unity characterized by a causal and temporal logic (Stibbe, *Gospel*, 34). Stibbe explains that John's plot helps the reader to expect his own story of faith and discipleship to follow a similar pattern (*Gospel*, 51-52).

[15] Cf. Culpepper, *Anatomy*, 87-89; *idem*, *Gospel*, 67-86; Stibbe, *Gospel*, 40-44; Tolmie, *Farewell*, 42.

[16] Cf. Stibbe, *Gospel*, 44; Tolmie, *Farewell*, 141. However, both Stibbe and Tolmie entirely neglect the role of the Spirit in Jesus' ministry. Stibbe contends that Jesus does not have any obvious, consistent helpers, not even the Holy Spirit (*Gospel*, 43-44), but see our view in ch. 4 section 2. Moreover, Stibbe and Tolmie differ about the identity of the receiver — for Stibbe the receiver is Jesus, for Tolmie it is the world — which is due to their different understanding of Greimas's theory (Stibbe, *Gospel*, 39; Tolmie, *Farewell*, 120). Tolmie's interpretation is more generally used. Stibbe also sees a counter-plot in John — the quest of 'the Jews' to kill Jesus (*Gospel*, 47-49). The term 'the Jews' denotes those Jews who are suspicious, hostile and opposed to Jesus, and refers especially to Jewish leaders (cf. Motyer, *Father*, 46-57; Hamid-Khani, *Revelation*, 232-51). 'World' is in some sense personified as the great opponent of Jesus; 'world' (as 'the Jews') denotes those people who are in opposition to Jesus (cf. H. Sasse, 'Κοσμέω, κτλ.' in *TDNT*, III:894; Harner, *Relation*, 115-20).

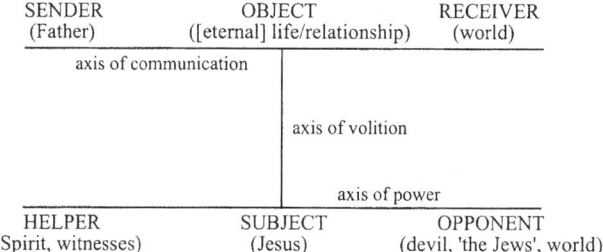

Moreover, the story of the Fourth Gospel is 'open-ended': after Jesus' glorification, the story of the disciples begins:[17]

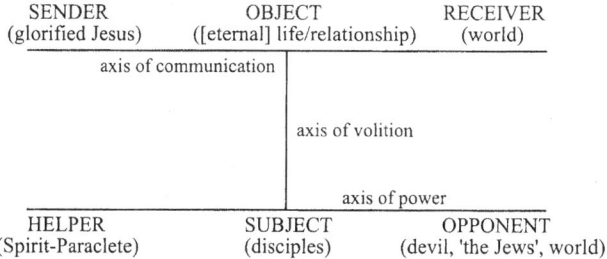

The *purpose* of the Gospel, the author's intended perlocutionary effect, is explicitly stated in 20.30-31. John 20.30 (cf. 21.25) reveals that the author has made a deliberate selection of Jesus' numerous signs for the twofold purpose stated in 20.31: ἵνα πιστεύ[σ]ητε ὅτι Ἰησοῦς ἐστιν ὁ Χριστὸς ὁ υἱὸς τοῦ θεοῦ, καὶ ἵνα πιστεύοντες ζωὴν ἔχητε ἐν τῷ ὀνόματι αὐτοῦ. There has been much debate whether the first purpose clause is evangelistic — taking πιστεύσητε as an aorist subjunctive denoting 'that you may come to believe (for the first time)' — or pastoral — taking πιστεύητε as a present subjunctive denoting 'that you may continue to believe'.[18] However, John is also able to use the tenses of the subjunctive

---

[17] This diagram is mainly based on Jn 13-21. Cf. Stibbe, *Gospel*, 52-53; Tolmie, *Farewell*, 141. This time Tolmie brought in the Spirit-Paraclete, but as sender instead of helper. However, it is Jesus who sends the disciples on their mission (17.18; 20.21), and it is precisely the Spirit-Paraclete who comes to the aid of the disciples (14.16-18).

[18] People line up on either side: scholars who propose primarily an evangelistic aim are, e.g., Dodd, *Interpretation*, 9; Carson, *John*, 662-63; Morris, *Gospel*, 755-56; Witherington, *Wisdom*, 29-32; Motyer, *Father*, 57-62. Amongst those who argue primarily for a pastoral purpose are Brown, *Gospel*, 2:1060; Barrett, *Gospel*, 575; Schnackenburg, *Gospel*, 3:338; Culpepper, *Gospel*, 244; Pryor, *John*, 90-91; Stibbe, *John*, 202. Most of them, however, allow for the other purpose in a secondary sense (see, e.g., Culpepper, *Gospel*, 244). Others argue more explicitly for a dual purpose (F.F.

differently — in 11.15; 13.19; 20.25 the aorist subjunctive is used with reference to the disciples' (continuous) belief, whereas in 6.29; 10.38; 17.21 John uses a present subjunctive to present Jesus' summons for people to come to belief for the first time — which should warn us against putting too much weight on the syntax.[19]

We nevertheless suggest that an evangelistic aim is more probable for three reasons. First, the purpose of John the Baptist's coming coincides with the purpose of the Gospel; the use of πιστεύσωσιν in 1.7, an aorist subjunctive denoting 'to come to believe for the first time', may support a similar reading for 20.31. Second, the aim especially of John 1-12 and John 20, but also of the work of the Spirit-Paraclete (through the witness of the disciples), seems to be to lead people to an adequate belief-response to Jesus and his revelation (see chs. 4-5). Third, 20.31 emphatically declares that Jesus is the Christ/Messiah, implying that the fundamental issue is the recognition of the true identity of Jesus; an issue it seems for non-believers rather than believers (cf. the theme 'people's response').[20]

The Fourth Gospel, however, also emphasizes the pastoral aspect (to strengthen and deepen an existing belief): an important issue is that disciples follow and stick with Jesus (6.66-69; 21.19, 22), and John 13-17 especially emphasizes also the need for continuous belief. This aspect might be reflected in the second purpose clause in 20.31, which contains the present participle πιστεύοντες, possibly denoting the need for continuous belief.[21]

In conclusion, both aspects (evangelistic and pastoral) are reflected throughout the entire Gospel and summed up in 20.31. Hence, we suggest

---

Bruce, *The Gospel of John: Introduction, Exposition and Notes* [Basingstoke: Pickering & Inglis, 1983] 395; Beasley-Murray, *John*, 387-88).

[19] Cf. Brown, *Gospel*, 2:1056; Schnackenburg, *Gospel*, 3:338; Carson, *John*, 662; Beasley-Murray, *John*, 387; Pryor, *John*, 90; Tovey, *Art*, 90; Motyer, *Father*, 58. Frey, in his impressive volume on John's use of tenses and time, states that the aorist subjunctives in 11.15 and 13.19 denote the *beginning* of faith (*Eschatologie II*, 93 n.83), but we would argue that in these passages Jesus seems to encourage his disciples to *continue* to believe.

[20] Carson argues that in the phrase ὅτι Ἰησοῦς ἐστιν ὁ Χριστός the subject is 'the Christ' and the complement is 'Jesus', implying that the fundamental issue is the identity of the Messiah rather than of Jesus; an issue, it seems, for unconverted Jews rather than converted (*Gospel*, 662). Although Carson's argument also supports an evangelistic purpose, we contend that 'Jesus is the Messiah' seems the normal reading, especially when 1 Jn 2.22; 4.15; 5.1, 5 is considered where Jesus is very probably also the subject. For a more detailed critique of Carson's view, see D.B. Wallace, *Greek Grammar Beyond the Basics: An Exegetical Syntax of the New Testament* (Grand Rapids: Zondervan, 1996) 46-47; Hamid-Khani, *Revelation*, 165 n.27.

[21] The majority of scholars recognize the need for continuous belief, but they do so solely on the basis of the first purpose clause (taking it as pastoral either in a primary or secondary sense).

that, according to 20.31 (and the whole of the Gospel), *the purpose of the Fourth Gospel is soteriological and the author seeks to bring people to initial adequate belief and to sustain this belief so that they may (continue to) have life* (cf. 1 Jn 5.13, which states the purpose of the letter).[22]

Motyer also sees the importance of the two purpose clauses in 20.31, but he argues that they express two distinct stages in salvation: faith is just a starting-point and should be supplemented by discipleship if it is to lead to life.[23] However, Motyer's theory has two hazards. First, Motyer is in danger of creating a false dichotomy between faith and discipleship, as if faith and discipleship are subsequent (complementary) stages leading to life. We will argue in this chapter that discipleship is itself a belief-response; it is a manifestation/demonstration of true belief. Second, Motyer is consequently also in danger of advocating a dual purpose for the Gospel — faith and discipleship — whereas it is more probable that the *single* purpose of the Gospel is to evoke belief — either initially or continuously — so that people may have life. To put it differently, the *single* purpose of the Fourth Gospel is that people may (continuously) have (eternal) life in Jesus' name through a continuous life of believing displayed in discipleship.

Tovey, although taking a different approach, comes to a similar position, by arguing for a double focus and a double ending of the Fourth

---

[22] 'To believe in his name' probably denotes to understand/recognize Jesus' true identity and character; 'his name' represents the whole person bearing that name (cf. 5.43; 17.6, 26). We should probably not take the phrase πιστεύω ἐν τῷ ὀνόματι αὐτου as a technical term for adequate belief; the phrase occurs in 1.12; 2.23; 3.18; 20.31; 1 Jn 3.23; 5.13, but in 2.23 it does not denote adequate belief (πιστεύω in 2.23 is contrasted by δὲ 'Ιησοῦς οὐκ ἐπίστευεν in 2.24). T. Okure argues that the whole debate on whether or not the Gospel was a missionary or a community document seems uncalled for by the Gospel; Jesus' life-giving mission is directed towards believers and non-believers, and includes both the aspect of 'to come to believe' and 'to continue to believe' (*The Johannine Approach to Mission: A Contextual Study of John 4:1-42* [WUNT II/31; Tübingen: Mohr Siebeck, 1988] 292-94; cf. A.J. Köstenberger, *The Missions of Jesus and the Disciples according to the Fourth Gospel: With Implications for the Fourth Gospel's Purpose and the Mission of the Contemporary Church* [Grand Rapids: Eerdmans, 1998] 200-10; Hamid-Khani, *Revelation*, 157-229).

Obviously, there were not hundreds of copies of the Fourth Gospel available to hand out as 'evangelistic tracts'. However, the Fourth Gospel was probably read out in the Johannine church(es) which possibly contained non-believers. Moreover, and more importantly, the believers (being familiar with the text of the Fourth Gospel) probably used this material as a basis to evangelize non-believers. In this sense, the Fourth Gospel is used evangelistically/missiologically. Of course, the Fourth Gospel would also be used pastorally, to deepen and strengthen an existing belief (see Area 2 in our model of John's soteriology in ch. 3 section 7; cf. also our constant emphasis on 'remaining in salvation', discipleship, and the continual mediation of life and wisdom/knowledge by the Spirit).

[23] Motyer, *Father*, 58-61.

Gospel. Tovey plausibly argues that in John 1-12 the implied author wants to evoke faith, and in John 13-21 the attention is upon those in whom faith has already been implanted.[24] Rather than restricting these foci of coming to faith and of discipleship exclusively to respectively John 1-12 and 13-21, Tovey has 'characterized these [two foci] as waves, for the themes surge and recede in both sections, more dominant at certain points than at others, bringing different aspects to the fore at different times.'[25] Moreover, it is this wavelike, doubling and repetitive effect which accounts for the Gospel's double ending found in John 20-21: John 20 brings, in the encounter with Thomas, the first of these thematic waves to its climax, and John 21 brings, in the reinstatement of Peter, the second thematic wave to a climax.[26] Although we agree with Tovey's analysis, we see these two thematic waves also in 20.31 itself, which would then function as the link between John 20 and 21.

3. A Thematic and Conceptual Approach to the Johannine Soteriological Language[27]

In this section, we will elucidate the main soteriological themes in the Johannine literature, i.e., those themes that are related to salvation.[28] We have identified the following soteriological themes, and the most important Greek terms associated with these themes are mentioned in brackets:[29]

---

[24] Tovey, *Art*, 91-92, 99-107.

[25] Tovey, *Art*, 108.

[26] Tovey, *Art*, 108, 111-12. Tovey defends Jn 21 as an integral part of the narrative (*Art*, 109-13). On Jn 20-21 as a double ending, see B.R. Gaventa, 'The Archive of Excess: John 21 and the Problem of Narrative Closure' in R.A. Culpepper and C.C. Black (eds.), *Exploring the Gospel of John: In Honor of D. Moody Smith* (Louisville: Westminster John Knox Press, 1996) 240-52.

[27] For a treatment of John's enigmatic language, see Hamid-Khani, *Revelation*, ch. 2.

[28] For more general themes of the Fourth Gospel, see Culpepper, *Gospel*, 117-19; Stibbe, *John*, 26-28; Tovey, *Art*, 99-103.

[29] Although we have found twenty-two soteriological themes, we do not claim to be exhaustive. 'Bigger' salvific themes, such as the cross and the Spirit, are dealt with in sections 4 and 6 respectively. Because we examine all these soteriological themes as a whole, it is impossible to interact with scholarship on any and every point. Nevertheless, we have interacted with scholarship on the most important matters. The Prologue sets the agenda for the rest of the Gospel (as most scholars assert), and thus provides in embryo the majority of the themes, which will then be developed as the Gospel progresses. Except for themes c, g, h, s, t and v, and possibly e and j (although part of Jesus' work and teaching is to reveal the Father [1.18]), all other themes are already present in the Prologue.

(a) the sending of Jesus, the Spirit, the disciples et al. (ἀποστέλλω, πέμπω)
(b) Jesus' journey (ὁδός, καταβαίνω, ἀναβαίνω)
(c) the love of the Father and Son (ἀγάπη, ἀγαπάω, φιλέω)
(d) the identity of the Father and Son
(e) Jesus' work (ἔργον, ἐργάζομαι, σωτηρία, σῴζω)
(f) the glorification of the Father and Son (δοξάζω, δόξα, ὑψόω)
(g) the Father draws people and gives them to Jesus (δίδωμι, ἕλκω)
(h) Jesus' signs (σημεῖον)
(i) Jesus' revelation (ἐξηγέομαι, ἐμφανίζω, φανερόω, γνωρίζω, ἀναγγέλλω)
(j) Jesus' teaching (διδάσκω, διδάσκαλος, διδαχή)
(k) Jesus' encounter with and invitation to people
(l) saving truth (ἀλήθεια)
(m) sensory perception (βλέπω, ὁράω, θεωρέω, θεάομαι, ἀκούω)
(n) cognitive perception (γινώσκω, οἶδα)
(o) people's response (πιστεύω, [παρα]λαμβάνω)
(p) divine birth (γεννάω)
(q) the intimate relationship of the believer with the Father and Son (κοινωνία, φίλος, ἕν εἶναι, 'x [μένει] ἐν y')
(r) the divine life (ζωή [αἰώνιος], ζάω, ζῳοποιέω)
(s) bearing fruit ([φέρω] καρπός)
(t) remaining in Jesus (μένω)
(u) witnessing to Jesus (μαρτυρέω, μαρτυρία)
(v) following Jesus (ἀκολουθέω).

Although many studies have been devoted to one or more of these themes,[30] scholars have not always shown the soteriological aspects of some themes, nor has an attempt been made to show how all of John's soteriological language functions as a whole. Our objective is not to do etymological word studies nor to give an exhaustive analysis of each

---

[30] E.g., Appold focuses on the oneness motif, Tolmie on discipleship, Segovia on abiding, Ibuki and de la Potterie on the theme of truth, O'Day on revelation, Thüsing on the themes of lifting up and glorification. Dodd, Scott and Willett, e.g., have examined more of our themes. For Stibbe, Jesus is quintessentially the elusive Christ, a sort of first-century Scarlet Pimpernel, since Jesus is not easily grasped either physically — he constantly evades the attempts of the Jews to arrest or kill him — or intellectually — he equally often seems to evade the comprehension of his audience (see *Gospel*, ch. 1). Dr Mark Stibbe consequently suggested to me the soteriological theme 'seeking Jesus' (ζητέω). However, although ζητέω frequently denotes the search of the Jews for Jesus in order to arrest or kill him (e.g. 5.18; 7.1, 30; 10.39), ζητέω is not really used to evoke the idea of seeking Jesus intellectually (although ζητέω in 1.38 arguably alludes to something more than its literal meaning). Rather, the attempt to grasp Jesus cognitively seems to be denoted by other terms (see esp. section 3.2, below). Hence, in our view, 'seeking Jesus' (based on ζητέω) does not seem an apparent Johannine soteriological theme.

theme, but (i) to elucidate the soteriological dimension of each of these themes, and (ii) to show how all these various soteriological themes are linked and work together (see esp. section 7, below).

The main soteriological themes of the Fourth Gospel can tentatively be grouped in *thematic clusters* or *concepts*: (i) the identity and mission of the Father and Son, and their relationship (themes a-l, q-u); (ii) people's perception of and responses to Jesus and his revelation (themes l-o); (iii) people in relationship with the Father and Son (themes p-r); (iv) discipleship (themes c, s-v). We will concentrate on (and hence only elucidate) those themes that are most vital for our investigation, whereas less relevant themes will simply receive brief mention. Appendix 1 presents the occurrences of the Greek terms associated with the soteriological themes in the Johannine literature, and appendix 2 contains some statistics.

3.1. The Identity and Mission of the Father and Son and Their Relationship

This thematic concept has many aspects and consists of numerous themes. The section starts with a brief treatment of themes a-f (for a summary, see p.117), but the centre of gravity of this section are the themes i-l because this cluster introduces the idea of people being confronted with Jesus and his revelatory teaching, which brings salvation.[31]

The sending of Jesus, the Spirit, the disciples et al. (theme a) (ἀποστέλλω, πέμπω). This theme is inextricably linked to soteriology. Jesus' sending into the world by God has a soteriological aim and is a token of God's salvific love for the world (3.16-17; cf. 12.47; 17.23; 1 Jn 4.9-10, 14).[32] The sending of the Paraclete, by the Father and Son (14.26; 15.26), has a soteriological aim because the Spirit-Paraclete will sustain one's salvation (14.18-23), and Jesus will continue his salvific mission through the Paraclete (14.16, 26; 15.26; 16.14). The disciples' sending into the world by Jesus also has a soteriological dimension because: (i) it is patterned upon Jesus' sending (17.18; 20.21); (ii) it is closely linked to the Paraclete's witnessing activity (15.26-27; 16.7-11); (iii) the aim of the disciples' sending is that through their message people will believe in Jesus and be

---

[31] Theme g is mentioned in n.100, below, theme h will be treated in section 4.2, below, and themes q-u are considered in sections 3.3 and 3.4, below.

[32] Cf. Scott, *Sophia*, 134; Willett, *Wisdom*, 59-60. For the concept of agency, see P. Borgen, 'God's Agent in the Fourth Gospel' in J. Ashton (ed.), *The Interpretation of John* (Edinburgh: T&T Clark, 1997[2]) 83-95; A.E. Harvey, 'Christ as Agent' in L.D. Hurst and N.T. Wright (eds.), *The Glory of Christ in the New Testament: Studies in Christology in Memory of George Bradford Caird* (Oxford: Clarendon Press, 1987) 239-50; Witherington, *Wisdom*, 140-41; Thompson, 'God', 223-31. The concept of agency upholds that the one who is sent *represents* the one who sends, and hence, Jesus represents God, and to relate to Jesus is to relate to God (cf. 3.17; 5.23; 12.44-45; 13.20; 14.7-9). In other words, an emissary is not simply someone who is sent, but also an envoy, a plenipotentiary; he speaks and acts in the name of the one who sent him (de Jonge, *Jesus*, 147).

brought into unity with the Father and Son (17.20-23; cf. the Baptist's sending by God [1.6-7]). Thus, the sending of Jesus, the Spirit-Paraclete, the Baptist and the disciples is soteriologically driven, and because God is the ultimate sender, he takes the initiative in salvation.[33]

Jesus' journey (theme b) (ὁδός, καταβαίνω, ἀναβαίνω). The intertestamental literature shows a so called V-pattern of Wisdom's journey: *1 Enoch* 42 tells that divine Wisdom pre-exists in heaven, comes to earth to God's people to find a dwelling place, but, having found none, goes back to heaven (cf. Prov. 8 and Sir. 24). The Fourth Gospel also reflects this journey. The Prologue evokes the first two stages, in that pre-existent divine Wisdom-Logos descended to earth and dwelled among us (1.1-2, 14). The rest of the Gospel unfolds these first two stages as well as the third stage — Jesus' return to the Father via the path of the cross (cf. 3.13; 6.33, 62; 20.17; see 16.28 for a summary of the whole journey).[34] Hence, the cross could be interpreted sapientially, in that Jesus' being lifted up at the cross denotes the start of the third stage of Wisdom's journey. Jesus' journey is, as Wisdom's journey, essentially a soteriological one (cf. the soteriological significance of Jesus' sending and of the cross).[35] The importance of understanding this journey is that it is directly linked to a proper understanding of Jesus' origin, identity and mission, which is necessary for salvation (3.13-15; 8.14-24; 14.4-6; 16.28-30).[36] Besides the concept of the journey of Wisdom (incarnate), there is also people's journey with Wisdom (incarnate), which is essentially a soteriological journey. In sapiential Judaism (esp. in Wis. and Philo), Wisdom functions as a travel companion on one's soteriological journey to God, providing divine guidance, assistance and life (see ch. 2). In the Fourth Gospel this concept is captured under two images: Jesus being 'the way' and Jesus' invitation to follow him. The concept of Jesus as ἡ ὁδὸς καὶ ἡ ἀλήθεια καὶ ἡ ζωή (14.6), in which ὁδός refers to a journey or way of life/conduct, probably identifies Jesus as ἡ ὁδὸς ζωῆς of Proverbs 5.6; 6.23; 10.17; 15.24 [LXX], as ἡ ὁδὸς σοφίας of Proverbs 4.11 [LXX], and as ἡ ὁδὸς ἀληθείας/κυρίου of Wisdom of Solomon 5.6-7 (cf. Sir. 37.15). Hence, it denotes that Jesus, as Wisdom incarnate, is the way of/to life or simply the way

---

[33] For sending as a soteriological concept, see also J. Ferreira, *Johannine Ecclesiology* (JSNT.S 160; Sheffield: SAP, 1998) ch. 6. In Wis., Solomon's request to God to send Wisdom (and the accompanying Spirit) has strong soteriological overtones (Wis. 9.4, 10, 17-18; cf. Wis. 6-10). The 'sending' of Wisdom by God in Sir. 24.8 also has salvific implications since Wisdom is understood as the source of life and life-giving wisdom (Sir. 1.20; 4.12; 24.25-27; 39.6-8). Dodd sees the prophetic tradition behind the theme of Jesus' sending (*Interpretation*, 254-55), but, without denying the influence of the prophetic tradition, Willett argues for a primary influence of the wisdom tradition (esp. Wis.) (*Wisdom*, 60-63).

[34] Cf. Nicholson's Descent-Ascent Schema (DAS) (see *Death*, ch. 2). Scott prefers the phrase Descent-Withdrawal (Going-Away) rather than Descent-Ascent to designate the journey of Jesus/Wisdom (*Sophia*, 138-39). Willett essentially adheres to Nicholson's DAS but also builds on Loader's christological model, and consequently explains Jesus' descent in terms of Wisdom, and Jesus' ascent via the cross in terms of the apocalyptic Son of Man (*Wisdom*, 56-66). Although Stibbe also sees a V-pattern in the Fourth Gospel (he calls it a U-pattern), based on the U-shaped plot of comedy (*Gospel*, 66-70), we contend that the background of Jesus' journey probably lies in the Jewish story of Wisdom.

[35] Cf. Scott, *Sophia*, 134-36. However, Scott does not really work out the soteriological parallel between Sophia and Jesus.

[36] Cf. Witherington, *Jesus*, 372-73; *idem*, *Wisdom*, 21-22.

that is life itself (cf. Wis. 10.15-17). The second image of people's soteriological journey in the Fourth Gospel is Jesus' summons to his disciples to follow him; those who (continue to) journey with Jesus will have life (see the theme 'following Jesus').

The love of the Father and Son (theme c) (ἀγάπη, ἀγαπάω, φιλέω).[37] The relationship between the Father and Son is one of, or characterized by, love (3.35; 5.20; 14.31; 15.9). This reciprocal love between the Father and Son, however, is not limited to themselves but finds an outlet to humanity and is the underlying motivational force of salvation (3.16-17; 6.51; 10.11, 17; 15.13; 1 Jn 3.16; 4.9-10).[38] The relationship of mutual love between the Father and Son is not only the basis for salvation, in that it is life-giving, but also the paradigm for believers. Believers are drawn into this life-giving relationship of mutual love between the Father and Son (see the theme 'the intimate relationship...'), and they should in turn love the Father and Son as well as reproduce this relationship of reciprocal love among the community of believers. This reproduction of love at a vertical and horizontal level has a soteriological dimension. At a vertical level, Jesus expects that believers will show/demonstrate their love for him (and the Father) by keeping his commandments, which guarantees to a person the love and indwelling presence of the Father and Son (14.15-23; cf. 1 Jn 3.23-24; 5.3). At a horizontal level, Jesus commands his disciples 'to love one another' (13.34-35),[39] which is not only the ultimate command (cf. 15.12, 17; 1 Jn 3.11), but also *the* characteristic of discipleship.[40] Both aspects — to love Jesus (and the Father) and to love one another — are then linked in John 15.1-17 (cf. 1 Jn 2.10-11; 3.10-15; 4.12, 16). In sum, the love between the Father and Son has soteriological implications for humanity, in that God's love for the world propelled the Son's salvific mission, and in that Jesus' love for his friends is ultimately expressed in his salvific death on the cross. Moreover, the love required from the believer at a horizontal and vertical level is soteriologically necessary because to love one another is the ultimate demonstration of obedience to Jesus' commandments and hence of love for Jesus. This demonstration of love is the characteristic expression of discipleship and sustains one's salvation because it maintains one's life-giving relationship of love with the Father and Son.[41]

---

[37] For an overall treatment of the doctrine of love, see D.A. Carson, *The Difficult Doctrine of the Love of God* (Leicester: IVP, 2000). See also Harner, *Relation*, 26-31, 62-72.

[38] Both Willett (*Wisdom*, 75-78) and Scott (*Sophia*, 140-41) recognize that, above all, love describes the intimate relationship between the Father and Son, but they do not draw out its soteriological aspect.

[39] It is not entirely certain whether καθώς in 13.34 indicates that Jesus' love for his disciples is the reason/basis ('because') or the pattern/measure ('just as', 'in the same manner', 'to the same extent') for the disciples' love for one another (1 Jn 4.10-11 seems to indicate that God's love for people is the reason for their love for one another).

[40] NB the Beloved Disciple, as the disciple whom Jesus loved, functions as a paradigm of discipleship; he is (not surprisingly) only introduced in the second part of the Fourth Gospel, which has a special emphasis on discipleship. Peter is also referred to as a paradigm of discipleship (cf. Jesus' testing of Peter's love for him in 21.15-19).

[41] The intertestamental wisdom literature reveals a similar picture. The relationship between God and Wisdom is characterized by love (Wis. 8.3), and God's love extends to all things that exist (Wis. 11.24, 26; cf. Jn 3.16). Moreover, God gives his Wisdom to those who love him (Sir 1.10). People are exhorted to love (and stay with) Wisdom, which is expressed/demonstrated in keeping her commandments (Wis. 6.17-18; cf. Sir.

The identity of the Father and Son (theme d). God is primarily known as the one who sent Jesus (cf. the many references to 'the one/Father/he who sent me').[42] God is also characterized by love (3.16; 1 Jn 4.8, 16), judgment/wrath (3.36), truth (17.17), life (5.21, 26), knowledge (10.15) and glory (11.4, 40; 13.31; 14.13). Numerous titles are given to Jesus: λόγος (1.1, 14), χριστός (1.17, 41; 11.27; 20.31; 1 Jn 5.1), προφήτης (4.19; 6.14; 9.17), σωτὴρ τοῦ κόσμου (4.42; 1 Jn 4.14), ὁ υἱὸς τοῦ θεοῦ (1.34, 49; 11.27; 20.31; 1 Jn 4.15), ὁ υἱὸς τοῦ ἀνθρώπου (1.51; 3.14; 6.62), ὁ ἀμνὸς τοῦ θεοῦ (1.29, 36), παράκλητος (14.16; 1 Jn 2.1), βασιλεύς (1.49; 12.13; 19.19), κύριος (6.68; 9.38; 20.28) and διδάσκαλος (1.38; 3.2; 8.4; 11.28; 13.13).[43] Although the title σοφία is never used for Jesus, there are reasons to believe that Jesus is presented as Wisdom incarnate (see ch. 1 section 2.2.1; cf. Jesus' offering life-giving water and bread, which are symbols of wisdom). Jesus is characterized by or as truth (14.6), light (1.4-5, 9; 8.12; 9.5), life (1.4; 5.21, 26; 11.25; 14.6), love (15.13), peace (14.27; 16.33), knowledge (10.15), glory (1.14; 17.5) and joy (15.11; 17.13). Related to Jesus' identity is his origin; he comes from God (7.29; 8.42; 16.28), from above/heaven (3.31-34; 8.23). Knowing, recognizing and understanding the true identity of the Father and Son (and their relationship) is salvific (17.3; 20.31; cf. the theme 'the intimate relationship...').[44]

Jesus' work (theme e) (ἔργον, ἐργάζομαι, σωτηρία, σῴζω). Jesus' work/mission is to finish the Father's work (4.34; 5.36; 17.4; 19.28, 30), which is to send the Son and save the world through him (3.17; cf. 1 Jn 4.14).[45] Hence, because the work of the Son is to finish the Father's salvific work, Jesus' work is necessarily also soteriological (cf. 12.47).[46] This is confirmed when one looks at aspects of Jesus' work. First, Jesus' miracles, which can evoke belief (2.11; 6.14; 7.31; 11.45; 12.10-11; cf. 20.30-31), are called works (7.3, 21; 9.3-4; 10.25, 32, 37-38; 14.11; 15.24). Second, Jesus' death on the

2.15-16), because this will result in blessing (Prov. 4.6-9; 8.17-21), (eternal) life (Wis. 6.12, 17-18; Sir. 4.12) and God's love (Sir 4.14; Wis. 7.28).

[42] Cf. W.R.G. Loader, 'The Central Structure of Johannine Christology', *NTS* 30 (1984) 190.

[43] For an elucidation of some of Jesus' christological titles, see, e.g., Dodd, *Interpretation*, 228-85; S. Smalley, *John: Evangelist and Interpreter* (Carlisle: Paternoster, 1998²) 238-48.

[44] In Judaism, Wisdom is also characterized by or as possessing life (Prov. 3.16, 18; 8.35; Wis. 8.13, 17; Sir. 1.20; 4.12), love (Prov. 8.17), peace (Prov. 3.17; cf. Sir. 6.28), truth (Prov. 8.6-8), wisdom (Sir. 15.3), knowledge/understanding (Prov. 4.5; 8.10, 12, 14; Wis. 8.4, 8, 18; 9.9, 11; Sir. 1.19; 3.25), glory (Prov. 8.18; Wis. 7.25; 9.11; Sir. 24.1-2), joy (Prov. 8.30-31; Wis. 8.16, 18; Sir. 6.28) and light (Wis. 6.12; 7.10, 26, 29; cf. Sir. 3.25). Concerning Wisdom's origin, she comes from and lives with God (Wis. 8.3; 9.4, 9-10; Sir. 24.2-4).

[45] Based on 4.34, P.W. Ensor argues that doing God's will and accomplishing his work was a *sine qua non* of Jesus' existence (*Jesus and His >Works<: The Johannine Sayings in Historical Perspective* [WUNT II/85; Tübingen: Mohr Siebeck, 1996] 151; cf. Riedl, *Heilswerk*, 48). For Jesus' mission, see Köstenberger, *Missions*, ch. 3. Riedl thinks that 6.29 refers to God's work of bringing people to belief (*Heilswerk*, 319-26), but this verse probably means that the work God calls for is to believe in Jesus, because 6.27-28 speaks about the work of people (cf. Ensor, *Jesus*, 281). Nonetheless, people can only come to belief in Jesus through God's initiative (6.44, 65).

[46] Okure, who elucidates the theme of mission in John, stresses that Jesus is the Father's exclusive agent of salvation, in that Jesus alone does and completes the Father's work (*Approach*, 286).

cross is salvific and marks the climactic completion of his and the Father's work (3.14-15; 12.32; cf. τετέλεσται in 19.28, 30).[47] Third, Jesus' testimony/teaching, which is part of or points to Jesus' work (5.36; 14.10-11), is salvific if it is accepted (3.32-36; 8.31-36; 17.8; cf. 1 Jn 5.10).[48]

The glorification of the Father and Son (theme f) (δοξάζω, δόξα, ὑψόω). 'To glorify' or 'to give glory' probably means to give praise/honour or to manifest divine presence and power.[49] The Father and Son mutually glorify one another (13.31-32; cf. 8.54; 14.13; 17.1, 4-5). For example, Jesus' completing the Father's (salvific) work and especially his being lifted up at the cross is part of his and the Father's glorification (3.14; 8.28; 12.23, 28, 32; 17.4). The Spirit-Paraclete, in turn, glorifies the Son by revealing him to the disciples (16.14). Jesus passes on to the disciples the glory that the Father gave him, so that they may be drawn and take part in this relationship of glorification between the Father and Son (17.22, 24). However, believers should also glorify the Father and Son by bearing fruit/showing discipleship (15.8; 17.10), and by praying according to Jesus' will/character in order to carry forward Jesus' work (14.13). In sum, glorification/exaltation has a soteriological dimension. First, Jesus' finishing the Father's salvific work glorifies the Father, and Jesus' salvific death is the start and part of his glorification. Second, Jesus' revealing his glory to people through his miraculous signs can evoke belief (2.11; 11.4, 45). Third, the believer is drawn and participates in the life-giving relationship of mutual glory/glorification between the Father and Son; the believer receives glory but is also expected to give glory to the Father and Son through the demonstration of discipleship.[50]

---

[47] Because τελειόω in 4.34; 5.36; 17.4 and τελέω in 19.28, 30 overlap semantically, and because ἔργον is the subject of τελειόω in 4.34; 5.36; 17.4, it seems likely that τελέω in 19.28, 30 also refers to God's work which was given to the Son to be completed.

[48] For a fuller elucidation of the salvific aspect of the theme ἔργον, see especially Riedl, *Heilswerk*. Ensor's monograph also touches on the soteriological aspect of Jesus' work (*Jesus*, 125-26, 153, 160-61, 191, 194, 221-22). Ensor, e.g., states that 'the ἔργα of Jesus include not only his miracles but also his entire ministry of life-giving and judgment, in short, the "work" which he was sent into the world to do' (*Jesus*, 222). In sapiential Judaism, Wisdom is also an associate in God's works, i.e., Wisdom has insight and is co-partner in what God is doing (Wis. 8.4; 9.9; cf. Wis. 14.5; Sir 1.9), and the primary work of God and Wisdom is to save, to give life (Wis. 16.7; 9.18; 10.4; Sir. 1.20; 2.11; 51.8, 12).

[49] Dodd, *Interpretation*, 206-207; Forestell, *Word*, 66. For a fuller elucidation of the theme 'to glorify/exalt' and 'glory', see Holwerda, *Spirit*, ch. 1; Nicholson, *Death*, 141-44, 149-51; Loader, *Christology*, 107-23; Smalley, *John*, 248-56.

[50] Thüsing elucidates more fully the themes of lifting up and glorification in relation to John's soteriology (see *Erhöhung, passim*). Ferreira also recognizes glory as a soteriological concept in John (see *Ecclesiology*, ch. 5). Glory in the Jewish wisdom literature is also a characteristic of Wisdom and God (Prov. 8.18; Wis. 7.25; 9.11; Sir. 24.1-2), and Wisdom (implicitly) glorifies God (Wis. 8.3). According to Sir. 3.3, 6 there is a direct relationship between the propitiation for sins, long life and giving glory. God's people receive glory from him (Sir. 24.12; 44.2, 7), and, in turn, people can give glory to God through humility (Sir. 3.20) and generosity (Sir. 35.7; cf. Sir. 43.30; Wis. 18.24). Moreover, there is also the concept of mutual glorification between Wisdom and her disciples (Prov. 4.8-9; Sir. 1.19; 4.13; 6.26-31; cf. Wis. 8.10; 10.14).

To partly summarize themes a-f, Jesus' soteriological journey consists of coming to, staying in, and leaving this world (via the cross). Jesus' sending into the world by God and Jesus' work/mission, which culminates at the cross, have a soteriological aim (3.14-17; 12.47; 19.28, 30). However, the sending of the Spirit-Paraclete by the Father and Son and the sending of the disciples by Jesus also have a soteriological dimension because Jesus will continue his salvific mission through the Paraclete and the disciples, and because it is the Paraclete who will sustain one's salvation (14.16-26; 15.26-27; 16.7-11; 17.18-23).[51] The underlying motivational force for Jesus' sending, and in fact for salvation itself, is love (17.23; cf. 3.16-17; 1 Jn 4.9-10). The reciprocal love between the Father and Son has soteriological implications for humanity, in that God's love for the world propelled the Son's salvific mission (3.16-17; 1 Jn 4.9-10), and in that Jesus' love for his friends is ultimately expressed in his salvific death on the cross (6.51; 15.13; 1 Jn 3.16). Besides love, the Father and Son are also characterized by truth/knowledge, life and glory. For people, knowing and understanding the true identity and work of the Father and Son and their relationship is salvific.

Jesus' revelation (theme i) (ἐξηγέομαι, ἐμφανίζω, φανερόω, γνωρίζω, ἀναγγέλλω). To reveal is to make known that which was not known before (1.18, 31; cf. 1 Jn 3.2); divine realities can only become known to people through revelation (by the Son) (1.18, 51; 3.3-5, 11-13). Negatively, the reason for Jesus' revelatory mission is to destroy the devil's work (1 Jn 3.8). Positively, Jesus' mission is to reveal the identity and work of the Father and Son, and the nature of their relationship.

According to Bultmann, Loader, Scott et al., there is little or no definable content to Jesus' revelation; he merely reveals that he is the Revealer.[52] At first sight this may be the case, but there are indicators which show there is more to it than meets the eye. Moreover, even when the term 'to reveal' does not appear the concept of revelation may still be

---

[51] The soteriological functions of the Spirit-Paraclete will be more fully elucidated in ch. 5.

[52] Bultmann, *Theology*, 2:62-66; Loader, *Christology*, 136-41, 147, 153; Scott, *Sophia*, 145; cf. Dunn, 'John', 331-32. Loader admits that there is some revelation content, namely the revelation that the Son has a unique relationship of oneness with the Father and speaks and acts for him (*Christology*, 143). Although Forestell criticizes Bultmann's 'empty' concept of revelation and attributes slightly more content to Jesus' revelation — the object of Jesus' revelation is the identity of the Father and Son and their mutual relationship — he still concludes that Jesus' revelation is primarily a communication of eternal life rather than of knowledge (*Word*, 17-57, 192). However, this seems an unnecessary distinction; we will argue that knowledge (of God and Jesus) leads to belief, and hence to life, i.e., the communication of saving knowledge *is* the communication of life.

present. First, Jesus reveals his own identity (4.25-26; 9.35-38; 20.27-28), origin and journey (8.23, 42; 16.28). The signs that Jesus performs reveal his identity (6.14; 7.31), aspects of his character (2.11), and the nature of the relationship between him and the Father (10.38; 14.11).[53] Through the seven 'I am'-sayings, their predicates and the corresponding discourses, Jesus reveals aspects of his character and of the life-giving nature of his work/mission. Second, Jesus also reveals the Father (1.18; 17.6). Jesus' testimony reveals what he has seen and heard in the Father's presence (3.11-13; 3.31-32, 34; cf. 8.28; 17.8). Jesus reveals the work of the Father (5.19; 9.3), as well as the Father's name, i.e., his being, nature, character (17.26). Jesus reveals the character/nature of the Father because anyone who knows or has seen Jesus knows or has seen the Father (8.19; 12.45; 14.7, 9).[54] Jesus can reveal the (identity, character and work of the) Father because: (i) of his intimacy with the Father, (1.18); (ii) Jesus has open access to revelation/heaven (1.51; cf. 3.12-13); (iii) Jesus reveals/communicates what he sees the Father doing and hears the Father speaking (5.19; 8.26, 28; 15.15). Third, the cross is the ultimate revelatory event, in that it reveals: (i) Jesus' identity (8.28); (ii) Jesus' glory (by virtue of the use of ὑψόω); (iii) the salvific nature of Jesus' work (3.14-15; 12.32); (iv) Jesus' love for his friends (15.13; 1 Jn 3.16); (v) God's giving and saving love (3.16).

In conclusion, contra Bultmann, Loader, Scott et al., there is more content to Jesus' revelation than the mere fact that he is the Revealer; *Jesus reveals the identity, character and mission of the Father and Son, as well as the nature of the relationship between the Father and Son.*[55] If eternal life is (the result of) the knowledge, the recognition of who the Father and Jesus are (17.3; 20.31), and if this knowledge/understanding of (the identity, nature, and work of) the Father and Son comes through revelation (1.18, 31; 17.6), then *salvation is mediated by revelation.*[56] Moreover, based on Jesus' intimate knowledge of the Father and that Jesus only reveals what he sees and hears from the Father, Jesus is not only the

---

[53] The theme 'Jesus' signs' will be more fully developed in section 4.2, below.

[54] Cf. Culpepper, *Anatomy*, 113.

[55] Willett also disagrees with Bultmann's slightly 'empty' concept of revelation, and attributes some content to it, although Willett admits that 'precisely what Jesus reveals remains a bit vague...it is a personal revelation which cannot be captured in propositions' (*Wisdom*, 81). Hamid-Khani also does not really spell out the content of Jesus' teaching/revelation after having criticized Bultmann (*Revelation*, 349-52). Carson, however, states that '[t]he demand for faith does not require a mere contentless *dass*, but belief in the highest christological propositions' (*Sovereignty*, 169).

[56] This now seems the consensus in Johannine scholarship.

mediator but also the content and locus of God's revelation.[57] Finally, the Spirit-Paraclete also has a revelatory function — to the world (16.8-11) and to the disciples (16.13-15).

Jesus' teaching (theme j) (διδάσκω, διδάσκαλος, διδαχή). Jesus' main activity is teaching (6.59; 7.14-17, 28; 8.2, 20; 18.19-20), and he is addressed as Teacher (1.38; 3.2; 8.4; 11.28; 13.13-14; 20.16). Jesus' revelatory teaching comes from God (3.34; 7.16-17), and is essentially the communication of what he sees the Father doing and of what he hears the Father speaking (see the theme 'sensory perception'). One of the main functions of the Spirit-Paraclete is also to teach (14.26; 16.12-15; cf. 1 Jn 2.27).[58]

Bultmann et al. deny any definable content to Jesus' teaching, and thus, it could be argued that John does not record so much (the content of) Jesus' teaching but rather the dialogues and discussions Jesus had. Hence, does John actually record the content of Jesus' teaching or does he merely assume/affirm *that* Jesus teaches and concentrate on Jesus' dialogues, perhaps arising out of his teaching? Can the discourses be called teaching? We argue that the answer may be affirmative for several reasons. First, at least once Jesus' public discourses are called 'teaching' (6.59-60; cf. 7.14, 28, 37). Second, the farewell discourses are Jesus' private teachings to his disciples. Third, Jesus teaches through short wisdom sayings (aphorisms) (2.19; 4.37; 7.37-38; 12.24-26; 13.16; 18.36-37). Fourth, the concept of teaching is evoked through the use of λόγος/ῥῆμα, which often denotes teaching (3.34; 8.31, 51; 10.35; 12.48; 14.23; 17.8), and frequently λόγος/ῥῆμα occurs during or shortly after a public discourse, implying a reference to teaching (4.41; 5.24, 47; 6.63; 7.40; 8.37, 47; 10.19; 12.47-48). Fifth, Jesus reveals aspects of his character and of the Father's, of the life-giving nature of his mission, and of his relationship with the Father, especially through the seven 'I am'-sayings, their predicates, and the corresponding discourses.[59] Thus, Jesus' discourses are the Johannine

---

[57] O'Day concludes that the locus of revelation is not Jesus but the text of the Fourth Gospel (*Revelation*, 89-92). However, we uphold that Jesus and his teaching are the primary locus of God's revelation, although other loci of revelation are the disciples' Spirit-informed witness (see ch. 5) and the text of the Fourth Gospel (expressing John's understanding of Jesus and his revelation).

[58] The Paraclete's anamnesis (ὑπομιμνῄσκω [14.26]) is closely related (if not an aspect of) the Paraclete's teaching (see ch. 5 section 3.3) and hence not treated as a separate theme.

[59] The predicates are the Bread of life (6.35), the Light of the world (8.12; 9.5), the Gate of the sheep pen (10.7, 9), the Good Shepherd (10.11, 14), the Resurrection and the Life (11.25), the Way, Truth and Life (14.6), the true Vine (15.1, 5). Moreover, Jesus also reveals (aspects of) the identity, mission, and relationship of himself and the Father in the discourses of Jn 3-4. For the presentation of Jesus as Wisdom in the 'I am'-

presentation of Jesus' teaching; the content of which reveals the identity and mission of the Father and Son, and the nature of their relationship (cf. the theme 'Jesus' revelation').[60]

Jesus' teaching is soteriologically orientated because: (i) revelation and teaching are inextricably linked — Jesus teaches through revelation and/or Jesus reveals through teaching (1.18; 3.12-13) — and salvation is mediated through revelation; (ii) people believe on the basis of Jesus' words or Jesus endorses this kind of belief (4.41, 48-53; 5.24; 7.40-41a; 8.30; 14.11); (iii) Jesus' teaching reveals the identity, mission and relationship of the Father and Son, and recognition or understanding of this leads to salvation; (iv) Jesus' words give life (6.63, 68); (v) in his teaching, Jesus presents himself, *inter alia*, as the source of life-giving water, the life-giving Bread, the Light of the world, the salvific Gate of the sheep pen; acceptance and understanding of these leads to life; (vi) acceptance of Jesus' teaching sets one free from sin, and hence gives life (8.31-36); (vii) Jesus' word cleanses (15.3); (viii) the disciples accepted Jesus' revelatory teaching/words and believed (17.6-8);[61] (ix) if God gave Jesus a commandment about what to speak, and if this commandment leads to life (12.49-50), then Jesus' teaching leads to life. However, Jesus' teaching can also cause offence, rejection and apostasy (6.41-42, 59-66; cf. 18.19).[62]

Further, in order to sustain one's salvation one must *continue* to adhere to Jesus' teaching. To remain (μένω) in Jesus' word/teaching is a necessary demonstration of discipleship, and leads to knowledge of the truth and freedom from sin, and hence to salvation (8.31-36). Moreover, continuous adherence to Jesus' teaching guarantees one's fellowship with the Father and Son, and hence sustains one's salvation (15.7; 2 Jn 9-10).

Jesus' encounter with and invitation to people (theme k). The Fourth Gospel records encounters of Jesus with, for example, 'the Jews', Nicodemus, the Samaritan woman, the royal official (4.43-54), the paralysed man at Bethesda and the man born blind. In these encounters Jesus presents himself as the one who will be lifted up, the source of life-giving water, the Bread of life, the Light of the world, the Gate of the sheep pen, accompanied with invitations to come, drink, eat, enter, etc. Jesus' encounter with people carries with it the intrinsic demand for a response; the person and ministry of Jesus confront people with the choice to accept or reject Jesus and his invitation. Moreover, one's destiny

---

sayings, see Scott, *Sophia*, 116-31; Willett, *Wisdom*, 86-92; Witherington, *Wisdom*, 157-58; Ringe, *Friends*, 61.

[60] Scott, who said that there was no content to Jesus' revelation, surprisingly gives content to Jesus' teaching (*Sophia*, 153).

[61] Moreover, the disciples' words (in the form of witness) may also cause other people to come to believe in Jesus (17.20).

[62] Cf. Dodd, *Interpretation*, 353; Scott, *Sophia*, 153-54.

depends on one's response to Jesus: accepting Jesus' invitation leads to eternal life/salvation, whereas rejection leads to judgment and death (3.15-18, 36; 5.24; 6.35; 9.41).[63] People's response of acceptance or rejection is part of John's soteriological dualism — light/darkness, from above/below, Spirit/flesh, God/devil as father, life/death, free/slave, truth/lie.[64]

Saving truth (theme 1) (ἀλήθεια). 'Truth' in John is very much a soteriological concept; indeed, it is 'saving truth'. Truth originates from God (8.40; cf. 17.17), and Jesus, as the source of life, is the embodiment (14.6) and dispenser of this truth (1.14, 17; 8.45-46). Jesus' life-giving teaching/word contains truth, which will set people free from sin (8.31-36; cf. Jesus speaks God's words, which are truth [3.34; 17.17]). The truth sanctifies, purifies, cleanses a person (through the word of Jesus/God) (15.3; 17.17), and this sanctification in truth is based on Jesus' sanctification, i.e., his death on the cross (17.19). Moreover, to do the truth (ὁ ποιῶν τὴν ἀλήθειαν) probably denotes something like 'to follow', 'to adhere to', 'to behave according to' the truth, and is necessary to sustain one's salvation — because if one does the truth, s/he has fellowship with God (3.21; 1 Jn 1.6-7; cf. περιπατέω ἐν ἀληθείᾳ [2 Jn 4; 3 Jn 3-4]). To remain in Jesus' word then enables one to know the truth (8.31-32), and the Spirit of truth will guide the disciples into all truth (16.13; cf. 1 Jn 5.6).[65] People are not only encouraged to know and do the truth, but also to have the truth (continuously) in them (1 Jn 1.8; 2.4; 2 Jn 2). The truth being or abiding in the believer indicates that s/he is indwelled by and in fellowship with the Father and Son (cf. 2 Jn 3).

Thus, the concept of 'saving truth' is essentially the idea that truth is the saving aspect or content of Jesus' word/teaching.[66] In this case, the reason for the life-giving dimension of Jesus' word/teaching is that it contains liberating, sanctifying, saving truth. Moreover, the *continuous* mediation of truth is needed to sustain fellowship with the Father and Son, and hence, one's salvation. Furthermore, 'truth' combines both cognitive and

---

[63] For the concept of judgment (κρίσις), see, e.g., Bultmann, *Theology*, 2:33-69; Dodd, *Interpretation*, 208-12. In John, judgment has, as salvation, an already-not yet dimension (cf. 3.18, 36 with 5.28-29; 12.48). Jesus' purpose for coming to the world was not to judge it, in the sense of condemning (3.17; 8.15; 12.47). Rather, judgment is the inevitable, immediate consequence of rejecting Jesus and his teaching; those people call judgment upon themselves. Jesus' paradoxical saying in 9.39, then, probably indicates that, although Jesus had not come for judgment, his coming divided people, and brought judgment for those who rejected him.

[64] Cf. Willett, *Wisdom*, 99-105; Bultmann, *Theology*, ch. 2 (although Bultmann of course argues that John's dualism is derived from Gnostic dualism).

[65] Cf. Dodd, *Interpretation*, 223-24.

[66] Although Hamid-Khani also elucidates the concept of 'truth', he stops short of defining it as the *saving content* of Jesus' word/teaching (*Revelation*, 340-45).

relational aspects, in that truth needs cognitively to be perceived and is, or results in, cognitive information, and this happens in relationship with the Truth (see section 3.2, below). In sum, *saving truth is the saving content of the revelation of the identity, mission and relationship of the Father and Son*, or perhaps even the saving understanding/information resulting from cognitively perceiving this revelation.[67]

Conclusion. Jesus' salvific mission is to reveal the identity and work of the Father and Son, and the nature of their relationship. Salvation (eternal life) then is the knowledge and understanding of the Father and Son, and this salvation is mediated primarily by Jesus' revelation/teaching because Jesus' revelatory teaching contains saving truth-knowledge.[68] People who encounter Jesus and his revelatory teaching need to respond — to accept or reject Jesus and his saving revelation. To sustain salvation one must continue to adhere to Jesus and his teaching.

In the Jewish wisdom literature we found a similar picture. Wisdom readily reveals herself, i.e., her character, origin and secrets, to those who seek/desire her (Prov. 1.23; 8.22-23; Wis. 6.13; Sir. 4.18; 24.1-4). Wisdom reveals God's intentions/purposes (Wis. 9.13, 17), and she can do this

---

[67] For Bultmann, the basic meaning of ἀλήθεια in John is not the teaching about God transmitted by Jesus but God's very reality revealing itself in Jesus (*Theology*, 2:18-19). Bultmann's denial of Jesus' teaching being the locus of truth is probably due to his view that there is no content to Jesus' revelation. Y. Ibuki argues that ἀλήθεια in John primarily denotes the nature of the Father, Son and Spirit, and only secondarily the content of Jesus' words (*Die Wahrheit im Johannesevangelium* [Bonn: Hanstein Verlag, 1972] 115, 310). We, however, hold together Jesus being the (embodiment of) truth and his revelation containing truth; Jesus is and brings the revelation of God. Similarly to Bultmann, Dodd argues that the dominant sense of ἀλήθεια in John is the Platonic concept of truth as (the knowledge of) eternal reality, that comes through Jesus Christ (*Interpretation*, 171-77). However, without denying possible points of contact in other literature, in our view Dodd interprets John too much through a Greek lens. Ladd criticizes Dodd and argues that the background of ἀλήθεια is the OT אֱמֶת, denoting the character of God's acts in dealing with his people, and is in John a soteriological concept, designating what God has done in Jesus (*Theology*, 300-305). I. de la Potterie argues that the background to ἀλήθεια lies in the late Jewish wisdom and apocalyptic literature, where it has the sense of revealed truth, the teaching of wisdom, and consequently, truth in John is the revelation and its content, which comes from God in the person and teaching of Jesus ('The Truth in Saint John' in J. Ashton [ed.], *The Interpretation of John* [Edinburgh: T&T Clark, 1997²] 54-57; cf. Witherington, *Wisdom*, 176-77). Although we tend to agree with de la Potterie and Ladd, we nevertheless allow ἀλήθεια is also an intellectual category (as in Greek thought), in that truth needs to be cognitively perceived and results in understanding.

[68] Knowledge, understanding and salvation can also come as a result of (perceiving) Jesus' signs (see section 4.2, below).

because of her intimacy with God (Wis. 8.4; 9.4, 9).[69] For Philo, σοφία is one of the intermediary figures that reveals God, and in the Qumran community, W/wisdom, through its association with Torah, also had a revelatory function.

Teaching is the main activity of Wisdom (and of the sages and teachers at Qumran as derivative sources of wisdom) (Prov. 1.23; 13.14; Wis. 7.21; 9.17-18; Sir. 4.11; 24.33). The concept of teaching (by Wisdom) is especially captured under the term 'instruction': in many instances παιδεία and σοφία are closely related (Prov. 1.2, 7; 8.10-11; Wis. 3.11; 6.17; Sir. 1.27; 4.17, 24; 6.18; 22.6; 23.2; 44.4), and Sirach 51.16, 26 mentions explicitly that Wisdom gives παιδεία. Wisdom's teaching is salvific, in that acceptance of and adherence to Wisdom and her revelatory teaching gives or leads to life, whereas rejection of Wisdom's teaching leads to death.

The wisdom literature also depicts Wisdom encountering and inviting people: Wisdom calls out and preaches in the streets in order that people may listen to her and accept her (Prov. 1.20-33; 8.1-36), and she invites people to her banquet to 'consume' her life-giving revelatory words/teaching (Prov. 9.1-6; Sir. 24.19-21).[70] Wisdom searches for and meets people who seek her (Wis. 6.12-25). Sapiential Judaism also knows the concept of soteriological dualism; one's destiny — life or death — depends on whether one accepts or rejects Wisdom's call/offer (Prov. 1.32-33; 8.35-36; 9.6).

In the wisdom literature, the term 'truth' is not frequently related to Wisdom/God (Prov. 8.6-8; Wis. 3.9; cf. Wis. 5.6-7; 6.22; Sir. 37.15). Philo elucidates the concept of liberating truth/wisdom; truth or wisdom leads to true freedom and friendship with God (e.g. *Prob.* 20, 40-44, 59). However, the Johannine concept of 'saving truth-knowledge' is essentially the intertestamental concept of 'saving wisdom', as the saving content of Wisdom's teaching (see ch. 2 and the theme 'cognitive perception'; cf. Prov. 23.23 and Sir. 4.24-25, where truth and wisdom are closely associated, if not identified). Only in the Qumran literature, truth (as part of the salvific nexus knowledge-wisdom-truth) is frequently used to denote the saving content of God's revelation/teaching.

---

[69] Willett also recognizes both Jesus and Wisdom as the *locus revelationis* (*Wisdom*, 83). Motyer contends that the presentation of Jesus as the Revealer draws not just on prophetic and wisdom traditions, but also on apocalyptic and 'heavenly journey' traditions (*Father*, 46).

[70] For the invitation to Wisdom's banquet and its parallel in John, see Braun, *Jean*, 4:121-23; Feuillet, 'Themes', 76-83; Willett, *Wisdom*, 87-91; Witherington, *Wisdom*, 22-23; McKinlay, *Wisdom*.

3.2. People's Perception of and Responses to Jesus[71]

Sensory perception (theme m) (βλέπω, ὁράω, θεωρέω, θεάομαι, ἀκούω). Seeing and hearing have strong soteriological overtones. To hear Jesus' teaching is to hear his life-giving words, which may lead to a recognition of his true identity (4.28-29; 5.24-25; 7.40-41a; cf. 9.35-38). To see the signs, which reveal Jesus' identity and the nature of relationship between the Father and Son, may lead to life (7.31; 11.45; 12.9-11). To look at the Son (in faith) leads to life (6.40), which denotes particularly to look at the Son lifted up on the cross to give his life for the life of the world (6.51, 62; cf. 3.14-15).[72] No one has seen God, except the Son, and hence, he can reveal God (1.18; 6.46). One can now see God in Jesus (12.45; 14.9; cf. those who sin cannot see God [1 Jn 3.6; 3 Jn 11]). To see Jesus, and in him the Father, probably denotes to recognize and understand their identity, work and relationship.[73] To see the glory of the Son and Father probably denotes to experience the manifestation of God's being, presence, and power (1.14; 11.40; 12.41; 17.24), which is salvific (cf. 2.11).[74] The climactic manifestation of divine glory is in Jesus' life-giving death on the cross (ὑψόω connotes to exalt in 3.14; cf. the theme 'the glorification of the Father and Son').

It seems, therefore, that John's usage of the categories of hearing and seeing operates on two levels — literal/physical hearing and seeing, and, based on this, cognitive or spiritual hearing and seeing, which recognizes and understands the true identity and mission of the Father and Son, and the nature of their relationship (5.24-25; 6.36, 40; 7.40-41a; 9.35-38; 10.3, 16, 27; cf. 1.29; 1 Jn 1.1-3; 2.24; cf. Jesus' perception of Nathanael, Nathanael's belief-response and Jesus' promise to Nathanael to see heaven opened [1.47-51]). People come to true understanding of the Father and Son, and hence salvation, through sensory and cognitive perception (cf. to 'see' heaven opened [1.51], to 'see' the kingdom of God [3.3] and to 'see' life [3.36] denoting the access to it through adequate perception). Some

---

[71] For the definitions of 'sensory perception', 'cognitive perception' and 'understanding', see ch. 1 section 3.

[72] Jn 3.14-15 evokes Num. 21.8-9, where those who looked (in faith) at the snake lifted up were saved (cf. Wis. 16.6-7). This seeing of the Son on the cross is at the same time the demonstration of God's salvific love for the world (3.16).

[73] John's concept of 'seeing' God probably does not refer to (or criticize) some sort of mysticism/apocalypticism because John does not seem to mention people undertaking heavenly journeys to catch a vision of God, preparatory ascetic practices or an angelic entourage. Moreover, one can now see God in the person of Jesus, which makes heavenly visions/journeys (if John refers to these at all) redundant.

[74] Cf. Dodd, *Interpretation*, 206-207. Jn 11.40 need not contradict the understanding that to see God's glory results in belief, but rather shows that seeing God's glory and belief are closely interrelated and evoke one another.

people, however, will not come further than the sensory perception and/or find what they see and hear too offensive (6.36, 41, 60-61, 66; 7.41-42; 8.43, 47; 9.39-41; 10.20). Seeing the signs can also happen at two levels; adequate sight is recognizing the true significance of Jesus' miraculous works followed by an adequate faith-response (4.48; 6.14; 11.45; 12.9-11), but true spiritual sight does not necessarily follow from literal sight (6.2, 36; 12.37-40; 15.24; cf. 2.23).

In conclusion, 'seeing and hearing' does not automatically lead to salvation. Sensory perception (hearing and seeing) should be followed by cognitive or spiritual perception (a recognition and understanding of the spiritual reality or significance of what is seen and heard) and result in an adequate response (believing) in order to give life.[75] This concept of a two-level seeing and hearing — the cognitive perception of the identity and work of the Father and Son, and their relationship, as the result of sensory perception — is confirmed by the semantic domain of βλέπω, ὁράω, θεωρέω, θεάομαι and ἀκούω, which allows for a connotative meaning of 'to come to understand'.[76]

It must be noted that Jesus reveals, communicates, does, speaks only what he has seen in the Father's presence and heard from the Father (5.19-20; 8.26-28, 38; 14.24; 15.15).[77] Jesus speaks God's words (3.34), and testifies to what he has seen and heard (in God's presence) (3.31-32; cf. 3.12-13). How is this possible? First, Jesus has an intimate relationship with the Father, and hence, it seems likely that during his earthly ministry Jesus was continuously in communication with his Father.[78] Second, Jesus has open access to the heavenly realm (1.51; 3.12). Third, Jesus received the Spirit as an empowerment for his salvific ministry (1.32-33; see ch. 4 section 2), and if the Spirit functioned in Judaism as the channel of communication between God and people (see ch. 2), then the Spirit might also have functioned as the link/mode of communication between the Father and Jesus.

---

[75] Cf. Bultmann, who argues that faith proceeds from hearing and seeing as a sense-perception, although he can also see believing as parallel or identical to hearing and seeing, in as far 'hearing' and 'seeing' denote faith-perception (*Theology*, 2:71-73). However, we maintain a distinction between sensory and cognitive perception (the latter is similar to Bultmann's faith-perception), as well as between cognitive perception and belief, in that cognitive perception is the basis for, but not identical with, belief.

[76] Cf. the Louw-Nida lexicon.

[77] This confirms the concept of Jesus' mission of finishing the Father's work (see the theme 'Jesus' work'), and also shows Jesus' obedience and faithfulness to and dependence on the Father, which is paradigmatic for the believers' total dependence on Jesus (15.5).

[78] There is not only communication from the Father to the Son, but also vice versa (11.40-41; 12.27-30; 17.1-26).

Thus, John may have understood that during his earthly ministry Jesus was continuously in communication with his Father — through the Spirit — in which Jesus received information concerning what to do, speak, reveal, etc., rather than a scenario in which, prior to the incarnation, the Son and the Father 'sat around the table' and talked through in great detail everything the Son was about to do in his mission on earth.[79] Similarly, the Spirit-Paraclete will only speak and reveal what he hears (from Jesus) (16.13-15).

Cognitive perception (theme n) (γινώσκω, οἶδα). The verbs γινώσκω and οἶδα can just mean 'to know, to have knowledge of', but in John, they frequently denote 'to understand', 'to perceive' (e.g. 1.48; 2.25; 5.42; 6.15; 8.43; 13.12; 17.3; 20.9; 21.17).[80] The primary *content* of γινώσκω and οἶδα is: (i) Jesus and the Father (10.4, 14; 14.7; 17.3); (ii) Jesus' identity (3.2; 4.42; 6.69; 16.30; 17.8);[81] (iii) Jesus' teaching and its origin (7.17; 8.43; 15.15; 17.7); (iv) the work of the Father and Son (8.28; 13.12; 17.7-8; 1 Jn 3.16);[82] (v) the nature of the relationship between the Father and Son (10.38; 14.20, 31; 17.7); (vi) the truth, which encompasses the revelation of the identity and work of the Father and Son, and their mutual

---

[79] Cf. Bultmann, *John*, 105-106. See also van der Watt (*Family*, 272-77), although he does not explain how the communication between Jesus and the Father was possible; namely, through the Spirit. Although Ensor mentions that Jesus is being 'assisted' in carrying out God's work, he explains this in terms of the Father himself acting in and through Jesus (*Jesus*, 284-89). Loader argues that what the Son has seen and heard from the Father refers to the received revelation in his pre-existence rather than to his time on earth (*Christology*, 148-54). Loader partly comes to this position because he wants to do justice to the concept of space-time. Other reasons might be that, according to Loader, Jesus' revelation lacks content, so that a continuous reception of information from the Father is deemed unnecessary, and that Loader's Jesus as the revealer-envoy is in no need of the Spirit. However, this would not do sufficient justice to the present dimension of Jesus' communication with the Father. Moreover, if only Loader had recognized the significance of the Spirit upon Jesus, he would have seen the possibility of the Spirit functioning as the channel of communication between the Father in heaven and Jesus on earth, and hence that it was the Spirit, rather than Jesus, who possibly transcended the space-time dimension. Nevertheless, we do not exclude the possibility that Jesus came to earth with previous, pre-existent knowledge of himself and his Father.

[80] Cf. the semantic domains of γινώσκω and οἶδα in the Louw-Nida lexicon. John does not differentiate between these two verbs (contra I. de la Potterie, 'Οἶδα et γινώσκω: Les deux modes de la connaissance dans le quatrième évangile', *Bib* 40 [1959] 709-25).

[81] The concept of understanding Jesus' true identity is sometimes also indicated by symbolic actions, such as the Samaritan woman's leaving her water jar (4.28), acts of worship (9.35-38; 12.3; 21.27-28), and possibly Nicodemus' giving Jesus a king's burial (19.39).

[82] The cross is a climactic event of knowledge because it reveals God's salvific love for the world (3.16), and Jesus' identity and co-mission with the Father (8.28). After the cross more knowing/understanding will follow (12.16; 13.7; 14.20; cf. 14.26; 16.13).

relationship (8.32; 1 Jn 2.21).[83] The *basis* of γινώσκω and οἶδα is sensory perception, i.e., people know/understand on the basis of seeing signs, seeing the Father (in Jesus), seeing the Son lifted up, hearing Jesus' words/teaching (3.2; 4.42; 6.68-69; 8.28, 43; 10.38; 14.7-9; 16.29-30; 17.6-8).[84] Thus, γινώσκω and οἶδα in John primarily denote 'to understand', and connote *cognitive perception* of the truth on the basis of sensory perception, i.e., the cognitive penetration of the deeper, spiritual significance of what has been heard and seen, resulting in an adequate understanding of the Father and Son.

However, not everyone comes to this cognitive perception; the world, including 'the Jews', does not know/understand Jesus and his teaching, nor do its people know the Father (1.10; 7.27-28; 8.14, 19, 27, 43, 55; 10.6; 16.3) or the Spirit (14.17), despite their claim that they possess knowledge of Jesus (6.42; 7.27) and of eternal life (5.39). Neither is all cognitive perception sufficient nor does it result in an adequate understanding. Nicodemus came to some cognitive perception of Jesus' identity on the basis of Jesus' signs (3.2), but his understanding was apparently not yet sufficient as the rest of the pericope indicates (cf. 2.23-25). However, Nicodemus' giving Jesus a royal burial (19.39) might indicate that he had later acquired saving understanding.[85] After another one of Jesus' signs, people came to some sort of cognitive perception of Jesus' identity, but the subsequent discourse shows that people's understanding was not adequate, and in the final analysis, many found Jesus' teaching offensive and deserted him (6.60, 66). Although the disciples apparently had an adequate understanding and belief, they often did not perceive cognitively everything Jesus had tried to teach them (14.5-9; 16.17-18; 20.9; cf. 6.5-7). It seems the work of the Spirit-Paraclete to bring the disciples to a higher level of cognitive perception (14.26; 16.12-15), which would trigger off, for example, further, continuous belief (2.22).

---

[83] Hence, Dodd can call ἀλήθεια the object of γινώσκω (*Interpretation*, 170).

[84] Dodd, however, equates knowing with seeing (*Interpretation*, 165-67). The *mode* of γινώσκω and οἶδα is revelation, i.e., an adequate knowing and understanding of the Father and Son comes by revelation (1.33; 15.15; cf. the revelatory connotation of γνωρίζω).

[85] Cf. Bultmann, *Gospel*, 680; Stibbe, *John*, 197. The amount of spices Nicodemus used in 19.39 was an amount typically used for kings, and hence it is at least possible (if not likely) that Nicodemus had perceived something of Jesus' significance (NB the emphasis on Jesus as King and his kingdom in Jn 18-19). Moreover, in 7.50-52, Nicodemus took a positive stance towards Jesus in the face of criticism/ridicule from his fellow religious leaders. Hence, it is possible to argue that Nicodemus gradually developed a more positive attitude towards Jesus, indicating cognitive progression in his understanding of the significance of Jesus and his work.

Γινώσκω and οἶδα have strong soteriological connotations, in that the cognitive perception of the identity and mission of the Father and Son, and their relationship is necessary to come into a saving relationship with the Father and Son.[86] Moreover, a *continuous* knowing and understanding of the Father and Son is needed to *remain* in this life-giving relationship (this is possibly also indicated by the aorist and present subjunctive of γινώσκω in 10.38 [cf. 15.7; 17.3; 20.31]). Furthermore, the relationship between the Father and Son is one of life, love, glory and knowledge/truth, in which the believer participates (see the theme 'people's response'). Consequently, the knowledge generated, received or made accessible in this relationship with the Father and Son is probably also precisely the knowledge needed to sustain the believer's relationship with the Father and Son.

This concept of the need for continuous knowledge can be explained as follows. The knowledge available to the believer in her/his relationship with the Father and Son forms the basis on which the believer can know the will of the Father and Son, be obedient to Jesus' commandments, and thus demonstrate discipleship (cf. 7.17; 8.31-32; 10.4; 13.17; 15.15; 15.27-16.4; cf. Jesus' obedience because he knows the Father [8.55; cf. 2.24-25; 13.1; 18.4]). This display of discipleship based on knowledge, guarantees and sustains the believer's participation in the relationship with the Father and Son, and subsequently guarantees to the believer the access to further knowledge, which is necessary to remain in salvation (cf. 1 Jn 2.3-6; 4.7).[87]

Thus, there is a *perpetual* flow of life, love, glory and knowledge/truth between the Father, Son and the believer (cf. 10.14-15; 14.20). Moreover, because γινώσκω and οἶδα form such an important soteriological category, we can label this concept of the cognitive perception of truth as 'saving knowledge'. 'Saving knowledge' can then be defined as *the saving content of what has been cognitively retrieved from what has been heard and seen*, or perhaps even as the saving understanding that results from cognitive and sensory perception. Hence, 'saving knowledge' is synonymous with 'saving truth'.[88]

Another significant observation is that γινώσκω and οἶδα have, besides a cognitive aspect, also a *relational* aspect. First, a continuous

---

[86] Willett only elaborates the concept of knowledge as expressing the intimate relationship between the Father and Son, but does not mention the saving aspect of knowledge (*Wisdom*, 70-75).

[87] The demonstration of discipleship may also produce or result in saving knowledge/understanding for the world (13.35; 17.23).

[88] The locus of cognitive perception is ἡ διάνοια, the mind, i.e., the faculty of understanding, reasoning, thinking, deciding, etc., so that a person is able to know and understand the Father and Son (1 Jn 5.20; cf. ch. 2). The locus of saving knowledge is Jesus' revelatory teaching (cf. Barton, *Spirituality*, 124).

knowing/understanding, necessary to sustain one's relationship with the Father and Son, occurs in relationship with the Father and Son. Second, knowledge/understanding is one of the characteristics which make up the intimate relationship between the Father and Son in which the believer partakes (see the theme 'the intimate relationship...').[89]

An important issue that still needs to be explained is *how* the believer can have access to this knowledge, or *how* this knowledge is mediated to the person. Tentatively, we suggest that the Spirit plays a role in this, although such an understanding comes mainly from the Epistles rather than from the Gospel. First, the believer seems to have knowledge because of the 'anointing', which probably refers to the Spirit (1 Jn 2.20, 27). This would tie in with our observation that the Spirit-Paraclete will teach and guide believers into all truth (14.26; 16.13). Further, the Spirit given to the believer is or gives the knowledge that a person is in a saving relationship with the Father and Son (1 Jn 3.24; 4.13; cf. 14.20). Moreover, the believer knows the Spirit (1 Jn 4.2, 6; cf. the disciples already knew the Paraclete as the Spirit of T/truth [14.17]). However, these explanations are somewhat vague and do not satisfactorily answer the question. Hence, all that can be said at this point is that *a* function of the Spirit-Paraclete will be to bring the believer to a higher level of cognitive perception and understanding.

People's response (theme o) (πιστεύω, [παρα]λαμβάνω). The theme of believing constitutes people's response to Jesus and his revelation.[90] Most belief-responses are expressed by the term πιστεύω (although it does not

---

[89] Cf. Dodd, who argues that γινώσκω in John has a cognitive aspect — derived from the Greek concept that to know God is to contemplate from a distance the ultimate reality in its changeless essence — and a relational aspect — the Hebrew concept that to know God is to experience God in his dealings with people in time (*Interpretation*, 152-53; cf. Brown, *Gospel*, 1:508; Barrett, *Gospel*, 82, 162, 504; Schnackenburg, *Gospel*, 1:565-66). Ladd, however, decides that the background to the Johannine concept of knowing is not to be found in Greek thought — knowledge being the apprehension of ultimate reality/God by the mind either through reason or through direct intuition and inner illumination — but in Hebrew thought, where knowledge involves relationship, fellowship, experience (*Theology*, 296-99). We, however, uphold (with Dodd et al.) that John combines elements of Greek and Hebrew thought, though in a qualified way: (i) John's 'vision of God' is neither ecstatic nor mystical; God can be 'seen' and encountered in a historical person; (ii) knowledge of God is mediated through the person and revelatory teaching of Jesus. Thus, John's concept of knowledge is revealed, historical information of God that illumines the mind and results in a new understanding of God, and subsequently brings one into an intimate relationship with God. Moreover, discussion whether John's thinking was influenced by either Greek or Hebrew thought might be misleading since first-century Judaism had been permeated (to various extents) by Hellenism for about 400 years.

[90] Cf. Schnackenburg, *Gospel*, 1:560.

always denote an adequate belief-response [2.23-25; 8.31]),[91] but sometimes also by λαμβάνω (1.12; 17.8; cf. 1.11; 3.11, 32; 12.48), by a recognition of Jesus' identity (e.g. 9.35-38; 20.28), or by deduction from certain actions (e.g., the Samaritan woman's successful witness to her fellow people, and possibly Nicodemus' giving Jesus a royal burial [19.39; cf. n.85, above]).

The Fourth Gospel presents a spectrum of various responses to Jesus and his revelation/teaching, but people ultimately either accept or reject Jesus and his revelation (1.11-12; cf. 3.18, 36) (cf. the theme 'Jesus' encounter with...').[92] The purpose of Jesus' coming is that people might come to believe, to have faith in Jesus, in order to have eternal life (1.7, 12; 20.31). To believe in Jesus, which is to believe in God (12.44; cf. 14.1), results in new birth and in being drawn in a saving relationship with the Father and Son (1.12-13; 3.5; 17.20-21; see also the theme 'the intimate relationship...'). The object of πιστεύω can be Jesus (e.g. 2.11; 3.15-16, 18, 36), the Father (5.24; 12.44; 14.1), Jesus' name (1.12; 3.18), Jesus' word (2.22; 4.50) or Jesus' signs (10.38; 14.11).

What constitutes an adequate faith-response, i.e., what kind of belief is sufficient for salvation? First, a belief that recognizes and understands the true identity of Jesus (e.g. 1.49-50; 4.39-42; 6.69; 9.38; 11.25-27; 20.28, 31) and that Jesus has come from and is sent by God (11.42; 17.3, 8). Second, a belief that understands the mission/work of the Father and the Son, especially that of the cross. Third, a recognition and understanding of the character of the relationship between the Father and Son (10.38; 14.10-11; 17.3). *'Adequate' belief, then, is an authentic belief-response to Jesus based on a true understanding that is sufficient to bring a person into a saving relationship with the Father and Son.*[93]

The *basis* for such belief can be: (i) Jesus' revelatory word/teaching (1.50; 2.22; 3.12, 34-36; 4.41-42, 50, 53; 5.24; 6.68-69; 8.30; 9.35-38; 14.10-11; 16.29-30; 17.8); (ii) the witness of people or Scripture to Jesus

---

[91] Looking at the various Johannine usages of πιστεύω — πιστεύω followed by εἰς with the accusative, πιστεύω with a ὅτι-clause, πιστεύω with the dative, the absolute use of πιστεύω — all forms can express an adequate faith-response, which prevents us from attaching different meanings to the different occurrences of πιστεύω or from distinguishing too sharply between them (contra Dodd, *Interpretation*, 182-86; Brown, *Gospel*, 1:512-13; Schnackenburg, *Gospel*, 1:559-63; Kysar, *John*, 93; Painter, *Quest*, 385-88; Hamid-Khani, *Revelation*, 373 n.167).

[92] For a taxonomy of belief-responses, see, e.g., Culpepper, *Anatomy*, 146-48.

[93] We will not attempt to probe further into the issue *when* exactly a person's understanding or belief is adequate. Moreover, although we contend that, e.g., children and the mentally retarded can attain adequate belief, it is beyond the scope of this study to analyze (if this is at all possible) the intellectual capacity or exact level of cognitive activity that is necessary for such belief-response.

(1.7; 4.39; 5.46; 10.41-42; 17.20-21; 19.35; 20.31); (iii) signs (2.11; 7.31; 10.37-38; 11.45; 12.11; 14.11; possibly 4.48); (iv) other sensory and cognitive perception, such as 'seeing the Son', especially as the one who was lifted up on the cross (3.14-15; 6.40, 62; 20.8, 27-28).[94] The *benefits* of adequate belief are: (i) eternal life; (ii) reception of the Spirit-Paraclete; (iii) becoming a child of God and part of his family (1.12-13; 8.35); (iv) being set free from sin, no darkness, no condemnation or wrath of God (3.18, 36; 8.12, 31-36; 12.46); (v) friendship, relationship, (comm)union, fellowship with the Father and Son, and all the benefits that brings (see the theme 'the intimate relationship...').[95]

However, not all belief-responses can be designated as 'adequate'.[96] In 2.23-25 it becomes clear that Jesus was at least suspicious about the kind of belief-response the people had made (the δέ...οὐ πιστεύω in 2.24 stands in contrast to the πιστεύω in 2.23). Further, a group of Jews who 'believed in' Jesus (8.30-31) are depicted as still enslaved to sin, children of the devil, and not belonging to God (8.31-59). The Fourth Gospel also mentions numerous reasons why some people reject or do not believe in Jesus: (i) Jesus speaks the truth but his teaching is too offensive or demanding (6.41, 60-66; 8.45); (ii) people remain stuck at the level of sensory perception; (iii) people's eyes are blinded and their hearts are hardened, i.e., their minds are closed for cognitive perception and understanding (12.39-40);[97] (iv) people do not belong to Jesus' flock (10.26); (v) they prefer to accept glory from people (5.44);[98] (vi) they are bound by sin which is virtually or primarily described as unbelief (8.24, 34-35; 16.9).[99] Interestingly, John does not explicitly mention that people do not believe because people have not been given/drawn by the Father to

---

[94] Frequently, however, the basis for belief is not mentioned (1.12; 6.29; 12.42; 14.1).

[95] Most of these benefits only become (fully) available after the cross (see sections 4 and 7, below).

[96] Cf. not all cognitive perception results in adequate understanding (in which 'adequate' knowing/understanding is an authentic understanding of God and Jesus that is sufficient to make an adequate belief-response).

[97] Jn 12.39-40 is probably not a description of the *general* condition of people (although lack of perception and incomprehension of divine reality is a general condition of humankind), but, more specifically, the condition of those who *oppose* Jesus. Moreover, 12.39-40 may simply refer to the resulting condition and inevitable consequence of rejecting Jesus rather than the result of divine predestination: by rejecting Jesus one *remains* blind (cf. 9.39-41). For a more substantial explanation of people's incomprehension, see Hamid-Khani, *Revelation*, 296-324.

[98] Hence, the belief of the many rulers does not seem adequate (12.42-43).

[99] Van der Watt defines sin in John as 'the existential position of guilt and alienation from God' (*Family*, 324). For a comprehensive treatment of the concept of sin in the Fourth Gospel, see R. Metzner, *Das Verständnis der Sünde im Johannesevangelium* (WUNT 122; Tübingen: Mohr Siebeck, 2000).

Jesus (*theme g*).[100] What John does say is that Jesus knew from the beginning those who would not believe in him because he knew what was in a person (2.24-25; 6.64). Thus, the main (and perhaps only) reason for people's unbelief appears to be found in people themselves (cf. 3.19-20).

What comes first, believing or knowing? It could be argued that, according to 10.38, belief results in knowledge (cf. 1 Jn 5.13), whereas 4.42 and 16.30 seem to say that belief follows knowledge, and in 6.69 'knowing' and 'believing' are put at the same level. It seems that John expresses both aspects: knowing facilitates or results in believing, and, if believing brings one into a relationship with God, then believing facilitates access to further knowledge of God, which in turn is necessary for further belief.[101]

Conclusion. We are now able to see some sequence or pattern in what may lead to life/salvation. Based on *sensory perception* (the literal/physical hearing of Jesus' words/teaching and seeing of his signs) a person comes to *cognitive perception* (the cognitive penetration of the deeper, spiritual significance of what has been heard and seen, resulting in an adequate understanding). This new understanding enables the person to make an *adequate belief-response*, which in turn results in a new birth and

---

[100] People can only come to Jesus (and hence find life) when the Father draws (ἕλκω) or gives (δίδωμι) them (5.40; 6.35, 44, 65; 17.9), and no one can snatch them out of the hands of the Father and Son (10.28-29). It is the Father's will that Jesus shall lose none of all those whom he has given Jesus (6.37-39), and that the Son gives eternal life to all of these (17.2, 6). Jesus guarded those the Father gave him, except Judas (17.12; cf. 18.9). This ties in with Jesus' knowledge; Jesus knew from the beginning those who would not believe in him because he knew what was in a person (2.24-25; 6.64) and he knew who would betray him (13.11; 18.9). Finally, at the cross Jesus will draw everyone to himself (12.32), implying the universal scope of his life-giving death (cf. 'the Greeks' in 12.20). This concept of the Father's drawing and giving of people shows that the initiative for salvation lies with God and not with humankind; it is the Father who *enables* people to come to (believe in) Jesus, and it is Jesus who gives them eternal life and *keeps* them in relationship with himself and the Father. For the concept of divine determinism or election, and the consequent tension with human free will and responsibility, see Carson, 'Predestination', ch. 5; cf. Bultmann, *Theology*, 2:21-26; Kysar, *John*, 70-74. Kysar calls this divine drawing/giving the first stage of faith — the openness to faith or embryonic faith (*John*, 85, 95-96).

[101] Although Bultmann states that the normal movement is from πιστεύω to γινώσκω ('Γινώσκω', I:712-13), what he probably means is that only in cases where πιστεύω means a first turning toward Jesus, not yet developed into full faith, can γινώσκω be distinguished from πιστεύω as a distinct act (cf. *Theology*, 2:74). Nevertheless, we think the 'normal' movement is from γινώσκω to πιστεύω. Hultgren, saying that 'faith leads to understanding and becomes knowledge', seems to have misunderstood Bultmann (*Christ*, 151).

being drawn into a life-giving relationship with the Father and Son.[102] An important question still to be answered, however, is *how* a person comes from sensory to cognitive perception, i.e., how a person recognizes and understands the true identity and work of the Father and Son, and their relationship.

In order to maintain this life/salvation, a person needs to *continue* to believe (cf. 20.31), and this need for faithfulness is essentially the need for a continuous demonstration of discipleship. In 2.22 we probably find a good example of a continuous belief-response: the belief of the disciples based on μιμνήσκομαι is probably the result of the Paraclete's ὑπομιμνήσκειν (14.26). Thus, adequate belief is an *initial* sufficient belief-response that is then sustained in discipleship. Moreover, πιστεύω has a cognitive and relational aspect. Cognitive, in that πιστεύω is based on and integrates/incorporates the cognitive perception of the Father and Son, and hence it is an *understanding belief*.[103] Relational, in that πιστεύω results in being drawn into a saving relationship with the Father and Son.[104]

---

[102] The concept of sensory perception→cognitive perception→adequate belief is of enormous importance: any (or more) of the nine words that make up this concept (ἀλήθεια, βλέπω, ὁράω, θεωρέω, θεάομαι, ἀκούω, γινώσκω, οἶδα, πιστεύω), occur in about 38% of the verses in the Johannine literature, and together account for approximately 39% of the entire Johannine soteriological vocabulary we examined (see appendices 1-2). Although we disagree with Kysar's stages of faith, he comes close to our position: seeing and hearing are the necessary prerequisites for believing and 'faith is a result...of understanding experience. One tries to grasp the meaning of...what is seen, heard, experienced' (*John*, 89). Despite the fact that Painter makes too much of the various uses of πιστεύω, he points in the right direction when he argues that πιστεύω followed by a ὅτι clause, and often used with verbs of seeing, hearing, and knowing, expresses the perception, recognition, understanding of authentic faith (*Quest*, 387-88). Unfortunately, according to Painter, this was only possible after Jesus' glorification (*Quest*, 414-15). Dodd does not make sufficient distinction between the concepts of believing, seeing, and knowing: 'faith therefore is the equivalent of the life-giving vision, or knowledge, of God' (*Interpretation*, 186; cf. 165-68, 185). Willett also does not distinguish sharply enough between sensory perception and belief (*Wisdom*, 82). Hamid-Khani argues that faith leads to spiritual perception. For example, he states that '[t]he movement from superficial understanding to spiritual perception ultimately takes place by faith' (*Revelation*, 373; cf. those mentioned in n.101, above), whereas we argue that faith occurs *on the basis of* spiritual perception. Hamid-Khani also says that 'people must believe in Jesus *in order to* perceive his identity and his words' (*Revelation*, 374 [my emphasis]), whereas in our understanding people must perceive Jesus' identity and words in order to believe. Nevertheless, continuous belief guarantees one's relationship with God and hence access to further spiritual perception.

[103] Although πιστεύω and γινώσκω are two distinct concepts, they are closely and inseparably related, in that πιστεύω is based on γινώσκω/οἶδα and integrates/absorbs the content of γινώσκω/οἶδα, but not vice versa (unless in the sense that adequate belief leads to a saving relationship with God, which gives access to further knowledge). See also Bultmann's concept of 'knowing faith', which denotes that γινώσκω is a constitutive

In the intertestamental wisdom literature, this concept of sensory perception leading to cognitive perception and understanding is well attested. In Philo, sensory perception leads to cognitive perception and to knowledge of God('s existence),[105] and the Qumran literature also expresses the concept of the acquisition of wisdom and understanding through sensory and cognitive perception, so that one may find life. Proverbs, Sirach and Wisdom of Solomon depict an unequivocal interplay between Wisdom and people.[106] Wisdom encounters people (she searches, calls out, tests, etc.), and invites them to accept her and her teaching, and essentially to enter into a relationship with her. The first step towards this is people's sensory perception of Wisdom's teaching/instruction, followed by a cognitive perception of what is perceived at a sensory level. Wisdom possesses wisdom/knowledge that she wants to dispense to people. This wisdom/knowledge, which is perceived cognitively (denoted by γινώσκω, οἶδα, νοέω), is or results in knowledge/understanding of God and Wisdom. Based on the acquired wisdom and understanding, people then make a response to Wisdom and her teaching — acceptance or rejection — which results either in 'salvation' (a long, blessed life [Prov., Sir.] or immortality [Wis.]) or in disaster and death.

Hence, we introduced the concept of 'saving wisdom-knowledge', in which saving wisdom-knowledge is either the saving content of Wisdom's teaching/instruction that is cognitively retrieved through sensory perception, or the saving understanding (of God and Wisdom) resulting from cognitive perception. This process also has a relational aspect, in that wisdom/knowledge/understanding is acquired within a relationship with Wisdom. People's response to Wisdom is a common feature at least in Proverbs, Sirach and Wisdom of Solomon, but, in contrast to the Fourth

---

element or structural aspect in πιστεύω ('Γινώσκω', I:713; *Theology*, 2:73-74; *Gospel*, 435 n.4; cf. Braun, *Jean*, 2:134; Schnackenburg, *Gospel*, 1:565; Kümmel, *Theology*, 304-306; Ladd, *Theology*, 313). However, we disagree with Bultmann that the knowledgeable content/aspect of faith is merely the re-cognition and (ac)knowledge(ment) that Jesus is the Revealer. Moreover, Bultmann seems in practice not to distinguish sufficiently between πιστεύω and γινώσκω; he can talk about 'knowing faith' and 'believing knowledge' (*Theology*, 2:73-74). Loader (*Christology*, 142) and Kysar (*John*, 91) do not distinguish sharply enough either between belief and knowledge.

[104] One could possibly also argue from syntax that πιστεύω expresses both aspects: πιστεύω εἰς indicates the relational aspect and πιστεύω ὅτι denotes the cognitive aspect, although it must be said that both aspects can also be expressed by other constructions of πιστεύω.

[105] Philo's concept of 'seeing', however, differs from that of John: (i) Philo's seeing of God in his Logos is philosophical, and does not refer to a historical person with whom fellowship is possible; (ii) sometimes Philo means by 'seeing' God the deification of the holy soul (Kanagaraj, *'Mysticism'*, 218-19).

[106] See ch. 2 for the different nuances between Prov., Sir. and Wis.

Gospel, the wisdom literature does not really use πιστεύω to denote a belief-response to Wisdom.[107]

3.3. People in Relationship with the Father and Son

Divine 'birth' (theme p) (γεννάω). Those people who accept/receive, i.e., believe in, Jesus are born of God, and hence born into a relationship with God, into the family of God (1.12-13; 1 Jn 2.29; 3.9-10; 4.7; 5.1; cf. 12.36). John 3.3, 5 elucidates this birth from God as a birth from the Spirit, which is the prerequisite for entry into the kingdom of God. People need to undergo a new birth in order to see/enter the kingdom of God, and hence, a new birth of the Spirit is a soteriological necessity (see ch. 4 section 3.1). Related to this is the question of one's origin — from below or above (3.31) — and of one's parenthood — God as father (1.13) or the devil (8.44; cf. 8.31-47).

The intimate relationship of the believer with the Father and Son (theme q) (κοινωνία, φίλος, ἐν εἶναι, 'x [μένει] ἐν y'). The relationship between the Father and Son is one of intimacy (1.1-2, 18; 10.30, 38; 14.10-11; 17.21-22), mutual love (3.35; 5.20; 14.31; 15.9), mutual knowledge (10.15, 8.55), one will (4.34), life (5.21, 26), truth (14.6; 17.17) and mutual glory/glorification (17.1-5).[108] This intimate relationship of love, life, knowledge/truth and glory between Father and Son is not exclusive; believers are drawn, have a share and partake in this saving relationship.[109] In this sense, the relationship between the Father and Son is not only paradigmatic but also *constitutional* for the relationship between the believer and the Father and Son. In relating to Jesus a person relates to the Father (14.7-9), so that s/he has a relationship with the Father (through Jesus) (1.12-13). Knowing, recognizing, and understanding the identity, mission and relationship of the Father and Son is salvific (17.3; 20.31), in that this enables one to make an adequate belief-response and to take part in this divine relationship of life, love, knowledge/truth and glory (1 Jn calls this participation 'κοινωνία with the Father and Son').[110] The *benefits* of being in a saving relationship with the Father and Son, then, are

---

[107] Only Sir. 4.16 and 34.8 indicate some relationship between (ἐμ)πιστεύω and Wisdom. Occasionally, the object of πιστεύω (and its derivatives), or its partial synonym πείθω, is God (e.g. Prov. 3.5; 16.20; 28.25; 29.25; Sir. 2.6, 8; 11.21; 32.24; Wis. 3.9; 12.2; 16.24, 26).

[108] Cf. Dodd, *Interpretation*, 194-95, 262. See also Loader, *Christology*, 155-73; Scott, *Sophia*, 140-42; Willett, *Wisdom*, 67-80.

[109] Cf. Willett, *Wisdom*, 105-25; Barton, *Spirituality*, 115.

[110] Turner arrives independently of us at a similar concept when he argues that κοινωνία with the Father and Son means 'the mutual sharing of believers in a personal *communion* with the Father and the Son, who *are* truth, love, light and life' ('Churches' [author's emphasis]).

essentially those things which characterize the Father and Son and their relationship: love (14.21; 16.27), life (3.15-16, 36), knowledge (14.7; 17.3), glory (17.22), peace (14.27; 20.19, 21, 26), joy (15.11; 17.13), truth (8.32; 16.13), the Spirit-Paraclete (7.38-39; 14.16, 26; 15.26), authority to forgive (20.23), friendship (15.13-15).[111]

This concept of intimacy (between the Father and Son, and between them and the believer) is also expressed in various other ways. First, in the oneness-language (10.30; 17.11, 21-23).[112] The oneness in relationship between the Father and Son is the basis or paradigm for the unity among the believers (17.11, 21-22).[113] Second, in the mutual indwelling-language: the formula 'x (μένει) ἐν y' is a relational metaphor for a (saving) relationship of mutual indwelling between persons 'x' and 'y', in which either 'x' or 'y' represents Jesus (e.g. 10.38; 14.10-11, 20; 17.21, 23). The phrase denotes the mutual indwelling of the Father and Son (and the believer), and are not statements about ontology but about intimate relationship.[114] The indwelling presence of the Father and Son in the believer (ποιέω μονή) is guaranteed by a demonstration of discipleship, i.e., love for Jesus and obedience to Jesus' teaching (14.23).[115] Third, in the flock and vine metaphor (10.16 [cf. Ezek. 34; Sir. 18.13 for God as shepherd]; 15.1-8 [cf. Sir. 24.17, 19]), which are not statements of ontology either but also of close relationship and unity (10.30; 17.11, 21-22). Fourth, Jesus' intimate relationship with his disciples is also characterized as one of friendship (15.13-15), which is based on knowledge of the Father('s doings), as revealed by Jesus (15.15).

---

[111] Cf. Willett, *Wisdom*, 105-25. Most of these benefits only become (fully) available after the cross. Bultmann calls this saving relationship between the believer and the Father and Son 'eschatological existence' (*Theology*, 2:78-88).

[112] The oneness between the believer, Father and Son should not be related to Hellenistic mysticism in which the person is deified. Appold also draws out the soteriological aspect of the oneness motif (*Motif*, 274-75, 284-85).

[113] Cf. Dodd, *Interpretation*, 195-96. The concept of unity is given rather than achieved, i.e., the people of God are one *because* of their unity with the Father and Son. Hence, people's responsibility is to maintain this existing unity (cf. 17.11, 21-22, which probably means 'so that they may continually be one'). The means of continuing this unity of God's people is to love one another (cf. 15.9-12). Thus, love and unity are closely related concepts, in which unity presupposes love (cf. 17.23, 26), and love maintains unity.

[114] Cf. A. Oepke, ''Eν' in *TDNT*, II:537-43; C.F.D. Moule, *The Origin of Christology* (Cambridge: CUP, 1977) 63-66; T.E. Pollard, 'The Father-Son and God-Believer Relationships according to St John: a Brief Study of John's Use of Prepositions' in M. de Jonge (ed.), *L'Évangile de Jean: Sources, rédaction, théologie* (BEThL 44; Leuven: Leuven University Press, 1977) 363-69.

[115] Cf. Brown, *Gospel*, 1:511.

Continuation of this friendship depends on the believer's obedience to Jesus (15.14).[116]

The divine life (theme r) (ζωή [αἰώνιος], ζάω, ζῳοποιέω). John's major soteriological term is 'life', which is available in Jesus (1.4; 5.21, 26; 11.25; 14.6; cf. 1 Jn 1.1-2; 5.11-12). 'Life' is also captured under the soteriological and revelatory symbols of water (4.10-11; 7.38), bread (6.33, 35, 51), light (1.4; 8.12) and gate (10.9).[117] '(Eternal) life' itself is a metaphor for partaking or having a share in the divine life of the Father and Son, and is the primary benefit or expression of being in relationship with the Father and Son.[118] Hence, John has very much a *symbolic soteriology*.[119]

Those who can give (eternal) life (ζῳοποιέω) are the Father, the Son and the Spirit (5.21; 6.63). Jesus' ability to give life is given to him by the Father (5.26), and the Spirit gives life (6.63a), in that the Spirit appears to be somehow active in or through Jesus' life-giving words/teaching (6.63c; cf. 6.68). The Father is the source of life for the Son (6.57; cf. 5.26), and Jesus is the source of life for the believer (6.57). The Spirit, then, appears to be the mediating agent of life to the believer (6.63; cf. the Spirit as the referent of the life-giving water in 4.10-15 and 7.37-39).[120] Moreover, if the Spirit is the communicative agent of the Father's words to Jesus (see

---

[116] Cf. Willett, *Wisdom*, 109.

[117] Willett merely elucidates the revelatory aspect of the images of light, bread and water, but not their soteriological dimension (*Wisdom*, 88-95).

[118] Cf. U.E. Simon, 'Eternal Life in the Fourth Gospel' in F.L. Cross (ed.), *Studies in the Fourth Gospel* (London: Mowbray, 1957) 97; A. Feuillet, 'Participation in the Life of God according to the Fourth Gospel' in A. Feuillet (ed.), *Johannine Studies* (Transl. T.E. Crane; New York: Alba House, 1964) 169-80; L. Goppelt, '"Ὕδωρ' in *TDNT*, VIII:326; Schnackenburg, *Gospel*, 2:355; Thompson, 'Life', 40; Beasley-Murray, *Gospel*, 4; van der Watt, *Family*, 202-204. Ζωή with and without αἰώνιος means the same (J.G. van der Watt, 'The Use of αἰώνιος in the Concept ζωή αἰώνιος in John's Gospel', *NT* 31 [1989] 217-28). The term ψυχή in John refers to the physical life, which can be laid down (10.11-24; 12.25; 13.37-38; 15.13; 1 Jn 3.16). Brown rightly observes that the crucial distinction between ψυχή and ζωή is that in contrast to the former the latter is imperishable and cannot be taken away, laid down, or given up (*Gospel*, 1:507; cf. Thompson, 'Life', 39). Various backgrounds have been proposed for the Johannine concept of ζωή (αἰώνιος): e.g., Gnosticism/Mandaism (Bultmann, *Theology*, 2:11-13; cf. Schnackenburg, *Gospel*, 2:356-60); the Jewish idea of the life of the age to come combined with Philo's Platonic concept of life in God's eternal To-day (Dodd, *Interpretation*, 144-50; cf. Ladd [*Theology*, 294] for a criticism).

[119] This is probably due to John's symbolic worldview (cf. Dodd, *Interpretation*, 143).

[120] Cf. Dodd, *Interpretation*, 224. Thompson's view, that Jesus is (merely) the mediating agent of and the gateway to (God's) life ('God', 246; cf. 'Life', 42), seems too limited; Jesus has life in himself and is as such its source (5.26). Moreover, Thompson does not explain the life-giving role of the Spirit (except for an unexplained statement that '[e]ternal life becomes a reality through the power of the Spirit of God' ['Life', 51]).

the theme 'sensory perception'), and if these words are life-giving (cf. 12.49-50), and if the Spirit is also the communicative agent of Jesus' life-giving words to people, then the Spirit appears to be the agent of life itself. Still, it will be necessary to explain further precisely how the Spirit mediates life and how this is related to Jesus' teaching.

Life becomes *available* to people through: (i) believing (in Jesus, in his name, in his word/teaching) (see the theme 'people's response');[121] (ii) 'consumption': to drink the life-giving water (4.14; 7.37-38), to eat Jesus' flesh and drink his blood (6.53-55), are metaphors for believing in Jesus; (iii) entering the sheep pen through the Gate (10.9); (iv) cognitive perception, i.e., the recognition, knowledge, understanding of the identity and teaching of Jesus, based on sensory perception. Life is *sustained* through: (i) continuous belief (cf. the conclusion of section 3.2, above, and Jn 6.54-58, which probably denotes continuous consumption [cf. the use of μένω and the present participles]); (ii) continuous knowing (cf. the theme 'cognitive perception'); (iii) remaining/abiding in Jesus, adherence to Jesus' teaching and a continuous demonstration of discipleship (see section 3.4, below).[122]

Conclusion. Based on an adequate belief-response, one enters, through a birth of the Spirit, into a saving relationship with the Father and Son. This life-giving relationship (salvation) is maintained through continuous belief, demonstrated in discipleship.

In sapiential Judaism the relationship between God and Wisdom is also one of intimacy, love, knowledge, life and glory (see esp. Prov., Sir., Wis.). All the Jewish wisdom writings we investigated depict the possibility of people having a relationship with Wisdom, which is or brings 'salvation', but especially Wisdom of Solomon and Philo emphasize that the ultimate aim is a relationship with God through his Wisdom. Only Philo knows of a metaphorical (re-)birth to describe the restoration of a person's relationship with God through his Wisdom.[123] The benefits of being in relationship with (God through) Wisdom are: love, life, glory, peace, joy and truth/wisdom/knowledge/understanding (see esp. Prov., Sir., Wis.). Wisdom of Solomon can also explain intimacy with God and Wisdom through the concept of friendship (Wis. 7.14, 27-28; 8.17-18; cf. Philo, *Prob.* 40-44, 59).[124]

---

[121] 'The Jews', in contrast, thought the study of Scripture rather than belief in Jesus ensured eternal life (5.39-40).

[122] Cf. Thompson, 'Life', 41.

[123] For the idea of divine begetting in Judaism, see Pryor, *John*, 173-74; Keener, 'Function', 161-76.

[124] For the testing of friends and friendship, see Sir. 4.17-19; 6.5-17.

Life (ζωή) originates from God (Wis. 16.13; Sir. 11.14; 18.1), but Wisdom also possesses life (Prov. 3.16, 18; 4.13; 8.35; Wis. 8.13, 17; Sir. 1.20; 4.12; cf. Qumran). Wisdom's life-giving qualities are also captured under the metaphors of Wisdom being depicted as a tree of life (Prov. 3.18), a spring of life (Prov. 16.22; cf. Sir. 24.23-34), the gate to life (Prov. 8.34-35), and as a vine producing life-giving fruits (Sir. 24.17, 19). The wise person, in turn, becomes also a spring of life and wisdom (Prov. 10.11; 13.14; Sir. 21.13; 39.6; cf. Jn 4.14). In Wisdom of Solomon and Sirach the term βίος (as ψυχή does in John) refers exclusively to the physical human life or daily life, whereas ζωή is used to refer to the life of God and Wisdom and to the gift of life to people. However, the gift of ζωή to people does not always denote eternal life; only Wisdom of Solomon has a theology of an afterlife (cf. ἀθανασία in Wis. 3.4; 4.1; 8.13, 17; 15.3; ἀφθαρσία in Wis. 2.23; 6.18-19; the righteous will live forever [Wis. 5.15]), and Philo has the concept of the immortality of the soul.

3.4. Discipleship

Discipleship is necessary to sustain salvation, which is emphasized by its various components, of which we mention a few.[125]

Loving Jesus (part of theme c). The love between the Father and Son is not only the basis for entering into salvation, but also the paradigm for believers to sustain their salvation. Jesus expects believers to show their love for him (and the Father), as well as to love one another (13.34-35; 14.15-23; 15.1-17). To love the Father and Son and fellow believers guarantees for the believer the saving love and the indwelling presence of the Father and Son, and thus sustains salvation (cf. the theme 'the love of the Father and Son').

Bearing fruit (theme s) ([φέρω] καρπός). Jesus' life/ministry bears fruit in that people come to belief in him (e.g., the fruit of Jesus' work in Jn 4 is the 'harvest' of the Samaritans [4.31-42]), but it is ultimately Jesus' death that produces fruit, in that it is life-giving (12.24-25). However, the concept of bearing fruit is not restricted to Jesus; it is also demanded from Jesus' disciples (12.24-26). Moreover, the illocution of 4.31-38 is to invite the disciples to take part in the harvest of the fruit for eternal life. In John 15, Jesus makes explicit the need to produce fruit; Jesus' disciples are meant to bear fruit (that remains), and they can only do so if they remain in (relationship with) Jesus (15.4-5, 8, 16). Bearing fruit is not only the

---

[125] For the theme of discipleship, see esp. Segovia and Tolmie, but also Kim, 'Church', 107-24. Scott elucidates the role of women as paradigms for discipleship (see *Sophia*, ch. 4).

purpose but also a 'test'/demonstration of true discipleship; a test which can be passed or failed (15.2, 5-6).[126]

Remaining in Jesus (theme t) (μένω). The concept of abiding/indwelling is closely related to the theme 'the intimate relationship...'; the Father remains/indwells the Son (14.10), the Father and Son indwell the believer (14.20, 23), the Spirit-Paraclete abides/remains with the disciples/believers (14.17; cf. 1 Jn 2.27).[127] Remaining in Jesus is guaranteed by continuous believing; the continuous consumption of Jesus' flesh and blood guarantees abiding in Jesus (6.56). To remain in Jesus' teaching is a demonstration of discipleship (8.31) and guarantees one's fellowship with the Father and Son (14.23; 2 Jn 9). The need for mutual indwelling — the believer in Jesus and vice versa — is illustrated by the vine-metaphor. Without being in a continuous relationship with Jesus there is no life (15.1-10). Moreover, only if one remains in Jesus will one bear fruit (that remains), which is a sign or expression of discipleship. Otherwise, there will be judgment for those who do not display discipleship (15.2) or who perpetrate apostasy/defection (15.6). Hence, to remain in Jesus and in his love is not an option but a necessity (15.4, 9; cf. 1 Jn 2.6; 3.24). In sum, the concept of remaining in Jesus denotes for the believer essentially the necessity to remain in a continuous relationship with the Father and Son in order to sustain her/his salvation.[128]

Witnessing to Jesus (theme u) (μαρτυρέω, μαρτυρία). The Fourth Gospel depicts a cosmic trial, in which the world brings Jesus to trial.[129] The reasons for Jesus' trial are Jesus' claim to have life in himself and to make this life available to those who believe (1.4-5; 8.12-13, 51-52; 10.17-20; 11.45-48; 1 Jn 5.11), and Jesus' claim to have an intimate relationship with the Father (5.18; 6.41; 10.33, 38-39). The vital issue is to have witnesses and John depicts five categories of witness of Jesus: (i) Jesus himself and the Father as the main witnesses (5.32, 37; 8.18; cf. 1 Jn 5.9-10); (ii) various people, such as the Baptist (1.6-8, 29-34), the Samaritan woman (4.39) and the disciples (15.27; cf. 1 Jn 1.2; 4.14); (iii) the Spirit-Paraclete (15.26; cf. 1 Jn 5.6-7);[130] (iv) the Scriptures (5.39); (v) Jesus' works (5.36; 10.25). The witness contains several aspects: (i) the Father has sent Jesus

---

[126] Okure says: '[m]issionary fruitfulness, then, in whatever way it is understood, forms an essential aspect of the Johannine conception of discipleship' (*Approach*, 212).

[127] The truth also indwells the believer (2 Jn 2).

[128] Surprisingly, Segovia's monograph on the Johannine call to abide (*Farewell*) highlights several aspects of discipleship, but does not bring out the need to abide in Jesus as the *conditio sine qua non* of sustaining salvation.

[129] See especially A.E. Harvey, *Jesus on Trial: A Study in the Fourth Gospel* (London: SPCK, 1976) and Lincoln, *Truth*.

[130] The Spirit-Paraclete will be sent to the disciples so that they will not be orphans/defenceless and so that the trial will not be lost (14.18).

(5.36); (ii) the things Jesus has seen and heard (in the Father's presence) (3.11-12, 31-32); (iii) sin, righteousness and judgment (16.8-11); (iv) truth (18.37; cf. 5.33); (v) God has given believers eternal life which is found in the Son (1 Jn 5.11). Witness to Jesus has soteriological overtones. First, the purpose of witness to Jesus is to evoke belief (1.7; 4.39; 19.35). Second, the content of the testimony is soteriological (1 Jn 5.11; cf. 18.37). Third, the ultimate aim of the witness of the Paraclete (and the disciples) is people's conversion (16.8-11; see ch. 5). Hence, disciples are expected to bear witness to Jesus, and the purpose of this witness is to convict and evoke belief.[131]

Following Jesus (theme v) (ἀκολουθέω). Jesus summons his disciples to follow him (1.43; 12.26; 21.19, 22). Following Jesus brings or leads to life (8.12; cf. 10.4, 10, 27-28). However, not all people continue to follow Jesus, because either their motives are wrong or because Jesus' demands are too hard/offensive, and they desert him (6.2, 24-26, 41, 60, 66; 13.27-30). Hence, there is a need for continuous discipleship, expressed by the concept of following; only those who continue to journey with Jesus and who continue to accept his, at times, offensive teaching and demanding commands, will remain in a saving relationship with him (cf. the theme 'Jesus' journey').[132]

Conclusion. Bearing fruit, loving, remaining in, witnessing to, and following Jesus are characteristics and demonstrations of discipleship, and also the means of remaining in a saving relationship with the Father and Son. Hence, it necessarily follows that *a continuous demonstration of discipleship is a (if not the) necessary means to sustain/maintain salvation.*[133]

The Jewish wisdom traditions also know the concept of discipleship and its various aspects. The concept of being a disciple of Wisdom is frequently alluded to (Prov. 3.13-18; 4.5-9; 8.32-34; 9.1-6; Sir. 4.11-18; 6.18-31; 14.20-15.10; 24.19-22; Wis. 7.8-14; 8.2, 9, 16-18). Moreover, Sirach 46.6-10 and 51.15 evoke the concept of following God and Wisdom. Wisdom saves and gives life to her disciples, to those who remain faithful to her (Prov. 8.32-35; Wis. 10.4, 9-10; Sir. 4.11-18), but those who cease to follow Wisdom instead will perish (Prov. 8.36; Wis.

---

[131] For a more comprehensive treatment of the theme 'witnessing to Jesus', see J. Beutler, *Martyria: Traditionsgeschichtliche Untersuchungen zum Zeugnisthema bei Johannes* (FTS 10; Frankfurt: Knecht, 1972).

[132] For the theme 'following Jesus', see also A.J. Köstenberger and P.T. O'Brien, *Salvation to the Ends of the Earth: A Biblical theology of mission* (NSBT 11; Leicester: Apollos, 2001) 219-20.

[133] Cf. Schnackenburg, *Gospel*, 1:566; Okure, *Approach*, 291. J.M. Lieu comments: 'behaviour is the test and expression of a relationship with God which is initiated by God' (*The Theology of the Johannine Epistles* [Cambridge: CUP, 1991] 118).

10.3; Sir. 4.19). God examines souls in search of fruit (Wis. 3.13), and fruit brings glory (Wis. 3.15). Wisdom, who herself produces life-giving fruit (Sir. 6.19; 24.17), also increases/makes grow the fruit of those who serve her (Wis. 10.10). A person with wisdom bears trustworthy fruit (Sir. 37.22-23) and the fruit of the righteous leads to life (Prov. 10.16; 11.30), but the ungodly are like branches broken off, whose fruit will be useless (Wis. 4.3-5; cf. Sir. 6.3; 23.25). Wisdom abides/dwells in or remains among people (Wis. 1.4; 7.27; Sir. 1.15; 24.7) and people abide/live with God and Wisdom (Wis. 3.9; Sir. 6.20). Philo speaks of the soul as a temple indwelled by God (*Som.* 1.149, 215). People are exhorted to love (and stay with) Wisdom, which is expressed/demonstrated in keeping her commandments (Wis. 6.17-18; cf. Sir. 2.15-16), because this will result in blessing (Prov. 4.6-9; 8.17-21) and (eternal) life (Wis. 6.12, 17-18; Sir. 4.12). Although sapiential Judaism does not strictly mention the concept of witnessing to Wisdom, one can find the idea of the Spirit of Wisdom being a witness of/before God (Wis. 1.6-9),[134] and of a witness/testimony being established on the basis of truth by those who have wisdom (Prov. 12.17-22; cf. 29.14). Moreover, a faithful witness even has salvific implications; he 'saves' lives from evil/bad morality (Prov. 14.25).

In section 7, below, we will elucidate how all the soteriological themes we have examined in section 3 work together.

4. The Role of Belief in Salvation

In this section, we need to deal with two paradoxes. First, on the one hand, eternal life seems to be available only after the cross, whereas, on the other hand, eternal life seems to be available in the person and revelatory teaching of Jesus, and hence already before the cross. Second, on the one hand, signs can evoke belief and such belief is sometimes recommended by Jesus, yet, on the other hand, belief that is not dependent on signs seems to be preferred.

In order to untangle these paradoxical issues, we may briefly state our findings thus far. First, we have suggested that an 'adequate' belief-response leading to life/salvation is constituted by a belief that sufficiently understands the true identity and mission (especially the significance of the cross) of the Father and Son and the nature of their relationship. Moreover, in order to sustain/maintain this life/salvation, there is the need for a

---

[134] God can most probably be a witness of the blasphemers' speech (Wis. 1.6), precisely because the Spirit of Wisdom knows what is said in the world, and will scrutinize the ungodly and report their words before God (Wis. 1.7-9). In this way, the Spirit will convict the unrighteous (cf. the Paraclete's ἐλέγχειν in 16.8-11).

continuous belief-response, which is predominantly the need for a continuous demonstration of discipleship, such as keeping Jesus' commandments (especially 'loving one another'), witnessing, bearing fruit, bringing glory to the Father and Son, serving Jesus (12.26) or praying (14.13-14). Thus, *adequate belief (leading to eternal life) is an initial sufficient belief-response that is sustained in discipleship* (cf. the purpose of the Fourth Gospel). Second, *an adequate belief-response is made on the basis of ample cognitive perception, which in turn is based on sensory perception.* In other words, the cognitive penetration of the deeper, spiritual significance of what has been heard and seen, results in a true understanding of the Father and Son, and this understanding forms the basis on which a sufficient belief-response can be made.

4.1. Belief and the Cross

Concerning the place of the cross in salvation, the consensus seems to be that the cross is integral/climactic and constitutional to salvation, which implies that salvation/life is only fully available after the cross (see ch. 1 section 2.1). Our suggestion that adequate belief includes a true understanding of Jesus' salvific mission, and hence of the significance of the cross, also implies that such belief, and thus life/salvation, could only be available after the cross (cf. 3.14-16; 6.51; 12.24). However, how does this relate to the fact that life/salvation seems available in the person and work of Jesus (1.4; 5.21, 26; 11.25; 14.6), and hence already before the cross, as indeed is indicated by Jesus' real offers of life-giving water, bread, and words/teaching (4.10-14; 6.35, 63, 68; 7.37)? We will elucidate this tension by examining the belief and understanding of 'the Twelve' (Jesus' inner circle of disciples [6.67-71; 20.24]).

Although the Fourth Gospel mentions at various points an authentic belief-response of the Twelve before the cross (1.41, 45, 49; 2.11; 6.68-69; 16.29-30), the question is whether this belief was adequate because it is only after the cross that the disciples seem to have been 'born again' and to have received the new life (20.22, 28).[135] Before this, we find that the disciples frequently misunderstand or fail to understand Jesus (2.19-22; 4.31-34; 6.5-9; 9.2-3; 11.11-16; 13.6-10, 36-38; 14.5, 8, 22; 16.17-18; 18.10-11; 20.9), i.e., they often do not have sufficient cognitive perception.[136] Prior to the cross, the disciples' understanding was limited (16.12), and even after the cross and resurrection misunderstanding still occurred (21.19-23). It seems especially the task of the Spirit-Paraclete to

---

[135] Cf. Bennema, 'Giving', section IV.7.

[136] Cf. D.A. Carson, 'Understanding Misunderstandings in the Fourth Gospel', *TynB* 33 (1982) 59-91. The misunderstandings of the characters frequently lead to more revelation/explanation, which benefits the reader.

bring the disciples to a further level of cognitive perception (14.26; 16.13-15; cf. the disciples' μιμνήσκομαι [2.22] and μνημονεύειν [16.4] with the Paraclete's ὑπομιμνήσκειν [14.26]; see also ch. 5). Nonetheless, there are a few indications of true understanding before the cross, leading to an adequate belief-response (6.68-69; 16.29-30). Moreover, Jesus himself indicated that the disciples had some satisfactory understanding and belief (17.6-8), and were in a saving relationship with him (13.10; 15.3; 17.12) (cf. ch. 5 section 3.5).[137]

Thus, it seems that the disciples had, at times, a sufficient, though not perfect, understanding, and that they had an adequate belief-response and were in a life-giving relationship with Jesus.[138] This is also confirmed by the fact that the Twelve continued in their discipleship — with the exception of Judas — whereas many other disciples defected (6.66-69).[139] No one could snatch the disciples out of their saving relationship with Jesus (6.39; 10.27-29; 17.12; cf. the strong bond between the disciples/believers and the Father and Son in 15.1-17; 17.21-23).

Still, we have not explained how the Twelve could be in a life-giving relationship with Jesus while the climax of the giving of life was only after the cross (20.22). The answer probably lies in what John conceives to be the uniqueness of the disciples' situation. Before the cross, the disciples were already in a life-giving relationship with Jesus, but this life was tied to the historical Jesus, who was soon going to leave them. Hence, the issue came up of how the disciples' relationship with the departing Jesus was going to be sustained. The solution is twofold. First, Jesus needs to go to the cross, partly in order to make widely and fully available the life within him. Second, this new life would be made available or mediated through the giving of the Spirit (20.22); the Spirit would sustain the disciples' relation with the glorified Jesus and the Father, and hence their salvation.[140]

---

[137] Cf. 3.11, where, through the use of 'we', Jesus seems to include his disciples as capable of adequate understanding. It must be noted that although the disciples were already clean (13.10), they still needed to have their feet washed (13.8), i.e., Jesus still needed to die for them (cf. Culpepper, *Anatomy*, 118).

[138] Culpepper puts the Twelve in the category 'commitment in spite of misunderstandings', and states that disciples/believers do not have to understand perfectly; as long as they follow the Revealer, revelation is in progress (*Anatomy*, 147). Cf. Segovia, 'Peace', 81-82. Hamid-Khani emphasizes the post-Easter illumination of the disciples to the extent that he virtually denies the possibility of adequate understanding before the cross (*Revelation*, 334).

[139] Peter's defection, expressed by his denial of Jesus, is only temporary (13.37-38; 18.17, 25-27; 21.15-19), whereas Judas' defection was permanent (17.12).

[140] See Bennema, 'Giving', section IV.7.

This would not be an unfamiliar concept because the Spirit was somehow already actively reaching out to people and mediating to them the life which was available in the person and words of Jesus (see the theme 'the divine life' and chs. 4-5). The cross, then, released and made available to people the life that was in the person of Jesus, in a way that was not possible before. Before the cross the availability of life and the activity of the Spirit were limited and tied to the historical Jesus (cf. οὔπω γὰρ ἦν πνεῦμα in 7.39), but after Jesus' glorification, the life of the glorified Son and the Father would become fully available through the Spirit. Thus, it appears that the life of the Father and Son and the life-giving Spirit could already be adequately (though partially) *experienced* during Jesus' ministry, but could only be '*given*', i.e., more fully experienced, after Jesus' glorification (cf. chs. 4-5).[141]

Further, John does not really portray a continuous or consistent progress of understanding or belief on behalf of the Twelve, so that any form of 'stages of faith' becomes increasingly unlikely. This does not exclude, however, the possibility of cognitive development or progression. First, Nicodemus may be an example of someone who shows cognitive progression: from someone who failed to understand the basics of the kingdom (3.1-10) to a possible recognition of Jesus as King (19.39). In John 4, the Samaritan woman shows cognitive progression in understanding Jesus' identity (vv.9, 19, 29) and his gift of life-giving water (the leaving of her water jar in v.28 might indicate her grasp of the significance of Jesus' offer). The man born blind in John 9 also progresses cognitively (through Jesus' revelation) to the point that he can make an adequate belief-response (9.38). Second, even when a person already is in a saving relationship with Jesus, progression in knowing/understanding the Father and Son will happen through the teaching of the Spirit-Paraclete (14.26; 16.12-15; see ch. 5). Based on this further and authentic understanding, a continuous adequate belief-response, expressed particularly in or through continuous discipleship, can be made in order to sustain one's life/salvation. Thus, cognitive development, i.e., progress in people's understanding of the Father and Son, towards sufficient understanding, on the basis of which an adequate belief-response can be made, is possible, and also continues within a person's relationship with the Father and Son.

4.2. Belief and Signs

A true understanding of the identity and mission of the Father and Son and the relationship between the Father and Son is necessary for salvation, i.e.,

---

[141] See Bennema, 'Giving', section IV.7. Cf. Turner, *Spirit*, ch. 4 (although see our criticism in the conclusion of our ch. 4).

for an adequate belief-response. The question is, however, on which bases such a belief-response can be made. One such basis is Jesus' revelatory teaching, but do signs also provide ground for saving faith? Can an adequate belief-response be made on the basis of signs alone? Can cognitive perception, resulting in true understanding and believing, be reached merely on the basis of signs?

Signs can (and should [20.30-31]) evoke belief (2.11; 2.23; 6.14; 7.31; 11.45; 12.10-11), but sometimes they do not (12.37).[142] Some of these belief-responses are not adequate or perhaps not even authentic (2.24-25; 6.66), or it is not certain whether this belief is sufficient or not (7.31; 11.45; 12.10-11). Hence, 2.11 may be the only occurrence of ample belief based on signs, and even then, it could be argued that John portrays the disciples as already in a saving relationship with Jesus. Thus, signs are not a guarantee for an adequate or even authentic belief-response. Nevertheless, belief based on signs can be recommended by both Jesus (10.37-38; 14.11; cf. 10.25-26) and John (20.30-31).[143] Moreover, Thomas seems to come to a true belief-response based on seeing and perceiving the miracle/sign of the resurrection (20.27-29).[144] What is criticized, is not belief based on signs but the *lack* of belief (12.37; cf. 6.26).[145] However, even if belief based on signs can be adequate, this belief should still be based on true understanding, and cannot bypass cognitive perception (10.38; 14.11).[146] Thus, as with Jesus' words/teaching, the signs also

---

[142] Dodd sees the background to the Johannine signs in the OT prophetic symbolic acts (אוֹת) and in Philo's σημεῖον or σύμβολον (*Interpretation*, 141-42). For an overall treatment of Jesus' signs, see esp. Bittner, *Zeichen, passim*, and Twelftree, *Jesus*, chs. 7-8. According to sapiential Judaism, Wisdom also performed miraculous signs (Wis. 10.16; cf. 8.8). For the parallel between Wisdom's and Jesus' signs, see Ziener, 'Weisheitsbuch (I)'; Clark, 'Signs'. Moreover, the lifting up of the serpent was a symbol/sign of God's salvation — σύμβολον σωτηρίας (Wis. 16.6-7; cf. Jn 3.14-15). Signs reveal God's glory and his identity (Sir. 36.4-7; cf. Jn 2.11).

[143] Although 10.37-38 and 14.11 mention ἔργα (of the Father) rather than σημεῖα, they are partially synonymous (cf. 6.30; 9.3-4, 16; cf. Bittner, *Zeichen*, 272-73, 287-88; Ensor, *Jesus*, 221-22).

[144] Even the recommended believing that is not based on seeing in 20.29b is still based on the seeing and believing of reliable *eye*-witnesses (as pointed out by Richard Bauckham during the annual Laing Lecture 'The Women at the Tomb: Is their Witness Credible?' [London Bible College, 27 February 2001]).

[145] Cf. Appold, *Motif*, 94; Thompson, *Word*, 79.

[146] It is significant that precisely on the basis of 10.38 even Twelftree, who argues that the signs are an adequate basis for salvation and a full understanding of Jesus, nonetheless admits that for John belief on the basis of Jesus' words is the ultimate form of belief-response (*Jesus*, 231-33).

contain or can provide revelatory information that can be cognitively perceived and result in a sufficient understanding and belief-response.[147]

Nonetheless, the signs are a much less secure basis for adequate understanding and belief than Jesus' words because, in contrast to Jesus' words, the signs are not explicitly linked with 'life', 'truth', 'cleansing', 'release from sin' or the Spirit.[148] Moreover, it was Jesus' teaching, especially his claim to be equal to God and the need for his death, which caused offence, not his miracles (6.41, 52, 60-62; 10.32-33; 18.19; 19.7).[149] Finally, there is no hint in the Fourth Gospel that a continuous belief that is exclusively based on signs can maintain a person's relationship with the Father and Son.[150] In conclusion, contra many scholars (see ch. 1 section 2.1.2), signs can be a basis for adequate belief. However, they are not a very secure basis and the reader is encouraged to continue and progress towards a belief that is less dependent on signs and more based on Jesus' words/teaching (4.48; 20.29).[151]

---

[147] Contra, e.g., Hamid-Khani, who thinks that signs-faith is spurious (*Revelation*, 367 n.145, 378-80).

[148] Although the Spirit is nowhere explicitly linked with the signs, we tentatively put forward a suggestion. First, Jesus' ministry is one of words and works, and, through an allusion to the Spirit-endowed Messiah in Isa. 11.2, Jesus is empowered by the Spirit with wisdom and *power* to carry out his total ministry, including his miraculous signs (cf. ch. 4 section 2.1). Second, Jesus' disciples will continue Jesus' ministry, including the performance of signs (14.11-12), and they will be empowered by the Spirit-Paraclete, so that it seems plausible to assume that the Spirit-Paraclete will also be the power behind the disciples' signs. Third, if the signs need to be perceived cognitively in order to grasp what they signify, and if the Spirit is depicted as the facilitator of cognitive perception, then the Spirit will be expected to facilitate this perception of the signs.

[149] Even in Jn 5, the offence was not the miracle, but the fact that the miracle was performed on the Sabbath, and Jesus' claim to be equal to God (5.16-18).

[150] This does not deny the ongoing significance of signs for believers. By meditating on the signs, e.g., the Spirit-Paraclete can give the believer a deeper understanding of their significance and of Jesus' identity and work, which may result in a continuous belief-response. However, a fuller exploration of Johannine spirituality is beyond the scope of our study.

[151] Appold concludes that signs 'do not constitute real faith since they do not penetrate through to an authentic recognition of who Jesus is' (*Motif*, 283). Turner's view echoes that of Appold. In a private conversation, Turner mentioned that signs cannot produce adequate faith; people cannot penetrate Jesus' revelation merely based on signs, but only get 'fractured images of Jesus'. Whereas Appold and Turner probably attribute slightly too little significance to the signs, Motyer surely attributes too much, when he says that '[s]igns are indeed an essential prerequisite for true faith' (*Father*, 65). Twelftree, defending that the signs are an adequate basis for salvation and a full understanding of Jesus, believes that the signs are the centre/heart of Jesus' life-giving ministry, which are then explained by Jesus' teaching (*Jesus*, 199, 235-36). However, it seems that both Jesus' teaching and signs are equally central and important (cf. Thompson, *Word*, 83-84). Moreover, although Jesus' dialogues with Nicodemus and the

5. The Role of Jesus as Wisdom in Salvation

The aim of this section is to elucidate John's functional Wisdom christology, i.e., to examine how Jesus functions as Wisdom in relation to salvation.[152] Although the term σοφία is not used in the Johannine literature, the concept of W/wisdom is evoked in various ways (see section 3, above). From all the soteriological themes, only one does not find a parallel in the intertestamental wisdom literature: the theme 'the Father draws people and gives them to Jesus'. The theme of 'divine birth' is only found in Philo. Other Johannine themes do find a parallel in the intertestamental wisdom literature, but the parallel is conceptual rather than verbal. The Johannine concept of 'truth', for example, is partially synonymous with the intertestamental concept of 'wisdom', since both truth and wisdom denote the (saving) content of the teaching of respectively Jesus and Wisdom.

Concerning the theme 'people's response' in sapiential Judaism, the term πιστεύω only occurs sporadically, and even then it expresses trust in God rather than in Wisdom (except Sir. 4.16). The *concept* of people's response to Wisdom, however, is well attested: (i) Wisdom calls out to and invites people to listen to her (instruction) and people's response is either to accept or to reject her and her teaching (Prov.); (ii) Wisdom invites people to come to her banquet; an invitation which can be accepted or rejected (Prov., Sir.); (iii) Solomon sincerely desired Wisdom and responded positively to her (Wis. 6.12-9.18); (iv) 'to love, seek, hold, serve, obey, listen to' Wisdom implies a positive response to Wisdom (Sir. 4.11-15; cf. Wis. 10.9); (v) the concept of being a disciple of Wisdom presupposes the acceptance of Wisdom. With regard to the theme 'witnessing to Jesus', although sapiential Judaism does not strictly mention the concept of witnessing to Wisdom, one can find the idea of the Spirit of Wisdom being a witness of/before God (Wis. 1.6-9), and of a

---

Samaritan woman are not connected with any sign, they make vital contributions to the Johannine concept of salvation. Finally, if the signs were the centre of Jesus' ministry and provided a full understanding of Jesus, why then would the signs need to be explained by the discourses (as Twelftree claims himself)? Hence, we maintain that, although an adequate belief-response based on signs is possible, signs remain a feeble and perhaps ambiguous basis for adequate belief. Our position also contrasts that of Koester, who argues that signs, rather than being a first step to genuine faith, would merely confirm and be received by genuine faith ('Hearing', 347-48; cf. Ladd, *Theology*, 310).

[152] Cf. ch. 1 section 2.2.1. For Jesus as Wisdom in general, see esp. Scott, *Sophia*; Witherington, *Wisdom*. For the role of Jesus as Wisdom in salvation, see esp. Willett, *Wisdom*.

witness/testimony being established by those who have wisdom (Prov. 12.17-22; cf. 29.14).

In conclusion, Jesus and his (soteriological) role in the Fourth Gospel find a powerful parallel or background in the Jewish figure of Wisdom and her function in the world. We may now also suggest a possible rationale for why John uses the concept of W/wisdom to present Jesus and his soteriology. John's purpose for writing the Gospel was soteriological (20.30-31); in fact, the whole Gospel is permeated by the issue of life and of Jesus as its dispenser. Moreover, the concept of divine W/wisdom had acquired strong soteriological overtones in the Jewish intertestamental wisdom literature. Especially in Wisdom of Solomon, Wisdom is depicted as a salvific figure who wants to dispense her saving wisdom/knowledge. Finally, the common denominator between the numerous parallels between Wisdom and Jesus seems to be the concept of salvation. Hence, it seems that soteriology is the *context* in which John's Wisdom christology should be interpreted, and the soteriological figure of Wisdom was especially appropriate to John's purpose to present Jesus and his salvific mission.[153]

6. The Role of the Spirit in Salvation

The theme of the Spirit has not been enlisted among John's soteriological themes because of its complexity and compass, which will be more fully elucidated in chapters 4-5. In this section, we merely seek to regroup the various soteriological activities of the Spirit that were identified in section 3, above.

The first group of the Spirit's soteriological activities has to do with the relationship between the Spirit and Jesus. The Spirit upon Jesus equips Jesus in order to accomplish his salvific mission (1.32-33; cf. ch. 4 section 2). Moreover, it is implicit that the Spirit functions as the channel or mode of communication between the earthly Jesus and his Father, so that Jesus is able to communicate to people what he sees and hears from the Father. The Spirit-Paraclete will also be the primary means through which the glorified Jesus continues his salvific mission in this world (see ch. 5; cf. 14.16, 26; 15.26; 16.14).

The remaining soteriological activities of the Spirit have to do with the relationship between the Spirit and people. First, the Spirit is the boundary-marker of God's people/family, in that being born of the Spirit facilitates entry into salvation, into a saving relationship with God (3.5; cf. 1.12-13). Second, the Spirit gives life (6.63a), in that the Spirit appears to

---

[153] For alternative explanations, see Scott, *Sophia*, 170-72, 244-45; Willett, *Wisdom*, 46-47; Thompson, 'God', 229 n.27; Ringe, *Friends*, 44-45, 62.

be active in or through Jesus' life-giving words/teaching (6.63c; cf. 6.68) and somehow mediates life to people. Third, if what leads to life/salvation is an adequate belief-response, as the result of sufficient cognitive perception and understanding, which, in turn, is the result of sensory perception, and if the Spirit is the mediating agent of life, then the Spirit is essentially the provider or facilitator of cognitive perception, and understanding. This concept of the Spirit as provider of cognitive perception and life is also evoked by the concept of the Paraclete. As the Spirit of truth, the Spirit-Paraclete will bring the disciples to a higher level of cognitive perception — through teaching and guidance into all truth (14.26; 16.12-15) — which would result in, for example, further, continued belief (cf. 2.22). Fourth, the believer will receive the Spirit-Paraclete, who will consequently sustain the believer's life-giving relationship with the Father and Son, and hence her/his salvation (14.16-23; see ch. 5).[154] Fifth, if the glorified Jesus continues his salvific ministry in this world through his disciples by means of the Spirit-Paraclete, who empowers and equips the disciples for their missionary and salvific task, then the Spirit-Paraclete will also somehow have a soteriological role towards the world.[155]

This leads to the preliminary conclusion that *the Spirit is a soteriological necessity,* in that the Spirit gives or mediates life in his function as provider or facilitator of cognitive perception. The Spirit enables a person to come from sensory to cognitive perception, which enables a person to come to a true understanding of the Father and Son and consequently to make an adequate belief-response in order to enter into and remain in a saving relationship with the Father and Son.

A possible explanation as to *why* John uses the concept of Spirit in combination with the concept of W/wisdom for his soteriology, is twofold. First, the Spirit was already soteriologically necessary in parts of Judaism. Second, Spirit and W/wisdom were already closely connected (in relation to 'salvation') in Jewish wisdom literature, as represented mainly by Sirach, Wisdom of Solomon, Philo and Qumran.

---

[154] Cf. Bennema, 'Giving', section IV.7.

[155] The words of Jesus/God that the disciples have accepted probably form the foundation of their witness through which people may come to believe in Jesus (17.6-8, 20). It is also likely that the teaching, anamnesis and witnessing function of the Paraclete (14.26; 15.26-27; 16.12-15) is the basis for and directly related to the disciples' witness (cf. ch. 5).

7. A Model of John's Pneumatic Wisdom Soteriology

The objective of this section is to demonstrate how all the various soteriological themes of the Fourth Gospel are linked and work together in an overall model of Johannine soteriology. The strategy to achieve this objective is to switch from themes to activities, in that the category of 'activity' will be the organizing principle. The reason for this approach is twofold. First, our agenda for this chapter is to discover how, for John, one can *enter* into and *stay* within salvation, and all the various activities involved in this. Hence, an overall model of Johannine soteriology can be constructed better by using 'activities' as the main building blocks rather than 'themes'. Second, most themes we examined are represented by Greek verbs, and hence express activities. However, we are not claiming that the category of 'activity' is a higher abstraction or occupies a higher place in the hierarchical order than 'theme'. Moreover, the relationship between activity and theme is complex; one activity may be related to one or more themes and vice versa.[156]

If we approach John's soteriological themes via our leading questions, we may tentatively identify *two main areas or concepts of soteriological activity*: (i) entering into salvation (themes a-s); (ii) remaining in salvation (themes c, f, j, l-o, q-v).[157] This division corresponds with the structure of the Gospel: Jn 1-12, 20 focuses primarily, though not exclusively, on cluster (i), whereas cluster (ii) is the primary focus of Jn 13-17, 21. We will first present all the soteriological activities in a diagram as a model of John's Pneumatic Wisdom Soteriology, and elucidate the various activities that make up these two main areas of coming into and remaining within salvation. Then, we will compare our model with especially those of Bultmann, Loader, Willett, Lee, Turner and Hamid-Khani (with the exception of Lee's model, see ch. 1 for the descriptions of the other models), and show where our model is similar to and where it is distinct from theirs.

---

[156] E.g., the love of the Father and Son (theme c) initiates the Son's sending and mission (activity A), is one of the believer's benefits (activity G), and also refers to Jesus' command to love one another (activity K). Activity A relates to, e.g., themes a-f.

[157] We have to bear in mind that sharp distinctions cannot always be made because the relationship between theme and activity is one of many-to-many.

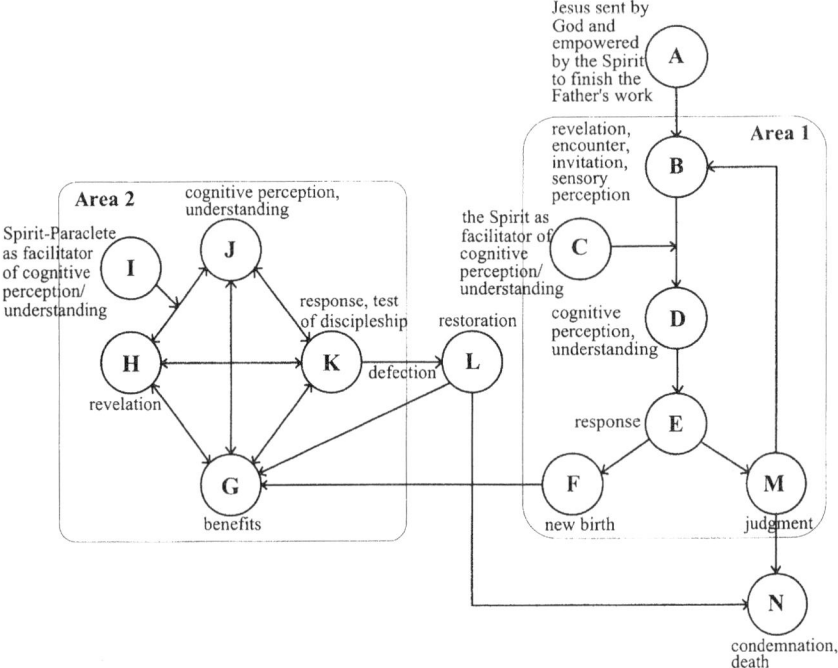

Area 1: Entering into Salvation. This is the area in which people are confronted by Jesus and his revelation (in words and works), which will bring salvation or judgment, dependent on one's response towards the Revealer. The initiative for salvation lies with the Father, who sent the Son into this world in order to save it. The underlying and foundational concept of salvation is the intimate relationship of life, love, knowledge/truth and glory between the Father and Son, in which the believer will be drawn and partake. In order to finish the Father's work Jesus is empowered by the Spirit. After Jesus has finished his earthly work and after his return to the Father, the disciples are sent by Jesus into the world and are empowered by the Spirit-Paraclete, who is sent by the Father and Son (activity A).

Jesus confronts people with his revelatory teaching and signs, and invites people to accept/believe him and his revelation. After Jesus' departure, people encounter Jesus' historical revelation through the witness of the disciples and the Spirit-Paraclete, and especially through the reading of the Fourth Gospel (activity B).[158] In this confrontation, the Spirit

---

[158] The reader of the Fourth Gospel has the advantage of having the narrator as a hermeneutical guide; information, such as 1.1-18; 2.23-25; 3.16-21, 31-36; 7.39 was not available to the historical disciples.

enables people to come from sensory to cognitive perception (activity C). Based on people's sensory perception of Jesus' words and signs — either directly, or indirectly through the witness of the disciples and the Spirit-Paraclete or the reading of the Fourth Gospel — and through the help of the Spirit in the function of facilitator of cognitive perception, people can come to a level of cognitive perception of Jesus' revelation. This perception may result in an adequate understanding of the identity and mission of the Father and Son and of their relationship (activity D). Subsequently, people will make a response to Jesus and his revelation, and John presents a spectrum of possible responses (activity E).[159]

Some people will make an adequate belief-response, based on true cognitive perception and understanding, which will bring the person, through a new birth of the Spirit (activity F), into a saving relationship with the Father and Son (area 2).[160] These are the people given or drawn to Jesus by God, such as the Samaritan woman and her fellow people, the royal official, the man born blind, Martha,[161] and the disciples. Others will make an inadequate response, either because they do not have sufficient understanding (Nicodemus in Jn 3, the lame man at the pool), or because they reject Jesus and his revelation ('the Jews', the world). They will come or remain under judgment (3.18, 36) (activity M), but they may be further confronted with Jesus and his revelation (back to activity B). Condemnation and death awaits those people who persist in rejecting Jesus (3.16; 8.21) (activity N).

Among those people who make an inadequate response to Jesus, some may still have gained some authentic understanding, and, through more exposure to Jesus' revelation and the Spirit's work, they may make further cognitive progression and come eventually to sufficient understanding and belief (possibly Nicodemus in 19.39).[162] Others, however, who are

---

[159] Cf. Moloney, 'Cana', 185-213; Culpepper, *Anatomy*, 146-48; Stibbe, *Gospel*, 124; Barton, *Spirituality*, 128-30.

[160] The new birth of the Spirit is only possible after the cross (20.22). However, already during Jesus' ministry people could receive life from Jesus and be in a saving relationship with him, and the new birth subsequently *secured* their life-giving relationship with Jesus through the Spirit.

[161] Scott points out the linguistic parallel between 11.27 and 20.31 (*Sophia*, 204-205).

[162] However, it could be argued that the Samaritan woman, her fellow Samaritans, the royal official and the man born blind also came to an adequate belief-response only after some cognitive development and exposure to Jesus' revelation rather than coming immediately to an adequate understanding and response on the basis of one encounter with Jesus. The Samaritan woman, e.g., struggles to come to an adequate understanding, and Jesus had to guide her through various stages of revelation before she grasped his identity and the nature of his offer. Similarly, the spiritual sight of the man born blind did not immediately follow the reception of his physical sight; he needed more exposure to Jesus' revelation in order to perceive cognitively who Jesus was.

portrayed as having some sort of belief but not authentic or yet adequate (as Jesus points out), do not show progression in cognitive perception and understanding, but find further exposure to Jesus' teaching offensive and they reject Jesus (8.30-59).

Area 2: Remaining in Salvation.[163] This is the area of salvation in which people are in relationship, fellowship, (comm)union, friendship with the Father and Son, and participate in the divine life of the Father and Son and all the benefits this gives. The benefits of being in a saving relationship with the Father and Son is primarily '(eternal) life', which includes also love, glory, joy, peace, future resurrection (6.4), freedom from sin and the giving of the Spirit-Paraclete (activity G).[164] In fact, it is the Spirit-Paraclete, who can only be fully 'received' after the cross, who mediates all these benefits: the Spirit mediates and sustains the new life, empowers for mission, witness, worship, etc.[165] Moreover, the Spirit-Paraclete will continue to teach the disciples, and thus lead them to further cognitive perception and understanding of Jesus' revelation (activities H-J).

Based on this deeper understanding, disciples can then make a further belief-response, particularly expressed in the demonstration of discipleship, such as serving Jesus (12.26) and others (13.12-17), bearing fruit, witnessing, maintaining unity, keeping Jesus' commandments (especially loving one another), bringing glory to the Father and Son, praying (14.13-14; 15.7; 16.23-26; 1 Jn 3.22; 5.14-16), suffering (15.18-16.4), etc. (activity K). Thus, in order to remain in a saving relationship with the Father and Son, a person needs to display continuous belief through a continuous demonstration of discipleship, i.e., discipleship is the *conditio sine qua non* of ongoing salvation. However, not everyone continues in discipleship, and defection (a denial or discontinuation of discipleship) or apostasy (defection and becoming part of an opposite

---

[163] The activities in this area are probably all interrelated and/or work simultaneously, rather than in a particular sequential order. Moreover, we have not attempted to produce an exhaustive list of all the possible activities in one's relationship with God.

[164] We differentiate slightly between the closely related concepts of salvation and eternal life. Eternal life denotes the life of the Father and Son, and a person 'having' eternal life denotes a person having a share or participating in this divine life. Salvation, however, denotes a particular state of a person; namely, a person who is liberated from sin, the devil and destruction, and who is brought into a relationship with the Father and Son, and who receives all the benefits from being in this relationship, such as eternal life, love, glory, knowledge, the Spirit, etc. Thus, salvation encompasses the gift of eternal life (cf. Schnackenburg, *Gospel*, 2:352-53).

[165] Cf. Bennema, 'Giving', section IV.7. However, before the cross the Spirit could already somehow mediate to people the life that was available in the person and teaching of Jesus.

group) can occur (the disciples in 6.66, Judas, Peter).[166] There is nonetheless the possibility of restoration: Peter's commissioning in John 21 implies his restoration after his temporal defection. Similarly, through the confession of sins one can be restored to fellowship with the Father and Son (1 Jn 1.5-10) (activity L). Judas portrays permanent apostasy (he left Jesus and 'joined' Satan), which led to destruction (17.12) (activity N).[167]

The activities which involve the Spirit, and which will be more fully elucidated in chapters 4-5, are A, B, C, F, G, H, I (and possibly L and M).[168] The careful observer will see the strong similarity between the activities B-C-D-E and H-I-J-K.

Some scholars have dealt with or touched upon certain activities of our model, without necessarily explaining them adequately. According to Bultmann, salvation is the reception of authentic self-understanding and in consequence the transition into eschatological existence in relationship with God through faith, i.e., the recognition/acknowledgement of Jesus as the Revealer (of God). However, Bultmann does not describe how this eschatological existence can be sustained, or what the role of the Spirit is in all this. Moreover, we emphasize the need for an adequate understanding of the Father and Son rather than of the self that is salvific.[169] Although Bultmann made a very valuable contribution in recognizing the cognitive element of salvation — the concept of 'knowing faith' — this cognitive aspect of salvation seems to be as empty as Bultmann's concept of revelation. Nonetheless, Bultmann's model has much to commend it, and Bultmann was probably the first to offer a

---

[166] In her reconstruction of the missionary *Sitz im Leben* of John and his audience, Okure argues that the situation of the Johannine audience was marked by defecting and disobedient disciples (*Approach*, ch. 7; 288).

[167] Contra Judas, the Beloved Disciple (BD) depicts the epitome of true discipleship. Even Peter could be seen as an embodiment of true discipleship, despite his temporary episode of non-discipleship (6.68; 21.15-19; cf. Culpepper, *Anatomy*, 120-23; T.J. Wiarda, *Peter in the Gospels: Pattern, Personality and Relationship* [WUNT II/127; Tübingen: Mohr Siebeck, 2000] chs. 5-7). K. Quast's study also concludes that both Peter and the BD represent the paradigmatic disciple — Peter models the Johannine understanding of what it means to become a believer and a true disciple, and the BD epitomizes the intimate and continuing relationship of a disciple to Jesus (*Peter and the Beloved Disciple: Figures for a Community in Crisis* [JSNT.S 32; Sheffield: JSOT Press, 1989] 160, 163).

[168] Harner seems to have reduced the role of the Spirit merely to a supportive one; the Spirit supports, enriches and strengthens the relationships that the Father and Son have established with the believer (*Relation*, 31, 37). However, our case is that the Spirit not only sustains but also *establishes* the believer's relationship with the Father and Son.

[169] For Bultmann, an adequate understanding of the Father and Son and their identity, mission and relationship is not possible because there was no content to Jesus' revelation — *kein Wass, nur ein bloßes Dass*.

coherent model of Johannine soteriology that combined relational and cognitive aspects.[170]

The central and foundational component of Loader's model of Johannine soteriology — the revealer-envoy model — also combines relational and cognitive aspects, but, because of Bultmann's influence, essentially also deprives the cognitive element of salvation of its content. Moreover, although Loader is able to integrate the Spirit into John's soteriology, for Loader the Spirit's soteriological functions only start after the cross. Loader has not recognized the significance of the Spirit upon Jesus and the Spirit's soteriological role during Jesus' ministry (see ch. 4). Nevertheless, Loader probably developed the first coherent model of John's pneumatic soteriology.[171]

Willett's model of John's Wisdom soteriology — the descending revealer-redeemer — is significant in that it integrates John's Wisdom christology with his soteriology. However, Willett does not really bring out the cognitive aspect of salvation, or how one's intimate saving relationship with Jesus can be maintained, nor the role of the Spirit in all this.[172]

Although Lee uses a different language and approach, her attractive model reveals many affinities with part of ours, and is generally convincing. Looking at six symbolic narratives, Lee detects a distinctive five-stage pattern, in which a person misunderstands (stage 2) the sign/image (stage 1) (and hence Jesus), but after a struggle for understanding (stage 3), the person either attains or rejects a symbolic understanding (stage 4), followed by either a confession of faith or a statement of rejection (stage 5).[173] However, whereas Lee understands the attainment of symbolic understanding as *representing* the attainment of faith,[174] we suggest that the attainment of sufficient understanding may *result in* or *lead to* adequate belief. Moreover, and more important, Lee has not included the Spirit in her model, whereas we suggested that it is

---

[170] In terms of our model, Bultmann's model would exist of activities A, B, D/E (Bultmann sees these as one), Area 2 (this area corresponds to Bultmann's concept of eschatological existence, although he does not really explain it much further). Dodd, Barrett and Forestell also recognize relational and cognitive elements in John's soteriology, but they basically do not add anything to Bultmann's model.

[171] In terms of our model, Loader's model touches on activities A, B, D/E (as Bultmann, Loader takes these as one: 'right understanding is belief' [*Christology*, 142]), F, Area 2 (Loader speaks about an ongoing faith relationship, but he does not describe in detail its facets), K.

[172] Willett's model relates to activities A, B, E, Area 2, K/L of our model.

[173] D.A. Lee, *The Symbolic Narratives of the Fourth Gospel: The Interplay of Form and Meaning* (JSNT.S 95; Sheffield: JSOT Press, 1994) 12-13, *passim*. Lee's model corresponds to activities B, D and E.

[174] Lee, *Narratives*, 13.

precisely the Spirit who helps a person to move from a literal to a symbolic understanding (using Lee's terms).

Turner made a significant contribution by elucidating the role of the Spirit in enabling authentic understanding and belief through the impartation of revelatory wisdom.[175] However, Turner's emphasis is primarily on the cognitive aspect of salvation rather than attempting to hold both the cognitive and relational aspects together, although he clearly implies the latter.[176]

The strength of Hamid-Khani's model of John's pneumatic soteriology is his insight that believers need to be aided by the Spirit to perceive and comprehend the revelation of God in Jesus.[177] However, his model also brings up several issues (cf. ch. 1 section 2.3). First, he does not explain precisely *how* the Spirit illuminates the truth to believers (unlike, e.g., Turner). Second, Hamid-Khani focuses almost exclusively on the Spirit's post-Easter illuminative role in the believing community at the expense of the Spirit performing this function already *during* Jesus' earthly ministry.[178] Third, our findings contradict Hamid-Khani's understanding that the necessary preconditions for access to the Spirit's illumination are a birth of God/the Spirit and abiding faith.[179] In our view, John advocates an *understanding* faith (even Hamid-Khani attributes cognitive content to faith),[180] and the Spirit's illumination is precisely needed to *come* to this faith. Thus, Hamid-Khani correctly identifies the Spirit's function of facilitating cognitive perception and understanding, but he neglects that this function was already operative before the cross, as well as being directed to both unbelievers and believers in order to enter into and remain in salvation respectively.

8. Conclusion

John's soteriology is a variety of Wisdom soteriology, in that John uses the soteriological figure of Wisdom to present Jesus and his salvific mission.

---

[175] See Turner, *Spirit*, chs. 4-6. Turner's model touches on activities A-F and Area 2.

[176] This is not a criticism but merely an observation that Turner's theory needs to be developed. Turner's purpose simply has not been to elaborate how a person's relationship with the Father and Son can be sustained, i.e., the need for discipleship, nor how the cognitive and relational aspects of John's soteriology can be held together, or how his theory would fit into the whole of John's soteriology.

[177] See Hamid-Khani, *Revelation*, ch. 6. Hamid-Khani's model relates to our activities A, B, E, F, H-K.

[178] Hamid-Khani, *Revelation*, 333-37, 360, 391-92.

[179] Hamid-Khani, *Revelation*, 331-33, 361-66, 369, 373-74, 383-84, 404.

[180] Hamid-Khani, *Revelation*, 373.

Moreover, John's soteriology is also a pneumatic soteriology, in that the Spirit has a primarily soteriological role in John. Finally, all but one of John's soteriological themes find a parallel in the Jewish wisdom traditions. In sum, John depicts a *pneumatic W/wisdom soteriology*, which can be understood against a Jewish sapiential background, in which the figure of Wisdom had acquired strong soteriological overtones and in which the soteriological Spirit was closely related to W/wisdom.

If our model of John's soteriology is sustained, salvation can then be defined as 'being brought and kept in relationship with the Father and Son through the Spirit'. This relationship is depicted as the dynamic, continuous process of reassessment and progression of belief, i.e., of cognitive perception and knowing/understanding (the revelation of) the Father and Son and of demonstrating this belief in discipleship, so that one may continuously be in relationship with and share in the divine life of the Father and Son and all the benefits it gives. In our view, John understands faith as a *Spirit-informed cognitive belief-response to Jesus and his revelation expressed in personal allegiance to Jesus*, i.e., in discipleship/faithfulness. Hence, this model of John's Pneumatic Wisdom Soteriology holds together the relational and cognitive aspects of salvation.[181]

---

[181] John has (of course) a broader view of salvation than 'merely' the personal salvation of individuals. The reason for being in relationship with the Father and Son is not merely to sustain one's personal salvation, but there is also an element of participation in the ongoing work of God and Jesus in this world. First, the purpose for sending the Paraclete to the disciples is not to leave them defenceless (14.18), but to perpetuate the cosmic trial (see ch. 5). Second, Jesus' sending the disciples into the world and the reception of the Spirit is not just for the disciples' salvation (20.22), but is, by being placed in a missionary cotext (20.21, 23), also for the salvation of others. Third, the Paraclete's teaching will inform the disciples' witness, which convicts the world and may lead to the conversion of some (see ch. 5). Fourth, the intimate relationship between the individual believer and the Father and Son serves a bigger purpose, namely as witness to the world (17.21, 23; cf. 13.34-35). Fifth, the purpose of the Gospel is partly evangelistic (20.31a). Thus, salvation has a twofold dimension/purpose: *salvation is a person's coming into and remaining in a personal relationship with the Father and Son so that (i) s/he may have a share in the divine life, and so that (ii) s/he can participate in the ongoing work of the Father and Son through the Spirit-Paraclete in this world.* This second purpose of participation in the continuous work of the Father and Son is not an option, but is essentially the display of discipleship — to love one another so that the world may believe, to witness in order to convict and convert the world, etc. — and the display of discipleship is necessary to sustain one's salvation. Moreover, there is also the *corporate aspect of salvation* in that the sustenance of one's personal salvation/relationship with the Father and Son helps to sustain the entire community of believers. This aspect of the community of believers is especially emphasized in 1 Jn (e.g. 1 Jn 2.9-11; 3.17; 4.20-21) (cf. Barton, *Spirituality*, 116-18; Turner, 'Churches', *passim*). In conclusion, salvation has a more extensive scope than the personal salvation

What we need to elucidate further is the particular function of the Spirit in salvation. Especially the soteriological concept of the Spirit giving/mediating life in the function of provider/facilitator of people's cognitive perception and understanding will be our primary interest, because through this function of the Spirit a person can come to and retain an adequate, saving understanding and belief-response.[182] In terms of our model, this implies a focus on activities B-C-D-E (and its parallel H-I-J-K). The most important questions concerning the role of the Spirit in salvation that still need to be answered are as follows. How does the Spirit enable a person to come from sensory to cognitive perception, and how is this linked with the concept of the Spirit mediating life through Jesus' teaching? How will the Spirit sustain one's salvation? What exactly is the Spirit's soteriological role in and towards the world? These questions will be addressed in chapters 4-5.[183]

---

of individuals. First, a person is also brought into a saving relationship with the Father and Son for being available to God to be used for his salvific purposes in this world. Second, a believer is part of the wider community of believers who are in fellowship with the Father and Son.

[182] One reason why this concept has not been developed earlier might be due to Bultmann's influence that there is no content to Jesus' revelation (accepted by, e.g., Forestell and Loader), and hence, there is no saving wisdom/truth/knowledge contained in Jesus' revelation, and people do not need information to come to a true acknowledgement of who Jesus is.

[183] The question of how and when the disciples (and future believers) will receive this soteriological Spirit, is addressed in Bennema, 'Giving'.

Chapter 4

Spirit, Wisdom and Salvation
in Jesus' Ministry (Jn 1-12)

1. Introduction

In chapter 3 we suggested that the soteriological function of the Spirit is to give/mediate life and to provide cognitive perception and understanding, but it still needs to be demonstrated how this is accomplished. Hence, the objective of this chapter is to elucidate *how* the Spirit functions as the facilitator of cognitive perception, understanding and life. The agenda for this chapter is set by two questions. How does the Spirit enable a person to come from sensory to cognitive perception and understanding? How is this linked with the concept of the Spirit mediating life through Jesus' teaching? Our strategy is to focus first on Jesus' ministry, as depicted in John 1-12, before we investigate the concept of the Spirit as Paraclete in chapter 5. We will start by explaining the relationship between the Spirit and Jesus, and its significance for John's concept of salvation (section 2). Then we will examine Jesus' revelatory encounters with Nicodemus, the Samaritan woman and the Jews in John 6 (section 3). We will also investigate to what extent our conceptual background of Spirit-W/wisdom-salvation in Judaism might possibly assist us in the elucidation of the relationship between John's pneumatology and soteriology. The originality of this chapter lies in the development of the concepts of 'saving wisdom' and of the Spirit as a (life-giving) cognitive agent, in that the Spirit seems to provide revelatory wisdom to both Jesus and his hearers.

2. The Spirit upon Jesus

In chapter 3 we indicated that the Spirit upon Jesus equips him to accomplish his salvific mission, but we still need to investigate more precisely *how* the Spirit equips Jesus. Moreover, we need to determine how Jesus is able to communicate to people what he sees and hears from the Father (see the theme 'sensory perception' in ch. 3). Hence, the aim of this section is to discover the (soteriological) *significance* of the Spirit upon Jesus by elucidating John 1.32-34 and 3.34.

2.1. Jesus Endowed with the Spirit

The christological section 1.29-34, as part of the testimony of John the Baptist (1.19-42), focuses on the identity of the Messiah, especially the revelation of the Messiah's identity to the Baptist and to Israel. On the lips of the Baptist, Jesus is referred to as 'Lamb of God',[1] one on whom the Spirit rests, 'Spirit-Baptizer' and 'Son/Chosen One of God'. We will focus on the significance of the Spirit's coming upon Jesus (1.32-34).[2]

The significance of the Spirit upon Jesus for the Baptist was that, based on prior divine revelation, he might recognize Jesus as the Messiah, and subsequently be able to reveal Jesus as such to 'Israel' and bear witness to him before 'Israel' (in order to evoke belief [cf. 1.7]).[3] However, what about the significance of the Spirit upon him for Jesus himself; why should the incarnate Logos need the Spirit? Scholars such as Bultmann, Kümmel, Käsemann and Schweizer think that for John the bestowal of the Spirit upon Jesus had no essential significance for Jesus himself.[4] These scholars have such an exalted view of John's Logos christology that they do not allow much place for the Spirit, but this is quite unnecessary. To begin with, Burge believes that both 'high' and 'low' christological concepts can stand side by side in John's Gospel; he argues that John knew and

---

[1] There are three possible intertextual backgrounds for the title 'Lamb of God' — the Suffering Servant of Isa. 53 who makes a guilt offering for the atonement of sin, the Passover Lamb of Exod. 12 as the means of escaping Yahweh's judgment, and the victorious Lamb of the apocalyptic traditions that will destroy the evil of the world (*1 En.* 90.38; *T.Jos.* 19.8; cf. Rev. although the word ἀρνίον is used instead of ἀμνός) — and 1.29 is possibly a creative fusion of all these three intertexts. Nevertheless, whatever the antecedents of the expression, the *function* of 'Lamb of God' is soteriological (ὁ αἴρων τὴν ἁμαρτίαν τοῦ κόσμου).

[2] Johnston rejects any reference to the divine Spirit of God for πνεῦμα in 1.32-33; 3.5-8, 34; 6.63; 7.39. He argues that πνεῦμα refers to divine power and fluctuates between the sense of divine hypostatized power and that of dynamic energy immanently active in people (*Spirit-Paraclete*, 9-12, 84, 123). Cf. Bultmann, for whom John's concept of πνεῦμα refers to the divine power that establishes and rules over the being of the believer (*Gospel*, 139-40 n.1). It seems inadequate, however, also in the light of our investigation of sapiential Judaism, to interpret πνεῦμα in terms less than the divine Spirit (cf. B.M. Newman and E.A. Nida, *A Translator's Handbook on the Gospel of John* [New York: UBS, 1980] 650-53). For a critique of Johnston's concept of πνεῦμα, see E. Malatesta, 'The Spirit/Paraclete in the Fourth Gospel', *Bib* 54 (1973) 540-43.

[3] The (implied) reader is already familiar with the Baptist's function as witness (1.6-9, 15). For the witness motif in 1.29-34, see J.D. Charles, '"Will the Court Please Call in the Prime Witness?": John 1:29-34 and the "Witness"-Motif', *TrinJ* 10 (1989) 71-83.

[4] Bultmann, *Gospel*, 92 n.4; Käsemann, *Testament*, 20-26; Kümmel, *Theology*, 314; E. Schweizer, 'Πνεῦμα, πνευματικός' in *TDNT*, VI:438. Cf. Loader, *Christology*, 129-32.

refashioned the (primitive) christology from the Synoptic tradition, but that even John's 'higher' christology still preserves a place for the Spirit.[5] Likewise, Kasper argues that the Logos was wholly a mould and receptacle for God's self-communication *because* of the Spirit.[6] Moreover, it seems natural to assume that Jesus needs to be anointed in order to anoint; in order to baptize people with Spirit (v.33) Jesus needs to have the Spirit imparted first (v.32) (cf. 1 Jn 2.20, 27). Further, in a Gospel that also emphasizes Jesus' humanity (e.g. 4.6-7; 11.33; 12.27; 13.21), it should come as no surprise that Jesus is endowed with the Spirit. Finally, the Jewish expectation was that the Messiah would be endowed with the Spirit.

Dunn argues for a fixed division of salvation-history, in which the Spirit's descent on Jesus marked his entry into the new covenant and into a new epoch of salvation-history. Moreover, the disciples, due to the various stages in the transition period between the old and new dispensation, could only experience the Spirit and the new life/birth after the cross.[7] However, Dunn's scheme seems too rigid. If Jesus only entered the new age and experienced new life at the Jordan, does Dunn imply that this occasion denoted Jesus' conversion experience and entry into new covenant sonship? Did the incarnation not mark the start of the new age, and was Jesus himself, as the incarnate Wisdom/Logos, not the bringer of new life (1.1-18; cf. 5.26)?[8] Moreover, although Dunn is right in saying that the

---

[5] Burge, *Community*, 71-73. However, it seems that Burge has exaggerated his case for a 'higher' Spirit-christology when he reduces the Spirit to merely an attribute of Jesus' person or to Jesus' breath/life (*Community*, 87-100, 110; cf. Scott, *Sophia*, 137, 164-65). For a critique, see M.[M.B.] Turner and G.M. Burge, '*The Anointed Community*: A Review and Response', *EvQ* 62 (1990) 261-63. E.C. Colwell and E.L. Titus go beyond Burge by stating that Jesus and the Spirit are fused into one person/nature (*The Gospel of the Spirit: A Study in the Fourth Gospel* [New York: Harper & Brothers, 1953] 120-37).

[6] W. Kasper, *Jesus The Christ* (Transl. V. Green; London: Burns & Oates, 1976) 250-68.

[7] Although Dunn's division of salvation-history is mainly based on the Synoptics, it is also implied in John (J.D.G. Dunn, *Baptism in the Holy Spirit: A Re-examination of the New Testament Teaching on the Gift of the Spirit in relation to Pentecostalism today* [London: SCM Press, 1970] 29 n.19, 180-81; *idem*, 'Spirit and Kingdom', *ET* 82 [1970-71] 39).

[8] Although the later Dunn seems to have slightly changed his view, he still maintains that for Luke Jesus' anointing with the Spirit was initiatory and marked the start of the new age ('Baptism in the Spirit: A Response to Pentecostal Scholarship on Luke-Acts', *JPT* 3 [1993] 3-27, esp. 16-22). Colwell and Titus put forward an adoptionist interpretation of 1.29-34; at his baptism, the man Jesus *became* the divine Son of God through the descent of the Spirit (*Gospel*, 109-11, 118, 136). However, apparently they have dismissed the incarnation described in the Prologue. Moreover, 1.29-34 is not about ontology (Jesus being/becoming divine) but about functionality (Jesus being empowered by the Spirit).

disciples' experience was limited to that which was possible at each stage, this chapter will show that the disciples' experience of Spirit and life was not exclusively confined to the time after the cross (cf. ch. 3 section 4.1).

It is also important to note that the language of the Spirit descending on Jesus and 'resting' or 'remaining' on him (vv.32-33) probably alludes to Isaiah 11.2, which presents the Davidic Messiah on whom the Spirit (of wisdom, understanding, knowledge and power) rests.[9] Another OT text which could serve as background to vv.32-34, if we accept the more difficult reading of ὁ ἐκλεκτός in v.34, is Isaiah 42.1, which depicts the Isaianic Servant as endowed with the Spirit to establish justice on earth (cf. Isa. 11.1-5).[10] The implication of recognizing Isaiah 11.2 (and 42.1) as the conceptual background to Jesus' endowment with the Spirit, is not only that the endowment would be permanent, but, more precisely, that Jesus would be *empowered* for his ministry.[11] Thus, Jesus' experience at the Jordan is an endowment as Messiah and the allusions to Isaiah 11.2 (and 42.1) would naturally assume that *Jesus would be equipped by the Spirit to accomplish his ministry exactly through the gifts of charismatic wisdom, understanding, knowledge and liberating power.*[12]

---

[9] Burge argues that ἔμεινεν denotes the 'permanence' of the Spirit on Jesus (*Community*, 54-56; cf. Schnackenburg, *Gospel*, 1:303-304; Porsch, *Pneuma*, 36, 41; Barrett, *Gospel*, 178; Carson, *Gospel*, 151; Morris, *Gospel*, 133 n.75; see also the theme 'remaining in Jesus' in ch. 3). Turner, however, criticizes Burge, and argues that here μένω ἐπί simply means 'to alight/settle upon' (*Spirit*, 59 n.5). However, even if the 'permanence' of the Spirit upon Jesus is not locked up in the meaning of μένω, it is nevertheless implied by the allusion to Isa. 11.2, which depicts the Messiah as endowed with the Spirit permanently.

[10] Porsch, *Pneuma*, 37-41; Burge, *Community*, 59-62. The more difficult reading ὁ ἐκλεκτός in v.34 is supported by most scholars (e.g., Porsch, Schnackenburg, Brown, Barrett, Lindars, Burge, Morris, S. Smalley, 'Salvation Proclaimed: VIII. John 1[29-34]', *ET* 93 [1981-82] 324-29).

[11] Contra H.-C. Kammler, who denies Isa. 11.2; 42.1 as the intertextual background to Jn 1.32-34 ('Jesus Christus und der Geistparaklet: Eine Studie zur johanneischen Verhältnisbestimmung von Pneumatologie und Christologie' in O. Hofius and H.-C. Kammler [eds.], *Johannesstudien: Untersuchungen zur Theologie des vierten Evangeliums* [WUNT 88; Tübingen: Mohr Siebeck, 1996] 157-58). Chevallier argues that Jesus is consecrated as the eschatological Temple through the presence of the Spirit, and that the Spirit has no further role in Jesus' ministry (*Souffle*, 2:425-26). However, we suggest that the Spirit upon Jesus is about empowerment for service rather than consecration (as if Jesus needed to be purified). Moreover, we will also demonstrate the vital role of the Spirit in Jesus' ministry.

[12] Cf. Turner, *Spirit*, 59.

2.2. Jesus Speaks the Words of God

The immediate cotext of 3.34 is 3.31-36, which is most probably the narrator's commentary rather than the words of the Baptist or Jesus.[13] Some scholars think that vv.31-36 are primarily intended to contrast Jesus and John the Baptist,[14] but this is too narrow an interpretation. Rather, the section 3.31-36 draws to its climax the supremacy of the revelation through Jesus over all other previous words of the prophets.[15]

An important issue is whether the subject of δίδωμι in v.34 is God or Jesus.[16] Although the majority of scholars take God as the subject, we cannot easily dismiss Porsch, who probably presents the best case for taking Jesus as the subject. Porsch argues that v.34 does not allude to 1.32 but to 1.33: 'der vom Himmel gekommene Gottgesandte gibt als der »ὁ βαπτίζων ἐν πνεύματι ἁγίῳ« das Pneuma nicht abgemessen!'[17] From v.34 onwards Jesus' 'Spirit-baptism' is identical with his function as Revealer, namely, the giving of the Spirit and the speaking of God's word are one event: when Jesus speaks the word of God, he also gives the Spirit.[18] However, although Porsch's view is grammatically possible, it can hardly be the point that 'Jesus speaks the words of God because *Jesus* gives the Spirit without measure'.[19] Moreover, the coming of the Spirit at Jesus' baptism is not merely a sign of Jesus' identity, but the empowerment of Jesus to fulfil his task as Revealer (cf. section 2.1, above), i.e., the Spirit is

---

[13] Burge, *Community*, 82; Beasley-Murray, *John*, 53; Carson, *Gospel*, 212; Stibbe, *John*, 59; Morris, *Gospel*, 215; Witherington, *Wisdom*, 110; H.N. Ridderbos, *The Gospel according to John: A Theological Commentary* (Transl. J. Vriend; Grand Rapids: Eerdmans, 1997) 148-49.

[14] Dunn, *Baptism*, 20; Brown, *Gospel*, 1:161; Barrett, *Gospel*, 219; Burge, *Community*, 82-83.

[15] Brown, *Gospel*, 1:157; Beasley-Murray, *John*, 53.

[16] Scholars who take God as subject are, e.g., Bultmann, *Gospel*, 164; Schnackenburg, *Gospel*, 1:386; Barrett, *Gospel*, 226; Burge, *Community*, 83-84; Beasley-Murray, *John*, 53-54; Carson, *Gospel*, 213; Morris, *Gospel*, 218-19; Witherington, *Wisdom*, 111; Ridderbos, *Gospel*, 150; Turner, *Spirit*, 59. Amongst those who take Jesus as subject are Thüsing, *Erhöhung*, 154-55; Brown, *Gospel*, 1:158; Porsch, *Pneuma*, 103-105; I. de la Potterie, 'L'Esprit-Saint dans l'Evangile de Jean', *NTS* 18 (1971-72) 448-49; *idem*, 'Parole', 182-84; J.-J. Suurmond, *The Ethical Influence of the Spirit of God: An Exegetical and Theological Study with Special Reference to 1 Corinthians, Romans 7:14-8:30, and the Johannine Literature* (Fuller Theological Seminary: Ph.D. dissertation, 1983; Ann Arbor: UMI, 1985) 235-36; W. Howard-Brook, *Becoming Children of God: John's Gospel and Radical Discipleship* (Maryknoll: Orbis, 1994) 98. E.C. Hoskyns allows for both referents (*The Fourth Gospel* [2 vols.; F.N. Davey (ed.); London: Faber and Faber, 1940] 1:250-51).

[17] Porsch, *Pneuma*, 104.

[18] Porsch, *Pneuma*, 104-105; 200.

[19] Turner, *Spirit*, 59. Cf. Burge for a criticism of Porsch (*Community*, 83 n.140).

a prerequisite for Jesus' activity as Revealer, because the Spirit provides Jesus with charismatic wisdom and power.

Thus, it is more probable that we should take God as the subject of δίδωμι, so that '**Jesus speaks the words of God** *because* **God gives** *Jesus* **the Spirit without measure'**, (cf. the Spirit-endowed messianic Servant speaking Yahweh's words in Isa. 50.4).[20] Therefore, contra Porsch et al., 3.34 alludes to Jesus' endowment with the Spirit in 1.32 rather than to his function as Spirit-Baptizer in 1.33, i.e., 3.34 is not talking about Jesus' 'giving' the Spirit.[21] Interestingly, the phrase οὐκ ἐκ μέτρου may be a possible (contrasting) allusion to *Leviticus Rabbah* 15.2, which teaches that the Spirit rested on the prophets *only by measure*, so that '*John's* point would then be that the *immeasurable* gift of the Spirit (of revelation) *to* Jesus corresponds to the perfection of revelation *through* Jesus — it provides a revelation which *transcends* the Law and the Prophets.'[22] Jesus and his revelatory ministry supersedes all God's messengers prior to him and their revelation, i.e., all the OT prophets as well as John the Baptist.[23]

2.3. The Significance of the Spirit upon Jesus

The soteriological significance of the Spirit upon Jesus can be drawn out further than Johannine scholarship has done so far, in that John already

---

[20] Cf. Turner, *Spirit*, 59. Cf. also the argument in v.35: πάντα in v.35 corresponds to οὐκ ἐκ μέτρου of v.34b, so that v.35 is the more generalizing comment of which the statement in v.34b is the more particular outworking (Bultmann, *Gospel*, 165; Schnackenburg, *Gospel*, 1:387; Brown, *Gospel*, 1:161; Carson, *Gospel*, 213).

[21] What Porsch means by Jesus' 'giving' the Spirit is not completely clear yet, but we will deal with that in section 3, below. Cf. Schnackenburg, who contends that 3.34 refers to Jesus' pouring out the Spirit in his revelatory words (*Gospel*, 1:387). Dunn (*Baptism*, 20, 32) and Morris (*Gospel*, 218-19) also see (at a secondary level) a reference to Jesus' gift of the Spirit to his disciples. However, with an eye on 7.39, it is unlikely that 3.34 refers to Jesus' 'giving' or communicating the Spirit to people. Moreover, we will argue in section 3, below, that although the Spirit is active in/through Jesus' words, i.e., the Spirit affects people through Jesus' words, the Spirit is not yet 'given' before the cross.

[22] Turner, *Spirit*, 59 (author's emphasis); cf. Hoskyns, *Gospel*, 1:250-51; Beasley-Murray, *John*, 53-54. Contra B.C. Aker, who argues that ἐκ μέτρου refers to regeneration by the Spirit ('John, Gospel of' in S.M. Burgess, G.B. McGee and P.H. Alexander [eds.], *Dictionary of Pentecostal and Charismatic Movements* [Grand Rapids: Zondervan, 1988] 504).

[23] The illocutionary force of 3.31-36 is to assert Jesus' superiority, through the use of spatial dualism — to the realm/sphere of heaven/from above belongs God, Jesus, the Spirit, revelation, life, light, grace, truth, glory; to the realm/sphere of the earth/from below belongs the devil, the world, 'the Jews', flesh, darkness, blindness, death, lies, sin — and to present people with a choice — to accept or reject Jesus and his revelation (cf. 3.18). Moreover, the intended perlocution is to persuade people to believe in the Son; by drawing out the consequences, the implied author recommends one choice (acceptance) above the other (rejection).

reveals something about the interrelation between Spirit, W/wisdom and salvation in 1.32-34 and 3.34. Jesus, as Wisdom incarnate, has come from ἄνωθεν, the realm of God, and he testifies to what he has seen and heard (in the realm of God) (3.31-32). In other words, Jesus is sent by God to speak the words of God, i.e., to bring God's revelation, which is not only the revelation that comes *from* God but is also the revelation *about* God (3.34a; cf. 1.18).[24] These revelatory words of God are the essence of Jesus' teaching. Thus, Jesus' purpose is to reveal God, namely, who God is, based on what Jesus himself has seen and heard (cf. 1.1-2, 14, 18).

Jesus can bring this revelation from and concerning God precisely *because* God has given Jesus the complete fullness of the Spirit (3.34b). The logical inference is then that Jesus can be the Revealer (and as such reveal God) because the *Spirit* provides Jesus with revelatory words, viz., with charismatic revelation/wisdom (cf. Jesus' endowment with the Spirit as described in 1.32-34). *Jesus' endowment with the Spirit is primarily an empowerment of revelatory wisdom in order to reveal God.*[25] Those who receive/accept this revelation have eternal life, whereas rejection leads to judgment (3.36). We suggest then that the interrelation between Spirit, W/wisdom and salvation can be tentatively expressed as: (i) the Spirit endows Jesus/Wisdom incarnate with revelatory wisdom; (ii) Wisdom incarnate brings to people the revelation from and about God; (iii) those who accept God's revelation in Jesus receive salvation/eternal life (whereas rejection of this revelation results in judgment).

This confirms our concept of 'the Spirit as the power of saving Wisdom'. The Spirit functions as the revealing power of Wisdom incarnate, in that the Spirit, through the mediation of revelatory wisdom to Jesus, is the power behind the saving revelation of God that Jesus brings primarily in his teaching. This concept of the Spirit providing Jesus with revelatory wisdom also confirms our suggestion regarding the issue of how Jesus is able to communicate what he has seen and heard from the Father (cf. the theme 'sensory perception' in ch. 3). Jesus is able to reveal to people what he has seen and heard from the Father precisely because the Spirit, functioning as the channel of communication between the Father and Son, provides Jesus with this 'information' and insight into the divine

---

[24] The genitive τοῦ θεοῦ denotes origin/source (the words that come from God) as well as content (the words that define/describe God). Cf. 1.51, which, alluding to Gen. 28.12, depicts Jesus as a mediator having free access to both the realm of God and the realm of man.

[25] This possibly explains how the incarnate Logos can reveal the Father (1.18). Burge (*Community*, 62) and Turner (*Spirit*, 57, 60) have also recognized that in John the Spirit is the Spirit/power of revelation.

reality.[26] More important, if salvation is based on God's work in Jesus at the cross (cf. ch. 3), then God's saving revelation in Jesus is not only the revelation of who God is but also includes what he does or has done in Jesus (especially at the cross). Moreover, if the significance of this event needs to be revealed to and understood by people (cf. ch. 3), and if it is the Spirit who functions as the power to reveal God through Jesus and his revelatory wisdom teaching, then the Spirit would be expected to mediate the significance of the cross and hence salvation.

In sum, the soteriological significance of the Spirit upon Jesus is threefold. First, the Spirit upon Jesus reveals him to be the expected Messiah, who would take away the sin of the world (1.29) and who would be expected to bring justice and deliverance (Isa. 11.4-5; 42.1-4). Second, the Spirit endows Jesus primarily with revelatory wisdom in order to accomplish his salvific mission. Third, Jesus brings God's saving revelation, i.e., what he has seen and heard from the Father and what the Father will do in Jesus at the cross, because he is endowed with the Spirit and wisdom. This insight into the relationship between Spirit, W/wisdom and salvation raises the following questions. How, and in what way, does the Spirit function as the power of Jesus and the revelation/salvation he brings? What precisely is the significance (in terms of its soteriological effect) of Jesus' endowment with the Spirit for the people? These questions will be addressed when we turn to the discourses in John 3, 4 and 6.

3. The Spirit and Salvation —
The Spirit as a Life-Giving Cognitive Agent

In this section we will look at three discourses and their respective metaphors — 'the birth of the Spirit' in John 3, 'living water' in John 4 and 'the bread of life' (in combination with 'the Spirit gives life') in John 6 — in order to discover how the Spirit functions as the facilitator of cognitive perception, understanding and life during Jesus' ministry.[27]

---

[26] Contra H. Windisch, who argues that the Spirit is scarcely to be regarded as a mediator, and that Jesus receives his instructions directly from the Father ('Jesus and the Spirit in the Gospel of John' in J. Reumann [ed.], *The Spirit-Paraclete in the Fourth Gospel* [Transl. J.W. Cox; Philadelphia: Fortress, 1968] 36).

[27] Jn 3-6 also depicts the main concentration of the terms ζάω, ζωή and ζῳοποιέω (see appendix 1). For a detailed analysis of John's metaphorical language, see van der Watt, *Family*.

3.1. Entrance into Salvation — The Birth of the Spirit

The pericope 2.23-3.21 can be divided into three units: the setting (2.23-3.1), the dialogue between Jesus and Nicodemus (3.2-15), and the narrator's commentary (3.16-21). The story starts with the statement that many people believed in Jesus on the basis of his miraculous signs (2.23), but, based on Jesus' revelatory knowledge of people, this belief-response seems to be inadequate (2.24-25).[28] The inadequacy of this belief is spelled out in 3.2-15 by virtue of Nicodemus being one of the πολλοί of 2.23.[29] Our focus is on the dialogue between Jesus and Nicodemus, which is centred on the image of birth that becomes, through the narrative, one of John's symbols for eternal life.[30] The story context is probably that the conversation took place in Jerusalem (2.23), at night (3.2), between Jesus and his disciples (plurals in 3.11-12) and Nicodemus with his disciples (οἴδαμεν in 3.2).[31] In this discourse Jesus is portrayed as Wisdom: just as Wisdom revealed to Jacob the kingdom of God (Wis. 10.10), so does Jesus to Nicodemus.

The Nature of the Birth of the Spirit (vv.2-8). Nicodemus' opening statement in v.2 probably reflects the type of belief-response of the πολλοί in 2.23 because both Nicodemus and the group he represents base their response on Jesus' miraculous signs. Jesus rejects Nicodemus' offer of the topic of identity (the implied question is 'Who are you?'),[32] and offers the topic of entry into the kingdom of God instead (v.3). Nicodemus accepts the new topic, and with it Jesus' superiority, but he misunderstands Jesus (v.4). Nicodemus understands the new birth literally and hence misses the

---

[28] Consequently, Moloney seems to remain critical towards the possibility of complete belief based purely on signs ('Cana', 192, 201). However, this seems unwarranted (see ch. 3 section 4.2).

[29] Ἄνθρωπος in 3.1 alludes to its double use in 2.25, and the antecedent of αὐτόν in 3.2 is Jesus in 2.24 (cf. Cotterell/Turner, *Linguistics*, 279; Stibbe, *John*, 53).

[30] Cf. Lee, *Narratives*, 36.

[31] Cf. F.P. Cotterell, 'The Nicodemus Conversation: A Fresh Appraisal', *ET* 96 (1984-85) 238. Although 'by night' probably reflects the rabbinic custom of using the 'night' for theological discussion (Cotterell/Turner, *Linguistics*, 282), it probably also symbolizes that Nicodemus is still in the dark and is invited to come into the light. Nicodemus and Jesus are contrasted in many ways: traditional Jewish wisdom encounters Wisdom incarnate, 'a man' meets the Son of Man.

[32] Stibbe contends that the implied question is one of origin (*John*, 53), whereas Bultmann thinks it is soteriological (*Gospel*, 134).

metaphorical meaning.[33] The solution to resolve the misunderstanding is further revelation provided by Jesus (vv.5-15). V.5 parallels and hence explains v.3: (i) the birth from above is a birth of water and Spirit (cf. the birth from God in 1.13); (ii) to 'see' the kingdom of God means to enter into it.[34] Thus, due to its parallels with 1.13 and 3.5, 'birth from above' is a circumlocution for 'birth from God/the Spirit'.[35]

There is much dispute about the meaning of the phrase γεννηθῇ ἐξ ὕδατος καὶ πνεύματος in v.5, to which the large number of possible interpretations testify. We will not present the whole spectrum of views, because in arguing for our own position we will offer evidence that implicitly excludes most others.[36] Because v.5 parallels v.3, ἄνωθεν is now interpreted by ἐξ ὕδατος καὶ πνεύματος, which implies that water and Spirit are not contrasted but in some way conjoined. This is also confirmed by the fact that both ὕδατος and πνεύματος are anarthrous, governed by the single preposition ἐκ, and conjoined by καί, indicating that the phrase is to be viewed as a conceptual unity, a hendiadys.[37] Thus, the metaphorical

---

[33] The passive of γεννάω can mean either 'to be born' or 'to be begotten'. Most scholars opt for the latter (e.g., Brown, *Gospel*, 1:130; Schweizer, 'Πνεῦμα', VI:439; E. Haenchen, *John: A Commentary on the Gospel of John* [2 vols.; Philadelphia: Fortress Press, 1984] 1:200; Beasley-Murray, *John*, 45; Carson, *Gospel*, 189). The word ἄνωθεν is an example of John's literary technique of ambiguity and double entendre, meaning either 'from above', denoting origin (spatial reference), or 'again/afresh/anew' (temporal reference). Scholars line up on either side, but the meaning 'from above' seems more likely because: (i) 'born of God' (1.13) parallels 'born from above/of the Spirit' (3.3, 5); (ii) Jesus is portrayed as one who came from above (3.2, 13, 31); (iii) as part of John's spatial dualism, the birth of the Spirit (from above) is contrasted with the natural birth of the flesh (from below) (3.6; cf. 1.13). Moreover, the meaning 'from above' implies and includes the meaning 'again/anew'; a birth from above is also a re-birth. Although Nicodemus misunderstands Jesus and chooses the meaning 'again/anew' (cf. δεύτερον in v.4), the real misunderstanding is in the *reference* of the new birth: Nicodemus thinks it refers to physical birth whereas Jesus refers to a spiritual birth (cf. Lee, *Narratives*, 50).

[34] Contra J.A. Trumbower, who argues that vv.3 and 5 are not parallels but two subsequent steps for participation in the kingdom of God: v.3 denotes a fixed and determinative category for human beings as a prerequisite for the subsequent rebirth from (water and) the spirit (v.5), which happens automatically to those who belong to the first category. Nicodemus does not and cannot belong to the first category, and hence, is not offered the possibility of rebirth (*Born from Above: The Anthropology of the Gospel of John* [HUTh 29; Tübingen: Mohr Siebeck, 1992] 71-74).

[35] Cf. Turner, *Spirit*, 67. Related to the concept of new birth is the question of parenthood; one's father is either God (1.13) or the devil (8.44). The concept of birth of God is well attested in 1 John (1 Jn 2.29; 3.9; 4.7; 5.1, 18).

[36] For an overview and assessment of major and minor interpretations, see L. Belleville, '"Born of Water and Spirit:" John 3:5', *TrinJ* 1 (1980) 125-34; Carson, *Gospel*, 191-95.

[37] Cf. Dunn, *Baptism*, 191-92; Montague, *Spirit*, 343; Belleville, 'Water', 134; Burge, *Community*, 166; Carson, *Gospel*, 194; Turner, *Spirit*, 67. H.M. Ervin's definition of a

birth of water-and-Spirit probably describes two different, although related, activities under one single concept, and not one activity or two identical activities.

Because vv.7 and 10 indicate that Jesus expected Nicodemus to be able to understand all this from his background as a Pharisee, the reader probably needs to look at the OT, the scriptures of first-century Judaism, in order to recognize the conceptual background to this birth of water-and-Spirit. The single most important intertext that closely combines ὕδωρ and πνεῦμα, and which could serve as the probable conceptual background to 3.5, is Ezekiel 36.25-27:[38]

> I will sprinkle clean water upon you, and you shall be clean from all your uncleannesses, and from all your idols I will cleanse you. A new heart I will give you, and a new spirit I will put within you; and I will remove from your body the heart of stone and give you a heart of flesh. I will put my spirit within you, and make you follow my statutes and be careful to observe my ordinances.

In this passage, we have a promise of Israel's eschatological cleansing (with water) from impurity and of her transformation through the impartation of Yahweh's 'indwelling' Spirit. Moreover, if we read Ezekiel 36.25-27 in conjunction with Ezekiel 37.1-14 (which most scholars do not do), we see that the Spirit sustains as well as causes this inner transformation of Yahweh's people.[39] Thus, Ezekiel 36-37 describes the

---

hendiadys, in which one element is absorbed into the other, is too narrow; he used a common language dictionary rather than a grammar. If, according to Ervin, ὕδατος καὶ πνεύματος were a hendiadys, the result would be 'spiritual water' (*Conversion-Initiation and the Baptism in the Holy Spirit: A critique of James D.G. Dunn, Baptism in the Holy Spirit* [Peabody: Hendrickson, 1984] 145). Aker ('John', 504) and Morris (*Gospel*, 191-93) actually use this narrow definition of hendiadys.

[38] Cf. Brown, *Gospel*, 1:140-41; Belleville, 'Water', 138-40; Bruce, *Gospel*, 84; Cotterell, 'Conversation', 241; Beasley-Murray; *John*, 49; S.M. Schneiders, 'Born Anew', *Theology Today* 44 (1987) 192; Burge, *Community*, 162-63; Carson, *Gospel*, 195; Turner, *Spirit*, 68. Surprisingly, Porsch almost completely dismisses the relevance of Ezek. 36.25-27 (*Pneuma*, 123). J.E. Morgan-Wynne even rejects Ezek. 36.25-27 as background to 3.5 because there is no specific reference to cleansing in Jn 3 ('References to Baptism in the Fourth Gospel' in S.E. Porter and A.R. Cross [eds.], *Baptism, the New Testament and the Church: Historical and Contemporary Studies in Honour of R.E.O. White* [JSNT.S 171; Sheffield: SAP, 1999] 122-23; cf. Bultmann, *Gospel*, 138 n.3). However, it seems that the general function of water in John is one of cleansing/purification (cf. Keener). Isa. 44.3 does not seem the primary referent of 3.5 because there 'water' and 'Spirit' are set in parallel, denoting one activity.

[39] Van Imschoot denies the role of the divine Spirit being the *agent* of the new life in Ezek. 36.25-27. According to van Imschoot, Ezek. 36.25-27 envisages the interior regeneration of individuals in three stages: (i) purification from sin (v.25); (ii) the renewal of the human heart and spirit (v.26); (iii) the gift of the divine Spirit, the principle of the moral life (v.27). The Spirit then, according to van Imschoot, is not

collective restoration of Israel, in which the divine Spirit is depicted as both the agent and as the sustaining power/principle of Israel's new life ('salvation'), i.e., in the eschatological age Yahweh will purify, transform and sustain his people by means of the Spirit.[40] Moreover, this spiritual purification and recreation is interpreted as a spiritual circumcision of the heart, alluding to that which Moses had already spoken about (Deut. 10.16; 30.6). Intertestamental Judaism picked up and developed this theme. *Jubilees* 1.23-24 understands Ezekiel's promise in terms of God's act of recreation and purification that ensures a life of true obedient sonship which is effectively a new birth.[41] The Qumran community also employs the concept of God cleansing and purifying the person by the Spirit (1QS 3.6-9; 4.20-22), and this purification of the heart by the Spirit is a prerequisite for grasping divine wisdom (see ch. 2).

Keener also recognizes a background of Ezekiel 36.25-27 to 3.5, and, due to his emphasis on purification in John, mentions that '[t]he Spirit functions as an eschatological *mikveh* in Ezek 36, and the water of John 3:5 thus is a picture of the Spirit, rather than representing something distinct from it.'[42] Moreover, Keener investigates the concept of 'rebirth' and argues that the clearest allusions to 'rebirth' are found in rabbinic literature concerning proselyte baptism.[43] Hence, Keener concludes that 'something more specific than the *mikveh* is in view: the Johannine Jesus is calling on Nicodemus to undergo a spiritual proselyte baptism, i.e., a conversion effected by the purifying Spirit of God, a new birth.'[44] Although Keener's conclusion may be correct, to take καί as epexegetical

---

involved in the first two stages ('Principe', 463-64; 'Alliance', 219-20). However, activities of cleansing and purification could be attributed to the Spirit (Isa. 4.4). Moreover, in the light of Ezek. 37.1-14 (esp. vv.5-6, 9-10, 14), it seems reasonable to assume that the inner transformation of Yahweh's people described in Ezek. 36 should also be attributed to Yahweh's Spirit (cf. L.C. Allen, *Ezekiel 20-48* [WBC 29; Dallas: Word, 1990] 187). Finally, would Judaism conceive the eschatological transformation to happen by any other means but Yahweh's Spirit?

[40] In the light of ch. 2, the 'new spirit' that Yahweh will put within Israel (Ezek. 36.26) probably denotes the renewal/restoration of Israel's covenantal relationship with Yahweh through his Spirit. Jn 3.8 probably also alludes to Ezekiel 37.1-14; both texts deliberately play on the double meaning of πνεῦμα/רוּחַ — 'wind' or 'Spirit'. The point of the pun is that although both wind and Spirit in themselves are invisible, their activities are perceived in their *effects*. Moreover, Nicodemus does not even know where the πνεῦμα comes from; it comes from ἄνωθεν.

[41] Turner, *Spirit*, 68.

[42] C.S. Keener, *The Spirit in the Gospels and Acts: Divine Purity and Power* (Peabody: Hendrickson, 1997) 151; *idem*, 'Function', 183.

[43] Keener, 'Function', 161-76; *idem*, *Spirit*, 143-49.

[44] Keener, *Spirit*, 151; cf. *idem*, 'Function', 183-84.

is mistaken; water and Spirit, though closely related, are distinct both in 3.5 and in Ezekiel 36.25-27.

Belleville, followed by Carson, argues that because πνεῦμα is anarthrous (cf. 4.23), πνεῦμα does not refer to the Holy Spirit but to God's nature: ὕδωρ and πνεῦμα constitute a twofold source which defines the nature of birth — ὕδωρ refers to the prophetic eschatological cleansing (Ezek. 36.26-27) and πνεῦμα to the impartation of God's nature as πνεῦμα (4.24) — rather than identifying a personal agent (τὸ πνεῦμα) for this birth.[45] Nevertheless, Belleville does acknowledge that this dual work of purification and impartation of God's nature is accomplished through God's Spirit (but based on 3.6).[46] Although Belleville has convincingly argued for the intertextual background of Ezekiel 36.25-27, her view is not entirely without difficulties. Her argument that πνεῦμα in 3.5 refers to spirit (as God's nature) because πνεῦμα is anarthrous, whereas τὸ πνεῦμα in 3.6 does refer to the divine Spirit, is not persuasive. The absence of the article is not determinative; in 1.33, 6.63 and 7.39, for example, πνεῦμα is used in each verse both with and without the article, and it would be unlikely that each time two different referents are in view.[47] Moreover, πνεῦμα referring to 'spirit' as God's nature does not seem to be Johannine terminology; even in 4.24, the phrase πνεῦμα ὁ θεός probably means something like 'God is represented or manifested by the Spirit', rather than a metaphysical statement concerning the nature of God.

Having suggested that the birth of ὕδωρ and πνεῦμα refers respectively to cleansing/purification and the transforming 'indwelling' of God's Spirit, which results in a new creation, we can then exclude several other views: (i) views that 3.5 denotes two births: the birth of water is natural birth of flesh from flesh, and the birth of spirit is spiritual birth of spirit from spirit;[48] (ii) views which take καί as epexegetical, i.e., the Spirit explains the water or the water refers to the Spirit;[49] (iii) views which take John the Baptist's baptism as a referent for the water.[50]

---

[45] Belleville, 'Water', 135, 139-40; Carson, *Gospel*, 195. Belleville takes πνεῦμα as 'spirit' also in the syntactical parallels in 4.23 and 6.63.

[46] Belleville, 'Water', 140.

[47] Cf. Newman/Nida, *Handbook*, 650-53. Harner also makes too much of the presence and absence of the article in relation to πνεῦμα (*Relation*, 34-37).

[48] Schneiders, 'Born Anew', 192; M. Davies, *Rhetoric and Reference in the Fourth Gospel* (JSNT.S 69; Sheffield: JSOT Press, 1992) 141-42; Lee, *Narratives*, 45-48, 52; Witherington, *Wisdom*, 97. However, because of the hendiadys, ὕδωρ and πνεῦμα are not set in contrast with each other. Moreover, both Witherington and Lee fail to see that Ezek. 36.25-27 is the conceptual background to 3.5, which could have led them in the right direction.

[49] Léon-Dufour, 'Reading', 450; Cotterell, 'Conversation', 240; S.M. Horton, 'Holy Spirit, Doctrine of the' in S.M. Burgess, G.B. McGee and P.H. Alexander (eds.), *Dictionary of Pentecostal and Charismatic Movements* (Grand Rapids: Zondervan, 1988)

It must be noted that the promise in Ezekiel was primarily referring to the corporate eschatological cleansing and transformation of Israel rather than to an individual's conversion. This is also implied in John 3: Nicodemus is one of the πολλοί and represents the group to which he belongs (cf. the plural usage in vv.7, 11-12). Nevertheless, Nicodemus is also presented as an individual, and individuals in general are referred to in vv.3-8, 15. Thus, John 3 depicts the birth of water-and-Spirit not only as a corporate but also as a personal metaphor for entrance into the kingdom of God, into the true 'Israel'.[51]

414; Keener, 'Function', 183; *idem, Spirit,* 151; L.P. Jones, *The Symbol of Water in the Gospel of John* (JSNT.S 145; Sheffield: SAP, 1997) 71, 74. However, water and Spirit do not have the same referent; καί points towards a relation between the two terms rather than denoting identity (cf. Ezek. 36.25-27, where water and Spirit also have two different functions). If water referred to the Spirit, 3.5 would be a tautology (cf. Lee, *Narratives,* 44-45). The point in 3.5 is that both terms have two distinct referents — 'water' refers to cleansing and 'Spirit' refers to transformation — even though the cleansing/purification itself is probably a work of the Spirit. Due to this epexegetical view, Jones wrongly argues that water does not appear to denote purification but functions as the *agent* of the new birth (*Symbol,* 74-75). Moreover, Jones's case, that in John water primarily symbolizes the Spirit (*Symbol,* 229), seems an oversimplification: e.g., in 7.39 water refers to the Spirit but not in 2.6-9; 5.7; 19.34 (for the latter assertion, see Bennema, 'Giving', section III), and in 3.5 water is 'merely' closely associated with the Spirit.

[50] Barrett, *Gospel,* 209; Burge, *Community,* 159-65; G.R. Beasley-Murray, 'John 3:3, 5: Baptism, Spirit and the Kingdom', *ET* 97 (1985-86) 168-69; *idem, John,* 49; Painter, *Quest,* 197 n.103; Ridderbos, *Gospel,* 127-28 (although he seems to read 3.5 through Pauline spectacles). Cf. Moloney, who argues that 3.5 refers to a baptism with water (similar to the Baptist's baptism), perfected with Jesus' baptism with the Spirit (cf. 1.33) (*Belief,* 111-12). However, this would still contradict ὕδωρ and πνεῦμα forming one single unitary event.

Many scholars see in 3.5 a reference to Christian baptism, either primarily or secondarily: e.g., C.K. Barrett, 'The Holy Spirit in the Fourth Gospel', *JThS* 1 (1950) 6-7; *idem, Gospel,* 209; Schnackenburg, *Gospel,* 1:369; I. de la Potterie and S. Lyonnet, *The Christian Lives by the Spirit* (Transl. J. Morriss; New York: Alba House, 1971) 1-36; Brown, *Gospel,* 1:141-44; Porsch, *Pneuma,* 101, 125-30; Schweizer, 'Πνεῦμα', VI:440 n.736; Bruce, *Gospel,* 84-85; Haenchen, *John,* 1:200; Burge, *Community,* 159-71; Culpepper, *Anatomy,* 193-94; Beasley-Murray, 'Baptism', 169-70; *idem, John,* 49; U. Schnelle, 'Johannes als Geisttheologe', *NT* 40 (1998) 26-27. Hoskyns allows for both the Baptist's baptism and Christian baptism (*Gospel,* 1:230-31). Dunn argues that water refers to Christian water-baptism and Spirit to Spirit-baptism, although both baptisms are closely connected (*Baptism,* 190-94; cf. Chevallier, *Souffle,* 2:504-509). However, a primary reference to Christian water-baptism would reduce Nicodemus to a mere foil in order to make a theological point for the Johannine community. Further, Nicodemus would never have been able to understand Jesus (contra 3.10). Moreover, even at a secondary level, a reference to Christian water-baptism remains problematic: would the Evangelist stress that Christian water-baptism is a prerequisite for salvation?

[51] John's movement of reinterpreting Ezek. 36.25-27 as a personal metaphor may also have consequences for his anthropology: if Ezek. 36.26 describes metaphorically a

In v.6 σάρξ is set over against πνεῦμα. Neither term refers to ontology but probably to their respective realms, worlds or spheres, so that v.6 would express the contrast between the realm of man (the world, the natural, the realm of below) and the realm of God (the realm of above, of heaven) (cf. 1.13; Isa. 31.3).[52] Birth of the flesh does not qualify for entrance into the kingdom of God; only birth of the Spirit. If the kingdom of God belongs to the realm from above, and if what is from the earth belongs to the realm from below and hence can never enter the kingdom of God (cf. v.31), then an agent from above (the Spirit) is needed to facilitate this entry. John's dualism comes very much to the fore in chapter 3: 'spirit' versus 'flesh' (v.6), light versus darkness (vv.19-21; cf. 1.5; 8.12; 9.4-5), above versus below (v.31; cf. 8.23), life versus death (vv.16, 36). This dualism has a soteriological dimension, denoting the two different realms — the realm of God and of man — and to which realm one belongs is dependent on one's attitude towards Jesus; namely, whether one accepts or rejects Jesus and his revelation.

The implication of Jesus' revelation in vv.3-8 is then that being born as a Jew is not sufficient to qualify for entry into the kingdom of God. The Spirit has now become the identity- or boundary-marker of the true 'Israel', and the metaphorical birth of the Spirit is the *conditio sine qua non* for entering into salvation, into the kingdom of God.[53]

The Manner of the Birth of the Spirit (vv.9-15). If entrance into the kingdom of God (salvation) requires a new creation/birth, *how* will this happen asks Nicodemus (v.9).[54] Jesus' question in v.10 functions as a rebuke for Nicodemus' misunderstanding of and inadequate response to his revelation in vv.5-8; Nicodemus should have grasped that Jesus referred to

---

radical change at the core of Israel's 'being' (denoted by 'new heart' and 'new spirit'), then 3.5 possibly also implies a change of a person's inmost being (at an ontological level). We interpret the Spirit's activities regarding people primarily in relational categories, but also allow the possibility of change at an ontological level, although we remain agnostic as to how and to what extent this operates. For 'Israel' understood as the new community constituted around Jesus as the true Israel, see Bennema, 'Giving', n.77. For the personal dimension in John, see C.F.D. Moule, 'The Individualism of the Fourth Gospel', *NT* 5 (1962) 171-90.

[52] Schnackenburg, *Gospel*, 1:371-72; Carson, *Gospel*, 196; cf. Bultmann, *Gospel*, 141.

[53] W.A. Meeks's conclusion that being (born) from above is the exclusive property of the Son of Man ('The Man from Heaven in Johannine Sectarianism', *JBL* 91 [1972] 52-53, 68), seems unwarranted.

[54] The question is not 'How can this be (true)?' but 'How can this come about (γενέσθαι)?'. Nicodemus is inquiring about the nature of this spiritual transformation. For the equation of entrance into the kingdom of God and entrance into salvation, see, e.g., the parallel between to 'see' the kingdom of God (v.3) and to 'see' (eternal) life (v.36).

some sort of spiritual conversion process.[55] Nicodemus' initial belief-response, as part of the group he represents (2.23-25), was not adequate, nor is his response to what Jesus says in vv.3-8; the problem for Nicodemus is that he had not been 'born from above'.

Although Johannine scholarship has recognized that Nicodemus has a problem, it has insufficiently analyzed its nature and the solution to it.[56] However, by examining vv.10-15 more closely, we can probe a little further. Jesus poignantly indicates in vv.11-12 that if Nicodemus does not even understand and believe the 'earthly things' Jesus has just spoken about in vv.3-8, then how can he grasp and believe the 'heavenly things' Jesus will speak about, which includes vv.14-15?[57] In vv.10-12, then, Jesus essentially points out that Nicodemus' problem is a cognitive one. The teacher of Israel fails or is unable to cognitively penetrate and understand the concept of entrance into salvation through a birth of the Spirit, nor to respond to this revelation with sufficient belief, and hence he does not experience the new birth.[58] Moreover, if Nicodemus is not able to produce an adequate belief-response on the basis of the cognitive information Jesus provided, how then will Nicodemus be able to respond adequately if Jesus starts to reveal even more (v.12)? How could Nicodemus overcome this cognitive barrier, especially in the light of v.10, which reveals that Jesus expected Nicodemus to have understood at least something of what he had revealed? Some important clues to the answer can be found in vv.13-15.

---

[55] Nicodemus should have grasped that Jesus referred to some sort of conversion process in order to enter the kingdom of God; proselyte baptism, effecting new birth, and the baptism of John the Baptist, as an extension of the practice of proselyte baptism to include the baptism of repentant Jews, could have occurred to him (Cotterell/Turner, *Linguistics*, 285). Culpepper points out the irony that a teacher of Israel cannot understand even earthly things (*Anatomy*, 169; cf. Stibbe, *John*, 57). Pryor, however, thinks that Jesus' response itself is irony, i.e., Jesus really never expected Nicodemus to understand his teaching; Nicodemus could have understood Jesus if he had spoken of cleansing or renewal by the Spirit rather than birth (*John*, 175, 218 n.58). It seems that Pryor has failed to recognize Ezek. 36 as the intertextual background, which explains this birth exactly in categories Nicodemus could have understood.

[56] Forestell, e.g., does not analyze vv.9-15 in relation to vv.3-8, and hence dismisses that the divine birth will come about through an understanding of the cross.

[57] Contra Thüsing, who, in line with his two-stage model (see ch. 1 section 2.3), argues that in vv.12-13 ἐπίγεια and καταβαίνω refer to Jesus' earthly work, whereas ἐπουράνια and ἀναβαίνω refer to the work of the ascended/exalted Jesus through the Paraclete (*Erhöhung*, 254-59). Bultmann (*Gospel*, 147-48), Beasley-Murray (*John*, 49-50) and O. Hofius ('Das Wunder der Wiedergeburt. Jesus Gespräch mit Nikodemus Joh 3,1-21' in O. Hofius and H.-C. Kammler [eds.], *Johannesstudien: Untersuchungen zur Theologie des vierten Evangeliums* [WUNT 88; Tübingen: Mohr Siebeck, 1996] 58-59) tend to agree with our interpretation of ἐπίγεια and ἐπουράνια.

[58] Vv.10-12 has a rich cognitive vocabulary (γινώσκω, οἶδα, ὁράω, λαμβάνω, πιστεύω).

In v.13 Jesus reveals his identity: he is the heavenly Revealer from the realm above who came to the realm below to testify to what he has seen and heard (cf. vv.31-32 and 1.51). The main problem of v.13 is the (perfect) tense of ἀναβέβηκεν, which seems to imply an ascent prior to a descent. Of the various possible explanations scholars have come up with,[59] the three most plausible ones are those of Borgen, Burkett and Kanagaraj.[60] Following their train of thought for a moment, whatever people might have been looking for (in heaven), the point is that Jesus brought it all down or had access to it. People do not need to ascend into heaven to gain knowledge of God and to catch a vision of God and his glory because: (i) to 'see' Jesus is to 'see' God (12.45; 14.9); (ii) Jesus revealed God and God's glory (1.14, 18); (iii) Jesus made God known and spoke the words of God (3.34; 7.16; 8.28; 12.49-50; 14.24; 17.6); (iv) Jesus testified about the 'heavenly things' (3.12, 31-32).

The main difficulty with all these positions is that there seems to be no indication in the entire pericope (2.23-3.21) that refers to people undertaking some sort of heavenly ascent. Moreover, perhaps v.13 does not even indicate temporal priority; 1.51 also mentions that angels ascended and descended, without implying that the angels' starting point was the earth. In this case, we may perhaps just assume the Johannine christological-revelation pattern of descent (incarnation) and ascent (via the cross) (cf. Wisdom's V-patterned journey). Bultmann also argues that the Evangelist did not think of people ascending into heaven (to bring back heavenly knowledge), nor that ἀναβαίνω precedes καταβαίνω. He suggests that, in answer to the question 'Who can enter the heavenly world?', 3.13 indicates that Jesus is the one who has come down from heaven.[61] Alternatively, Cadman argues that Jesus' ascent to heaven denotes his access to the immediate presence of God and to the self-knowledge, brought by the Spirit, of his heavenly origin.[62] In any case, the point is that

---

[59] For an overview and assessment, see D. Burkett, *The Son of the Man in the Gospel of John* (JSNT.S 56; Sheffield: JSOT Press, 1991) 16-37.

[60] P. Borgen interprets 3.13, against the background of God's revelation to Moses at Mt Sinai, as a polemic against those who claim to have ascended into heaven (*Philo, John and Paul: New Perspectives on Judaism and Early Christianity* [Atlanta: Scholars Press, 1987] 104-14; *idem*, 'Gospel', 103-106). Burkett argues, contra Borgen, that 3.13 refers not to revelation (to gain knowledge of 'heavenly secrets') but to salvation (ascent to live with God in the kingdom in heaven) (*Son*, 73-92). Contra Burkett, we suggest that because salvation is mediated by revelation, we do not need to choose; probably both are in view in 3.13. Kanagaraj suggests that 3.13 is a polemic against Merkabah mystics (*'Mysticism'*, 194-200).

[61] Bultmann, *Gospel*, 150-51; cf. Hofius, 'Wunder', 60-61.

[62] W.H. Cadman, *The Open Heaven: The Revelation of God in the Johannine Sayings of Jesus* (Oxford: Basil Blackwell, 1969) 28-30.

Jesus, in his function of Revealer, brought down and embodied the revelation of God (cf. section 2, above).

Further, there are reasons to assume that behind vv.12-15 lies some sort of sapiential background.[63] First, Jesus' showing Nicodemus the kingdom of God parallels Wisdom's showing Jacob the kingdom of God (Wis. 10.10; cf. Philo's concept of 'seeing' the Logos). Second, the descent of Jesus in 3.13b, and his ascent via the cross in 3.14 evokes the story of Wisdom's journey. Third, John's 'comparison' of the lifting up of Jesus on the cross to the lifting up of the serpent is also attested by the wisdom tradition (Wis. 16.5-7).[64] Fourth, Wisdom of Solomon 9.16 may provide a parallel to v.12: both speak about 'earthly' and 'heavenly things'. Fifth, the concept of spiritual (re-)birth is also present in Philo (see ch. 2). Hence, Jesus, as Wisdom incarnate, brings down from heaven wisdom in the form of (or as the basis for) God's revelation; a wisdom that has salvific consequences.[65]

Subsequently, vv.14-15(16) show that the culmination of God's revelation in Jesus is the 'lifting up' of the Son of Man on the cross, which displays God's love for the world and brings salvation for those who perceive the significance of the event and respond adequately.[66] Ὑψόω in v.14 has both the literal sense of 'to lift up' (on the cross) as well as the

---

[63] Contra Burkett (*Son*, 30-33), who may be right in refuting the idea of identifying the Johannine Son of Man with the figure of Wisdom, but wrongly rejects the theory that the figure of Wisdom stands behind the Logos of John's Prologue.

[64] Cf. J. Frey, '"Wie Mose die Schlange in der Wüste erhöht hat..." Zur frühjüdischen Deutung der "ehernen Schlange" und ihrer christologischen Rezeption in Johannes 3,14f.' in M. Hengel and H. Löhr (eds.), *Schriftauslegung im antiken Judentum und im Urchristentum* (WUNT 73; Tübingen, Mohr Siebeck, 1994) 153-205.

[65] Contra Meeks, who argues that the point of Jn 3 is to indicate Jesus' superiority over against Nicodemus (or any 'earthly' person) rather than the communication of supraterrestrial knowledge ('Man', 56). However, Jesus is superior *because* he comes from above, and *because* he brings down heavenly saving knowledge. The concept of Jesus' bringing revelatory wisdom down from heaven need not contradict the concept of the Spirit's providing Jesus with revelatory wisdom. Jesus was in continuous communication/fellowship with his Father (through the Spirit), and it seems unlikely that Jesus came to earth with a detailed, worked-out plan of his mission (cf. the theme 'sensory perception' in ch. 3). Nonetheless, it is possible that the Johannine Jesus had previous (pre-existent) knowledge of himself, his Father and of their relationship and mission, although we do not know to which extent. We should probably not distinguish too sharply between what Jesus brings down (or had access to) and what the Spirit provides because both Jesus and the Spirit are 'from above' and they both communicate 'heavenly things'. Perhaps the wisdom that Jesus had access to or brought down from heaven (in the form of revelation) is precisely Spirit-imbued revelatory wisdom.

[66] In the light of 3.14-15, the supreme revelatory act of God's love referred to in 3.16 must be Jesus' death on the cross, and Gen. 22.1-19 is the most appropriate intertextual background (Stibbe, *John*, 57-58). Note the irony of life through death (cf. 6.51).

metaphorical meaning of 'to exalt'.[67] Thus, the answer to Nicodemus' question of how this spiritual renewal can come about is finally explained in vv.14-15 in terms of Exodus typology (Num. 21.4-9; cf. Wis. 16.5-7); everyone who 'looks' in faith on the One 'lifted up' on the cross will be saved.[68] The 'lifting up' of Jesus is the anti-type of the lifting up of the serpent in the wilderness, and brings salvation to those who 'see' it, which probably means that the crucifixion of Jesus brings salvation to those who cognitively perceive its true significance, (cf. the themes 'sensory perception' and 'cognitive perception' in ch. 3).[69] Wisdom of Solomon 16.5-7 also makes clear that the Israelites were not saved by the literal seeing of the bronze snake, but by perceiving its significance (ἐπιστρέφω denotes cognitive change); the bronze snake was merely a *symbol* of the salvation that came from God.

Thus far, we have seen that Jesus is the locus of heavenly wisdom and revelation, and that the culmination of this revelation is Jesus' lifting up on the cross, which brings salvation (eternal life) to those who believe. Moreover, Jesus' revelation needs to be penetrated cognitively, and one needs to perceive the true significance of the cross, in order to enter into salvation through a new birth. How can people truly understand the meaning and significance of Jesus' revelation and of the cross? How can people have access to and obtain the 'saving wisdom' present in Jesus' revelation? We suggest that the clue to resolving these questions lies in the concept of the Spirit.

First, we return to Wisdom of Solomon 9.16-18. Wisdom of Solomon 9.16 and John 3.12 depict the same thought: if 'earthly things' are already difficult to understand, then what about 'heavenly things'?[70] Wisdom of Solomon 9.17-18 then continues to explain how Solomon can have access to and acquire knowledge of 'heavenly things': Solomon will be able to understand the 'heavenly things' if God sends Wisdom and the

---

[67] Cf. Holwerda, *Spirit*, 8-11; Thüsing, *Erhöhung*, 9-12. Kanagaraj understands the cross as a throne, which replaces the chariot-throne of Jewish mysticism (*'Mysticism'*, 205).

[68] Cf. Thüsing, *Erhöhung*, 4-15, 254; Forestell, *Word*, 62, 89 (although Forestell does not interpret vv.14-15 as the answer to Nicodemus' question); Burge, *Community*, 169; Turner, *Spirit*, 69.

[69] Although the literal term 'to see' does not occur in vv.14-15, the Johannine concept of seeing (including its connotative meaning 'perceiving') is evoked by the use of 'to see' in the cotext (vv.3 and 36) and in Num. 21.8-9; Wis. 16.7.

[70] The terminology used is virtually identical: Wis. 9.16 uses τὰ ἐπὶ γῆς and τὰ ἐν οὐρανοῖς whereas Jn 3.12 uses τὰ ἐπίγεια and τὰ ἐπουράνια. Moreover, both passages (including their cotexts) are concerned with the access to and the acquisition of heavenly saving W/wisdom. Surprisingly, Johannine scholarship has not really elucidated this parallel (Keener [*Spirit*, 150], e.g., just mentions Wis. 9.15-16 but does not do much with it; Forestell [*Word*, 42, 126], as an exception, makes more of it).

accompanying Spirit, which leads to salvation. According to Wisdom of Solomon, saving knowledge/wisdom is available in the figure of Wisdom and provided by the Spirit of Wisdom (cf. ch. 2 section 5). Second, Jesus could bring God's saving revelation *because* he is endowed with the Spirit that provides him with revelatory wisdom (see section 2, above). As an extrapolation, the implication could be that the Spirit also mediates this revelatory saving wisdom to people, and thus reveals the meaning and significance of Jesus' revelation and the cross. Third, if the Spirit is the agent of the new birth/life, and if this new birth/life comes about through a true understanding of the cross, then the Spirit might be considered to provide this cognitive perception and understanding, and hence life.

In sum, we suggest that the Spirit would be understood to act as a *life-giving cognitive agent* who mediates to people the saving wisdom present in Jesus' revelation in order to communicate to people the significance of this revelation (as seen especially at the cross). The Spirit enables one to 'see' the kingdom of God by enabling one to 'see' the one lifted up on the cross (cf. to 'see' life in 3.36). In this case, 'birth from above/the Spirit' is accomplished through some sort of spiritual understanding of the demonstration of God's love for the world at the cross, which (in Ezekiel's categories) replaces the heart of stone with a new heart. In other words, it is that new saving knowledge and understanding of God, as a result of the Spirit's activity, which recreates the person and brings him into a saving relationship with the Father and Son (cf. ch. 3 sections 6-7).[71]

A subsequent question is *when* this salvation, when this birth from above brought about by the Spirit, will be available. Vv.14-15 make clear that salvation/eternal life in the full Johannine sense is only available *after* the cross, *after* Jesus' glorification.[72] However, if the 'we' in v.11 includes the disciples, then somehow the disciples must already have been capable of knowing and experiencing something of this new life that is available in

---

[71] Cf. Turner, *Spirit*, 69. Does the birth of the Spirit precede faith or vice versa? Porsch contends that the begetting of the Spirit is also the begetting of faith; being born of the Spirit depicts the beginning of faith (*Pneuma*, 113-14). Carson argues, on the basis of 1.12-13, that 'faith...is the *evidence* of the new birth, not its cause' (*Sovereignty*, 182 [author's emphasis]; cf. 'Predestination', 227-29). However, this seems to go against a natural reading of 1.12-13, namely, that the prerequisite for being born of God (which is paralleled by being born of the Spirit in Jn 3) is to receive Jesus, i.e., to believe in him (cf. Trumbower, *Born*, 69). Moreover, Jesus' answer (vv.14-15) to Nicodemus' question (v.9) suggests that belief precedes the birth from above (cf. Burge, *Community*, 170). Thus, it seems that the prerequisite for entrance into the kingdom of God is a birth of water-and-Spirit, and the prerequisite for this birth is belief in the Son of Man (cf. our model of John's soteriology in ch. 3 section 7).

[72] Holwerda argues convincingly that each of the three events — crucifixion, resurrection, ascension — constitutes an aspect of the single glorification of Jesus (see *Spirit*, ch. 1).

Jesus, although salvation and the new birth would be fully available only after Jesus' glorification (cf. ch. 3 section 4.1).[73]

In vv.16-21, then, the narrator sets out the basic problem of humankind (love of darkness, doing evil deeds and fear of exposure), the solution to it (God sending his Son in order to save the world that he loves), and the consequences of people's choice (unbelief in the Son results in judgment and ultimately death, belief in the Son results in escaping God's judgment and in eternal life).

Conclusion. Against the backdrop of Ezekiel 36-37, the birth of water-and-Spirit is an *initiation metaphor* for entering into salvation, into the kingdom of God, through the cleansing, purifying and renewing work of the Spirit. Moreover, the Spirit functions as the agent and power/principle of salvation, in that the Spirit effectively causes and sustains the new life. Hence, the Spirit is not only the means of entry into salvation, but also functions as the identity- or boundary-marker of those who belong to the true 'Israel'.

How does this birth of the Spirit, which leads to salvation, come about? Jesus, as Wisdom incarnate, brings down from heaven God's revelation, which contains saving wisdom. The culmination of this revelation is the lifting up of Jesus on the cross, which displays the love of the Father and Son for the world, and which brings salvation (eternal life) to those who 'see' and believe. That is, to those who cognitively perceive and understand the true significance of the cross, and who respond appropriately. The Spirit, acting as a cognitive agent, facilitates this cognitive perception and understanding (and hence life) through the mediation of saving wisdom present in Jesus' revelation. This saving understanding of God, as a result of the Spirit's activity, and a subsequent adequate belief-response recreates the person and brings her/him through a 'birth of the Spirit' into a life-giving relationship with the Father and Son. In sum, John 3 depicts the Spirit as a *life-giving cognitive agent*, as the agent of life-bearing wisdom and understanding.

At the level of story, the intended perlocution of vv.2-15 — to persuade Nicodemus to move beyond a literal/material towards a symbolic/metaphorical understanding of the means of entering the kingdom of God, and to persuade Nicodemus to respond in belief to Jesus' revelation — failed.[74] Although Nicodemus was attracted to Jesus because

---

[73] At the level of narrative, 'we' probably includes the implied author and those who truly believe (cf. Tovey, *Art*, 257).

[74] Cf. Lee, *Narratives*, 36. Lee also argues that John the Baptist provides a foil for the character of Nicodemus and makes the confession of faith which Nicodemus is unable to make (*Narratives*, 36-37, 58-60). Cf. Moloney, who sees in 2.13-3.36 a spectrum of belief-responses within Judaism — from no belief ('the Jews') to incomplete belief (Nicodemus) to complete belief (the Baptist) ('Cana', 193-96; *Belief*, ch. 5).

of the signs and believed that Jesus was 'from God', he failed to grasp the significance of the signs and of Jesus being 'from above'. Nicodemus failed to see the realm that the signs represent and to which Jesus belonged. Nicodemus neither accepts nor rejects Jesus; he remains interested but there is no commitment of faith, and hence he remains in the dark and an outsider.[75]

At the level of narrative, Nicodemus represents a group of people with a particular belief-response to Jesus. These people 'believe' on the basis of Jesus' miraculous signs, but they have not penetrated/understood Jesus' revelation. Nicodemus represents those people who are attracted to Jesus and who desire to believe but who are unable to produce an adequate belief-response to him because they still operate at an earthly level and are unable to accept/grasp Jesus' revelation, and hence remain in the dark as an outsider.[76] The overall illocutionary force of 2.23-3.21 (taken as a speech act addressing the reader), then, is that Nicodemus' misunderstanding and dullness serves to warn the (implied) reader not to be like Nicodemus, and to call her/him to respond to Jesus and his revelation in belief. The implied author's intended perlocutionary effect is to persuade and encourage the reader to believe in Jesus, the Son of God.

3.2. The Offer of Living Water

John employs the term (τὸ) ὕδωρ (τὸ) ζῶν three times: in 4.10, 4.11 and 7.38. Hence, we shall elucidate the concept of 'living water' in 4.1-42 and 7.37-39, but we will concentrate on the discourse in John 4.

John 4.1-42. As in the case of Nicodemus, the discourse of the Samaritan woman's meeting with Jesus at the well in 4.1-42 is primarily a story about belief, and both narratives are bound by the common themes of water, Spirit and witness.[77] Moreover, just as the Nicodemus discourse

---

[75] Jn 7.50-52 and 19.19 possibly indicate, on Nicodemus' behalf, cognitive progression and eventually adequate understanding and belief (cf. Lee, *Narratives*, 57; Moloney, 'Cana', 194). For a different view, see D. Rensberger, *Johannine Faith and Liberating Community* (Philadelphia: Westminster Press, 1988) 39-40.

[76] Martyn sees in Nicodemus a symbolic figure representing a local Jewish leader at the time John was writing, a sort of secret Christian who remains in the synagogue (Martyn, *History*, 87, 121-23, 161-63). Cf. Culpepper, *Anatomy*, 135-36; idem, *Gospel*, 135; Rensberger, *Faith*, 40-41, 55. However, Carson finds Martyn's view anachronistic (*Gospel*, 185; cf. Cotterell, 'Conversation', 237-42). Moreover, it seems unlikely that Nicodemus was a secret believer: in Jn 3 Nicodemus' disciples were present, and in 7.50-52 Nicodemus was willing to defend Jesus before the religious authorities. Rather, Nicodemus is a type of the sympathetic seeker, yet one who is still seeking (Stibbe, *John*, 54; Witherington, *Wisdom*, 93).

[77] Lee, *Narratives*, 64-66; C.R. Koester, *Symbolism in the Fourth Gospel: Meaning, Mystery, Community* (Minneapolis: Fortress, 1995) 48. In fact, the whole 'Cana to Cana' section (2.1-4.54) deals with entry into eternal life and the obstacles which hinder or

portrayed a personal and corporate element, so the Samaritan woman is depicted as an individual, as well as a representative for the Samaritan people. However, Nicodemus and the woman are also contrasted: Nicodemus is a prominent, influential Jewish man whereas the main character in 4.1-30 is, from a Jewish reader's perspective, an unimportant, sinful Samaritan woman. In fact, Jesus had to cross several barriers — geographical, ethnic, religious, gender — in order to have a conversation with the woman.[78]

The discourse can be divided into four episodes: the setting (vv.1-7a), Jesus and the Samaritan woman (vv.7b-30), Jesus and his disciples (vv.31-38), and Jesus and the Samaritans (vv.39-42). Vv.5-7a evoke (by drawing attention to the patriarchs, a well and a woman) the story of an OT betrothal type-scene (e.g., Abraham, Isaac, Jacob, Moses).[79] Our focus will be on Jesus' revelatory encounter with the Samaritan woman (vv.7b-30), which in itself can be subdivided into three parts: the first dialogue (vv.7b-15), the second dialogue (vv.16-26), and the woman's response to Jesus' revelation (vv.27-30).

The First Dialogue (vv.7b-15). Jesus' encounter with the Samaritan woman (vv.7b-30) is dominated by the dual theme of the gift of 'living water' and the identity of its giver. Initially, Jesus requests the Samaritan woman to give him a drink (v.7b), but the woman implicitly refuses although she remains co-operative (v.9).[80] In v.10 Jesus offers her then two related topics: the gift of God ('living water') and the identity of the giver (Jesus).[81] Jesus hereby moves from a literal/material to a symbolic/metaphorical level, but the woman does not recognize this and remains at an earthly level, struggling for understanding (vv.11-12). In v.11 the woman misunderstands the nature or referent of ὕδωρ ζῶν — the phrase ὕδωρ ζῶν is an example of double entendre, meaning 'running water' (as opposed to the standing water of the well) or 'life-giving water'

---

prevent it (Lee, *Narratives*, 64-65; chs. 2-3; Moloney, *Belief, passim*). Stibbe, in contrast, argues that the focus of Jn 4 is true worship (*John*, 63).

[78] J. Gundry-Volf, 'Spirit, Mercy, and the Other', *Theology Today* 51 (1995) 509-10; Keener, *Spirit*, 152.

[79] Culpepper, *Anatomy*, 136; Botha, *Jesus*, 109-12; Scott, *Sophia*, 185-86; Stibbe, *John*, 68; Lee, *Narratives*, 67; Witherington, *Wisdom*, 118; Keener, *Spirit*, 152-53.

[80] Although v.9 has the form of an interrogative, it functions as a negative statement. The narrator's aside in v.8 may stress the parallel with the OT betrothal type-scene. In v.9b, the narrator indicates the alienation between Jews and Samaritans (for the relationship between Jews and Samaritans, see Okure, *Approach*, 316-18).

[81] V.10 is an example of chiasmus (inverted parallelism): the gift of God is matched by the gift of 'living water' and Jesus is implicitly identified as the giver. In v.14 Jesus explicitly identifies himself as the giver/source of this 'living water', and hence, equates himself with God (contra Botha's interpretation that the gift of God refers to Jesus himself [*Jesus*, 123]).

(cf. v.14) — thinking that it still refers to physical water.[82] In v.12, then, she mockingly asks whether Jesus thinks he is superior to the patriarch Jacob.[83] The illocutionary force of the two questions in vv.11-12 is to challenge Jesus' proposal and the authority he claims and to request further justification.[84]

The woman's misunderstanding is about two things: the nature/referent of the gift and the identity of the giver. Jesus resolves her misunderstanding concerning the gift in vv.13-14 and concerning his identity in vv.16-26, but the woman will only grasp at a later stage the meaning of Jesus' revelation. We then need to resolve two questions. What is the referent of the metaphor 'living water'? Who is the giver or source of this 'living water'? The answer to these questions lies partly in the cotext and partly in the conceptual background of ὕδωρ ζῶν in the OT and ITP, i.e., how '(living) water' is used metaphorically in Judaism.[85]

Concerning the meaning of the metaphor ὕδωρ ζῶν, we find four possible referents in Judaism.[86] First, '(living) water' is used to denote *life* or (eschatological) *salvation* (Isa. 12.3; 35.6-7; 41.17-18; 43.19-20; 55.1-3; Jer. 2.13; 17.13; Ezek. 47.1-12; Joel 3.18; Zech. 14.8; 1QH 16.4-23).[87]

---

[82] We should probably not attach too much significance to the different words used for well/spring by the woman (φρέαρ) and by Jesus (πηγή) because πηγή is also used by the narrator in v.6 (cf. also Carson, *Gospel*, 217). The real ambiguity lies in the meaning of the metaphor ὕδωρ ζῶν. Lee correctly comments that the woman perceives the absurdity of Jesus' proposition if taken at a literal level (v.11), but the collapse of the literal understanding is necessary and opens the way to a metaphorical understanding (*Narratives*, 72).

[83] The use of μή implies the answer 'no'. Culpepper notes the irony in v.12, in that the reader already knows the right answer while the Samaritan woman implies the wrong one (*Anatomy*, 172).

[84] Botha, *Jesus*, 125-26.

[85] We will not merely look for the literal term 'living water' but also how 'water' is used metaphorically in Judaism. Bultmann finds the meaning of 'living water' principally in the Gnostic *Odes of Solomon* (*Gospel*, 184-85), but we think it is unnecessary to go beyond Judaism.

[86] Surprisingly, Botha does not deal at all with the possible referents of the metaphor 'living water', and it stresses again the need to combine a synchronic approach of the text with a diachronic approach (historical-criticism). Similarly, H. Boers, taking a literary-critical approach, believes that the meaning of Jesus' offer of living water is unclear (*Neither on This Mountain Nor in Jerusalem: A Study of John 4* [SBL.MS 35; Atlanta: Scholars Press, 1988] 163-64).

[87] Cf. Barrett, *Gospel*, 233; Carson, *Gospel*, 218-20; Turner, *Spirit*, 61. Brown mentions that in 4.10-14 'living water' is not to be equated with eternal life, but *leads* to it (*Gospel*, 1:178). This may be a correct observation (although see Isa. 12.3), but 'living water' and eschatological salvation, here in Jn 4 and in Judaism, are so closely associated that it naturally invites to take salvation as a referent for 'living water'. It would seem far-fetched to make a sharp distinction between 'living water' *symbolizing* eschatological salvation and 'living water' *resulting in* this salvation. Water has a life-giving function,

Consequently, we may paraphrase ὕδωρ ζῶν as 'water that mediates/communicates life' or 'life-giving water'. A second potential referent, which ties in with and is closely related to salvation, is that of *cleansing and purification* (Exod. 29.4; 30.18-21; Lev. 8.6; 14.5-9, 49-52; Num. 8.7; 19.7-9, 17; Ezek. 36.25; Zech. 13.1; 1QS 3.4-9; 4.21).[88] Third, 'living water' is a metaphor of the eschatological gift of *the Spirit* (Isa. 44.3; 1QS 4.21; cf. *Gen.R.* 70.8).[89] This is confirmed by 7.38-39, where the Spirit is made the explicit referent of 'living water' (cf. a reference to the Spirit in 4.23-24).[90] Fourth, 'living water' is also a metaphor for *divine wisdom* or *teaching* (Prov. 13.14; 18.4; Isa. 11.9; 55.1-3; Sir. 24.23-29; 1QH 12.11; *Som.* 2.241-242; *Det.* 117; *Fug.* 166; *Quaest. in Gn.* 4.97-107; cf. Bar. 3.12; *4 Ezra* 14.47; *1 En.* 48.1; 49.1; *Gen.R.* 54.1; *Exod.R.* 31.3; *Sifre Deut.* 11.22 §48).[91] Perhaps the best example is Sirach 15.3, where it is said that Wisdom will give her disciple ὕδωρ σοφίας to drink. In John, this fourth denotation of 'living water' then designates the revelation or wisdom teaching that Jesus brings.

---

and it would only be a small step for the OT and intertestamental authors to use 'water' metaphorically for 'life' and eschatological salvation. The book of Revelation, which possibly belongs to the Johannine literature, also depicts ὕδωρ ζῶν as a symbol for salvation, of which Jesus is the source (Rev. 7.17; 21.6; 22.1, 17).

[88] In fact, for special purifications ὕδωρ ζῶν was required (Lev. 14.5-6, 50-52; Num. 19.17). Keener thinks that because water in 3.22-4.3 has a purification motif, it is very likely that the water of Jacob's well also has to do with purification ('Function', 189). However, in our view, the water of Jacob's well is nothing else than ordinary drinking water; it is the 'water' that Jesus offers that has the aspect of purification.

[89] Cf. Brown, *Gospel*, 1:179; Porsch, *Pneuma*, 139-42; Montague, *Spirit*, 345-46; Turner, *Spirit*, 61. Although Isa. 32.15, Ezek. 39.29, Joel 2.28-29 and Zech. 12.10 do not directly use the term 'water', they possibly evoke the imagery of water by mentioning the Spirit being 'poured out' *like water*. Burge recognizes the reference to the Spirit (*Community*, 97-98), but we disregard most of his evidence. First, in Ezek. 36.25-27 water is not a metaphor for the Spirit because they have different functions (see section 3.1, above). Second, although ἅλλομαι (4.14) is used for the Hebrew צלח in Jdg. 14.6, 19; 15.14; 1 Sam. 10.10 [LXX], the picture of the Spirit suddenly taking hold of a person and 'jumping' on him, is entirely different from the Spirit becoming a fountain of water in the believer springing up to eternal life (Porsch, *Pneuma*, 141; also contra Suurmond, *Influence*, 237). Third, it is inappropriate to use Acts to say that 'the gift of God' in 4.10 was a technical term for the Spirit. Fourth, the use of δίδωμι with reference to the Spirit (3.34; 14.16) can hardly be an argument that another subject of the verb δίδωμι (such as 'living water' in 4.10-14) therefore must also refer to the Spirit.

[90] Forestell, however, only sees a reference to the Spirit in a secondary sense (*Word*, 27-30). Moloney even denies a reference to the Spirit because the implied reader has not yet reached 7.38-39 (*Belief*, 140-41). However, we assume that the reader has knowledge of Jewish literature. Moreover, in a *re*-reading of the Gospel, the reader will have picked up the explicit reference to the Spirit in 7.38-39.

[91] Cf. Brown, *Gospel*, 1:178; Porsch, *Pneuma*, 142; Montague, *Spirit*, 345; Turner, *Spirit*, 62.

There is no need to choose between these different metaphorical meanings because water in the Fourth Gospel cannot be narrowed to a single meaning, and hence, all referents are probably in view.[92] Thus, salvation, purification, the Spirit and Jesus' revelatory wisdom teaching are all referents of the metaphor 'living water', and consequently closely connected. Johannine scholars may have recognized some of the referents, but they have not always asked themselves the obvious question of how these four referents of 'living water' are interrelated.

How then can the various meanings of ὕδωρ ζῶν be combined in one single Johannine concept? First, Jesus brings God's saving revelation which contains saving wisdom (see section 3.1, above). Second, Jesus' word/teaching cleanses and purifies (15.3). Hence, saving wisdom is the purifying content of Jesus' revelatory word/teaching (cf. 17.17 and ch. 3). Third, the Spirit purifies (cf. Isa. 4.4; Ezek. 36.25-27), in that the Spirit mediates saving wisdom to people and thus facilitates cognitive perception and understanding of Jesus' teaching, and subsequently entrance into salvation. We suggest, then, that the metaphor ὕδωρ ζῶν denotes *Jesus' Spirit-imbued revelatory wisdom teaching that cleanses and purifies and leads to eternal life (salvation).*[93] In other words, the Spirit purifies the person with Jesus' word (and hence leads the person into salvation) by mediating the significance of Jesus' teaching in the form of saving wisdom/truth to the person, i.e., by enabling the person cognitively to perceive and understand Jesus' wisdom teaching. Based on this new understanding, the person can then make an adequate belief-response, which leads to a birth of the Spirit into a saving relationship with the Father and Son.

Coming back to our second question (who is the giver/source of 'living water'?), we find three possible sources for 'living water' in Judaism: *God* (Isa. 12.2; 55.1-3; Jer. 2.13; 17.13; Joel 3.18), *Wisdom* (Prov. 16.22; 18.4; Sir. 15.3; 24.19-22; *Quaest. in Gn.* 4.97-107) and *Torah* (Sir. 24.23-29; CD 3.16; *Gen.R.* 54.1; *Cant.R.* 1.2 §3; *Sifre Deut.* 11.22 §48). In Judaism, God is understood to be the source of the eschatological salvation, but in 4.10-14 it becomes evident that Jesus is depicted as its source (cf. 5.26).

---

[92] Brown, *Gospel*, 1:178-79; Montague, *Spirit*, 346; Culpepper, *Anatomy*, 192-95; Lee, *Narratives*, 76-77; Koester, *Symbolism*, 171; Jones, *Symbol*, 109-13; Turner, *Spirit*, 61-63. Contra Burge, *Community*, 97-98.

[93] Cf. esp. Turner, *Spirit*, 61-63; but see also Burge, *Community*, 103-104; Willett, *Wisdom*, 93; Lee, *Narratives*, 77. Beasley-Murray argues that 'living water' denotes '*the life mediated by the Spirit sent from the (crucified and exalted) Revealer-Redeemer*' (*John*, 60 [author's emphasis]), and thus seems to deny the possibility of the availability of the gift during Jesus' ministry; an issue we will address shortly. Ridderbos argues that what is central in 4.10-14 is not a specific meaning of 'living water' but that in Jesus the gift of God is present (*Gospel*, 157-58). However, this seems too easy a dismissal.

Moreover, Jesus supersedes not only Torah (cf. 1.14, 17; 5.38-40) but also Wisdom. In Sirach 24.21, for example, Wisdom says: 'Those who eat of me will hunger for more, and those who drink of me will thirst for more.' However, Jesus makes an even higher claim than divine Wisdom; those who drink from the divine wisdom Jesus gives are permanently satisfied (v.14).[94] Jesus is Wisdom incarnate, and his revelatory teaching contains divine wisdom and transcends the Torah.[95] In sum, Jesus, acting for God and superseding Wisdom-Torah, is depicted as the source/locus of 'living water'/salvation.[96]

Porsch, although recognizing that 'living water' refers to the Spirit and to Jesus' revelatory word, takes a different position. Based on 7.37-39 (with which we will deal below), Porsch seems to distinguish *two periods/stages* in 4.7-15: (i) the period of Jesus' earthly ministry, in which 'living water' can only refer to Jesus' revelatory word; (ii) the period after Jesus' glorification, in which an additional reference to the Spirit comes in view.[97] Porsch concludes, then, concerning the fundamental relationship between Spirit and word (=Jesus' revelation), that:

> Joh scheint in dem Gespräch (VV.7-15) bewußt zwei »Zeiten« zu unterscheiden: die Zeit des irdischen Wirkens Jesu und die Zeit nach Jesu Verherrlichung...*Das »lebendige Wasser« symbolisiert also beides: das Offenbarungswort Jesu und das Pneuma, aber es symbolisiert sie im Nacheinander, entsprechend der beiden >Stadien< der Offenbarung...* obwohl in der Zeit des Evg, also in der Zeit nach Jesu Verherrlichung und damit des Geistes, die beiden, Wort und Pneuma, als Einheit erfahren wurden.[98]

However, although it is correct to say that the Spirit can only be given after Jesus' glorification (cf. 7.39), it seems incorrect to deduce that therefore 'living water' could not refer to the Spirit during Jesus' ministry. The Spirit is already active within Jesus' ministry (as we will show below; cf. also section 3.3, below, and ch. 3). Hence, it seems legitimate to argue that 'living water' refers to *both* Jesus' revelatory word *and* Spirit at the

---

[94] Barrett, *Gospel*, 234; Witherington, *Wisdom*, 119; Turner, *Spirit*, 62.

[95] Cf. Brown, *Gospel*, 1:179; Turner, *Spirit*, 62-63.

[96] Burge argues that Jesus *is* the living water (*Community*, 98; cf. Moloney, *Belief*, 143; van der Watt, *Family*, 231-33). However, this would lead to the false identification that 'living water' refers to both Jesus and the Spirit; rather, Jesus is the *source* of the life-giving water, and the life-giving water can be equated with Jesus' Spirit-imbued revelation, but not with Jesus himself.

[97] Porsch, *Pneuma*, 140-44. This insight came first from de la Potterie (cf. 'Parole', 187-92; *Vérité*, 2:684-96). Porsch acknowledges this (*Pneuma*, 144 n.37), but develops it more fully. De la Potterie, in his article 'Parole', reveals in turn a strong dependence on Porsch. Chevallier essentially follows de la Potterie (and Porsch) (*Souffle*, 2:450-51, 454, 502).

[98] Porsch, *Pneuma*, 144 (author's emphasis).

same time, i.e., *both* before *and* after Jesus' glorification. Moreover, Porsch's argument creates an unwarranted dichotomy between word and Spirit, as if the Spirit was hardly active through Jesus' revelatory word during Jesus' ministry. Porsch seems to undervalue or dismiss the activity of the Spirit during Jesus' ministry, whereas we have argued that the Spirit mediates saving wisdom to people through Jesus' revelatory word.

Thus, in vv.13-14 Jesus reveals to the woman the nature of the gift, namely the life-giving qualities of the water that will become an internal spring in those who drink from the source of the life-giving water (Jesus). 'To drink' the living water, then, is to receive the gift of saving wisdom mediated by the Spirit. V.15 reveals that the woman has grasped the superiority of the water Jesus has to offer, although she still moves at an earthly level; she still struggles to penetrate cognitively Jesus' revelation.[99] Nevertheless, she has made more progress and is more responsive than Nicodemus.[100] At the level of story, the illocutionary force of vv.7b-15 is that Jesus explains to the woman the source and nature of life-giving water and that he offers this water to her. The intended perlocutionary effect is to persuade the woman to accept this offer and (implicitly) to recognize Jesus' identity. Realizing that the intended perlocution has not been achieved, Jesus now shifts the emphasis to the revelation of his identity (vv.16-26).

The Second Dialogue (vv.16-26). It is not that the conversation has failed,[101] because the desire and the progress of the woman shows that Grice's co-operative principle is still operating. Nor is this a form of discontinuous dialogue in which Jesus radically changes the conversation from the topic of water to that of worship.[102] The governing idea that holds vv.7b-15 and vv.16-26 together is the overall intended perlocution that the woman will confess adequate belief in Jesus through the recognition of Jesus' identity and the acceptance of his offer of life-giving water.[103]

---

[99] The woman, who as a Samaritan could only have known the Pentateuch, would perhaps not be expected to grasp everything. However, the woman's misunderstanding, and the consequent need for more revelation on Jesus' part, benefits the implied reader.

[100] For the contrast between the story of Nicodemus and the Samaritan woman, see Stibbe, *John*, 62.

[101] Contra Bultmann, *Gospel*, 187; Botha, *Jesus*, 127; Moloney, *Belief*, 145. Certainly, Botha's statement that '[t]he author does not intend the woman to grasp the meaning of the words, since the aim is actually the *failure* of the conversation in 4:10-15' (*Jesus*, 133 [author's emphasis]) seems to be out of place.

[102] Possibly contra Moloney, 'Cana', 196; *idem*, *Belief*, 132-34; Scott, *Sophia*, 187; Stibbe, *Gospel*, 18.

[103] Boers also perceives that, despite an apparent discontinuation at the surface level, at the deeper level Jesus continues to respond to the woman's need for miraculous knowledge, although Boers thinks the woman will not come to adequate belief (*Mountain*, 165, 169-71).

When the woman did not grasp the (metaphorical) meaning of Jesus' offer, Jesus started to focus on the revelation of his identity to her, so that if she recognizes his identity she might also recognize the nature of what he has to give. Hence, Jesus' aim in vv.16-18 is not to start to discuss ethics or the woman's moral life, but to reveal his identity.[104] Jesus' revelatory knowledge of the woman's (past and present) situation caused her to recognize him as a prophet; a progress Nicodemus never made. In v.15 the woman recognized the superiority of the water Jesus can give; in v.19 she also acknowledges the superiority of the giver (over Jacob).[105] Seeing Jesus as a prophet, the woman takes the opportunity to raise a theological issue about the locus of worship (v.20).[106] Although she now moves from a material to a spiritual topic, she remains at an earthly level, and hence more revelation is needed.

Vv.21-24 reveal four things. First, a new τόπος of worship: true worship will not be dependent on any geographical location or physical place but finds its locus in Jesus, as the new Temple (cf. 2.19-21).[107] Second, a new mode of worship: this new eschatological worship is characterized by Spirit and truth, i.e., worship in Spirit-and-truth is a metaphor for worship that is facilitated and empowered by the Spirit and characterized by truth, which is revealed in Jesus (cf. 1.14, 17; 3.21; 14.6).[108] The phrase πνεῦμα ὁ θεός is not a metaphysical statement, a definition of his being, rather it describes God manifesting/revealing himself or the way in which God is present; it is God's mode of action and dealing with people, God's mode of

---

[104] Cf. Botha, *Jesus*, 142-43; Lee, *Narratives*, 75.

[105] Stibbe comments on v.19 that 'she now begins to see things "from above"' (*John*, 66).

[106] V.20 has the form of a declarative but functions as a request (for explanation).

[107] Keener argues that the Spirit is the location of true worship and replaces the temple as the location of divine activity ('Function', 193-94; *Spirit*, 154). However, this seems to be a misrepresentation; rather, Jesus is the new Temple, and hence the locus of true worship, and the Spirit, functioning as the power of Jesus, will naturally be the *power* behind true worship.

[108] Cf. Schnackenburg, *Gospel*, 1:436-37; Porsch, *Pneuma*, 153-60; J.D.G. Dunn, *Jesus and the Spirit: A Study of the Religious and Charismatic Experience of Jesus and the First Christians as Reflected in the New Testament* (London: SCM Press, 1975) 354; Montague, *Spirit*, 346-47; Burge, *Community*, 193-97; S.S. Stuart, 'A New Testament Perspective on Worship', *EvQ* 68 (1996) 217. Ἐν πνεύματι καὶ ἀληθείᾳ is to be taken as a hendiadys. Ἐν can be taken as either spherical (worship 'in the realm of the Spirit and of Jesus and his saving truth') or instrumental (worship 'by means of the Spirit and the truth that one experiences through Jesus'). E.D. Freed argues that the main point of 4.23-24 is ethical ('The Manner of Worship in John 4:23f' in J.M. Myers et al. [eds.], *Search the Scriptures: New Testament Studies in Honor of Raymond T. Stamm* [Leiden: Brill, 1969] 33-48).

communication with people.[109] Third, a new revelation/dimension of worship, in that God is worshipped as Father, which implies that believers can stand in an analogous relationship to God as Jesus.[110] The prerequisite for this worship of God as Father seems to be adoption as a child of God, i.e., having a new relationship with God through the regeneration by the Spirit (1.12-13; 3.5).[111] Moreover, πνεῦμα ὁ θεός denotes that God belongs to the realm from above, and only those who are born from above will be able to worship him. Furthermore, the new mode of worship by or in the Spirit is available only to those who have experienced the Spirit through Jesus. Fourth, this eschatological worship in Spirit-and-truth has already become (partly) a present reality in Jesus' ministry by virtue of Jesus being the new Temple and by his announcement of the arrival of the 'hour' (ἔρχεται ὥρα καὶ νῦν ἐστιν).[112]

The Responses of the Woman, the Disciples and the Samaritans. The woman recognizes that Jesus is talking about eschatological issues that the Messiah will reveal (ἀναγγέλλω), but she still does not link Jesus to the Messiah nor does she perceive the significance of καὶ νῦν ἐστιν. Hence, Jesus reveals plainly and straightforwardly that he is the Messiah (v.26).[113] The implied reader now expects a confession of the woman but is again held in suspense because the disciples intrude on the scene (v.27). Only in vv.28-29 do we find the implicit evidence that the woman has begun to understand the identity of Jesus as well as the meaning of his gift. The leaving behind of her water jar in v.28 possibly symbolizes that the woman is no longer in need of physical water but that her thirst has been quenched

---

[109] H. Schlier, *Besinnung auf das Neue Testament, Exegetische Aufsätze und Vortrage II* (Freiburg: Herder, 1964) 264; Brown, *Gospel*, 1:172; B. Lindars, *The Gospel of John* (NCeB; London: Oliphants, 1972) 190; Porsch, *Pneuma*, 150; Dunn, *Jesus*, 353; Montague, *Spirit*, 347; Burge, *Community*, 192; Beasley-Murray, *John*, 62; Keener, *Spirit*, 154. Πνεῦμα in 4.23-24 refers to the divine Spirit (cf. Schnackenburg, *Gospel*, 1:437; Brown, *Gospel*, 1:180; Porsch, *Pneuma*, 152; Newman/Nida, *Handbook*, 650-55) rather than to the human spirit (so Morris, *Gospel*, 239) or to spirit as God's nature (so Carson, *Gospel*, 225-26; Harner, *Relation*, 35). Carson has to take this line in order to be consistent with his interpretation of 3.5, but his view (based on Belleville's) has already been questioned in section 3.1, above.

[110] Stibbe points out the contrast between the fathers in v.20 and the Father in v.23 (*John*, 64).

[111] Cf. Brown, *Gospel*, 1:180.

[112] The 'hour' refers to the hour of the messianic age, rather than to the hour of Jesus' glorification (contra Culpepper, *Gospel*, 142), because Jesus' hour only starts at 12.23; 13.1.

[113] Cf. de la Potterie's perceptive comment that the living water promised to the woman in v.10 is now, in v.26, actually communicated to her in the form of revelation; to receive the living water is to discover Jesus' identity ('Parole', 188). Botha states that the use of ἐγώ εἰμι prepares the reader for the ἐγώ εἰμι utterances in the rest of the Gospel (*Jesus*, 153).

by the 'living water'.[114] She now feels the urge to tell her fellow people about the Messiah, and consequently the Samaritans come to Jesus (vv.29-30).[115] That is, she demonstrates discipleship in witnessing about Jesus to her own people (cf. the 'come and see' in v.29 with that in 1.39, 46).[116] Thus, after Jesus' straightforward revelation of his Messiahship, vv.28-30 might indicate the woman's acceptance and understanding of Jesus and his revelation, and, combined with the manifestation of discipleship, probably implies a confession of adequate belief.

Meanwhile Jesus explains in vv.31-38 to his disciples certain things about discipleship and mission.[117] Although the disciples knew Jesus had been conversing with a Samaritan woman (v.27), they had missed its spiritual dimension and were moving at a literal/material level (v.31). Even when Jesus tries to move them to a spiritual level by virtue of referring to food metaphorically (v.32), the disciples misunderstand him and remain at an earthly level (v.33). Consequently, Jesus reveals in v.34 that his 'food' (vehicle) metaphorically means to do God's will and to finish his work (tenor) (cf. 6.38; 9.4; 17.4).[118] Jesus' 'food' is his mission, which would be brought to completion at the cross (19.30). The illocutionary force of vv. 35-38 is to invite the disciples to participate in Jesus' mission. The 'harvest' is the bringing into the kingdom of God, into eternal life, those people who are ready to confess belief in Jesus. The disciples can already (ἤδη) start with this harvest (vv.35-36).[119] The irony is that the Samaritan woman, rather than the disciples, participates in Jesus' mission of harvesting: the disciples do not bring anyone with them from the village whereas the woman brings the whole village (v.30; cf. the gathering of fruit in v.36 with the bearing of fruit in 15.1-8).[120]

---

[114] Cf. Botha, *Jesus*, 163-64; Lee, *Narratives*, 84. Contra Bultmann, *Gospel*, 193.

[115] The question 'Could this be the Christ?' does not perhaps denote doubt but suggestion; she tentatively suggests that Jesus might be the Messiah with the intended perlocution that the people will find out for themselves (and they do) (cf. Boers, *Mountain*, 183-84; Botha, *Jesus*, 164-65; Lee, *Narratives*, 86).

[116] Scott (*Sophia*, 190-91, 196) and Witherington (*Wisdom*, 119) observe that the Samaritan woman is depicted as assuming the role of Wisdom's maidservant in Prov. 9.3. For the woman as a witnessing disciple, see Scott, *Sophia*, 192-97. Boers characterizes the woman in her activity of a witness as the metaphoric sower and Jesus' co-worker (*Mountain*, 82-83, 182-86).

[117] Lee even comments that the theological heart of Jn 4 is the motif of mission (*Narratives*, 64). Cf. also Bultmann, *Gospel*, 194-200; Okure, *Approach*, *passim*.

[118] The disciples' misunderstanding is the reader's gain (Botha, *Jesus*, 171).

[119] Botha suggests that the disciples' baptizing the followers of Jesus (v.2) is in fact a realization of harvesting (*Jesus*, 176).

[120] Cf. Stibbe, *John*, 65. The woman is also contrasted with Nicodemus, who as a representative of Judaism made no impact on his fellow-Pharisees (7.45-52) (Lee, *Narratives*, 65-66). For the use of irony in the Fourth Gospel, see P.D. Duke, *Irony in the*

Many Samaritans believed in Jesus on the basis of the woman's words (v.39),[121] and, when Jesus granted their request to remain (μένω) with them, many more believed on the basis of Jesus' words (vv.40-41). V.42 then indicates the peak of the discourse in the communal confession of the Samaritans (including that of the woman) of the true identity of Jesus: ὁ σωτήρ τοῦ κόσμου.[122] Thus, the Samaritan woman confesses adequate belief and is also depicted as a model disciple; in her witness about Jesus to her people she participates in his mission and actualizes the challenge of vv.35-38.[123] Ironically, the Samaritan woman achieves what Nicodemus was unable to do (to confess adequate belief) and what the disciples were unable to do (to actualize Jesus' challenge to participate in his mission and so to display true discipleship). John 4 thus also shows the universal scope of Jesus' mission (cf. 3.16).

The Availability of 'Living Water'. An important issue to resolve is whether (and to what extent) this life-giving water was already available during Jesus' earthly ministry. There are several things that possibly point to the present reality of 'salvation' within Jesus' ministry. First, Jesus' offer of 'living water' can hardly have been a future promise or a theoretical possibility; he says he would have given her this 'living water' if she had asked him for it. In fact, vv.28-30 imply that she has probably tasted the 'living water' by virtue of the leaving behind of her water jar and her witness to her fellow people. Second, v.23 mentions that ἔρχεται ὥρα καὶ νῦν ἐστιν to worship in Spirit-and-truth. Most scholars recognize that Jesus has brought the eschaton into the present; the νῦν of the 'hour' is

---

Fourth Gospel (Atlanta: John Knox Press, 1985); R.A. Culpepper, 'Reading Johannine Irony' in R.A. Culpepper and C.C. Black (eds.), *Exploring the Gospel of John: In Honor of D. Moody Smith* (Louisville: Westminster John Knox Press, 1996) 193-207.

[121] Stibbe notices that this is a proleptic echo of 17.20 (*John*, 67).

[122] The οἴδαμεν of the Samaritans stands in sharp contrast with that of Nicodemus in 3.2, who ironically did not really understand the implications of his own statement. The cognitive progression in discovering Jesus' identity is shown in the titles given to him: Ἰουδαῖος (4.9), Κύριε (4.11-12, 15), προφήτης (4.19), Χριστός (4.29), σωτήρ (4.42) (cf. Culpepper, *Gospel*, 143). Boers, however, thinks that 4.42 does not include the woman's confession and that she never comes to a full expression of faith in Jesus (*Mountain*, 165). Boers merely sees the woman as an example of obedience, and the living water springing up to eternal life means for the woman partaking in Jesus' mission of doing the Father's will (*Mountain*, 165-91).

[123] Cf. Culpepper, *Anatomy*, 137; Scott, *Sophia*, 192-97; Stibbe, *John*, 67. R.E. Brown even talks about an 'apostolic role' (*The Community of the Beloved Disciple: The Life, Loves, and Hates of an Individual Church in New Testament Times* [London: Chapman, 1979] 187-88). Moloney contends that the Samaritan woman merely reaches incomplete/partial belief (over against the complete belief of the Samaritan villagers) ('Cana', 196-99; *Belief*, 156-58). However, Moloney does not seem to have recognized the importance of the woman's leaving behind of her water jar, her display of discipleship, and that the villagers' confession probably included hers.

based in the presence of Jesus, i.e. this worship in Spirit-and-truth was proleptically present in the ministry and person of Jesus (cf. 5.25).[124] Consequently, since worship in Spirit-and-truth can only happen when one has experienced the Spirit, i.e., when one has tasted the 'living water', 'salvation' must also have been proleptically present during Jesus' ministry. Third, vv.35-36 show that the harvester is *already* (ἤδη) employed, the harvest is *already* present in Jesus' ministry.[125] Fourth, the belief of the Samaritans *is* the 'harvest' (vv.39-42) and the woman is incorporated into their confession of faith.[126]

Coming back to the intertextual image of betrothal, we see that the implied author has subverted the OT betrothal story in two major ways. First, the eschatological wedding between Yahweh and his people is now being realized in the union between Jesus and those who believe in him. Second, instead of a Jewish bride, the narrative presents a Samaritan one; the spiritual betrothal between Jesus and his people is not based on ethnic but on spiritual birth.[127] We now turn to the other passage that refers to ὕδωρ ζῶν.

John 7.37-39.[128] Vv.37-38 present us three problems: (i) the punctuation of the Greek text; (ii) the antecedent of αὐτοῦ in v.38, which depends on the punctuation of the Greek text; (iii) the passage of Scripture cited in v.38. Regarding the punctuation of the Greek text, the principal options are two: (i) the Eastern or 'traditional' interpretation places a full stop after πινέτω, and the phrase ὁ πιστεύων εἰς ἐμέ is then a *nominativus pendens* (cf. 6.39; 8.45; 15.2; 17.2) resumed in αὐτοῦ; i.e. 'streams of living water' will flow from within the believer; (ii) the more recent Western or 'christological' interpretation places a comma after πρός με, and a full stop after ὁ πιστεύων εἰς ἐμέ, resulting in the αὐτοῦ referring to Christ.[129]

Most scholars prefer the 'christological' interpretation,[130] but there are various problems with this view, which are addressed most extensively and

---

[124] Porsch, *Pneuma*, 148; Barrett, *Gospel*, 237; Burge, *Community*, 98; Carson, *Gospel*, 224; Turner, *Spirit*, 62-63.

[125] Cf. Lee, *Narratives*, 88-89.

[126] Lee, *Narratives*, 91-92.

[127] Cf. Stibbe, *John*, 69.

[128] For the background to the Feast of Tabernacles, including the water-pouring rite, see Lev. 23.33-43; Num. 29.12-39; Deut. 16.13-15; Brown, *Gospel*, 1:326-27; B.H. Grigsby, '"If Any Man Thirsts...": Observations on the Rabbinic Background of John 7,37-39', *Bib* 67 (1986) 101 n.1; Beasley-Murray, *John*, 113-14; Carson, *Gospel*, 321-22; Morris, *Gospel*, 371-73; Keener, *Spirit*, 157.

[129] Barrett, *Gospel*, 326-27; Carson, *Gospel*, 323.

[130] Bultmann, *Gospel*, 303; Dunn, *Baptism*, 179; Brown, *Gospel*, 1:320; Porsch, *Pneuma*, 57-58; Forestell, *Word*, 28; Montague, *Spirit*, 348; L. Nereparampil, 'Holy Spirit as Living Water', *Bible Bhashyam* 2 (1976) 150-51; de la Potterie, 'Parole', 189-90; Schnackenburg, *Gospel*, 2:154; Haenchen, *John*, 2:17; Grigsby, 'Man', 101; Burge,

adequately by Cortés.[131] First, Cortés establishes some common ground. Both interpretations assert that Christ is the ultimate source of life-giving water, which is the Spirit (cf. 4.14), and although the 'traditional' interpretation makes believers the source of life-giving water, the emphasis is not on an overflow of the Spirit from the believer to others, but on the life-giving quality of the Spirit in the believer.[132] Subsequently, Cortés points out that the basic problem would seem to lie in v.38b: whether or not *in addition to* Christ being the source of life-giving water for the believer, this water will also keep on flowing from within the believer.[133] The 'traditional' interpretation endorses this and hence seems preferable. Cortés' most persuasive arguments are: (i) the 'traditional' interpretation parallels 4.13-14: the one who drinks from Jesus will never be thirsty, for he will have within him a spring of living water that never fails and that leads to eternal life; (ii) it seems more natural and coherent to invite one who is thirsty to drink than the one who already believes because the one who believes in Jesus *has already drunk* and cannot be thirsty again.[134]

Porsch disagrees with Cortés and argues that faith is not something static; the one who believes in Jesus need not thirst any more *because* he can always drink, and indeed does.[135] However, Cortés does not deny the continual drinking of the believer, only that he will be thirsty again. Jesus invites the thirsty to come to him and to drink, and then streams of living water will flow from within the believer, from which s/he can continue to drink (cf. 4.14). The believer need not be thirsty again because after s/he has drunk from the source of living water (Jesus) the life-giving water (the

---

Community, 89-91; Beasley-Murray, *John*, 115; Willett, *Wisdom*, 93-94; Koester, *Symbolism*, 175; F.J. Moloney, *Signs and Shadows: Reading John 5-12* (Minneapolis: Fortress Press, 1996) 86; Keener, 'Function', 209; *idem, Spirit*, 160. Hoskyns allows for both interpretations (*Gospel*, 2:365-67).

[131] J.B. Cortés, 'Yet another look at Jn 7,37-38', *CBQ* 29 (1967) 75-86.

[132] Cortés, 'Look', 76-77.

[133] Cortés, 'Look', 76.

[134] For a complete defence, see Cortés, 'Look', 77-83. Those who follow Cortés are Turner, 'Concept', 29-31; Carson, *Gospel*, 323-25; Morris, *Gospel*, 375-76. Cf. also J. Blenkinsopp, 'John vii. 37-9. Another Note on a Notorious Crux', *NTS* 6 (1959-60) 95-98; Witherington, *Wisdom*, 174; Ridderbos, *Gospel*, 273; Jones, *Symbol*, 153-55. M.J.J. Menken finds himself in deadlock: he favours the punctuation of the traditional interpretation but also believes that αὐτοῦ refers to Jesus. Menken's way out of the impasse is that the pendent nominative itself is not resumed later in the sentence, and hence, αὐτοῦ does not refer to the believer but to Jesus ('The Origin of the Old Testament Quotation in John 7:38', *NT* 38 [1996] 166-67).

[135] Porsch, *Pneuma*, 58 n.22.

Spirit) will become in her/him a spring of water welling up to eternal life.[136]

Moreover, the believer in turn becomes a source of living water for others (cf. the Samaritan woman in 4.39). If we were to ask how this is possible, the answer would probably be because of the Spirit, in that the Spirit through the believer actively reaches out to others (cf. the sage becoming a derivative source of wisdom in Sir. 39.6-11 [cf. 21.13; 24.30-34] *because* he received the Spirit of wisdom).[137] The disciples, for example, become sources of living water to others, in that the Paraclete will reach out to people *through* the disciples' Paraclete-imbued witness (see ch. 5).

The answer to the question which passage(s) of Scripture is (are) cited in v.38 seems to depend on one's view of vv.37-38: the defenders of the 'traditional' interpretation tend to propose a *sapiential* background, whereas the defenders of the 'christological' interpretation normally find a background in *prophetic* literature.[138] However, if Jesus is the source of 'living water', and if the believer in himself is also a source of 'living water', then these backgrounds need not be completely mutually exclusive.[139] Nevertheless, we suggest, without denying a possible prophetic background to 7.37-38, that a sapiential background is probably more in view. First, John 4 already reflected a sapiential background. Second, the looking-finding theme of 7.34a is a wisdom theme (Prov. 1.28b; Wis. 6.12).[140] Third, Jesus' standing up and crying out in a loud voice to invite people to come to him evokes the story of Wisdom (Prov. 1.20-21; 8.1-3; 9.3; Sir. 24.19; 51.23-24).[141]

John 7.37-39 is also important to us because we find here the basis for Porsch's two-stage model. He argues: (i) the offer of living water, which refers originally only to Jesus' revelatory word, is a present reality to Jesus' audience; (ii) after Jesus' glorification, the Spirit is to complete and deepen the knowledge of Jesus' word, and hence, John can now (but only

---

[136] Cf. S.H. Hooke, 'The Spirit was not yet', *NTS* 9 (1962-63) 378. Burge argues from vv.37-38, as in 4.10-15, that Jesus *is* the living water (*Community*, 93), but he seems to exaggerate the intimate union of Jesus and the Spirit (cf. n.96, above).

[137] Although there is no evidence in Judaism for people being a source of Spirit to others, sapiential Judaism frequently depicts sages as sources of *wisdom* to others (see ch. 2).

[138] Cortés, 'Look', 84-85; Brown, *Gospel*, 1:321-23; Montague, *Spirit*, 348; Burge, *Community*, 90-93; Koester, *Symbolism*, 174-76. Others suggest a rabbinic background (Grigsby, 'Man', 102-107) or Neh. 9 (Carson, *Gospel*, 326-28).

[139] Cf. Schnackenburg, *Gospel*, 2:155-56; Beasley-Murray, *John*, 116-17.

[140] Cf. Brown, *Gospel*, 1:318.

[141] For a sapiential background behind the whole Tabernacles discourse in 7.1-8.59, see C. Cory, 'Wisdom's Rescue: A New Reading of the Tabernacles Discourse (John 7:1-8:59)', *JBL* 116 (1997) 95-116.

now) also interpret the living water in terms of the Spirit, in that the Spirit unlocks Jesus' word.[142] However, in this way Porsch reduces (or virtually denies) the activity of the Spirit during Jesus' ministry.[143] We suggest that, as in John 4, the issue is not that living water refers to Jesus' revelatory word during Jesus' ministry, while only including a referent to the Spirit after Jesus' glorification, but that the living water (=the Spirit) was not yet *fully* available before Jesus' glorification: it did not yet 'stream' in and from the believer. The phrase οὔπω γὰρ ἦν πνεῦμα, ὅτι Ἰησοῦς οὐδέπω ἐδοξάσθη in 7.39b probably means something like 'the Spirit was not yet active/available in the same way that is possible only after Jesus' glorification.'[144]

Conclusion. The metaphor 'living water' denotes Jesus' Spirit-imbued revelatory wisdom teaching, which cleanses, purifies and leads to eternal life. Jesus is the source of 'living water' (and believers become a derivative source), in that Jesus' life-giving revelation/teaching contains saving wisdom, which is mediated to people by the Spirit. The Samaritan woman struggles to penetrate Jesus' revelation, but she slowly overcomes the cognitive barriers by taking in the saving wisdom of Jesus' revelation provided by the Spirit. Her abandoning the water jar (v.28), her testimony (v.29) and the Samaritans' confession (which includes hers) (vv.39-42) may hint that she has 'tasted' of the 'living water' and consequently even become a source of living water herself (cf. 7.37-38). That is, she made an adequate belief-response to Jesus and his revelation (on the basis of the Spirit's cognitive activity) that brings her into a saving relationship with the Father and Son, which is demonstrated in a display of true discipleship. The woman's belief and her expression of discipleship are two integrated aspects of salvation; her discipleship *is* her belief-response. The point of the irony of taking a non-Jewish female character as an example to follow is that Jesus' offer of living water is a universal offer for everyone.

Although salvation in the Johannine sense is only fully available after Jesus' glorification, a partly realized dimension of this salvation is already present within Jesus' earthly ministry through his Spirit-imbued revelatory life-giving word, i.e. through Jesus' teaching people have already started to experience the Spirit leading them to eternal life.[145] This experience of the

---

[142] Porsch, *Pneuma*, 69; cf. de la Potterie, 'Parole', 190-91. Porsch then sees the same two stages in 4.10-15 and 6.32-40, 60-65 (*Pneuma*, 70).

[143] Prior to the cross, the Spirit's activity is temporary and symbolic (*zeichenhaft-vorläufig*) whereas after the cross it is real and definite/conclusive (*eigentlich-endgültig*) (Porsch, *Pneuma*, 72).

[144] Bennema, 'Giving', section II. Contra Howard-Brook, who says that 'Jesus is clearly referring to an entity that *does not yet exist* at the moment being narrated' (*Children*, 325 [author's emphasis]).

[145] Cf. Turner, *Spirit*, 62-63.

Spirit is essentially the experience of people coming from sensory to cognitive perception and understanding of Jesus' revelation, on the basis of which they can then produce an adequate belief-response and enter into a life-giving relationship with Jesus.

The illocutionary force of John 4, taken as a speech act addressing the readers, is to invite them to recognize Jesus' identity and accept his offer of life-giving water, and to challenge them to discipleship and participation in Jesus' universal mission.[146] The implied author's intended perlocutionary effect is to persuade the implied reader to adopt the example of the Samaritan woman. She represents those who confess adequate belief in Jesus and display true discipleship.

3.3. The Spirit Gives Life

John 6 forms a coherent literary unit,[147] and its theme is that Jesus is the true bread from heaven who gives life to the world through his self-giving.[148] Evoking God's providence in the wilderness, Jesus symbolically presents himself as the heavenly food and invites people to feed on him so that they may have eternal life. The narrative can be divided into four episodes: the sign (vv.1-15), the interlude (vv.16-21), the discourse (vv.22-59), and the response (vv.60-71).

The Sign (vv.1-15). Vv.1-15 describe the sign and set the stage for the 'bread of life' discourse. V.2 narrates that a great crowd of people 'followed' Jesus because of his miraculous signs, which probably indicates that the crowd had incipient (signs-)faith and potential towards discipleship. This initial belief and potential discipleship of the crowd will be explored and tested by Jesus in the remainder of the narrative. Vv.10-13 describe the miraculous feeding but the implied reader will soon discover that this miracle serves as a sign revealing something about Jesus' identity. The people perceived through it something about Jesus' identity (the Mosaic Prophet of Deut. 18) and his mission (vv.14-15), but their concept of Jesus was still limited and from 'below': for John, Jesus was not merely a prophet like Moses nor was his kingship of this world (cf. 18.36).[149]

---

[146] Cf. Lee, *Narratives*, 93.

[147] J.D.G. Dunn, 'John vi - A Eucharistic Discourse?', *NTS* 17 (1970-71) 329-30; F.J. Moloney, *The Johannine Son of Man* (Roma: Libreria Ateneo Salesiano, 1976) 106; Beasley-Murray, *John*, 86-87; M.J.J. Menken, 'John 6,51c-58: Eucharist or Christology?', *Bib* 74 (1993) 6-7; Lee, *Narratives*, 130; Ridderbos, *Gospel*, 221-22.

[148] Surprisingly, Keener does not deal at all with the discourse in Jn 6; he may have been too focused on the water-motif.

[149] Cf. Lee, *Narratives*, 139-40. The purpose of the interlude (vv.16-21) is unclear. Lee thinks that it fits the Passover imagery by alluding to the crossing of the Red Sea (*Narratives*, 140), but this seems a bit far-fetched. Stibbe argues that vv.16-24 contribute to the portrayal of Jesus as the elusive Christ (*John*, 84).

The Bread of Life Discourse (vv.22-59). In v.26, Jesus declares that the people still move at an earthly level: their search is essentially materialistic. Even to seek Jesus because of his signs would have been more spiritual. Their signs-faith seems hardly 'faith' at all. In v.27, Jesus moves from physical/material food to the spiritual/symbolic 'food' that leads into eternal life.[150] Although the hearers move to a more theological level, they still misunderstand the meaning of 'to work' in terms of human achievement (v.28). Jesus consequently explains that 'to work' means 'to believe' (v.29). The crowd's response in vv.30-31 shows that they remain at an earthly level and perceive Jesus only as a miracle worker; they had not grasped that the physical feeding was a sign of Jesus' ability to feed them spiritually.[151] The crowd demands from Jesus a greater miracle than the manna given by Moses; Moses gave bread from heaven, Jesus just gave ordinary bread.[152]

In vv.32-33 Jesus corrects their wrong understanding and subverts the Jewish expectation in four ways: (i) it was not Moses but God who gave bread from heaven in the past; (ii) the giving of the bread is not restricted to the past but is a present reality; (iii) the manna was not the true bread from heaven but he who comes down from heaven (Jesus); (iv) the true Bread gives life to the world.[153] The real contrast then is between two different kinds of bread, between manna and the *true* bread from heaven, between the historical and the eschatological manna. Indeed, this true bread from heaven (the bread of God/life) is Jesus (vv.33, 35). Jesus is not the giver of the bread of life, as the crowd expects (v.34), but the bread of

---

[150] The absurdity of the literal meaning should point to the metaphorical meaning (Lee, *Narratives*, 142).

[151] Still, the crowd shows progressive understanding; they set the feeding and the bread within the interpretative framework of the manna in the wilderness (Lee, *Narratives*, 143).

[152] V.30 has the form of two interrogatives, but its illocutionary force is that of a command/request. Ironically, Jesus had just done in vv.1-15 the kind of sign the crowd is now asking for in v.30 (Culpepper, *Gospel*, 161). The quotation in v.31 is probably a combination of Exod. 16.15 and Ps. 78.24 (Lee, *Narratives*, 135; cf. Neh. 9.15; Ps. 105.40; Wis. 16.20-21). The request of the Jews in vv.30-31 for a miraculous sign from Jesus alludes to the idea that in the eschatological age the Messiah would again provide manna from heaven (*Qoh.R.* 1.9; cf. *2 Bar.* 29.8).

[153] Cf. Borgen's analysis (except for point [iii]): P. Borgen, 'Observations on the Midrashic Character of John 6' in P. Borgen (ed.), *Logos Was the True Light and Other Essays on the Gospel of John* (Trondheim: Tapir Publishers, 1983) 24-25; *idem, Bread From Heaven: An Exegetical Study of the Concept of Manna in the Gospel of John and the Writings of Philo* (NT.S 10; Leiden: Brill, 1965) 61-69. Borgen failed to recognize that Jesus' main point in vv.32-33 is not that God, as against Moses, was the true giver of manna, but that the manna is not the true 'bread from heaven' at all (Lee, *Narratives*, 144).

life itself.[154] The wrong expectation of the crowd in v.34 is caused by the phrase ὁ καταβαίνων in v.33, which is again an example of Johannine ambiguity, meaning either 'he who comes down' (Jesus) or 'that which comes down' (manna) (cf. ἄνωθεν in 3.3 and ὕδωρ ζῶν in 4.10). The crowd misunderstands Jesus and opts for a materialistic interpretation, desiring merely a perpetual supply of this miraculous bread (v.34), whereas on a metaphorical level it refers to Jesus. Jesus then plainly reveals that he is the bread of life, who will sustain those who believe in him (v.35).[155]

When we examine the way 'manna' or 'bread (from heaven)' is used in Judaism, there is more to discover than 'merely' that Jesus is the eschatological food. Originally, 'manna' or 'bread (from heaven)' certainly had a purely literal meaning (Exod. 16.4, 15, 31; Neh. 9.15; Pss. 78.24; 105.40; Wis. 16.20-21), but it was soon turned into a metaphor, signifying Torah or the divine word/wisdom/instruction (Deut. 8.3; Amos 8.11; Wis. 16.20, 26; *Mek. Exod.* 13.17; *Exod.R.* 25.7; *Gen.R.* 70.5).[156] By virtue of the assertion that Torah is the locus of Wisdom (Sir. 15.1; cf. 24.23), the way is then paved to associate 'bread' with divine wisdom/understanding in Sirach 15.3: Wisdom will feed her disciples with ἄρτος συνέσεως. In Philo, 'manna' or 'bread from heaven' is also used metaphorically to signify divine wisdom/word (*Mut.* 259; *Det.* 115-118; *Her.* 191; *Cong.* 173-174; *Leg. All.* 3.161-162; *Quaest. in Gn.* 4.102; cf. *Sac.* 86).

Thus, 'manna' or 'bread from heaven' had become a metaphor for divine wisdom/teaching, which is life-giving.[157] In vv.33, 35 Jesus then transfers this metaphorical meaning of 'manna' as divine wisdom/teaching and its life-giving function to himself: Jesus' identification with the true bread from heaven indicates the locus of God's wisdom/revelation which leads to life.[158] Moreover, if 'manna' or 'bread from heaven' denotes divine wisdom/teaching, then Jesus' identification with this bread implies a claim to personified divine wisdom/revelation: Jesus is Wisdom incarnate bringing saving wisdom/revelation from heaven (cf. our exegesis of Jn 3-4). Jesus consequently modifies the metaphor 'bread from heaven' (who gives life to the world) into the more accurate metaphor 'bread of life' (vv.33, 35), denoting 'bread' that gives/communicates/mediates life (cf. ὁ ἄρτος ὁ ζῶν in v.51 with [τὸ] ὕδωρ [τὸ] ζῶν in 4.10-11).

---

[154] Cf. Bultmann, *Gospel*, 227; Koester, *Symbolism*, 96.

[155] V.31 may provide the key OT text for the discourse, but Jesus' self-revelation in v.35 is the narrative and theological centre of the entire discourse (Lee, *Narratives*, 135-36; cf. J. Painter, 'Tradition and Interpretation in John 6', *NTS* 35 [1989] 438 n.4).

[156] For parallels with Wis., see Ziener, 'Weisheitsbuch (I)', 407-409.

[157] Cf. Borgen, *Bread*, 148-58; Burge, *Community*, 105; Koester, *Symbolism*, 96-97; Witherington, *Wisdom*, 149-50; Turner, *Spirit*, 63.

[158] Cf. Brown, *Gospel*, 1:265-66, 272; Turner, *Spirit*, 64.

A sapiential interpretation of the metaphor 'manna' or 'bread of life' seems also justified by the intertextual background to v.35.[159] The words 'to come',[160] 'hunger' and 'thirst' (as well as 'to eat' and 'to drink' in vv.50-58) evoke the invitation of Wisdom to come to her banquet:

> She [Wisdom] has slaughtered her animals, she has mixed her wine, she has also set her table...she calls...'Come, eat of my bread and drink of the wine I have mixed' (Prov. 9.2-3, 5).[161]

> 'Come to me, you who desire me...Those who eat of me will hunger for more, and those who drink of me will thirst for more' (Sir. 24.19, 21).

What Wisdom is offering to people, is her life-giving wisdom/teaching (cf. Sir. 15.3; Isa. 55.1-3; *Jos&As.* 8.5; 15.5; 16.15-16).[162] To 'eat' and 'drink' from Wisdom are metaphors for accepting and learning from God's wisdom. To have table-fellowship with Wisdom is another way of denoting being in union with Wisdom, and the result of feeding on Wisdom is (eternal) life (see ch. 2). Moreover, as in John 4, Jesus even transcends the offer of Wisdom: Jesus' invitation in v.35b describes a one-for-all satisfaction of hunger and thirst (the double negatives, οὐ μή, in v.35 and 4.14 deny the need of repetition).[163] In conclusion, *'bread of life' is a metaphor for Jesus who, as Wisdom incarnate, came down from heaven to give life to the world in the form of divine wisdom/revelation.*[164]

In v.36 Jesus perceives that the crowd will not come to adequate belief — the intended perlocution will fail — and is proleptic for their negative response in vv.41 and 52.[165] The nature of the scandal is Jesus' identity and origin: he claims to have a divine origin whereas 'the Jews' think they

---

[159] For a careful reading of Jn 6 from a sapiential perspective, see Feuillet, 'Themes', 76-102; Thompson, 'God', 221-46.

[160] 'To come' to Jesus means to believe in Jesus (v.35), which is made clear by the parallelism (cf. Bultmann, *Gospel*, 227).

[161] In contrast to the 'bread of godlessness' and the 'lawless wine' in Prov. 4.17.

[162] For the parallel with *Jos&As.*, see J. Kügler, 'Der König als Brotspender. Religionsgeschichtliche Überlegungen zu JosAs 4,7; 25,5 und Joh 6,15', *ZNW* 89 (1998) 118-24.

[163] Cf. Morris, *Gospel*, 324; Turner, *Spirit*, 64.

[164] 'From heaven' indicates not only the origin of the bread, but also the quality of the life (eternal life) (vv.32-33, 35, 50-51) (Painter, 'Tradition', 440). Although Jesus' offer of life seems a present reality (vv.33, 35, 40, 47, 54) (cf. Borgen, *Bread*, 168), it can only be partial because Jesus had not yet gone to the cross; Jesus had not yet given his life for the life of the world (v.51). Moreover, 'salvation' awaits its full consummation in the future (vv.39-40, 44, 54).

[165] V.36 stands in ironic contrast to 20.29. Vv.37-40, 44 reveal the priority of divine election over human response (cf. the theme 'the Father draws people...' in ch. 3 section 3.2. n.100).

know his origins (vv.41-42).[166] In vv.48-51 Jesus explains, as an exposition of v.33, *how* he will give life to the world — namely, through his self-giving in death on the cross. In v.51c, we have a reference to Jesus' self-giving on the cross; life is given through death,[167] or to put it differently, Jesus *gives* what he *is*: the bread of life.[168] This implies that the 'bread of life' is not just a metaphor for Jesus as life-giver, but, more precisely, a metaphor for *Jesus crucified*, i.e., for Jesus' giving his life for the world on the cross.[169] The Jews continue to move at a level 'from below' and misunderstand the metaphorical meaning of 'eating' Jesus' flesh (v.52). They take even greater offence to Jesus' words than in v.41, and show their increasing alienation and rejection of Jesus.[170] Vv.53-55 explain, as an exposition of v.35, that to 'eat his flesh' and 'drink his blood' are metaphors respectively for coming to and believing in Jesus.[171]

In the light of 'bread of life' being a metaphor for Jesus crucified, we can now also define more sharply the metaphors of 'eating' Jesus' flesh and 'drinking' Jesus' blood; they do not just denote coming to/believing in Jesus, but more particularly, to come to and believe in the one who is lifted

---

[166] From now on the crowd will increasingly alienate itself from Jesus and ultimately reject him (cf. Lee, *Narratives*, 147). Cf. the use of the term 'the Jews' instead of 'the crowd', which was used up to v.41. The murmuring of the Jews echoes that of the rebellious Israelites in the wilderness (Exod. 16.2, 7-9, 12).

[167] Dunn, 'John', 331; Lee, *Narratives*, 149-50; Koester, *Symbolism*, 98; Turner, *Spirit*, 64-65.

[168] Menken, 'John', 15.

[169] Cf. Menken, 'John', 12; Turner, *Spirit*, 64-65.

[170] The tragic irony is that, even though the Jews study the Scriptures of Moses, they have not recognized the one about whom Moses was really writing (cf. 5.39-40, 45-47) (Stibbe, *John*, 88).

[171] If the 'bread' is to be understood metaphorically, then it is natural to interpret its consumption also metaphorically (cf. Dunn, *Baptism*, 184; Burge, *Community*, 180; Beasley-Murray, *John*, 94; Carson, *Gospel*, 288-89; Burkett, *Son*, 136-37; Koester, *Symbolism*, 99, 260; Witherington, *Wisdom*, 150; Turner, *Spirit*, 65). Many scholars believe that vv.51(53)-58 refer to the eucharist, either primarily or secondarily (*inter alios* Bultmann, *Gospel*, 234-37; Borgen, *Bread*, 90-97; Brown, *Gospel*, 1:284-93; Porsch, *Pneuma*, 162-64; Barrett, *Gospel*, 283-84; Schnackenburg, *Gospel*, 2:54-69; Burge, *Community*, 181-82; Culpepper, *Gospel*, 163; Beasley-Murray, *John*, 95-99; Lee, *Narratives*, 136, 152-53; Koottumkal, *Words*, 79). However, although John uses eucharistic language, we doubt whether he had the sacrament of the eucharist in mind (cf. Dunn, *Baptism*, 185-86; *idem*, 'John', 332-38; Burkett, *Son*, 135-36; Ridderbos, *Gospel*, 236-42; Turner, *Spirit*, 65; see also Léon-Dufour, 'Reading', 451-52). Moreover, even if sacramentalism were present at a secondary level, for example, it would merely express something that is already there at a primary level: if the sacrament of the eucharist denotes the continual remembrance of and participation in Jesus' death, this meaning was already suggested by a non-sacramental reading of the text. Finally, if sacramentalism was so important to John or the Johannine church, why then do the Johannine letters not (clearly) refer to the sacraments?

up (3.14-15).[172] Moreover, to 'consume' Jesus' flesh and blood denotes reception (and perception) of Jesus' revelatory teaching concerning his death, and making an adequate response to it, so that, as a result, an enduring relationship with Jesus of mutual indwelling is created (v.56).[173] This presupposes that people will be able to comprehend Jesus' revelation. V.57 stresses again that Jesus is the source of (eternal) life, i.e., the shared life between the Father and Son (cf. 5.26; 14.10; 17.21).[174] V.58 shows that the Feeder has become the food: John 6 shows a subtle progression from Jesus as giver of bread to Jesus as bread.[175] The illocutionary force of vv.22-59, taken as the narrator's 'utterance' to readers, is to challenge or invite them to accept Jesus' revelation of himself as the life-giving bread who will give his life for the life of the world.

We now seem to have defined two ways in which Jesus, as the Bread of life, gives life; an observation Johannine scholarship does not seem to have made. On the one hand, 'bread of life' functions as a metaphor for Jesus' coming down from heaven to be and to bring God's life-giving revelation in the form of his revelatory wisdom teaching (vv.30-35). On the other hand, Jesus will give life to the world through his self-giving in death on the cross (vv.48-59). The obvious question then is: how are these two concepts related? How can both Jesus' wisdom teaching and Jesus' death be life-giving? From John 3 we know that these two concepts have already been linked: Jesus, as Wisdom incarnate, brings down from heaven saving wisdom in the form of God's revelation, which culminates in the cross. To put it differently, Jesus reveals God in his wisdom teaching, and the climax of this revelation is (displayed on) the cross. Thus, there is still one concept of salvation: God's saving revelatory wisdom has come down as the 'bread from heaven' by and in the person of Jesus, and the culmination of God's revelation which contains saving wisdom is displayed on the cross, where this 'bread' is given in order to provide life for those who 'feed' on it. We also believe that a further explanation lies in the salvific role of the Spirit, as is mentioned in v.63, to which we will turn shortly.

The Response (vv.60-71). Vv.60-71 reveal the sifting of Jesus' disciples. After the first scandal concerning Jesus' origin and identity (vv.41-42), the second scandal is the invitation to 'eat' Jesus' flesh (v.52). Many even of

---

[172] Cf. Painter, 'Tradition', 445. J.A. Grassi interprets vv.51-58 in the context of the Jewish Passover (cf. 6.4) ('Eating Jesus' Flesh and Drinking His Blood: The Centrality and Meaning of John 6:51-58', *BTB* 17 [1987] 24-30; cf. Painter, 'Tradition', 448).

[173] Cf. Turner, *Spirit*, 65. Since 6.56 parallels 6.54a, eternal life consists essentially in the remaining of the believer in Jesus, and vice versa.

[174] Cf. Lee, *Narratives*, 151.

[175] Culpepper, *Anatomy*, 196; Stibbe, *John*, 86. If the present participles in vv.54, 56 and 58 indicate a continuous aspect, John might even indicate the need for a continuous 'consumption' of Jesus' flesh and blood (cf. the use of μένω in v.56).

Jesus' disciples found his teaching hard to accept (v.60), to which Jesus replied that if this offended them, then how much more would they be offended when they would see the Son of Man ascend to where he was before, implying his return to the Father, which would start at the cross (vv.61-62).[176] Burkett does not believe that ἀναβαίνω includes the crucifixion; he argues that v.62 addresses the disciples' problem in believing that Jesus had descended from heaven, and that v.63 addresses the problem of how Jesus can give his flesh to eat.[177] However, it is unlikely that v.62 refers back to vv.33 and 35; rather, vv.62-63 taken together probably explain the supreme scandal of 'eating' Jesus' flesh. Moreover, although in Johannine terminology ὑψόω is connected with the cross, whereas ἀναβαίνω is linked with the Easter event, Porsch suggests that the choice of ἀναβαίνω here may be chosen to correspond with the καταβαίνω in vv.31-58.[178] This agrees with 3.13-15, where Jesus depicts himself as the Son of Man, descending from heaven and ascending via the cross. Hence, Jesus' ascent should be understood as the culmination of the entire series of events that was inaugurated by the cross; the cross is the path of Jesus' return to the glory he had with the Father before the beginning of the world.[179]

V.63 is for us the most important verse of the whole discourse because it explains the interrelation between John's pneumatology and soteriology.[180] That the Spirit gives life (v.63a) has already been asserted in John 3-4, in that the Spirit facilitates entry into eternal life and that

---

[176] Because v.62 is an aposiopesis (a conditional clause which has the protasis but not the apodosis), it can be interpreted in two ways: (i) Jesus' ascent will make the offence even greater, or (ii) Jesus' ascent will reduce/remove the offence, although these interpretations are not mutually exclusive (Porsch, *Pneuma*, 206-207; Moloney, *Son*, 120; Carson, *Gospel*, 300-301). Scholars who argue that seeing the ascent could increase or dispel the offence, depending on the individual response, include, e.g., Barrett, *Gospel*, 303; Schnackenburg, *Gospel*, 2:71; Beasley-Murray, *John*, 96; Morris, *Gospel*, 339-40. Moloney argues that there is no need for Jesus to ascend into heaven because he has been there τὸ πρότερον, i.e., in his pre-existence (*Son*, 121-23). However, Moloney is mistaken in taking v.62 as a rhetorical question; the point is *how* people respond to the supreme scandal of Jesus' ascent, not *whether* Jesus' ascent is necessary.

[177] Burkett, *Son*, 138-39.

[178] Porsch, *Pneuma*, 206.

[179] Porsch, *Pneuma*, 205-207; Carson, *Gospel*, 301; Morris, *Gospel*, 339; Turner, *Spirit*, 65. An exclusive reference to the crucifixion (so Painter, 'Tradition', 445) is unlikely because that would not correspond with the ὅπου ἦν τὸ πρότερον.

[180] According to Koottumkal, v.63 is the centre of vv.60-66 (*Words*, 86-87; cf. de la Potterie, 'Parole', 184).

Jesus' Spirit-imbued wisdom teaching gives life.[181] However, it was not indicated *how* the Spirit gives life. This is elucidated in 6.63b and 6.63c.

V.63b mentions that 'the flesh benefits no one', and the dispute is about the referent of σάρξ. A number of scholars think σάρξ should be interpreted anthropologically and not christologically: σάρξ and πνεῦμα stand in contrast to each other, referring, as in 3.6, to their respective spheres or realms.[182] Porsch, for example, thinks that σάρξ refers not to Jesus' flesh but to the unbelieving person who is locked in his fleshly/human thinking, whereas the life-working activity of the Spirit is the awakening of faith and the recognition of the truth.[183] However, this anthropological interpretation causes an unnatural distinction between σάρξ in vv.51-58 and v.63. We suggest that it is much more natural to take σάρξ christologically as referring to Jesus' life, in particular to the giving of Jesus' life delivered on the cross, because: (i) in vv.51-58 σάρξ also refers to Jesus' death; (ii) v.62 refers to Jesus' ascent, starting at the cross, and v.63 then sheds further light on this event.[184]

If σάρξ refers to Jesus' death on the cross, however, how can Jesus say that this benefits no one? In John 3, we suggested that Jesus' death on the cross is the supreme expression of God's love for the world, and that it is the Spirit who mediates to people the revelatory significance of this event. This insight may help us to explain v.63b and its connection with v.63a: Jesus' death on the cross can be understood and hence be life-giving, only if the significance of this event is revealed to people by the Spirit.[185] Thus,

---

[181] The verb ζωοποιέω occurs only three times in the Johannine literature: in relation to the Father (5.21a), the Son (5.21b) and the Spirit (6.63a).

[182] Borgen, *Bread*, 181-82, 187-89; Brown, *Gospel*, 1:299-300; Menken, 'John', 25; Ridderbos, *Gospel*, 246-47. Cf. Barrett, *Gospel*, 302; Burge, *Community*, 106, 185; L. Schenke, 'The Johannine Schism and the "Twelve" (John 6:60-71)' in R.A. Culpepper (ed.), *Critical Readings of John 6* (BIS 22; Leiden: Brill, 1997) 211-15.

[183] Porsch, *Pneuma*, 186, 191; cf. J. Pascher, 'Der Glaube als Mitteilung des Pneumas nach Joh. 6,61-65', *Theologische Quartalschrift* 117 (1936) 310-16; Hoskyns, *Gospel*, 1:338-40; Feuillet, 'Themes', 55; de la Potterie, 'Parole', 185; Koottumkal, *Words*, 112; Moloney, *Signs*, 62.

[184] Although for Bultmann σάρξ refers to Jesus, he argues it refers to the incarnation (ὁ λόγος σὰρξ ἐγένετο), which causes offence, rather than to the cross (*Gospel*, 446-47).

[185] Turner, *Spirit*, 66. Lee argues that the contrast in v.63 is between a symbolic and materialistic understanding of 'flesh'; σάρξ in itself is 'useless' to bring eternal life; only when suffused with the divine πνεῦμα does it become the means of attaining life (*Narratives*, 155-57). Although Lee points in the right direction, we believe that, instead of generalizing σάρξ, the primary referent is Jesus' σάρξ given on the cross. Nevertheless, Porsch's and Lee's interpretation need not be ruled out completely. It could be argued, at a secondary level, that Jesus' death on the cross remains soteriologically ineffective to the 'fleshly' mind of the unbeliever unless the Spirit illuminates the event at the cross to the person as God's saving wisdom and thus brings about life (cf. Porsch, *Pneuma*, 191; Lee, *Narratives*, 156-57; Morris, *Gospel*, 340).

the Spirit gives life precisely in that the Spirit discloses the revelatory significance of the Christ-event on the cross.[186]

If we probe deeper into the function of the Spirit in salvation, we might ask ourselves the following question: how does the Spirit reveal the soteriological significance of Jesus' death on the cross to people? The means by which the Spirit accomplishes this is through Jesus' revelatory wisdom teaching: 'the words I have spoken to you are Spirit-and-life' (6.63c).[187] The event at the cross is only understood by revelation, i.e., the revelation which Jesus brings and which the Spirit discloses. In fact, the revelation Jesus brought consists of the words that Jesus speaks, i.e., his revelatory wisdom teaching. Thus, *the Spirit gives life by disclosing the saving wisdom of Jesus' revelatory teaching.*[188] To elucidate this concept a little further, we will examine the positions of Porsch and Turner.

On the basis of 3.34, Porsch had already argued that the giving of the Spirit and the speaking of God's words are not two different activities, but should be understood as one single event, i.e., when Jesus speaks/reveals the words of God, he also gives the Spirit at the same time.[189] According to Porsch, v.63c parallels 3.34 and defines further the identification of God's/Jesus' words with the Spirit: the words of Jesus are life because in them the life-giving Spirit is active, i.e., the effectiveness of the Spirit is

---

[186] Although W. Stenger is thinking in the right direction, he concludes that only the believer understands the event at the cross in such a way that it becomes for him life-giving Spirit ("'Der Geist ist es, der lebendig macht, das Fleisch nützt nichts' [Jo 6,63]', *Trierer Theologische Zeitschrift* 85 [1976] 122). However, we cannot reduce the role of the Spirit to such a passive one; it is precisely the *Spirit* who *enables* the person to understand the crucifixion.

[187] Turner, *Spirit*, 66. We take 'Spirit-and-life' as a hendiadys (with Dodd, *Interpretation*, 342; Brown, *Gospel*, 1:297, contra Malatesta, 'Spirit/Paraclete', 545; Johnston, *Spirit-Paraclete*, 26-28). Burkett rejects a reference to the Holy Spirit in v.63c, and argues that the life-giving 'spirit' is Jesus' breath on which his spoken words are carried (cf. 20.22) (*Son*, 140; cf. Johnston, *Spirit-Paraclete*, 42, 69; Forestell, *Word*, 116). However, if τὸ πνεῦμα in v.63a clearly refers to the divine Spirit, why not then πνεῦμα in v.63c? Further, although Burkett rightly points out that πνεῦμα cannot refer to the Holy Spirit given after Jesus' ascension because v.63b denotes a present reality (*Son*, 140), πνεῦμα can refer to the Holy Spirit who is *experienced* through Jesus' words.

[188] Koottumkal seems a bit confused concerning the concept of Jesus' life-giving words: on the one hand, Jesus' words are life-giving because Jesus has life in himself (*Words*, 110); on the other hand, Jesus' words are life-giving because the Spirit in them is the life-giving power (*Words*, 119). Moreover, although Koottumkal rightly observes *that* the life-giving Spirit is active in Jesus' word, he does not explain *how* the Spirit gives life. Finally, does Koottumkal perhaps not attribute too much to the Spirit, when he says that Jesus' word is life because in it is the life-giving power of the Spirit? Is the Spirit not 'merely' *mediating* the life that is available in Jesus' words (in the form of saving wisdom)?

[189] Porsch, *Pneuma*, 200.

linked with Jesus' words; 'Wirksamkeit des Wortes ist Wirksamkeit des Pneuma durch das Wort.'[190] The Spirit is the life-giving power in Jesus' words, and the words without the Spirit are, in regard to life, of no use; only in combination with the Spirit are they words of eternal life.[191] Thus, Porsch qualifies his interpretation of 3.34 by 6.63: the affirmation 'when Jesus speaks God's words he also gives the Spirit' means for Porsch that the Spirit is active in Jesus' words; one cannot separate the Spirit from Jesus' words because the effectiveness of Jesus' words is the effectiveness of the Spirit *through* Jesus' words.[192] However, according to 7.39, it seems that the Spirit can only be given after Jesus' glorification, and here the ways of Porsch and Turner part.

Porsch argues that v.63c characterizes what Jesus' words are in themselves and how they can be experienced *later*. Although Jesus' words already carried the power of the Spirit in them at that time, and although the Spirit was already given, the Spirit was (in its special effectiveness) *not yet* experienced, i.e., the Spirit had not yet unlocked these words.[193] Turner, however, argues that v.63c indicates that people *began* to experience in Jesus' ministry the eschatological realities that they were more fully to comprehend and experience after Jesus' glorification.[194] Thus, Porsch argues that the Spirit was already 'given', i.e., proleptically present, in Jesus' words, but these words would only become life later because the Spirit would only become active/be experienced later (after Jesus' glorification) to unlock these words, whereas Turner suggests that the Spirit was not yet 'given' but was already experienced through Jesus' words.[195]

Turner's view seems to be more in line with the picture that emerges out of the Fourth Gospel than that of Porsch for various reasons. First, Porsch creates an artificial distinction between ontological and functional categories; it would seem strange that the Spirit is given in an ontological sense but not yet active functionally.[196] Rather than using the category

---

[190] Porsch, *Pneuma*, 200-203 (quotation from p.203).

[191] Porsch, *Pneuma*, 203; cf. Turner, *Spirit*, 66.

[192] Koottumkal essentially follows Porsch (*Words*, 117-19).

[193] Porsch, *Pneuma*, 209. Cf. Schlier, *Besinnung*, 265.

[194] Turner, *Spirit*, 66. Cf. Burge, *Community*, 106-107.

[195] Surprisingly, Turner does not interact with Porsch on this important point, also because here Porsch lays the basis for his 'embryonic' interpretation of 20.22 where he argues that the Spirit-Paraclete is given but who will only function as the Paraclete in the future (*Pneuma*, 376; see Bennema, 'Giving', section IV.5 for an assessment of Porsch's interpretation).

[196] In our understanding, to interpret 'the Spirit is given' ontologically would denote something like the Spirit becoming part of a person, people 'having' the Spirit, or the Spirit indwelling people as divine essence/substance, whereas a functional interpretation points more to a meaning in terms of the Spirit's activities.

ontology/functionality, we suggest a relational interpretation of the Spirit, i.e., how the Spirit is experienced in terms of his activities in relation to a person. Second, Porsch seems to diminish the role/activity of the Spirit during Jesus' (earthly) ministry; according to Porsch, not only are Jesus' words locked up (until the Spirit opens them up), but also the Spirit itself is locked up (in Jesus' words until after Jesus' glorification). Only after Jesus' glorification can the Spirit, and hence also Jesus' words, be experienced in its and their life-giving effectiveness. Turner, however, has rightly understood (we have argued) that the Spirit is already actively reaching out to people and already transforming them through Jesus' revelatory wisdom teaching.[197] Third, besides 4.10-15 and 7.37-39, Porsch also uses John 6 to support his two-stage model — the Spirit is already 'given' proleptically in Jesus' words but can only be experienced in its special life-giving effectiveness later — which we have already criticized in the previous section.[198]

Coming back to the remainder of the people's response, according to John, Jesus foreknows who, even among his disciples, do not believe (v.64; cf. v.36), and indeed many of his disciples rejected him and became 'non-disciples' (v.66).[199] On Jesus' challenge to the Twelve (v.67), Peter, as a spokesman for them (note the plurals in vv.68-69), confesses adequate belief and commitment to discipleship (vv.68-69). Yet, even one of the Twelve will turn his back on Jesus, as vv.70-71 proleptically show. Again, the problem with the crowd and the disciples seems to be a cognitive one.[200] Jesus' words cause offence, are hard to accept and cause defection, precisely because (but especially when) they are not properly perceived cognitively: Jesus' words are offensive to those who do not understand and reject them (vv.41-42, 52, 60, 66), but they are life-giving to those who

---

[197] Turner, *Spirit*, 67, 69, 75.

[198] Like Porsch, Dunn also seems to have overlooked that the life-giving power of the Spirit could already, though partially, be experienced during Jesus' ministry ('John', 332). See also Turner's criticism on Dunn (*Spirit*, 66-67 n.21). Barrett represents the other extreme, when he states: 'Jesus *imparts* the Spirit, and thus imparts life, to the world by his words' ('Spirit', 7 [my emphasis]; cf. Congar, *Spirit*, 1:51). Although Barrett probably makes this assertion because he understands John to be addressing a post-Easter situation (cf. *Gospel*, 304), it would be more accurate to say that the Spirit was being *experienced* through Jesus' words rather than being imparted.

[199] Cf. 8.(30)31-59, where the 'faith' of 'the Jews' (8.30-31a) proved to be inadequate and resulted in the final rejection of Jesus. V.65 answers the question of v.60b: those who can 'hear', i.e., perceive and accept, Jesus' words are those who are given to Jesus by the Father (cf. vv.44-45) (Koottumkal, *Words*, 86-87).

[200] Note the cognitive vocabulary in vv.60-71: ἀκούω, γινώσκω, θεωρέω, οἶδα, πιστεύω.

understand and accept them (vv.63, 68-69).[201] The illocutionary force of vv.60-71 to the readers is to assert the implications of Jesus' revelation (especially of his life-giving death), in that Jesus' Spirit-imbued revelatory life-giving teaching confronts people and requires them to make a choice.[202] Jesus confronts his followers with the reality of his mission and the implications of this for discipleship.[203] The intended perlocution is to persuade people to enter into a deeper commitment to/relationship with Jesus.

Conclusion. John 6 tells again the story of Jesus' identity and mission: he is the bread of life who will give life to the world through his death on the cross. John 6 is essentially an invitation to Wisdom's 'banquet', and tells, in showing the various belief-responses to Jesus' revelation, the tragic story of the rejection of Jesus, to which the Prologue had already hinted (1.10-11). The crowd initially showed (signs-)faith and some indication of discipleship, but they stumbled over the revelation of Jesus' identity and mission, and consequently, rejected Jesus and became increasingly alienated from Jesus.[204] The crowd represents the struggle of those who are open to believing but who fall back into rejection and ultimately remain part of the hostile world.[205] In addition, a major sifting took place too among his disciples: many of them defected.[206] Only the Twelve made a confession of adequate belief and a commitment to discipleship.[207] However, even among the Twelve there would eventually

---

[201] Contra Koottumkal, who believes that σκληρός (v.60) does not mean 'difficult to understand' but 'unacceptable/harsh/offensive' (*Words*, 104). However, Jesus' words are probably unacceptable/offensive because, or when, they are misunderstood (cf. v.60b, 'who is able to "hear", i.e., understand [and accept], it?').

[202] R. Kysar is less certain whether it is within human ability alone to respond to Jesus in faith. For him, 6.25-71 performs the demolition of any confidence in faith conceived as a human decision ('The Dismantling of Decisional Faith: A Reading of John 6:25-71' in R.A. Culpepper [ed.], *Critical Readings of John 6* [BIS 22; Leiden: Brill, 1997] 161-81). However, although we emphasized the Spirit's role, we have also pointed out the Father's drawing in the process of people coming to adequate belief.

[203] Cf. Koottumkal, who states that adherence to Jesus and to his words makes one a true disciple (cf. 8.31; 15.8), and the initial enthusiasm of many disciples fades away when they are tested in their allegiance to Jesus (*Words*, 103).

[204] Although signs attract people and can lead to adequate belief, one also needs to be prepared to accept Jesus' revelatory teaching, which is apparently much harder (cf. Culpepper, *Anatomy*, 117).

[205] Culpepper, *Anatomy*, 132, 147.

[206] The disciples' defection is perhaps also a proleptic echo of the possible problem of defection in the Johannine church(es) (1 Jn 2.19; 4.1; 2 Jn 7-8).

[207] This is of course not the first confession of the Twelve (cf. 1.35-51; 2.11), but this confession could be seen as a renewed confession based on the disciples' progressive understanding of Jesus' identity and mission.

be a defector.[208] Thus, besides the revelation of Jesus' identity and mission, discipleship is a dominant theme in John 6: what is involved in coming to Jesus, and then in remaining as a follower.[209] Moreover, we have demonstrated that John 6 also depicts the Spirit in the role of facilitating cognitive perception, understanding and life. The Spirit gives life by disclosing Jesus' revelatory teaching of its saving wisdom and mediating it to people so that they may cognitively perceive and understand Jesus' revelation (especially that of the cross), which may lead to an adequate response and hence to life.

4. Conclusion

In this chapter, we have elucidated the (soteriological) function of the Spirit within Jesus' earthly ministry. With regard to Jesus, the Spirit functions as a cognitive agent, in that the Spirit endows Jesus primarily with revelatory wisdom in order to provide life-giving teaching/revelation.[210] With regard to other people, the Spirit functions as a life-giving cognitive agent, in that the Spirit facilitates cognitive perception, understanding and life. How does the Spirit accomplish this? Each of the narratives we have investigated (Jn 3, 4 and 6) contributes to the answer. According to John 3 and 6, Jesus brings down the revelation of God, which culminates in the cross. This revelation needs to be perceived cognitively in order to be life-giving. It is precisely the Spirit that facilitates this cognitive perception and understanding, which results in a saving relationship with the Father and Son through a birth of the Spirit. The basis for the Spirit's life-giving cognitive function is Jesus' word/teaching (John 4 and 6).

How is the role of the Spirit with regard to Jesus and to people related? What is the common denominator? The answer lies in the concept of the Spirit as a cognitive agent: the Spirit provides revelatory wisdom to both Jesus and other people. The revelatory wisdom provided to Jesus by the Spirit is the basis of/for his revelatory teaching that leads to life, and this wisdom (as the content of Jesus' life-giving teaching) *becomes* 'saving

---

[208] Harner sees in the responses of the four groups of people in Jn 6 (the crowd, the Jews, the disciples, the Twelve) the possible responses of believers within the community of faith (*Relation*, 86-87). However, this extrapolation is incorrect; John certainly disapproves of the first three responses (or finds them at least wanting) as an adequate response for a believer. This does not imply that within the community of faith there are no 'degrees' of faith and understanding.

[209] Cf. Stibbe, *John*, 86.

[210] As the mode of communication between the Father and Jesus, the Spirit functions in a relational way too.

wisdom' mediated to people by the Spirit. This saving wisdom is the basis on which people can cognitively perceive and understand the significance of Jesus' revelatory teaching, which can subsequently lead to an adequate belief-response that brings one into a saving relationship with the Father and Son. Thus, the Spirit facilitates understanding and life in its function as a *life-giving cognitive agent.*

We are now also in a position to give a sharper definition of the Spirit's soteriological function than in chapter 3 section 6: the Spirit enables a person to come from sensory to cognitive perception precisely *through the mediation of revelatory saving wisdom that is present in Jesus' life-giving teaching.* The Spirit, in the function of the agent of life-bearing wisdom, thus combines the cognitive and relational aspects of salvation: (i) the Spirit acts as the facilitator of true 'relational' understanding, i.e., the understanding of the Father and Son — their identity, work, relationship, etc. — that is obtained in relationship to Jesus (and the Spirit); (ii) the Spirit brings a person into a life-giving relationship with the Father and Son (through a new birth). The concept of discipleship has also come to the fore: the witnessing of the Samaritan woman and the allegiance of the Twelve (over against rejection, defection [6.66], etc.). Thus, John wants to emphasize the need for adequate belief and a commitment to discipleship (as a continuous belief-response).[211] Moreover, if a commitment to discipleship is the ongoing expression or result of adequate belief, then the life-giving knowledge provided by the Spirit as the basis for such adequate belief might affect people's will, attitudes and motivations. Hence, the Spirit acts as an *affective agent* too.

Our exegesis of John 3, 4 and 6 also agrees with the concept of 'the Spirit as the power of saving W/wisdom'. First, the Spirit empowers Wisdom incarnate for his mission through the provision of revelatory wisdom. Second, the Spirit functions as the revealing power of Wisdom incarnate, in that the Spirit unlocks/discloses the saving wisdom of Jesus' revelatory teaching, and mediates it to people in order to give them a new understanding of God, which results in a saving/life-giving relationship with the Father and Son. The findings in this chapter are in continuation with our background (ch. 2), in that: (i) both depict the concept of 'the Spirit as the power of saving W/wisdom'; (ii) both combine the cognitive and relational aspects of salvation; (iii) both understand Wisdom (incarnate) as the source of salvation and the Spirit as the agent. The extent to which John's soteriology reflects the Jewish model of salvation in terms

---

[211] Cf. Rensberger, who, based on Jn 3, argues that belief in the full Johannine sense requires (from Jewish secret sympathizers [symbolized by Nicodemus]) a *public* transfer of allegiance — a dangerous social relocation (from synagogue Judaism to adherence to the community of faith) (*Faith*, 60-61, 113-14).

of degrees of intensity and quality of W/wisdom and Spirit, will be addressed in chapter 6 (excursus 4).

Our conclusion, emphasizing the significance of the soteriological role of the Spirit *within* Jesus' ministry, seriously undermines the two-stage models of Porsch and Loader, which both play down the work of the Spirit in Jesus' ministry and dichotomize the life-giving ministry of Jesus from that of the Spirit (see ch. 1 section 2.3 for a description of these models).[212] Loader's model essentially implies that the Spirit has no soteriological role in the revealer-envoy christology (because life is fully available in the person of Jesus), and according to the Son of Man christology, the soteriological work of the Spirit only starts after Jesus' glorification in its role as Paraclete.[213] However, why would John supplement an already established and sufficient revealer-envoy model for portraying Jesus' ministry with the Son of Man material? Looking at passages where revealer-envoy christology and Son of Man christology stand side by side (1.49-51; 3.1-12; 6.60-62; 7.37-39), Loader's rationale is that, '[t]he author…employed the Son of Man cluster of ideas to point readers to the appropriation of all that Jesus already was in his earthly ministry now through the Spirit in the Church's mission and in its community.'[214] However, although we agree, of course, that the Spirit appropriates after Easter all that Jesus was and offered in his earthly ministry, the point we need to reassert is that the Spirit already did so *during* Jesus' ministry. Our main disagreement with Loader is not so much about content but about timing. We agree with his somewhat incomplete description of the soteriological function of the Spirit, but we disagree with his setting the *terminus a quo* of such at 20.22 instead of within Jesus' ministry. If Loader had recognized to a greater extent the significance of the Spirit upon Jesus (for Jesus himself as well as for other people), it could have led him to

---

[212] We have already interacted with Porsch's model throughout this chapter, so that we will now only assess Loader's model.

[213] Although Loader claims that the Spirit was present and effective through Jesus during the ministry (*Christology*, 129), he does not explain how. According to Loader, although 3.1-11 refers primarily to the post-Easter situation, this does not mean that no rebirth and no seeing of the kingdom had been possible during Jesus' earthly ministry. Further, although 6.63 refers primarily to the words Jesus spoke during his earthly ministry, John may also have in mind the work of the Spirit after Easter. With regard to 7.37-39, Loader argues that Jesus' offer of living water in 7.37 was a real offer during Jesus' ministry, yet 7.38-39, in relation to 4.14, expands this promise in view of its future abundance made possible through the future coming of the Spirit (*Christology*, 129-31). However, Loader does not explain how this rebirth is possible during Jesus' ministry. Moreover, Loader, influenced by Porsch, unnecessarily dichotomizes the work of the Spirit and the work of Jesus in 6.63 and 7.37-39, instead of attributing an active role to the Spirit in Jesus' work.

[214] Loader, *Christology*, 209-10 (quotation from p.210).

attribute more importance to the role of the Spirit in Jesus' ministry. Moreover, if Loader had recognized the sapiential influence on the Fourth Gospel, it might also have helped him to give more substance to the cognitive aspect of his model.

Concerning Turner's model, with which we agree to a great extent and for which we have given further substantiation in this chapter, we can make one further critical remark (besides the ones we made in ch. 1 sections 2.3-2.4). Turner argues that during Jesus' ministry the disciples had life-giving *experiences* of the Spirit, which would give the disciples a *taste* of what was to come and bring them *towards* 'authentic (Christian) faith and understanding'. The disciples' belief during Jesus' ministry was only 'partial', and they will only be able to come to true authentic faith (or full Christian belief) *after* the cross.[215] We agree with Turner concerning the soteriological significance of the cross. We contend that the cross is climactic and constitutional for John's concept of salvation, in that the cross: (i) releases the life that was available in Jesus (3.14-16; 6.51; cf. 12.25); (ii) depicts the judgment of the prince of this world (12.31; cf. 16.11); (iii) 'releases' the Spirit;[216] (iv) reveals God's love (3.16; cf. 1 Jn 4.10); (v) constitutes the 'objective' atonement of sin, putting into effect Jesus' (proleptically) taking away of sin during his ministry (1 Jn 1.7; 2.2; 3.5; 4.10; cf. Jn 1.29).[217]

Nevertheless, Turner's description of the disciples' relationship with Jesus during the ministry in terms of life-giving *experiences* and *foretastes* of authentic faith seems too weak. We argued that the disciples already had an *adequate* belief-response during Jesus' ministry, and were already in a *saving* life-giving relationship with Jesus through the Spirit before the cross (ch. 3 section 4.1).[218] Our formulation might be due to the fact that we try to hold in better balance the cognitive aspect (saving wisdom) and the relational aspect (relationship with Jesus) of salvation, whereas Turner seems more focused on the former. Moreover, we are not completely certain whether Turner's categories of partial versus full/true authentic (Christian) faith are sufficiently accurate. Instead, we prefer to use the term '*adequate*' belief (defined as authentic *and* soteriologically sufficient, but not as 'perfect'), which is, in our view, already available *before* the

---

[215] Turner, *Spirit*, 69, 75, 97-99.

[216] See Bennema, 'Giving'.

[217] If life was already available during Jesus' earthly ministry, then the taking away of sin could possibly also have taken place already during Jesus' ministry (at least proleptically or partially) (cf. 1.29; 8.31-34; 13.10; 15.3; cf. also the pronouncements of forgiveness of sins during Jesus' ministry in the Synoptics).

[218] Nevertheless, not all the benefits of such a saving relationship (e.g., the new birth) were already available before the cross, due to the unique situation the disciples were in (cf. ch. 3 section 4.1).

cross. Hence, we suggest that the disciples' belief was adequate already during the ministry, though continuous progression in this belief would certainly be possible and indeed be expected (even after the cross) (cf. ch. 3).[219]

Although we have suggested that the Spirit is depicted as soteriologically active already during Jesus' ministry, we need to recognize the eschatological tension in the Fourth Gospel, which requires very careful and accurate navigation between two hazardous soteriological cliffs — the cross and the giving of the Spirit. First, although the cross is climactic and constitutional for salvation, adequate belief and life (based on the Spirit's activity) was already available during the ministry within a relationship with Jesus. We make a slight differentiation in the way we use 'salvation' and 'life', in that salvation encompasses the gift of eternal life (as the divine life of the Father and Son in which the believer participates) but also denotes the liberation/removal from sin, change of father, etc. As a result, within Jesus' ministry a life-giving relationship with Jesus was already available, but not yet all its benefits (cf. ch. 3 section 7 activity G). Second, although the eschatological 'not yet' of 7.39 indicates that the giving of the Spirit is dependent on Jesus' glorification, the Spirit was already soteriologically active during Jesus' ministry.[220]

---

[219] Cf. Thomas's criticism of Turner, and Turner's reply (J.C. Thomas, 'Max Turner's *The Holy Spirit and Spiritual Gifts: Then and Now* [Carlisle: Paternoster Press, 1996]: An Appreciation and Critique', *JPT* 12 [1998] 16-17; M.[M.B.] Turner, 'Readings and Paradigms: A Response to John Christopher Thomas', *JPT* 12 [1998] 32-33). We agree with Turner that Thomas exaggerates the availability of salvific experience during Jesus' ministry. Nonetheless, Turner still leaves unexplained the exact difference between 'real faith' during Jesus' ministry and 'fully authentic Christian faith' after the cross. We have no problem if the latter phrase (so Turner seems to imply) denotes a faith that understands the significance of the cross, but our point is that 'real faith' (using Turner's category) in Jesus' ministry could already be adequate, in that this belief already brought the disciples into a life-giving relationship with Jesus (without denying the need for progressive understanding of the significance of the cross, and of the Father and Son and their mission). Turner may not necessarily disagree with our category of 'adequate belief', but we suggest that it is perhaps a more helpful one than the category 'authentic belief' with its division into partial and fully Christian.

[220] For the giving of the Spirit in 20.22, see Bennema, 'Giving'.

Chapter 5

Paraclete, Truth and Salvation
after Jesus' Departure (Jn 13-17)

1. Introduction

In chapter 3 we saw that the relationship between the Father and Son is primarily characterized by love, life, knowledge/truth and glory, and that the believer is drawn into and participates in this relationship on the basis of cognitive perception, understanding and an adequate belief-response. Moreover, in order to sustain one's salvation, one needs to remain/continue in this saving relationship with the Father and Son. In chapter 4, we then developed the concept of the Spirit as a life-giving cognitive agent, who brings a person into such a saving relationship through the mediation of saving wisdom. In the present chapter, we shall examine to what extent the concept of the Spirit as Paraclete fits this picture, or perhaps even adds to it. Besides, in chapter 3 section 6, we had already suggested that the Paraclete performs soteriological functions — providing truth, sustaining salvation, empowering the disciples' salvific mission — which need to be tested. Hence, the objective of this chapter is to elucidate the Paraclete's soteriological role and, more precisely, the extent to which the Paraclete is depicted as a life-giving cognitive agent, i.e., as a facilitator of cognitive perception, understanding and life. The agenda for this chapter is constituted by three questions. How does the Paraclete bring people from sensory to cognitive perception and understanding? How does the Paraclete give or mediate life? What is the role of the Paraclete in creating and sustaining a saving relationship between the believer and the Father and Son? Our strategy is to examine the interrelationship between Paraclete, T/truth (=W/wisdom) and salvation in the farewell discourse (Jn 13-17), which depicts the projected time, events and activities after Jesus' departure.

Where is Johannine scholarship concerning the Paraclete at the moment? The concept of the Johannine Paraclete has been the object of much research,[1] but its soteriological dimension seems almost forgotten. The studies of, for example, Holwerda and Franck focus respectively on eschatology and on the didactic dimension of the Paraclete (without mentioning its soteriological potential), and Johnston and Burge seem to concentrate on several things except soteriology. Segovia and Tolmie have given a detailed overall literary analysis of the farewell discourse, and both develop the important concept of discipleship in the Fourth Gospel, but they fail to bring out its soteriological dimension, nor do they develop the salvific aspects of the Paraclete's functions.[2] Segovia argues that the *genre* of 13.1-17.26 is that of a testament or farewell discourse, and that within the context of a farewell gathering with his disciples at a meal, Jesus is portrayed as launching into a farewell speech, in which also the Paraclete's function is revealed.[3] Keener claims that the Spirit-Paraclete parallels the Jewish category of the Spirit of wisdom and prophecy, but he fails to bring out the significance of these parallels and to present a coherent concept of the soteriological function of the Paraclete.[4]

Consequently, we fall back again on the contributions of Porsch and Turner. Porsch contributes to our understanding of the soteriological dimension of the Paraclete in arguing that the Paraclete interprets and

---

[1] E.g., Holwerda, *Spirit*; O. Betz, *Der Paraklet: Fürsprecher im Häretischen Spätjudentum, im Johannes-Evangelium und in neu gefundenen gnostischen Schriften* (Leiden: Brill, 1963); H. Windisch, 'The Five Johannine Paraclete Sayings' in J. Reumann (ed.), *The Spirit-Paraclete in the Fourth Gospel* (Transl. J.W. Cox; Philadelphia: Fortress, 1968) 1-26; R.E. Brown, 'The Paraclete in the Fourth Gospel', *NTS* 13 (1966-67) 113-32; *idem*, 'The "Paraclete" in the Light of Modern Research' in F.L. Cross (ed.), *Studia Evangelica Vol. IV* (Berlin: Akademie-Verlag, 1968) 158-65; Johnston, *Spirit-Paraclete, passim*; Porsch, *Pneuma*, 215-324; J.T. Forestell, 'Jesus and the Paraclete in the Gospel of John' in J. Plevnik (ed.), *Word and Spirit: Essays in Honor of David Michael Stanley, S.J. on his 60th Birthday* (Willowdale, Ontario: Regis College Press, 1975) 151-97; I. de la Potterie, 'The Paraclete', *Bible Bhashyam* 2 (1976) 120-40; *idem*, *Vérité*, ch. 5; Ferraro, *Spirito*, chs. 7-10; Franck, *Revelation, passim*; Burge, *Community*, chs. 1 and 5; Chevallier, *Souffle*, 2:468-500; Keener, 'Function', ch. 4; A. Billington, 'The Paraclete and Mission in the Fourth Gospel' in A. Billington, T. Lane and M.[M.B.] Turner (eds.), *Mission and Meaning: Essays presented to Peter Cotterell* (Carlisle: Paternoster, 1995) 90-115; Kammler, 'Jesus', 87-190; Turner, *Spirit*, ch. 5.

[2] See Segovia, *Farewell* and Tolmie, *Farewell*. Although Tolmie briefly mentions the soteriological implications of the themes of unity and sanctification in the truth, he does not relate them to the Paraclete (*Farewell*, 64-65, 75-76, 91, 228-29). Both Segovia (*Farewell*, 20, 48) and Tolmie (*Farewell*, 12) contend that Jn 13-17 is a coherent unified literary unit. For an outline of the structure of Jn 13-17, see Segovia, *Farewell, passim*; Tolmie, *Farewell*, 28-32; cf. Stibbe, *John*, 144.

[3] Segovia, *Farewell*, 4, 20-23, 313. For an overview of research on Jn 13-17 and of investigations of farewell type-scenes, see Segovia, *Farewell*, 5-18, 25-47.

[4] See Keener, 'Function', ch. 4.

opens up Jesus' revelation.[5] However, Porsch does not go further than this, and leaves us with the questions of the exact content of Jesus' revelation, and of the soteriological significance of opening up Jesus' revelation (cf. ch. 1 section 2.3). Turner again provides a possible answer by arguing that the Paraclete's opening up of Jesus' revelation is none other than the Spirit affording both charismatic revelation and wisdom, which is salvific.[6]

We will not only attempt to test and substantiate Porsch's and Turner's arguments, but also show that the soteriological dimension of the Paraclete has a broader basis/scope than Turner and others have presented. In general, scholars have recognized *that* the Paraclete has a salvific dimension, but they have not investigated the full *scope* of the Paraclete's soteriological function, nor *how* the Paraclete achieves this salvific function. We start with an introductory section on the Paraclete, exploring its meaning, background and relationship to Jesus (section 2). Then we will examine, with the assistance of our conceptual background of the Spirit in sapiential Judaism, the soteriological role of the Paraclete (section 3), after which we will be able to formulate to what extent the Paraclete will act as the agent of life-giving understanding (section 4). The originality of this chapter lies in drawing out the soteriological functions of the Paraclete under the label of a life-giving cognitive agent, and in the development of the concept of 'saving truth'.

2. The Concept of the Paraclete

This introductory section looks at the meaning of the title 'Paraclete', the background of the Paraclete, and the relationship between the Paraclete and Jesus.[7] Many scholars seem to detect a hiatus between the title and the functions of the Paraclete; they contend that the forensic title παράκλητος does not cover the multiplicity of the Paraclete's functions (e.g., the revelatory teaching and prosecution function).[8] However, Turner adequately demonstrates that there is no justification for this assumed hiatus,[9] as our own analysis will also confirm.

---

[5] Porsch, *Pneuma*, 300-303.

[6] Turner, *Spirit*, 83-84, 88.

[7] Some scholars have doubted whether the Paraclete is identified with the (Holy) Spirit and argued that the Paraclete was once an independent salvific figure later (con)fused with the Holy Spirit (Betz, *Paraklet*, 147-49, 209; Windisch, 'Paraclete', 14, 20, 35; Bultmann, *Gospel*, 566-72).

[8] E.g., J. Behm, 'Παράκλητος' in *TDNT*, V:803-804; Johnston, *Spirit-Paraclete*, 80-81; Porsch, *Pneuma*, 216, 305; K. Grayston, 'The Meaning of PARAKLĒTOS', *JSNT* 13 (1981) 68; Franck, *Revelation*, 9-10; Burge, *Community*, 7.

[9] See Turner, *Spirit*, ch. 5.

2.1. The Meaning and Background of the Paraclete

Establishing the meaning of παράκλητος seems a difficult enterprise because there is no linguistic background for it in Hebrew or Aramaic, and hence we must depend on the Greek term for its analysis.[10] The major translations of παράκλητος are: 'Intercessor/Spokesman/Mediator',[11] 'Helper',[12] 'Representative',[13] 'Supporter/Sponsor',[14] 'Exhorter/Comforter/Consoler',[15] 'Counsellor',[16] 'Teacher/Preacher',[17] 'Paraclete',[18] 'Advocate'. Formally παράκλητος is a passive verbal adjective meaning 'one called alongside' especially to offer counsel, support or assistance in a court, thus an advocate or a 'defence attorney'.[19]

Because παράκλητος acquired in time an active meaning of one who spoke on behalf of someone, it seems appropriate to give a broad forensic sense to the term παράκλητος, defining it as a legal assistant in court who could have a defending as well as a prosecuting role, and which is best translated by 'advocate'.[20] Most scholars who object to this translation have too narrow a definition of 'advocate' (favouring either the passive or active meaning) and therefore see a hiatus between the Paraclete's title and

---

[10] Later Rabbinic Judaism used פרקליט as a loan-word for παράκλητος (Brown, 'Paraclete', *NTS*, 115-16; Burge, *Community*, 7).

[11] Brown, *Gospel*, 117.

[12] Bultmann, *Gospel*, 569; Isaacs, *Concept*, 95; Newman/Nida, *Handbook*, 466-67.

[13] Johnston, *Spirit-Paraclete*, 87, 120.

[14] Grayston, 'Meaning', 67, 75.

[15] J.G. Davies, 'The Primary Meaning of *ΠΑΡΑΚΛΗΤΟΣ*', *JThS* 4 (1953) 35-38; Barrett, 'Spirit', 1-15; *idem*, *Gospel*, 462.

[16] Dunn, *Jesus*, 350; Lindars, *Gospel*, 468, 478; RSV; NIV.

[17] Franck, *Revelation*, 36.

[18] Brown, 'Paraclete', *NTS*, 119; Burge, *Community*, 9; cf. Ridderbos, *Gospel*, 500-504. Although this suggestion is attractive, it does not really solve anything.

[19] Brown, 'Paraclete', *NTS*, 116; Turner, *Spirit*, 77. However, παράκλητος was by no means merely a technical term for a professional legal functionary, as, e.g., the Latin *advocatus* and the Greek σύνδικος or συνήγορος, (Behm, 'Παράκλητος', V:801; Turner, *Spirit*, 77).

[20] Cf. the majority of scholars: Holwerda, *Spirit*, 29; Behm, 'Παράκλητος', V:803; Porsch, *Pneuma*, 228; de la Potterie, 'Paraclete', 120-21; Bruce, *Gospel*, 301; Carson, *Gospel*, 499; Keener, 'Function', 222-32, 260-61; Morris, *Gospel*, 590-91; Witherington, *Wisdom*, 251-52; Billington, 'Paraclete', 94-95; Turner, *Spirit*, 77-79. This translation does not rule out a comforting, consoling or counselling role of the Spirit-Paraclete for the grief of the disciples (14.1, 27; 16.6, 20-22) nor for later believers; nonetheless, John presents the Paraclete primarily as Advocate. Although C.A.J. Pillai also defends the translation 'Advocate', he applies his results incorrectly to the contemporary profession of a Christian advocate ('Advocate — Christ's Name for the Holy Spirit', *Bible Today* 30 [1967] 2078-81). Hoskyns opts for both 'Advocate' and 'Comforter' (*Gospel*, 2:549-54; cf. Howard-Brook, *Children*, 320).

functions.[21] Moreover, most proposed translations do not do (sufficient) justice to the forensic aspect of παράκλητος (15.26-27; 16.7-11) and the forensic context.[22] Only if the normal meaning of παράκλητος cannot account for the tasks ascribed to the Paraclete, should we then attempt to discover another meaning for παράκλητος, and only then can we speak of a true hiatus or discrepancy between title and functions.[23]

The quest for a historico-religious background for the concept of the Paraclete seems to produce even more confusion, seeing the rich diversity of proposals and the lack of consensus.[24] Scholars who accept the sense 'advocate' have generally found the conceptual background for the Paraclete in Judaism, especially in the Jewish concepts of advocacy, intercession and succession, as highlighted by Mowinckel, Johansson, Bornkamm and Müller, although none of their theories is without difficulties.[25]

---

[21] Brown, 'Paraclete', *NTS*, 116-17; Burge, *Community*, 8; cf. S. Smalley, '"The Paraclete": Pneumatology in the Johannine Gospel and Apocalypse' in R.A. Culpepper and C.C. Black (eds.), *Exploring the Gospel of John: In Honor of D. Moody Smith* (Louisville: Westminster John Knox Press, 1996) 291.

[22] For the presentation of the Fourth Gospel as a trial, see esp. Harvey, *Jesus* and Lincoln, *Truth*.

[23] Cf. Holwerda, *Spirit*, 29. Several explanations have been offered for this assumed hiatus. Schnackenburg argues that John extended the meaning of the existing term παράκλητος, and hence not all the functions of the Paraclete go back to the term itself (*Gospel*, 3:140-41). Porsch, arguing that the Paraclete's main activity is one of revelation, suggests that John borrowed an appropriate title from his environment to express better the Spirit's work in a forensic situation (*Pneuma*, 305, 318-24). Cf. Franck, who believes that John used the title παράκλητος merely to draw attention to the association of the Spirit with the trial motif (*Revelation*, 9-10, 22-23). However, both Porsch and Franck undervalue the forensic aspects of the Paraclete, and thus only emphasize the assumed discrepancy between the Paraclete's title and functions. Moreover, this chapter will show that the translation 'Advocate', properly understood, covers all the functions of the Paraclete.

[24] For overviews of background studies see Johnston, *Spirit-Paraclete*, ch. 7; Burge, *Community*, 10-31. See also Brown, 'Paraclete', *NTS*, 119-26; Behm, 'Παράκλητος', V:806-12; Porsch, *Pneuma*, 308-17; Schnackenburg, *Gospel*, 3:144-50. The problem with most of these studies is that they involve a high degree of 'parallelomania' and/or, based on hypotheses concerning a Johannine community, indulge in excessive speculation (Billington, 'Paraclete', 94).

[25] S. Mowinckel, 'Die Vorstellungen des Spätjudentums vom heiligen Geist als Fürsprecher und der johanneische Paraklet', *ZNW* 32 (1933) 97-130; N. Johansson, *Parakletoi. Vorstellungen von Fürsprechern für die Menschen vor Gott in der alttestamentlichen Religion, im Spätjudentum und Urchristentum* (Lund: Gleerup, 1940) (Johansson developed Mowinckel's thesis); Bornkamm, 'Paraklet', 68-89; U.B. Müller, 'Die Parakletenvorstellung im Johannesevangelium', *ZThK* 71 (1974) 31-77 (cf. E. Bammel, 'The Farewell Discourse of the Evangelist John and Its Jewish Heritage', *TynB* 44 [1993] 103-16). Betz finds the background of the Paraclete concept in the Qumranian

Other scholars have found a possible background for the Paraclete in the Jewish wisdom tradition. Isaacs, for example, states: 'we can claim a correspondence between the spirit-paraclete of the Fourth Gospel and the figure of σοφία as developed in Hellenistic Judaism.'[26] Brown makes a similar observation: 'just as the figure of the Johannine Jesus is patterned upon personified divine Wisdom, so also is the figure of the Paraclete.'[27] However, the correspondence is probably not so much between the *figures* of Wisdom and the Paraclete, but rather between the *functions* of the Spirit in the sapiential traditions and the Paraclete in the Fourth Gospel. Moreover, Jesus is presented as Wisdom incarnate, and the Paraclete is modelled on Jesus (see section 2.2, below), but we cannot deduce from this that the Paraclete is modelled on Wisdom.

Witherington offers a more persuasive argument. First, Witherington interprets John 13-17 against a sapiential background: 13.1-30 corresponds to a Graeco-Roman banquet complete with a closing *symposium*, in which Jesus acts as the sage who offers the teaching and the religious rites

---

Spirit of Truth (*Paraklet*, 36-116; cf. A.R.C. Leaney, 'The Johannine Paraclete and the Qumran Scrolls' in J.H. Charlesworth [ed.], *John and Qumran* [London: Chapman, 1972] 38-61; Forestell, 'Jesus', 175-86). However, it is more likely that 'the similarities between the pneumatology of John and that of the Qumran community may be due to the fact that both have drawn independently upon Jewish wisdom traditions' (Isaacs, *Concept*, 137; cf. R.E. Brown, 'The Qumran Scrolls and the Johannine Gospel and Epistles' in R.E. Brown [ed.], *New Testament Essays* [London: Chapman, 1967] 128). Ashton seems to think that the Paraclete is more like the *angelus interpres* of the apocalyptic tradition (*Understanding*, 394, 423-24). However, although the Paraclete and the *angelus interpres* have a similar function (mediating wisdom to interpret teaching and visions respectively), the Spirit and the *angelus interpres* could both appear (as distinct beings) in the apocalyptic tradition and sometimes had different functions. Moreover, it seems that in the earlier 'apocalyptic' books (Ezek. and Dan.) the *angelus interpres* 'replaced' the Spirit rather than the Spirit being modelled on the *angelus interpres* (see Bennema, 'Strands', 66, 74-77, 79 n.73).

[26] Isaacs, *Concept*, 137. M.E. Isaacs sees also striking parallels between the functions of the Paraclete and the OT prophet ('The Prophetic Spirit in the Fourth Gospel', *Heythrop Journal* 24 [1983] 393-99). However, rather than comparing the Paraclete and the OT prophet, it would be more appropriate to compare the Spirit as the inspirational power of the OT prophet and the prophetic word with the Paraclete. M.E. Boring argues that the Paraclete (as the Spirit that inspires prophecy) is a more particularized function of the Spirit than that represented in Jn 1-12, and that John portrayed both Jesus and the Paraclete with traits taken from the Christian prophets in the Johannine church ('The Influence of Christian Prophecy on the Johannine Portrayal of the Paraclete and Jesus', *NTS* 25 [1979] 113-23). However, Boring's picture of the Paraclete is too narrow; this chapter will show that the Spirit as Paraclete includes all the functions of the Spirit as depicted during Jesus' earthly ministry. Moreover, the Paraclete may have 'created' or empowered the prophetic office in the Johannine church, but it seems unlikely that this office had shaped John's portrayal of Jesus and the Paraclete (cf. Burge, *Community*, 39).

[27] Brown, *Gospel*, 2:715; cf. 2:1139.

associated with such meals (13.31-17.26).[28] Jesus is depicted here as Wisdom (cf. Prov. 9.5-6) who gives his 'after-dinner speech', and the function of such farewell discourses in a Graeco-Roman setting is the preservation and handing on of wisdom to the next generation shortly before death or departure.[29] Second, Witherington shows that both the teaching and the forensic functions of the Paraclete are also ascribed to the Spirit in Wisdom of Solomon.[30] Nevertheless, although we do detect functional parallels between the Paraclete and the Spirit in the Jewish wisdom traditions (see section 3, below), we would still be hesitant to argue that John's entire concept of the Paraclete was derived from it.[31]

In conclusion, the attempt to find a historico-religious background for the concept of the Paraclete chiefly results in a labyrinth of proposed theories without a satisfactory solution.[32] It seems, however, that the most plausible and probable conceptual background for the Paraclete is found (i) in the concept of advocacy/intercession/succession in Judaism, as well as (ii) in the Jewish sapiential traditions. Nevertheless, John's understanding of the Paraclete goes beyond the mere sum of all the elements in the Jewish background, and the uniqueness of the Paraclete concept must be sought in John's own description of the Paraclete, in which the relationship of the Paraclete to Jesus is dominant.[33] Therefore, before we turn to the soteriological functions of the Paraclete (section 3, below), we will first outline the relationship between Jesus and the Paraclete.

2.2. The Paraclete and Jesus

The correspondence between Jesus and the Paraclete is evidenced in several ways. First, the implication of ἄλλον παράκλητον (14.16) is that Jesus himself is the first 'Paraclete' during his earthly ministry and that the

---

[28] Witherington, *Wisdom*, 231-34.

[29] Witherington, *Wisdom*, 231-34, 244-45.

[30] Witherington, *Wisdom*, 251.

[31] Keener essentially rejects a wisdom background for the Paraclete because he believes that a connection between Spirit and Wisdom is rarely demonstrable outside Wis. (to which John does not even clearly allude) ('Function', 257). However, the connection between Spirit and Wisdom is clearly much more widespread than just Wis. (see ch. 2). Moreover, we are not claiming that the personhood and entire background of the Spirit(-Paraclete) lies in the Jewish wisdom traditions; what we are claiming is that most, if not all, of the *functions* of the Spirit(-Paraclete) can be found in and explained from the Jewish sapiential traditions. John dwells on a general Jewish background of the Spirit but seems to develop his *specific* concept of the Spirit (as the power of Wisdom) especially from the Jewish wisdom traditions.

[32] Cf. Turner, *Spirit*, 79.

[33] Brown, 'Paraclete', *NTS*, 126. B. Vawter, who also acknowledges that the person of Jesus provides the meaning of the Paraclete, sees Ezekiel as a type of the Johannine Christ-Paraclete ('Ezekiel and John', *CBQ* 26 [1964] 450-58).

Paraclete is of the same kind/type as Jesus (cf. also 1 Jn 2.1).[34] Second, based on Bornkamm's theory (and Müller's corrective) that in the tandem relationship Jesus-Paraclete a successor motif is present, we would expect that the Paraclete is the continuation of Jesus' presence and of his work.[35] Third, as Bultmann and Brown were first to point out, there are numerous functional parallels between Jesus and the Paraclete.[36] In short, the Paraclete is modelled on Jesus; Jesus has acted as the Paraclete so far, and the Spirit is to take over that role, i.e., the Spirit will replace Jesus and take over his 'Paraclete' functions.[37] Moreover, the Paraclete will also mediate the personal presence of Jesus (and the Father) to the believer while Jesus is with the Father.[38]

Thus, we could say that παράκλητος *is a functional label*; Jesus has acted as the first Paraclete, and the Spirit, operating as the second Paraclete, will continue Jesus' presence and 'Paraclete' functions when Jesus is absent. Additionally, if the one who is sent is a genuine representative of the one who sends,[39] if the Paraclete not merely replaces Jesus when Jesus is absent but also mediates the presence of the Father and the exalted Son, then the Paraclete is the *mode of communication*, i.e., the

---

[34] Cf. Holwerda, *Spirit*, 26-27; Porsch, *Pneuma*, 242; Brown, 'Paraclete', *NTS*, 127; Beasley-Murray, *John*, 256; Turner, *Spirit*, 79. Contra W. Michaelis, 'Zur Herkunft des johanneischen Paraklet-Titels' in A. Fridrichsen (ed.), *Coniectanea Neotestamentica XI* (Lund: Köpenhamn, 1947) 152-54.

[35] Cf. Isaacs, 'Spirit', 402; Burge, *Community*, 137-39.

[36] Bultmann, *Gospel*, 566-67; Brown, 'Paraclete', *NTS*, 113-14, 126-27. See also Bornkamm, 'Paraklet', 68-89; Porsch, *Pneuma*, 237-40; Franck, *Revelation*, 83-84; Burge, *Community*, 139-42; Smalley, 'Paraclete', 292; Turner, *Spirit*, 79-80.

[37] Brown, 'Paraclete', *NTS*, 126-28; Turner, *Spirit*, 79-80; cf. Behm, 'Παράκλητος', V:813; Dunn, *Jesus*, 350; de la Potterie, 'Paraclete', 121; Isaacs, 'Spirit', 404; Burge, *Community*, 41. Contra Schweizer, 'Πνεῦμα', VI:443. Contra Willett (*Wisdom*, 147), who thinks that the Beloved Disciple was the first Paraclete for the Johannine community, and that after his death the Spirit continued his presence in the community. Malatesta may have overstated his qualification of Brown's position by reducing (the role of the) Paraclete to merely (that of) a medium ('Spirit/Paraclete', 547-50). Turner seems to have found a better balance when he qualifies the concept of the Paraclete's coming merely as a replacement/substitute when Jesus departs in three ways (see *Spirit*, 80-81). Brown slightly blurs the distinction between the Paraclete and Jesus, when he states: '[a]s "another Paraclete", the Paraclete is, as it were, another Jesus' ('Paraclete', *NTS*, 128; cf. Burge, *Community*, 33, 198; Ashton, *Understanding*, 469). However, the Paraclete represents Jesus rather than being Jesus present in another form, i.e., *the Paraclete is not another Jesus, but the Spirit is another Paraclete*. For a defence of the Spirit-Paraclete as a distinct 'Person', see Turner, *Spirit*, 175-76.

[38] Brown, 'Paraclete', *NTS*, 128; R.E. Brown, 'The Kerygma of the Gospel According to John', *Interp* 21 (1967) 392; Turner, *Spirit*, 80-81. Contra Forestell, 'Jesus', 162-63.

[39] For the Paraclete as an agent, see Witherington, *Wisdom*, 140-41; Smalley, 'Paraclete', 292.

most important bond of union, between the believer, the Father and the glorified Jesus.[40]

3. The Paraclete and Salvation —
The Soteriological Functions of the Paraclete

The two objectives for this section are to elucidate the content of salvation and the scope and content of the role of the Spirit-Paraclete in salvation. We shall attempt to achieve these objectives by answering four questions. Is the Spirit-Paraclete soteriologically necessary? If so, what is the exact scope and nature of the Spirit-Paraclete's role in salvation? Does the concept of W/wisdom have any significant role in the interrelation between the Spirit-Paraclete and salvation? Is there any evidence in John 13-17 that salvation was already available/experienced within Jesus' earthly ministry?

With regard to the first question, Windisch, for example, believes the Spirit-Paraclete is a *donum superadditum*. According to Windisch, the disciples have been sufficiently enlightened and comforted with regard to Jesus' departure and absence; they possess spiritually all that they need (e.g., communion with the Father, faith, the mystical indwelling), so Windisch concludes that 'the Spirit is not needed at all, either now or in the future.'[41] However, in the previous chapter we suggested that the disciples 'possess' faith and communion with the Father and Son precisely because of (the work of) the Spirit. Nevertheless, in this section we have to investigate whether the Spirit as Paraclete also performs these soteriological functions or whether the Paraclete (or Spirit's 'Paraclete' function) is superfluous.

In order to answer the above questions we will examine the concept of relationship-friendship with the Father and Son (section 3.1), and the Paraclete in his function of Spirit of Truth, revelatory Teacher, and Advocate (sections 3.2-3.4).

3.1. The Paraclete as the Means of a Relationship-Friendship with the Father and Son

In chapter 3, we argued that the main soteriological concept is of entering into and remaining in a saving relationship with the Father and Son. We believe that there are several clues that indicate that a person remains in such a saving relationship precisely through the Spirit-Paraclete. First,

---

[40] Cf. Bultmann, *Gospel*, 615; Dunn, *Jesus*, 351; Brown, 'Kerygma', 392, 395; Boring, 'Influence', 117.

[41] Windisch, 'Paraclete', 2-3 (quotation from p.3).

based on the previous section, if the Paraclete mediates to people the personal presence of Jesus while Jesus is absent, if the Paraclete is modelled on Jesus and will continue Jesus' work, and if the Paraclete is the mode of communication, the bond of union, between the believer, the Father and the glorified Son, then it is natural to assume that the Paraclete is not merely a *donum superadditum* but a soteriological necessity. After Jesus' departure, the only way to know the Father and Son is through the Paraclete.[42] In addition, this knowledge of the Father and Son is, or results in, eternal life (17.3). Still, two subsequent questions need to be answered in the following sections. Where is this saving knowledge located? How does the Paraclete mediate this saving knowledge to people?

Second, the concept of relationship/unity is also expressed in the typical Johannine oneness-language (ἐν εἶναι) and mutual indwelling-language (denoted by the formula 'x [μένει] ἐν y'), and we suggested these expressions should be interpreted not literally or ontologically but metaphorically or relationally (see the themes 'the intimate relationship...' and 'remaining in Jesus' [ch. 3]).[43] How is this intimate relationship between the believer and the Father and Son realized and sustained? We suggest that the answer lies in the concept of the Spirit-Paraclete. The point of 14.9-11, for example, is that to see, know and have fellowship with Jesus is to see, know and experience fellowship with the Father, because of the unity and oneness in relationship between the Father and Son. Hence, the Paraclete 'in' the disciples in 14.17 should probably also be interpreted in terms of the Paraclete being in close relationship with the believer, rather than the Paraclete physically indwelling the person.[44]

In addition, the pericope 14.15-24 reveals that the Father and Son relate to and indwell the believer by means of the Spirit-Paraclete. Jesus and the Father come to the believer and make a dwelling place with the believer (14.23), which parallels the believer being indwelled by the Paraclete (14.17), and Jesus' coming to his disciples (in the Paraclete) (14.18).[45] The

---

[42] Cf. Turner, *Spirit*, 88.

[43] Cf. Moule, *Origin*, 63-66; Appold, *Motif, passim.*

[44] De la Potterie states that the three prepositions παρά, μετά and ἐν (14.16-17) mark a nice progression of the interior character of the Paraclete's action ('Paraclete', 124; cf. Barrett, *Gospel*, 463). However, the prepositions do not appear in the linear order as de la Potterie suggests: μετά occurs in 14.16, παρά and ἐν in 14.17.

[45] There is disagreement about whether Jesus' 'coming' in 14.18 refers to Jesus' post-resurrection appearances (e.g., Forestell, 'Jesus', 158-63, 175; Schnackenburg, *Gospel*, 3:76-77; Beasley-Murray, *John*, 258-59; Carson, *Gospel*, 501-502), to the Parousia, to his coming in the coming of the Spirit-Paraclete, or to various combinations of them (Dodd, *Interpretation*, 395; Bultmann, *Theology*, 2:57; *idem, Gospel*, 617-25; Betz, *Paraklet*, 149-50; Windisch, 'Paraclete', 25; Barrett, *Gospel*, 464; Burge, *Community*, 138-39, 147; Ashton, *Understanding*, 463). However, except for Carson, those who advocate a reference to Jesus' resurrection appearances in 14.18, do not explain how the Father and

Paraclete will mediate, as the mode of communication, Jesus' presence and life to the believer so that they will 'see', i.e., perceive, Jesus and participate in his life (14.18-19).[46] Thus, we suggest that the indwelling of the believer by the Father and Son (14.23) is (experienced by) the indwelling of the believer by the Paraclete (14.17). This suggestion seems confirmed by 1 John, which explains that the believer's κοινωνία is with the Father and Son, and that the Father and Son remain in the believer by means of the Spirit (1 Jn 1.3; 2.27; 3.24; 4.13). Moreover, the believer's indwelling of the Father and Son through the Spirit-Paraclete is precisely the kind of relationship that gives life.[47] The concept of being in relationship/union with the Father and Son through the Spirit-Paraclete corresponds to the concept of being in relationship/union with God/Wisdom/Logos through the divine πνεῦμα in Wisdom of Solomon and Philo (see ch. 2).

The third indicator that a person remains in a saving relationship through the Spirit-Paraclete is found in John 15.13-15, which introduces the important concept of friendship. Although this concept has received some recent attention from Johannine scholarship (by Ford and Ringe [see ch. 1]), the soteriological dimension of friendship has not yet been

---

Son are supposed to manifest themselves in 14.23 (cf. Turner, *Spirit*, 81). Moreover, in this case, the disciples would be orphans again after Jesus' ascension, and further, in the cotext of 14.18 there is no reference to Jesus' resurrection appearances (Holwerda, *Spirit*, 67-72). Furthermore, if 14.18 refers to the Parousia, the disciples would continue to be orphans until the End (Holwerda, *Spirit*, 67). Finally, the Parousia is the visible coming of Jesus whereas 14.19 emphasizes that the world cannot see this coming (cf. Brown, *Gospel*, 2:645; Turner, *Spirit*, 81). Hence, the only viable interpretation for 14.18 seems to be a reference to Jesus' coming back to the disciples in and through the Spirit-Paraclete (so Holwerda, *Spirit*, 65-76; Brown, *Gospel*, 2:645-46; *idem*, 'Kerygma', 392; Porsch, *Pneuma*, 383-84; Dunn, *Jesus*, 350-51; D.B. Woll, 'The Departure of "The Way": The First Farewell Discourse in the Gospel of John', *JBL* 99 [1980] 234; Ladd, *Theology*, 330, 339; Turner, *Spirit*, 81).

[46] The gift of the Spirit-Paraclete (14.16), Jesus' coming back in the Spirit-Paraclete (14.18), Jesus' revealing himself to the believer (14.21), and Jesus' and the Father's coming to the believer and making a dwelling place with her/him (14.23), probably indicate the same reality: it is only through the Paraclete that one can know and experience the Father and Son (Holwerda, *Spirit*, 67-76; D. Wenham, 'Spirit and Life: Some Reflections on Johannine Theology', *Themelios* 6 [1980] 5; Burge, *Community*, 138-39; Kammler, 'Jesus', 91-93).

[47] Although Bultmann, comments on 14.17 that 'the Spirit is the *how* of believing existence' and on 14.18 that it refers to Jesus' coming in the Spirit (*Gospel*, 617 [author's emphasis]), regarding 14.23 he surprisingly dismisses that the Paraclete is the means by which the Father and Son abide with the believer (*Gospel*, 623-24). Tolmie notices that the theme of unity has important implications for John's soteriology because salvation is described as being drawn into the unity between Father and Son (*Farewell*, 76 n.33).

explored adequately.[48] The concept of friendship has already been established in the Jewish sapiential traditions.[49] Wisdom facilitates friendship with God (Wis. 7.14, 27; cf. Philo, *Prob.* 40-44, 59),[50] and the benefits of friendship with Wisdom are, for example, understanding and immortality (Wis. 8.17-18). The friendship between Wisdom and her disciples is characterized by (reciprocal) love (Prov. 8.17; Wis. 6.12; 7.10; 8.2). In an important chapter on friendship, Sirach's advice and principle is to acquire friends through testing (6.7), and, after some examples of negative (6.8-13) and positive (6.14-18) friendships, Sirach reveals that Wisdom also tests those who want to be her disciples (6.21).

The concept of friendship in the Fourth Gospel is in continuation with its possible background. Several people are called Jesus' friends — John the Baptist (3.29), Lazarus (11.11), the disciples (15.14-15). Friendship is based on revealed knowledge (of the Father and Son and their work), and obedience guarantees continuation of friendship with Jesus (15.14-15). However, love is *the* hallmark of friendship and finds its ultimate expression in the laying down of one's ψυχή for one's friends (15.13).[51] Friendship (love) also denotes intimacy: the Father and Son have an intimate love-relationship (1.18), and Jesus has an intimate love-relationship with his friends/disciples (11.3, 36; 13.1; 15.9; cf. the Beloved Disciple as the disciple whom Jesus loved),[52] and the believer has an intimate relationship with the Father and Son (14.23). Further, ὁ δοῦλος is contrasted with ὁ φίλος (15.15), and if we recall a similar contrast between ὁ δοῦλος (τῆς ἁμαρτίας) and ὁ υἱὸς (ἐλεύθερος) (8.34-36), then Jesus'

---

[48] Ford merely touches on the soteriological aspect of friendship and Ringe only shows awareness of the salvific dimension of friendship in the conclusion of her ch. 5: '[h]is [Jesus'] friendship unites his followers with himself, and with God who sent him, in an indestructible bond that is life itself' (*Friends*, 82-83).

[49] For a brief overview of friendship in the whole of Judaism, see Ringe, *Friends*, 71-74.

[50] It is then not surprising that Philo calls Abraham and Moses, who are ultimately endowed with wisdom by the divine πνεῦμα, 'friends of God' (*Sob.* 55; *Mos.* 1.156).

[51] In the Fourth Gospel there is no substantial difference in meaning between φιλέω and ἀγαπάω (cf. Segovia, *Relationships*, 134). Love is mystical in that it needs to be revealed and demonstrated (3.16; 14.15; 15.13; 1 Jn 3.16; 4.9; 5.3). Love is one of the main characteristics/attributes of the intimate relationship between the believer and the Father and Son, and any demonstration of love — obedience, witness, service, laying down one's life — confirms at the same time that love-relationship. For the soteriological aspect of love, see the theme 'the love of the Father and Son' in ch. 3. NB if people (are prepared to) lose their ψυχή, they will keep/gain ζωή (12.25).

[52] Culpepper (*Anatomy*, 121-22) and Stibbe (*John*, 149) notice the parallel between the Beloved Disciple ἐν τῷ κόλπῳ τοῦ Ἰησοῦ (13.23) and Jesus εἰς τὸν κόλπον τοῦ πατρός (1.18).

friends are the children of God (cf. 1.12).[53] Jesus also 'tests' his disciples (e.g., in 4.31-38 Jesus challenges his disciples to already partake in the 'harvesting', and 6.60-71 reveals the sifting of disciples) and warns them of the hardship that is to come (15.18-16.4a).

There is a strong link, if not an identification, between the concepts of friendship and discipleship: (i) John the Baptist is both a witness to Jesus and his friend, and the disciples are also called Jesus' friends; (ii) love, epitomized by 'the laying down of one's ψυχή for one's friends', is the characteristic of both discipleship and friendship; (iii) obedience, knowledge and intimacy are characteristics of both friendship and discipleship. Hence, as with discipleship, a (continuous) demonstration of friendship maintains one's saving relationship with Jesus. In fact, the intimate relationship of love, life, knowledge and glory between Jesus and the disciples/believer *is* one of friendship.

This leads to an important question. How is the Spirit-Paraclete involved in friendship? First, those in a life-giving relationship with Jesus are his friends, and such a saving relationship is created and maintained by the Spirit-Paraclete, as we have just seen. Moreover, if the Paraclete represents Jesus when Jesus is absent and mediates Jesus' presence to the believer, then the Paraclete, as the mode of communication, will also be expected to mediate Jesus' friendship. Hence, the Paraclete is the *bond of friendship* between Jesus and the believer.

In conclusion, the concepts John wishes to convey with his use of oneness- and mutual indwelling-language are essentially relational, and use metaphors that denote close relationship/fellowship/communion/unity. This intimate saving relationship between the believer and the Father and Son is realized (and naturally sustained) by means of the Spirit-Paraclete as the bond of union. Moreover, the concept of friendship also has soteriological overtones, and the Paraclete functions as the bond of friendship between Jesus and the believer.

3.2. The Paraclete as 'Spirit of T/truth'

In order to understand what the 'Spirit of truth' means, we first need to understand the concept of 'truth'. In chapter 3, we proposed that 'truth' in the Fourth Gospel is primarily a soteriological concept. We also mentioned that Jesus is the embodiment (14.6) and the dispenser of truth (8.31-32, 40; cf. 17.6-8, 17), so that the depiction of Jesus as the Truth, who offers life-giving truth, is similar to the concept of Jesus as Wisdom who confers

---

[53] Cf. Käsemann, *Testament*, 31; Ringe, *Friends*, 67.

saving wisdom.[54] Hence, we defined 'saving truth' either as the saving content of Jesus' word/teaching, which needs cognitively to be perceived, or as the saving understanding of the Father and Son resulting from this cognitive perception.[55] Thus, 'saving knowledge', 'saving wisdom' and 'saving truth' essentially denote the same concept.[56] We had also observed that from this it follows that truth needs cognitively to be perceived in relationship with the Truth.[57] The subsequent question (which Johannine scholarship has not always raised) is how this truth is mediated and cognitively perceived, and we suggest that the answer lies in the concept of 'the Paraclete as Spirit of T/truth'.

Two functions are explicitly attributed to the Spirit of T/truth: witness and guidance. In relation to the world, the Spirit of T/truth will witness (μαρτυρέω) about or on behalf of the Truth to the world (15.26). In relation to the disciples, the Spirit of T/truth will guide (ὁδηγέω) them into all T/truth (16.13). In sections 3.4 and 3.5, below, we will elucidate these two functions and see that they correlate with one another: the Paraclete as Spirit of T/truth will witness to the world through the witness of the disciples by means of 'guiding' them into the T/truth. That is, *as the 'Spirit of T/truth' the Paraclete mediates or communicates saving truth to people:*

---

[54] Truth and life are closely associated in 14.6, which can be paraphrased as: 'the way of truth that leads to life.' Alternatively, it may mean '[b]ecause Jesus is the life and the truth, he is the Way' (Scott, *Sophia*, 126).

[55] I. de la Potterie argues that, for John, truth is the revelation and its content, which comes from God in the person and teaching of Jesus, and that John's theme of truth is derived from the apocalyptic and wisdom traditions, where 'truth' denotes the revealed truth, i.e., the teaching of wisdom and the meaning of apocalyptic visions ('L'arrière-fond du thème johannique de vérité' in K. Aland et al. [eds.], *Studia Evangelica: Vol. I* [Berlin: Akademie-Verlag, 1959] 277-94; 'Truth', 54-57). Elsewhere, de la Potterie defines 'truth' in John as 'le *principe intérieur de la vie morale*' (*Vérité*, 632 [author's emphasis]). Others also confirm 'truth' as a soteriological concept (S. Aalen, '"Truth", a Key Word in St. John's Gospel' in F.L. Cross [ed.], *Studia Evangelica Vol. II* [Berlin: Akademie-Verlag, 1964] 20-23; Schnackenburg, *Gospel*, 2:228, 237; Tolmie, *Farewell*, 91 n.51). Both Aalen ('Truth', 24) and Schnackenburg (*Gospel*, 2:235), however, criticize de la Potterie's theory of the background to the concept of truth because John never describes truth as a 'mystery', neither does he combine directly truth with the idea of 'revelation' or 'knowledge', nor do hidden decrees occur about salvation and future events. However, there are some difficulties with their criticism. First, truth is related to revelation by virtue of being the content of Jesus' revelation. Second, the saving truth/wisdom in Jesus' revelatory teaching is 'hidden' and needs to be revealed to people (cf. chs. 3-4). Third, the need for truth to be revealed may also be implied by ὑπομιμνῄσκω (14.26), ἀναγγέλλω (16.12-15), ὁδηγεω (16.13) and παροιμίαις (16.25), all of which have revelatory connotations (cf. section 3.3, below).

[56] In Judaism, 'truth' and 'wisdom' are sometimes used synonymously (Ps. 51.6; Prov. 23.23), and Wisdom's word/teaching contains truth (Prov. 8.6-9; cf. Wis. 6.22).

[57] Cf. Bultmann, *Gospel*, 606-607.

to the disciples/believers directly and to the world indirectly (through the disciples/believers). 'Spirit of truth' then functions as an objective genitive or genitive of quality, describing the characteristic function of the Spirit — to mediate saving truth.[58]

Thus, people will cognitively perceive the T/truth through the mediation of saving truth by the Spirit of T/truth. Based on this cognitive information and understanding, people can then make an initial belief-response and enter into a saving relationship with the Truth. Moreover, the mediation of saving truth also maintains/sustains one's relationship with the Truth, in that this cognitive perception (i) increases the believer's knowledge and understanding of the Father and Son, which is salvific (17.3), and (ii) informs the disciples' witness to the world, which is essentially a demonstration of discipleship (cf. ch. 3 for the need of a continuous belief-response).

In sum, 'Spirit of truth' is, as it were, a *soteriological title/label* for the Paraclete.[59] This observation corresponds with our analysis of John 1-12, where the Spirit mediates to people the saving wisdom present in Jesus' revelatory life-giving teaching, and so we would naturally expect the Spirit-Paraclete to continue this function by mediating saving truth. The title 'Spirit of T/truth' also reflects the intimate relationship between the Paraclete and Jesus, who is the Truth (14.6; cf. 1.14, 17). 'Truth' then is the saving content or understanding of the revelation from and about God in Jesus, illuminated and mediated by the Paraclete functioning as the Spirit of T/truth.[60]

If the Spirit-Paraclete as 'Spirit of T/truth' then essentially continues the same function of revealing and mediating saving truth/wisdom to people as is ascribed to the Spirit in John 1-12, then it comes as no surprise that Jesus tells his disciples that they already know this Spirit-Paraclete

---

[58] Cf. Chevallier, *Souffle*, 2:473. Ibuki emphasizes that 'truth' in 'Spirit of truth' primarily denotes the nature (*das Wesen*) of the Spirit (*Wahrheit*, 306-10).

[59] As we said in n.25, above, we believe that John and Qumran developed their concept of 'Spirit of truth' independently of each other. Nevertheless, there is a strong conceptual parallel: both the Fourth Gospel and the Qumran literature depict the concept of increase in cognitive perception and understanding, which corresponds to an increase in the intensity of truth mediated by the Spirit of truth (cf. ch. 2 section 7).

[60] Cf. de la Potterie, 'Truth', 63. Johnston argues that the paraclete is secondary or adjectival to the spirit of truth because 'paraclete' merely denotes a particular kind of functionary (*Spirit-Paraclete*, 84, 120). However, both 'Paraclete' and 'Spirit of T/truth' are functional labels for the Spirit, denoting certain characteristics of his functions, especially the soteriological ones. Moreover, the scope of 'Spirit of T/truth' is narrower than that of 'Paraclete', i.e., one of the functions of the Spirit-Paraclete is to act as 'Spirit of T/truth'.

(14.17).[61] The world cannot receive the Paraclete as Spirit of T/truth because it does not 'see' or know him, i.e., it cannot cognitively perceive the Paraclete (and his work), but the disciples already know the Paraclete as Spirit of T/truth because of their experience of the Spirit through Jesus' revelatory teaching. Hence the disciples' future reception of the Paraclete already has a kind of realized dimension: ὁ παράκλητος is already (partly) known by the disciples as the Spirit of T/truth and is already alongside (παρά) them, although in the future they will experience a more intimate relationship with the Paraclete (denoted by ἐν).

3.3. The Paraclete as Teacher/Revealer

The Paraclete's teaching function is elucidated in John 14.26 and 16.12-15.

John 14.26. In this passage, the Paraclete teaches (διδάξει) and 'reminds' (ὑπομνήσει) the disciples of 'all things' (that Jesus had spoken to them). Διδάσκω means 'to teach', but is in John practically a verb of revelation.[62] The revelation Jesus brought was the revelation from and about God, and Jesus only spoke what the Father ἐδίδαξέν him (8.28; cf. 7.16), i.e., Jesus revealed the Father in his teaching. The Spirit-Paraclete, who will take over Jesus' 'Paraclete' functions, will naturally also take over the revelatory teaching function from Jesus (cf. 16.12-15; 1 Jn 2.27). This implies that the Paraclete will not bring any new revelation independent of Jesus' revelation. Also on textual grounds it becomes clear that the Paraclete will (continue to) reveal Jesus' teaching: the word πάντα occurs twice in 14.26b, once with διδάσκω and once with ὑπομιμνήσκω, and is on both occasions qualified or limited by the phrase ἃ εἶπον ὑμῖν (ἐγώ), i.e., as Jesus' own teaching/revelation. Jesus taught many things but (δέ) the Paraclete then further reveals Jesus' teaching. The Paraclete interprets Jesus' revelation; he explains and draws out the significance of the historical revelation.[63]

Ὑπομιμνήσκω in the active form literally means 'to remind (someone of something)', 'to recall (something)', and in 14.26 this 'something' refers to Jesus' revelatory teaching. However, anamnesis is not just to recall or to be reminded of Jesus' teaching, but more precisely, to *understand* Jesus' words, i.e., the aim of the Paraclete's anamnesis is to provide a deeper or new understanding of Jesus' revelation.[64] That is, the Paraclete's

---

[61] Cf. Porsch, *Pneuma*, 246-47, 251-53; Turner, *Spirit*, 80. However, the textual tradition also allows a future tense for the last two verbs in 14.17. Beasley-Murray, consequently, takes γινώσκετε as a present with future meaning (*John*, 242-43).

[62] De la Potterie, 'Paraclete', 126; cf. K.H. Rengstorf, 'Διδάσκω, κτλ.' in *TDNT*, II:143-44; Porsch, *Pneuma*, 258-59.

[63] Turner, *Spirit*, 82-83; cf. Bultmann, *Gospel*, 626; Dunn, *Jesus*, 352-53.

[64] De la Potterie, 'Paraclete', 127; cf. Porsch, *Pneuma*, 262-65. Anamnesis was the key to the learning process in Jewish education (Keener, 'Function', 287).

anamnesis brings the disciples to further cognitive perception (of the Father and Son), and based on this deeper understanding, they can then make a further belief-response. In Wisdom of Solomon, anamnesis also has a soteriological dimension (Wis. 12.2; 16.11).[65] The goal of the Paraclete's anamnesis, namely, a deeper cognitive perception and understanding of Jesus' revelatory teaching, and hence of the Father and Son, corresponds with the concept in John 1-12 of the Spirit giving people a new understanding of God by revealing the significance of Jesus' revelatory wisdom teaching. The Paraclete will *open up* and give insight into the (up to that moment) hidden meaning of Jesus' revelation.[66] John actually records three explicit examples of anamnesis (2.17, 22; 12.16 [cf. 15.20; 16.4]), of which 2.22 and 12.16 mention that the recalling happens respectively after Jesus' resurrection and after Jesus' glorification, which makes it more likely to ascribe these examples of anamnesis to the Paraclete. Moreover, 2.22 mentions that anamnesis, and the resulting cognitively perceived information, had led to belief.

How are διδάσκω and ὑπομιμνήσκω related in 14.26? We suggest that διδάσκω and ὑπομιμνήσκω are not two different functions but, taking καί epexegetically, aspects of the same function; they are complementary and reinforce each other.[67] According to Porsch, διδάσκω primarily refers to an active, internal teaching, emphasizing the internalization of Jesus' words, whereas ὑπομιμνήσκω emphasizes more the aspect of a new understanding which is obtained through the anamnesis activity of the Paraclete.[68] Hence, ὑπομιμνήσκω refers to the Paraclete's function of reminding the disciples of, or enabling them to recall, Jesus' words in order to perceive their significance. Thus, the Paraclete teaches the disciples to grasp the revelation of God brought by Jesus; ὑπομιμνήσκω is the method or means by which the Paraclete διδάσκει.[69]

John 16.12-15. In 16.12 it becomes clear that the disciples had not fully grasped the significance of Jesus' teaching, nor were they capable of doing so; it was to be the Paraclete's task to explain and reveal these things, and hence to increase the disciples' relational understanding of Jesus' words (16.13-15). The rationale for the necessity of the Paraclete's revelatory teaching function is twofold. The first reason is the unbelief of the world; the world does not believe Jesus and his testimony (e.g. 3.12, 19; 5.47;

---

[65] Cf. Forestell, 'Jesus', 164.

[66] Porsch, *Pneuma*, 265.

[67] Bultmann, *Gospel*, 626 n.6; Porsch, *Pneuma*, 265; Newman/Nida, *Handbook*, 474; Beasley-Murray, *John*, 261. Cf. Schnackenburg, *Gospel*, 3:83.

[68] Porsch, *Pneuma*, 265; cf. de la Potterie, 'Paraclete', 126-27.

[69] Newman/Nida, *Handbook*, 474; Chevallier, *Souffle*, 2:483; Beasley-Murray, *John*, 261. Cf. Porsch who says: 'das Lehren des Geist-P vollzieht sich im Erinnern' (*Pneuma*, 265).

6.36; 8.24, 45-46; 10.25-26). We shall show in the next section that as Teacher/Revealer the Paraclete will also be Advocate, and in this capacity he will convince the world of its guilt with regard to unbelief (16.8-9). The second reason is people's regular misunderstanding of Jesus (e.g., Nicodemus, the Samaritan woman, the Jews [6.42, 52; 7.35-36; 8.22], even Jesus' own disciples [4.31-38; 6.60-66; 14.5-9, 22; 16.17-18]). It will be the Paraclete's task to interpret Jesus' words and actions and to facilitate cognitive perception.

The reason for people's dullness may be the fact that Jesus spoke in 'riddles' (παροιμίαι) (16.25; cf. 10.6). Παροιμία denotes, in Johannine usage, a dark saying or figure of speech, in which especially lofty ideas are concealed,[70] or "hidden, obscure speech' which stands in need of interpretation.'[71] This corresponds with our observation that saving wisdom/truth is hidden or locked up in Jesus' revelatory teaching/words, and it will then be the task of the Paraclete to unlock, reveal and mediate this saving wisdom/truth to people.[72] Thus, there seem to be two modes of mediation of revelation: (i) Jesus brings God's revelation, though veiled, in the form of παροιμίαι; (ii) the Paraclete will, as Teacher/Revealer, uncover the meaning and significance of Jesus' revelatory teaching, i.e., the Paraclete will open up Jesus' teaching and mediate its saving truth/wisdom to people.[73] Consequently, when Jesus says that he will no longer speak to the disciples ἐν παροιμίαις but will proclaim to them plainly/publicly (παρρησίᾳ)[74] of the Father (16.25b), he probably refers to the Paraclete's revelatory teaching function as described in 16.12-15. Jesus will provide clear understanding through the revelatory teaching function of the Spirit-Paraclete.

---

[70] W. Bauer, *A Greek-English Lexicon of the New Testament and Other Early Christian Literature* (translated and edited by W.F. Arndt, F.W. Gingrich and F.W. Danker; Chicago: University of Chicago Press, 1979²) 629. The παροιμίαις in which the Johannine Jesus speaks correspond with the παραβολή in the Synoptics.

[71] F. Hauck, 'Παροιμία' in *TDNT*, V:856. Cf. van der Watt, *Family*, 158-60.

[72] Cf. the sage in Sirach, who devotes himself to careful examination of the secrets or hidden meaning of παροιμίαις (39.3), but who can only cognitively penetrate them if he receives the Spirit of understanding, i.e., if the Spirit unfolds for the sage the meaning of the παροιμίαις (39.6).

[73] Cf. Porsch, *Pneuma*, 291-92; de la Potterie, 'Paraclete', 125; *idem*, 'Truth', 62; Witherington, *Wisdom*, 265-66; Tolmie, *Farewell*, 263-64. These two stages of revelation might also be indicated by δέ in 14.26 and 16.13, showing a slight contrast between Jesus' teaching and that of the Paraclete. The contrast probably does not refer to the content of revelation, but to the way revelation is mediated, i.e., whereas Jesus' revelatory teaching was partly veiled, the Paraclete will disclose its meaning.

[74] Παρρησία is a reference to an enlightenment about the whole revelation in Jesus (Tolmie, *Farewell*, 88 n.47).

Ὁδηγέω (16.13) means 'to guide (someone on a way)', and is frequently used in the LXX in a religious/ethical sense through its connection with 'truth' (Pss. 24.5; 42.3; 85.11; cf. 142.10).[75] In Wisdom of Solomon, besides God being called the guide of W/wisdom (7.15) and of his people in the wilderness (18.3), Wisdom herself also functions as a guide in the wilderness (10.10, 17). In the light of Wisdom's salvific role in Israel's history (10.1-11.1), Wisdom's guidance probably has a soteriological dimension. Moreover, Wisdom will give Solomon ethical guidance and teach him what is pleasing to God (7.21-22; 8.7; 9.10-11), so that people can be saved through the ruler endowed with (the Spirit of) Wisdom (9.17-18). Wisdom can function as an ethical guide (with soteriological consequences) because she knows and understands all things, and understands God and his will (8.4, 8; 9.9, 11). In Philo, the divine Spirit is said to guide into the way of truth (*Mos.* 2.265; cf. *Gig.* 54-55).

In John 16.13, the phrase ὁδηγεῖν ἐν[76] τῇ ἀληθείᾳ also has a soteriological dimension; it is a metaphor for leading people to or keeping people in salvation through the mediation of saving truth (which is found in Jesus' revelatory wisdom teaching) by the Paraclete.[77] Thus, the Paraclete, in his capacity as 'Spirit of truth', guides people (further) in(to) this saving truth, and hence the Paraclete is soteriologically necessary. The revelatory teaching function of the Paraclete, then, is a further instruction or guidance/insight into the fullness of truth as revealed in the person and teaching of Jesus; 16.13 is concerned with a more profound penetration in(to) the content of Jesus' revelation.[78]

Concerning the meaning of πάσῃ, this does not denote new truth, a quantitative 'more' of revelation, but a 'more' of understanding and insight into Jesus' revelation, so that the Paraclete will lead the disciples into a more perfect knowledge of Jesus' teaching.[79] The Paraclete does not bring independent revelation but interprets Jesus' revelation; he draws out the significance of the historical revelation in Christ.[80] Hence, the Paraclete *continues* the revelatory life-giving work of Jesus.

---

[75] Cf. Forestell, 'Jesus', 171-72.

[76] Whether we read ἐν (so Carson, *Gospel*, 539) or εἰς (so Porsch, *Pneuma*, 293-94, 303), the main meaning is to denote a deeper penetration of the truth.

[77] Although Tolmie does not go this far, he points in the right direction when he argues that ὁδηγεῖν ἐν τῇ ἀληθείᾳ involves not only a deeper intellectual understanding of 'truth' (salvation), but also a way of life in conformity with 'truth' (*Farewell*, 86-87 n.45).

[78] Forestell, 'Jesus', 171; Porsch, *Pneuma*, 293-94; Schnackenburg, *Gospel*, 3:135.

[79] Porsch, *Pneuma*, 292, 303.

[80] Bultmann, *Gospel*, 574-76; Porsch, *Pneuma*, 294-95; Barrett, *Gospel*, 467; Burge, *Community*, 213-16; Turner, *Spirit*, 82-83; cf. Beasley-Murray, *John*, 283. Contra J. Painter, who thinks the Paraclete is to bring new truth that Jesus was not able to

'Αναγγέλλω, which occurs three times in 16.13-15, means 'to proclaim/announce', and virtually connotes 'to reveal/disclose'.[81] The Paraclete does not bring new, independent revelation but speaks what he hears (from Jesus) (16.13), and takes/receives from Jesus' revelation (16.14-15). Hence, ἀναγγέλλω probably denotes the interpretation or explanation of a previous revelation that has heretofore been hidden and mysterious.[82] John's use of ἀναγγέλλω may betray the influence of apocalyptic tradition (Ezek. 24.19, 26; 37.18; Dan. 2.2, 4, 6; Dan. 2.24, 27; 5.12 [Th]). Moreover, the usage of ἀναγγέλλω draws attention to the parallel task between the Paraclete and the *angelus interpres* in the apocalyptic wisdom tradition (e.g. Dan. 9.23; 10.21; 11.2 [Th]); both interpret previous revelation through the mediation of revelatory wisdom in order to reveal the meaning/significance of the revelation.[83] Porsch observes that, as in apocalyptic literature, the reception of revelation is presented in two stages: (i) the actual reception of revelation mediated by Jesus; (ii) the interpretation of this revelation by the Paraclete.[84] Again, we are not dealing with tandem figures in a succession of revelation (contra Bornkamm), but with one single revelation of the Father in Jesus, illuminated by the Paraclete to the believer.[85]

Synthesis. The revelatory teaching function of the Paraclete seems to be an internal one: the Paraclete will enable the disciples to recall Jesus' revelatory teaching and to cognitively perceive and understand it more fully (14.26); the Paraclete will provide a new and deeper understanding of the meaning and implications of Jesus' revelation (16.12-15).[86] The

---

communicate to the disciples during his earthly ministry ('The Farewell Discourses and the History of Johannine Christianity', *NTS* 27 [1981] 540; *Quest*, 431-32).

[81] Cf. Brown, *Gospel*, 2:708; Carson, *Gospel*, 540.

[82] Cf. de la Potterie, 'Truth', 62; *idem*, 'Paraclete', 130; Suurmond, *Influence*, 249.

[83] Cf. Boring, 'Influence', 115; Ashton, *Understanding*, 423-24. However, the Paraclete is not modelled on the *angelus interpres* (see n.25, above).

[84] Porsch, *Pneuma*, 296. Cf. the two modes of mediation of revelation we mentioned above.

[85] Forestell, 'Jesus', 173. Some scholars argue that the phrase τὰ ἐρχόμενα ἀναγγελεῖ ὑμῖν in 16.13 refers to a prophetic activity/office of the Paraclete (Betz, *Paraklet*, 191-92; Windisch, 'Paraclete', 12; Johnston, *Spirit-Paraclete*, 137; Montague, *Spirit*, 361). However, the phrase probably does not refer to apocalyptic prophecy, an exact foreknowledge of the future or to new revelation, but to a deeper understanding of Jesus' revelation for one's own time (Brown, *Gospel*, 2:715-16). The Paraclete reinterprets and applies the original revelation of the historical Jesus in any new context to give it contemporary significance. Nevertheless, this recontextualization of Jesus' historical revelation may have a 'prophetic' dimension. Moreover, if the Paraclete is the mode of communication between the exalted Jesus and the believer, then we cannot completely exclude the possibility that the Paraclete also has a prophetic function.

[86] Cf. Forestell, 'Jesus', 172; de la Potterie, 'Paraclete', 127; *idem*, *Vérité*, 437-38.

Paraclete's task as Teacher is to reveal the meaning and intent of Jesus' words, and the aim of the Paraclete's revelatory teaching function is a deeper internalization/interiorization of Jesus' revelation.[87] What the Paraclete does, then, is neatly summed up by Porsch: 'Jesus bringt die Wahrheit, macht sie durch sein Kommen in der Welt präsent, – der Geist-P *eröffnet* diese Wahrheit, schafft für die Glaubenden den Zu-gang zu ihr.'[88] However, Porsch (and Johannine scholarship in general) does not explain the soteriological significance of this opening up. The reason why the Paraclete opens up Jesus' words is that they contain saving wisdom/truth.

Thus, the Paraclete will guide people (further) in(to) all truth exactly by opening up Jesus' revelatory teaching, disclosing its saving truth/wisdom and mediating it to people, so that they may enter or remain in a saving relationship with the Father and Son.[89] Consequently, if the Paraclete recalls Jesus' words, which are life-giving (6.63), and opens them up to disclose their saving truth/wisdom, i.e., if the Paraclete reveals the saving truth/wisdom which is wrapped up in Jesus' revelatory words, and if the Paraclete reveals in this way the full meaning of Jesus' words, then the Spirit-Paraclete as Teacher/Revealer is soteriologically necessary.[90] Thus, as a revelatory Teacher, the Paraclete has soteriological consequences, in that the Paraclete brings people to a higher level of cognitive perception of Jesus' teaching, and hence to a deeper understanding of the Father and Son, on which basis an initial or continuous belief-response can be made.[91] The concept of the Paraclete as Teacher/Revealer corresponds to the concept of the Spirit as the power of Wisdom: as Teacher/Revealer the

---

[87] Cf. Holwerda, *Spirit*, 60; Schnackenburg, *Gospel*, 3:83; Burge, *Community*, 213-14; Carson, *Gospel*, 505; Turner, *Spirit*, 82. Suurmond observes that this is a fulfilment of the eschatological promise in Ezek. 36.27, which says that the indwelling Spirit will enable people to keep God's commandments (cf. Jer. 31.33-34) (*Influence*, 245-46, 253).

[88] Porsch, *Pneuma*, 300 (my emphasis). Cf. Schnelle, 'Johannes', 22; Schnackenburg, *Gospel*, 2:237.

[89] Turner rightly observes that the Paraclete is none other than the Spirit providing charismatic revelation and wisdom, which brings true comprehension of the significance of the historical revelation in Christ, and hence the Paraclete's illumination is soteriologically necessary (*Spirit*, 83, 88).

[90] Contra Forestell, who diminishes the Paraclete's soteriological dimension by arguing that there is no evidence in the Paraclete-sayings as such that he is the agent of that communion of knowledge and love between Father, Son and disciples, known as eternal life. The Paraclete's function is merely to guarantee, maintain and foster this communion among the disciples on earth as Jesus enjoys it in heaven ('Jesus', 175, 196-97). However, we have argued that the Paraclete, as the only way to know the Father and Son, precisely does communicate knowledge/truth in order to create and sustain communion between the believer, Father and Son; the Paraclete *is* the agent who creates this saving communion.

[91] Cf. Kammler, 'Jesus', 111.

Spirit-Paraclete functions as the disclosing power of Jesus' revelatory wisdom teaching in order to provide knowledge and understanding of the Father and Son.[92]

3.4. The Paraclete as Advocate

The forensic functions of the Paraclete are explicit in 15.26-27 and 16.8-11, and an elucidation of these passages will show why the Spirit is called an 'Advocate'. We will also show how the Paraclete's teaching functions can be combined with his forensic functions. However, our main concern is to elucidate to what extent the Paraclete as Advocate has a soteriological dimension.

To begin with, the Fourth Gospel presents a lawsuit between God/Jesus and the world, and the issue under debate is the Messiahship and divine Sonship of Jesus.[93] More precisely, the dispute between Jesus and the world/'Jews' is about Jesus' claims to have life in himself, to make this life available to people and to have an intimate relationship with God (cf. the theme 'witnessing to Jesus' in ch. 3 section 3.4).[94] Among the witnesses on behalf of Jesus are the disciples (15.27; cf. 1 Jn 1.2; 4.14) and the Paraclete (15.26; cf. 1 Jn 5.6-7). In the farewell discourse, Jesus prepares his disciples for what lies ahead; the trial with the world cannot cease and the witness cannot fall silent, because then the case would be lost by default.[95]

After Jesus' departure, the cosmic trial continues by means of the Paraclete and the disciples, and Jesus will hand over his 'advocacy' to the Spirit. Through their relationship with Jesus, the disciples have become identified with Jesus and hence also with the trial. The confrontation between Jesus and 'the Jews' is paradigmatic for the trial between the believers (assisted by the Paraclete) and the world.[96] In 14.18, Jesus assures the disciples that he would not leave them as ὀρφανοί, i.e.,

---

[92] For the significance of the Paraclete's function as Teacher/Revealer for the church, see, e.g., Johnston, *Spirit-Paraclete*, 16, 119, 126-28 (although we disagree with Johnston that church leaders are depicted as 'paracletes'); Schnackenburg, *Gospel*, 3:150-54; Turner, *Spirit*, 84-85.

[93] Harvey, *Jesus, passim*; A.A. Trites, *The New Testament Concept of Witness* (SNTS.MS 31; Cambridge: CUP, 1977) 20-22, 35-47, 78-90, 118; A.T. Lincoln, 'Trials, Plots and the Narrative of the Fourth Gospel', *JSNT* 56 (1994) 3-30; *idem, Truth, passim*. See also Porsch, *Pneuma*, 222-27; Ashton, *Understanding*, 220-32, 523-27; Billington, 'Paraclete', 95-102.

[94] Cf. Turner, *Spirit*, 85-86.

[95] Billington, 'Paraclete', 100.

[96] Cf. Porsch, *Pneuma*, 224. Hence, it is not necessary to limit the controversy in the Fourth Gospel to that between the Johannine church and the Jewish synagogue (*pace* Martyn and his many followers); rather, the Fourth Gospel presents a confrontation between the church versus the world at large.

defenceless in the face of the world's oppression, because Jesus would come to them; they would have an Advocate in the judicial process.[97] In sum, if the issue at stake in the cosmic trial is the person and life-giving work of Jesus, if the purpose of Jesus' coming and ministry is primarily salvific, and if the Paraclete as Advocate has to continue and sustain the case, then the Spirit-Paraclete in his role as Advocate will also be expected to have a soteriological dimension. Hence, we now turn to the two passages that mention explicitly the forensic functions of the Paraclete.

John 15.26-27. This passage emphasizes the Paraclete's role as witness in a world that would hate and persecute the disciples (15.18-16.4). Windisch believes that the witness of the Paraclete is independent of that of the disciples.[98] Porsch argues that the Paraclete's witness has to be differentiated from the witness of the disciples, in that the former is 'ein inneres Zeugnis vor dem Gewissen der Glaubenden...und *daher* nicht an die Welt gerichtet.'[99] De la Potterie also emphasizes that the Paraclete's witness is formally distinguished from the disciples' witness; the Paraclete's witness is a completely interior one, directed, not to the world, but to the conscience of the disciples to enlighten and strengthen them in times of adversity/persecution.[100] However, it seems that Windisch, Porsch and de la Potterie bifurcate too much the witness of the Paraclete and that of the disciples. There are probably not two distinct kinds of witness but rather two modes of witness, i.e., there is co-ordination rather than separation (cf. the two modes of revelation).

In this case, the Paraclete bears witness to Jesus in and through (the witness of) the disciples, and although the Paraclete's witness will strengthen the believer, the primary direction of the Paraclete's witness is to the world (cf. 16.8). Nevertheless, the Paraclete cannot aim his witness directly to the world because the world as 'world' does not perceive and know the Paraclete (14.17); hence, the disciples and their witness are a medium for the Paraclete's witness. Therefore, the Paraclete's witness is not exclusively interior; the Paraclete is engaging the world through the mission of the disciples.[101] The disciples' and Paraclete's witness, then, are not two distinct activities but essentially one: the Paraclete's witness is

---

[97] Holwerda, *Spirit*, 43-48; cf. Turner, *Spirit*, 85-86. Ridderbos rejects the idea of the Paraclete acting as Advocate in a cosmic trial before God, because the Paraclete is not depicted as acting before God as prosecutor or public defender in a trial that is still undecided (*Gospel*, 531-32). However, although the courtroom is primarily terrestrial rather than celestial, God can still act as judge, the Paraclete can still carry out his forensic functions, and the case is not settled since it needs to be sustained continuously.

[98] Windisch, 'Paraclete', 9.

[99] Porsch, *Pneuma*, 274-75 (my emphasis).

[100] De la Potterie, 'Truth', 60-61; *idem*, 'Paraclete', 133, 135.

[101] Suurmond, *Influence*, 246; Billington, 'Paraclete', 108-109.

directed to the world but mediated through the witness of the disciples, because (i) the Paraclete is sent to the disciples (15.26), and (ii) the world cannot receive the Paraclete (14.17).[102]

Holwerda argues it is probably not so much that the Paraclete presents his witness to the disciples and that they in turn pass it on to the world, but rather that the witness of the disciples is at the same time the active witnessing of the Paraclete.[103] Although we largely agree with this, it may be somewhat simplistic; the Paraclete's anamnesis and revelatory teaching could also result in (later) witness by the disciples. It seems more correct to say that the witness of the disciples is either the result of the simultaneous parallel witnessing of the Paraclete, and/or the result of an earlier, related (teaching) activity of the Paraclete.

We can take things even further. Negatively, the witness of the Paraclete and the disciples ensure the continuation of the cosmic trial, but there is also a positive side to it. The world as 'world' is not able to perceive and know the Paraclete (14.17), and the world persecutes Jesus and (consequently) the disciples because it does not know God (15.21). Hence the problem of the world is partly one of cognition; the world has not cognitively perceived and understood the Father and Son, and their work. Part of the solution lies in the combined witness of the Paraclete and the disciples, namely, that through their witness some people of the world will come to believe (cf. 17.20). Thus, the disciples' Paraclete-imbued witness, i.e., the correlated witness of the Paraclete and the disciples, directed to the world, has essentially a soteriological direction — to increase the world's cognitive perception and understanding of the Father and Son so that people may come to belief. Nevertheless, Jesus foretells that the world as 'world' will reject the Paraclete-imbued life-giving witness of the disciples because of its lack of cognition (16.2-3; cf. the rejection of Jesus' Spirit-imbued life-giving teaching).

John 16.8-11. The forensic functions of the Paraclete are most explicit in 16.8-11, which is exegetically a difficult passage. We will see that the forensic functions of the Paraclete are extended from defending/witnessing to accusing/prosecuting, which corresponds to the functions of παράκλητος in late Judaism. The first issue is the precise nuance of ἐλέγχω (περί). The basic meaning of ἐλέγχω is 'to expose', and when the object being exposed

---

[102] Holwerda, *Spirit*, 52. Cf. Hoskyns, *Gospel*, 2:568-69; Brown, *Gospel*, 2:690; Schnackenburg, *Gospel*, 3:117-18; Burge, *Community*, 204; Morris, *Gospel*, 607. Bultmann sees the Paraclete as the power of the community's proclamation of the word; the Paraclete's μαρτυρεῖν (15.26) and ἐλέγχειν (16.8-11) is accomplished in the community's preaching (*Gospel*, 553-54).

[103] Holwerda, *Spirit*, 52. Cf. Segovia, *Farewell*, 201 n.51; contra Chevallier, *Souffle*, 2:489.

is evil it means 'to convince' or 'to convict'.[104] 'To expose' seems to convey too little in this forensic context because the world is opposed to Jesus and hence in the wrong;[105] but 'to convict' in the sense of condemning the world communicates too much, because the Paraclete is nowhere depicted as judge.[106] The aim in a lawsuit is to establish the guilt of the party which is the object of ἐλέγχω, and to elicit a surrender from one's legal adversary.[107] Therefore, it seems best to translate ἐλέγχω by 'to expose (the guilt of)' or 'to convince (of guilt)', and it comes very close to 'convict' (cf. 3.20; 8.46).[108]

Having established that the most secure meaning for ἐλέγχω in this context is 'to expose the guilt of' or 'to convince of guilt', we now have to decide whether this activity refers: (i) to an objective presentation of arguments against the world, either (a) before the world through the disciples, or (b) before the conscience of the disciples; or (ii) to a subjective persuasion within the mind of the accused.[109] Choosing the first interpretation, Porsch and de la Potterie argue again that this activity of the Paraclete is not directed to the world but is an exclusively interior activity directed to (the consciences of) the disciples.[110] However, there are difficulties with the position of de la Potterie, Porsch et al. First, although the Paraclete will be sent to the disciples (16.7), he will convince the *world* of its guilt (16.8). It can hardly be the point that the disciples have to be reassured that the world is wrong; rather, the opposing world needs to be convinced of its guilt and needs to be brought to silence.[111] Second, Jesus' ministry was directed to the world, and if the Paraclete continues Jesus' ministry, the Paraclete's activity will naturally also be directed to the world. Thus, the forensic function of the Paraclete that is depicted in 16.8 is that of prosecuting the world (through the disciples). To choose exclusively the second interpretation seems not tenable either, because the

---

[104] Holwerda, *Spirit*, 53; cf. Forestell, 'Jesus', 168-69.

[105] Contra Painter, *Quest*, 429.

[106] Harvey takes a *via media* and opts for 'to accuse' (*Jesus*, 113).

[107] Mowinckel, 'Vorstellungen', 104-106; Trites, *Testament*, 118.

[108] Cf. Holwerda, *Spirit*, 53-54; Brown, *Gospel*, 2:705; Trites, *Testament*, 118; D.A. Carson, 'The Function of the Paraclete in John 16:7-11', *JBL* 98 (1979) 558; Beasley-Murray, *John*, 280-81; Billington, 'Paraclete', 104; Turner, *Spirit*, 86-87. Since ἐλέγχω is employed differently in 3.20 ('to expose') from its use in 8.46 ('to convict'), we cannot derive too much from these verses for the meaning of ἐλέγχω in 16.8.

[109] The analysis of this problem is helpfully outlined by de la Potterie, 'Paraclete', 136. Cf. Porsch, *Pneuma*, 280-82.

[110] Porsch, *Pneuma*, 285 (cf. 279-85); de la Potterie, 'Paraclete', 136-37; *idem*, *Vérité*, 405-406. Cf. Bultmann, *Gospel*, 561-62; Brown, *Gospel*, 2:712; Kammler, 'Jesus', 129-30; Hoegen-Rohls, *Johannes*, 187-88 (although she admits that, in a sense, the Paraclete's ἐλέγχειν is also directed to the world); Frey, *Eschatologie III*, 183-84.

[111] Turner, *Spirit*, 86 n.31.

Paraclete would be sent to the disciples (16.7); further, a direct relationship between the Paraclete and the world is not possible (14.17).

We suggest, then, a synthesis between interpretation (i.a) and (ii). To arrive at this synthesis we need to answer an important related question, namely, whether the *aim* of the Paraclete's ἐλέγχειν is the condemnation or conversion of the world. Johannine scholarship has not sufficiently explored this aspect, but we argue that a few things speak for the latter option. First, if the Paraclete takes over Jesus' 'Paraclete' functions, and if the Paraclete continues Jesus' ministry, then we may ask ourselves whether the aim of Jesus' ministry was condemnation or conversion. Jesus confronted people with his revelatory wisdom teaching, and salvation or judgment is the consequence of one's response to Jesus. Jesus came to bring salvation (cf. 3.17), and judgment was the (indirect) consequence of rejecting Jesus and the life that he offered. Jesus did not come to judge but to expose the sinful reality of the world and to redeem the world. Consequently, we would expect that the Paraclete's ἐλέγχειν also has a soteriological dimension, and that judgment would be the consequence of rejecting the Paraclete's ἐλέγχειν. Second, ἐλέγχω is also used in a moral and pedagogical sense, meaning to show someone his sin and to summon him to repentance, i.e., by exposing someone's guilt and sin, one is led to conversion.[112] Third, if the problem of the world is partly a lack of cognition (14.17; 15.21; 16.3) and consequently a lack of believing, since believing is based on cognitive perception and understanding (16.9), then we would expect the Paraclete's ἐλέγχειν to provide cognitive information, which might then enable a person to produce an adequate belief-response.

Thus, it seems that the context is more than forensic; *the Paraclete's ἐλέγχειν also has a soteriological dimension.* The Paraclete convinces the world of its guilt through the witness of the disciples but does not condemn the world; the Paraclete shows and convinces the world as 'world', so that some may repent and be saved. This soteriological aspect of the Paraclete's ἐλέγχειν does not contradict what is said in 14.17; the world as 'world' cannot accept the Paraclete and his ἐλέγχειν because it loves darkness (3.19; cf. 1.10-11), but a convinced person can. How else could people as part of the 'world' come to see themselves as they are, namely, in opposition to Jesus, and come to repentance and belief, if not being convinced by the Paraclete (through the disciples)? In conclusion, the aim of the Paraclete's ἐλέγχειν is twofold: (i) the Paraclete convinces the world as 'world', i.e., the sinful reality of the world, through (the witness of) the disciples (the objective proof of the world's guilt); (ii) those in the world

---

[112] F. Büchsel, 'Ἐλέγχω, κτλ.' in *TDNT*, II:474-75; Schnackenburg, *Gospel*, 3:128. Nevertheless, Schnackenburg rejects this interpretation for 16.8 because John uses ἐλέγχω forensically in order to condemn and punish the world.

who are convinced and repent will believe and be saved (the soteriological dimension).[113]

In this case, we pose the following four propositions. First, the *object* of the Paraclete's ἐλέγχειν is ὁ κόσμος — this is virtually assured grammatically. Second, the *medium* of the Paraclete's ἐλέγχειν are the disciples — the Paraclete works first in the disciples and prepares their witness, but through their witness the Paraclete will engage the world and convince the world of its guilt. Third, the *aim* of the Paraclete's ἐλέγχειν is soteriological — to convict the world so that some may believe. Fourth, the disciples' minds/consciences are the *locus* primarily of the Paraclete's teaching rather than the Paraclete's ἐλέγχειν (although these two activities are related). The 'court of justice' for/in which the Paraclete principally testifies is probably not the disciples' minds or the Johannine church but the world at large, in that the Paraclete performs his forensic functions (indirectly) before/in the world through the disciples and their witness.[114]

An interesting parallel to the Paraclete's ἐλέγχειν can be found in Wisdom of Solomon 1.7-9. The Spirit knows what is said in the world (Wis. 1.7), and hence, the unrighteous cannot escape judgment (Wis. 1.8). Subsequently, an inquiry will be made (by the Spirit) among the unrighteous and a report of their words will come before God in order to convince (ἐλέγχω) them of their guilt (Wis. 1.9; cf. God's ἐλέγχειν of people in Wis. 12.2, which has a soteriological dimension).[115]

The second issue is the interpretation of ὅτι, and the meaning of 'sin', 'righteousness' and 'judgment' in 16.9-11.[116] The question is whether ὅτι should be taken as explicative ('in that'), explaining or defining the nature of sin, righteousness and judgment, or as causal ('because'), providing the

---

[113] Only a few scholars have recognized the soteriological aspect of the Paraclete's ἐλέγχειν, and then they do not really spell it out (Forestell, 'Jesus', 168-70; Carson, 'Function', 561; Morris, *Gospel*, 619-20; cf. H. Schlier, 'The Holy Spirit as interpreter according to St. John's Gospel', *Communio International Catholic Review* 1 [1974] 137; Tolmie, *Farewell*, 84 n.42). A statement like 'the Paraclete...continues his [Jesus'] ministry of salvation *through* judgment' (Smalley, 'Paraclete', 292 [my emphasis]), seems to miss the point; judgment is the consequence of rejecting the offer of salvation by Jesus (and the Paraclete).

[114] It would not even be unthinkable that occasionally the Spirit convinces non-believers of their guilt without the medium of believers: e.g., through visions/dreams, the reading of the Hebrew Scriptures or the Fourth Gospel, etc.

[115] Bultmann, however, rejects this parallel with Wis. 1.7-9 because he thinks that John is not concerned with the conviction of sinful individuals (*Gospel*, 561).

[116] See Carson's overview and assessment of six major interpretations of 16.8-11 ('Function', 549-58). Carson's own argument for the necessity of symmetry, so that that all three nouns (sin, righteousness, judgment) should refer to the world ('Function', 548, 553, 560; cf. Howard-Brook, *Children*, 345-46), has received several criticisms (Franck, *Revelation*, 58 n.79; Segovia, *Farewell*, 230 n.18; Billington, 'Paraclete', 103).

reason or basis for the world's conviction. Scholars line up equally on each side, which makes the decision difficult.[117] Although the view that takes ὅτι as causal is attractive,[118] it may still be too simplistic; the causal reading of 16.9-11 seems somewhat forced, and an epexegetical reading seems as valid and maybe even more natural. First, taking ὅτι as explicative does not rule out the reasons or grounds for the world's conviction. A causal interpretation of ὅτι answers the question of *why* (for what reason, on what basis) the Paraclete will convince the world of its guilt with respect to sin, righteousness and judgment. An explanatory interpretation of ὅτι answers the question of *how* (in what way) the Paraclete will convince the world of its guilt with respect to sin, righteousness and judgment, and to answer this question presupposes or implies knowledge of the grounds for conviction. In other words, an explicative interpretation of ὅτι includes and assumes the reasons or bases of conviction; by defining the nature of sin, by explaining what sin is, one also indicates implicitly the ground or reason for the world's conviction with respect to sin. The three grounds on which the Paraclete will convince the world of its guilt (sin, righteousness, judgment) are already mentioned in 16.8; in 16.9-11, then, the nature of these three grounds is spelled out.

Second, ὅτι is interpreted as explicative after verbs that denote cognitive perception or the transmission of such perception, or an act of the mind, to indicate the content of what is said (e.g., after διδάσκω, μαρτυρέω, ὑπομιμνήσκω, πιστεύω, κρίνω).[119] It is not difficult to see that ἐλέγχω would fit this concept well: ἐλέγχω denotes cognitive perception (of the Paraclete's conviction) or the transmission of such perception (by the Paraclete's mediation of this conviction), and the three ὅτι-clauses explicate the Paraclete's ἐλέγχειν.

Taking ὅτι as explicative, 16.9-11 then denotes that the very essence of the world's sin is its disbelief in Jesus, that Jesus' death, resurrection and exaltation are the vindication of Jesus' righteousness, and that the nature of

---

[117] Those who hold ὅτι as explicative include: Bultmann, *Gospel*, 562-63; Brown, *Gospel*, 2:706; Harvey, *Jesus*, 113; Schnackenburg, *Gospel*, 3:129; Chevallier, *Souffle*, 518; Beasley-Murray, *John*, 281; Keener, 'Function', 302-303; Ridderbos, *Gospel*, 532; Turner, *Spirit*, 86-87. Those who take ὅτι as causal include: Hoskyns, *Gospel*, 2:572-74; Holwerda, *Spirit*, 56; Windisch, 'Paraclete', 10; Lindars, *Gospel*, 501; Schlier, 'Spirit', 137-38; de la Potterie, 'Paraclete', 138-39; Barrett, *Gospel*, 487-88; Carson, 'Function', 561; Suurmond, *Influence*, 247; Burge, *Community*, 210; Segovia, *Farewell*, 231-32; Morris, *Gospel*, 619; Witherington, *Wisdom*, 264-65; Billington, 'Paraclete', 104-105.

[118] This view is best presented by, e.g., Holwerda, *Spirit*, 56-57; Carson, 'Function', 561-63; Billington, 'Paraclete', 104-107.

[119] Bauer, *Lexicon*, 588. Cf. R.W. Funk, *A Beginning-Intermediate Grammar of Hellenistic Greek* (3 vols.; Missoula: SBL, 1973²) 509-10.

the world's judgment is the judgment of the prince of this world.[120] In conclusion, taking ὅτι as explicative does not contradict but rather also embraces the interpretation given by taking ὅτι as causal.[121]

Synthesis. The conflict between Jesus and the world is portrayed as a cosmic trial; after Jesus' departure the disciples would not be left defenceless as orphans but would receive the Spirit-Paraclete, who in his role as Advocate would continue the case. The Paraclete functions as both witness and advocate; as a prosecutor the Paraclete convinces the opposition concerning the truth, and as a witness the Paraclete brings forward evidence that substantiates the case for Christ.[122] The Paraclete, then, has both a defending and a prosecuting role; he defends Jesus and the disciples, and he prosecutes the unbelieving world.[123] In fact, these are not distinct activities or functions but various aspects of the Paraclete's dual legal function: the Paraclete is both witness and advocate, provides evidence to sustain the case and *thus* convinces the world of its guilt. In other words, as Advocate, the Paraclete defends Jesus and the disciples (and thus the case) *by means of* prosecuting the world and exposing its guilt.

How does the Paraclete fulfil this task? Because the disciples are instruments used by the Paraclete in presenting his witness to the world, they must know the meaning of that to which they are witnessing. Hence, the Paraclete reminds the disciples of and reveals to them the meaning and intent of Jesus' words (14.26; 16.12-15), and thus substantiates the case.[124] The Paraclete will convince the world of its guilt precisely by revealing the truth, and teaching its significance, to and through the disciples, and therefore, as Teacher and Revealer the Spirit-Paraclete will also be Advocate.[125]

We have also seen that a process of judgment had already started during Jesus' earthly ministry for those who rejected Jesus' teaching, and we find the same concept in 16.11. Jesus' witness is continued in the correlated witness of the Paraclete and the disciples, the disciples' teaching is

---

[120] Turner, *Spirit*, 86-87.

[121] Cf. Forestell, 'Jesus', 168.

[122] Trites, *Testament*, 85; Burge, *Community*, 205.

[123] Holwerda, *Spirit*, 48, 59; Harvey, *Jesus*, 110; Billington, 'Paraclete', 108.

[124] Holwerda, *Spirit*, 52, 63-64; Burge, *Community*, 208-10, 221.

[125] Turner, *Spirit*, 87; cf. Turner, 'Concept', 28; Porsch, *Pneuma*, 323-24; Burge, *Community*, 37-38, 210-21; Segovia, *Farewell*, 244. Contra Franck, who argues that although the forensic dimension forms the background, the didactic dimension is dominant, and because the Paraclete is a Teacher there is not much space to be Advocate (*Revelation*, 17-36, 75). The reference to anamnesis in 16.4, sandwiched between the two forensic Paraclete-sayings, may also draw attention to the Paraclete as revelatory Teacher in a forensic context.

identified with Jesus' teaching (15.20; 17.14), and the mission of the Paraclete and the disciples is modelled on Jesus' mission (17.18; 20.21). Hence, those who reject the disciples' Paraclete-imbued witness are essentially rejecting Jesus' witness and therefore judged already.[126] On the other hand, those who accept the conviction of the Paraclete (and the disciples) pass from judgment into eternal life (15.20; 17.20). Thus, to accept or reject the witness/teaching of the Paraclete/disciples will result in salvation or judgment, and is essentially the same as accepting or rejecting Jesus' teaching/words. In sum, the Paraclete's conviction of the world, through the disciples' witness, results in either salvation or judgment, dependent on whether one accepts or rejects this Paraclete-imbued witness. Hence, the Paraclete as Advocate is depicted as a soteriological necessity.

3.5. The Availability of Salvation

The question which has remained unanswered, however, is whether there is any evidence in John 13-17 that salvation was already available within Jesus' earthly ministry, and to that we now turn. Although salvation in the full Johannine sense of the word was not available before Jesus' glorification (see ch. 3 section 4.1), and although it seems that, according to 16.7 and 15.26, the Spirit-Paraclete can only be given after Jesus' departure and exaltation in the Father's presence, there are some indications that 'salvation' in a qualified sense was already available during Jesus' ministry. First, although there are textual uncertainties about μένει and ἔσται, which prevent us from building too much on these words, the phrase ὑμεῖς γινώσκετε αὐτό (14.17) strongly suggests a present reality. The disciples already knew the Paraclete as the Spirit (of T/truth) whom they had already begun to experience through Jesus' revelatory life-giving teaching (see section 3.2, above).

Second, Turner argues that 13.10, taken with 15.3, implies that the disciples are already cleansed by Jesus' word.[127] However, 15.3 is too far removed from 13.10, and both verses have different contexts.[128] Nonetheless, both texts speak of cleansing, namely, through water and through the word; and both are dependent on the cleansing effects of Jesus' death on the cross.[129] The illocution of 13.1-20 (taken as a speech act addressing the readers) is to assert on behalf of the disciples the need for (i) some sort of (spiritual) cleansing (13.1-11) and (ii) a continuous demonstration of discipleship (in this case servanthood) (13.12-20) in order to partake in Jesus, i.e., to participate in a saving relationship with

---

[126] Cf. Holwerda, *Spirit*, 58-59; Ashton, *Understanding*, 223.
[127] Turner, 'Concept', 31.
[128] Thomas, *Footwashing*, 101-102.
[129] Thomas, *Footwashing*, 102.

Jesus.[130] Although the footwashing may point to Jesus' death and signify the disciples' spiritual cleansing,[131] it is not purely symbolical, nor does 13.10 imply that the disciples are being initiated into salvation. Rather, the footwashing would signify the *continuation* of the disciples' belief and fellowship with Jesus.[132] The implication of 15.3 is that the disciples have already experienced the efficacy of Jesus' word, and that word has purified and sanctified them.[133] This is confirmed by 17.8, where Jesus states that the disciples have accepted his revelatory words.

In sum, the disciples were already clean and in a life-giving relationship with Jesus, and in this relationship they had already begun to experience life and the Spirit-Paraclete through Jesus' revelatory words.

3.6. Conclusion

The objective of this section was to elucidate the content of salvation and the role of the Paraclete in salvation. With regard to the content of salvation, we suggested that 'saving truth' is the cleansing life-giving content of Jesus' word/teaching. Moreover, the concept of the Truth (=Jesus) providing saving truth is synonymous with the concept of Wisdom incarnate providing saving wisdom.

With regard to the role of the Paraclete in salvation, we argued, contra Windisch, that the Spirit as Paraclete is soteriologically necessary. First, the intimate saving relationship between the believer and the Father and Son is realized and maintained by means of the Paraclete as the organ of communication and bond of union/friendship between the Father, Son and

---

[130] According to the Louw-Nida lexicon, πόδας νίπτω (13.5-6, 8, 10, 12, 14), which means literally 'to wash the feet' with the purpose of showing hospitality, denotes figuratively 'to perform humble duties on behalf of someone.' NB the devil prompts Judas to defect, i.e., to non-discipleship (13.2, 30), whereas Jesus exhorts the disciples to partake in him, i.e., to discipleship. Moreover, the devil indwelling Judas is contrasted with the Father and Son indwelling the disciples (cf. 13.27 and 14.23) (cf. Culpepper, *Anatomy*, 124).

[131] Other scholars who recognize that the footwashing symbolizes Jesus' salvific death on the cross are: J.D.G. Dunn, 'The Washing of the Disciples' Feet in John 13:1-20', *ZNW* 61 (1970) 249-50 (although Dunn's relating this cleansing to the Spirit and to 19.34 is doubtful); Pryor, *John*, 171; Stibbe, *John*, 150; Witherington, *Wisdom*, 237; Tolmie, *Farewell*, 70-71 n.26; Jones, *Symbol*, 186-97.

[132] Thomas, *Footwashing*, 105. That the disciples' entry into salvation is not in view but the continuation of it is confirmed by Jesus' explicit confirmation καὶ ὑμεῖς καθαροί ἐστε (cf. 15.3).

[133] Schnackenburg, *Gospel*, 3:98; cf. Barrett, *Gospel*, 474. Segovia, interpreting 15.3 as the disciples having already attained *full* understanding and belief (*Farewell*, 139 n.26), probably goes too far; rather, the disciples had reached an *adequate* level of understanding and belief, with scope for still more cognitive development. The ambiguity of καθαίρω in 15.2 (meaning 'to prune' or 'to cleanse') must be noted in combination with καθαρός in 15.3.

a person. Second, as the 'Spirit of T/truth', the Paraclete mediates saving truth to people in order to increase their cognitive perception of the Truth so that they can make an (initial or continuous) adequate belief-response. Third, as Teacher/Revealer, the Paraclete opens up Jesus' life-giving teaching and mediates its saving truth/wisdom to people. Fourth, as Advocate, the Paraclete's witness, mediated through the disciples' witness, is directed to the world to convict it, with salvation or judgment dependent on one's attitude towards this correlated witness.

If we accept that as Teacher the Paraclete is also Advocate, then the following picture emerges. The Paraclete cannot prosecute the world directly because the latter cannot see or know him. Consequently, the Paraclete teaches the disciples the significance of Jesus' revelation to prepare their combined witness to the world. Thus, the Paraclete prosecutes the world indirectly through the disciples and their witness, in order to convict the world of its guilt so that some may accept this Paraclete-imbued witness.

With regard to a possible realized dimension of salvation, we argued that, similarly to John 1-12, John 13-17 contained certain clues which seem to indicate that the disciples were already in a life-giving relationship with Jesus, and were thus already experiencing the Spirit-Paraclete through Jesus' words of saving truth.

4. The Paraclete as a Life-Giving Cognitive Agent

This section essentially provides a synthesis of all the soteriological functions of the Paraclete (as described in section 3, above) under the concept of the Paraclete as the mediator of life-bearing wisdom. The Paraclete functions as a life-giving cognitive agent at two levels: at the level of the disciples/believers and at the level of the world.

4.1. The Paraclete as a Life-Giving Cognitive Agent in Relation to the Disciples/Believers

For the disciples, as well as later generations of believers, the reception of the Spirit-Paraclete is envisaged not merely as a *donum superadditum* of empowerment for mission but also as a soteriological necessity. The Paraclete will maintain the believers' saving relationship with the Father and Son in various ways. First, the disciples/believers will make cognitive progression/development in their knowledge and understanding of the Father and Son through the continuous mediation of saving truth by the Paraclete in his role as revelatory Teacher, on which basis they can make a continuous adequate belief-response (cf. 13.7; 14.20). Second, the

Paraclete continuously mediates the presence of the Father and Son to the disciples/believers, and so maintains their saving relationship/union with the Father and Son. Third, one of the main themes of John 13-17 is discipleship (cf. especially Segovia's and Tolmie's studies), and the importance of discipleship for salvation is that (a) continuous (demonstration of) discipleship maintains salvation (see ch. 3).[134]

The subsequent question then is to what extent the Paraclete is involved in discipleship. First, obedience/adherence to Jesus' words/commandments guarantees Jesus' abiding in the disciples/believers, i.e., a continuation of their saving relationship through the Paraclete. Moreover, one can only adhere to Jesus' words/commandments if s/he understands (the significance of) them, which is precisely the work of the Paraclete (as Teacher). In addition, Jesus' commandments seem to be epitomized in the commandment 'to love one another', which in turn is ultimately expressed in laying down one's life for one's friends (15.12-13; cf. 1 Jn 3.16), so that self-giving love seems to be *the* hallmark/characteristic of discipleship (13.34-35).[135] It would probably not be too wide of the mark to expect that the Paraclete, who mediates knowledge/truth and the life of the Father and Son to people, also mediates the love of the Father and Son to people and enables them to love one another. 'To love one another', then, presupposes and at the same time guarantees the presence of the Paraclete.[136]

Further, to witness is a demonstration of discipleship, and it is the Paraclete who will inform and empower the witness of the disciples/believers. Furthermore, to bear fruit is also a demonstration of discipleship,[137] and one aspect of bearing fruit is possibly to reproduce

---

[134] Cf. Stibbe (*John*, 162), who remarks that the disciples' *coming* to Jesus is not sufficient for salvation; they must *continue* in their discipleship. It is then not surprising that the Beloved Disciple, who functions as a model/paradigm of discipleship, is only introduced in Jn 13-17 (13.23).

[135] In 13.37-38 it becomes clear that Peter is not yet ready to give the ultimate demonstration of love/discipleship; only later (13.36b; 21.18-19). Moreover, just as discipleship is characterized by love, so is non-discipleship characterized by hate (15.18-25).

[136] Contra Segovia, who contends apropos, e.g., 14.15-16 that the coming of the Paraclete is dependent upon the love of the disciples, although Segovia admits that 'proper love for Jesus on the part of the disciples clearly cannot exist without the presence and assistance of the Spirit-Paraclete among them' (*Farewell*, 105-106 n.87). However, what is dependent on the disciples' love for Jesus is probably not so much the *coming* of the Spirit-Paraclete but the *continuation of the relationship* between the exalted Jesus and the disciples by means of the Spirit-Paraclete (cf. Carson, *Gospel*, 498-99).

[137] Although γίνομαι in 15.8 can mean 'to become', it may also have the sense of 'to be', 'to behave/conduct oneself'. In the light of 15.4-5, it seems that 15.8 denotes that bearing fruit *demonstrates* rather than constitutes discipleship; it is the one who is

disciples (cf. Jn 4), which happens on the basis of the Paraclete-imbued witness of the disciples/believers (cf. 17.20). Besides, in order to bear fruit one needs to remain in Jesus and his words, which we have argued is by means of Paraclete-activity. Finally, unity among believers is also an important aspect of discipleship (17.11, 20-23), especially because it may lead people to belief, and this unity is created and sustained by the Paraclete as the bond of union (cf. 1 Jn 4.13).

Thus discipleship, as the continuous expression or result of adequate belief, is the *conditio sine qua non* of sustaining salvation, and the Paraclete enables believers to demonstrate discipleship. Moreover, the Paraclete probably also affects the believers' will and attitude to motivate and commit themselves to discipleship, and hence functions also as an *affective agent*.

4.2. The Paraclete as a Life-Giving Cognitive Agent in Relation to the World

The Paraclete is not only of soteriological significance for the disciples/believers but also for the world. The Paraclete's conviction of the world has a soteriological aim, but the world cannot perceive the Paraclete directly (as can the disciples); only indirectly can it perceive him via the disciples' witness. Hence, the Paraclete, as Advocate, co-witnesses with the disciples/believers, and so mediates saving truth/wisdom to the world. Thus the aim is that people may believe on the basis of the disciples' Paraclete-imbued word (cf. 15.26-27 and 16.8-11 with 17.20; cf. also 4.39), which is based on and informed by Jesus' Spirit-imbued teaching, i.e., the disciples' word (17.20) is Jesus' own Spirit-imbued life-giving word (17.6-8, 14).

If the disciples are to receive the Paraclete, then it would be reasonable to assume that the way the Spirit was active upon Jesus (providing wisdom) and in Jesus' ministry (mediating this saving wisdom) would be extrapolated in the time after Jesus' departure. In this case, we can expect that the Paraclete would mediate saving truth to the disciples, so that 'truth' was not merely the saving content of Jesus' words, but, through the identification of Jesus' word with the disciples' word, also the saving content of the disciples' witness. In other words, people who are confronted with the disciples' Paraclete-imbued truthful witness are in fact confronted with Jesus' Spirit-imbued wisdom teaching itself, and hence, the disciples' witness is potentially life-giving. In fact, *the disciples' words are 'Paraclete' and 'life'* (cf. 6.63).

---

engrafted into Jesus as the true 'Israel'/Vine who is called to bear fruit, rather than that bearing fruit causes engrafting (cf. Segovia, *Farewell*, 146-47). Jn 15.6 may hint at the situation of the defector/apostate (e.g., Judas).

Thus, the significance of the disciples'/believers' reception of the Paraclete in terms of its soteriological effects is twofold. First, the Paraclete, in the role of Teacher, will mediate to the disciples saving truth and so inform and empower their life-giving witness to the world.[138] Second, the Paraclete, in the role of Advocate, will co-witness with the disciples in order to convict the world so that some may come to believe.[139] Finally, the believers' oneness may cause knowledge and belief for the world (17.21-23),[140] and this unity is created and sustained by the Paraclete, as the bond (of [comm]union and friendship) between the believer and the Father and Son.

5. Conclusion

In this chapter we elucidated the soteriological functions of the Paraclete. First, as the Spirit of T/truth and revelatory Teacher, the Paraclete will bring the disciples/believers to a higher level of cognitive perception and understanding — through the mediation of saving truth — which may result in, for example, further, continuous belief.[141] Second, the reception of the Paraclete will maintain one's life-giving relationship with the Father and Son, and hence one's salvation. Third, the Paraclete is also expected to act as an affective agent to encourage and empower discipleship. Fourth, the glorified Jesus will continue his salvific ministry in this world through his disciples by means of the Paraclete, who will empower and equip the disciples for their missionary and salvific task towards the world. Hence, John 13-17 also evokes the concept of the Spirit as provider of cognitive perception, understanding and life; *the Spirit as Paraclete is also depicted as a life-giving cognitive (and affective) agent.* Moreover, the Paraclete functions as a life-giving cognitive agent at two interrelated levels — that of the disciples/believers and that of the world.

Our elucidation of John 13-17 agrees with the concept of 'the Spirit as the power of saving W/wisdom', in that the Spirit as Paraclete opens up Jesus' wisdom teaching, and mediates its saving truth/wisdom to people in order to increase their understanding of the Father and Son, which results in or maintains a saving relationship with the Father and Son. Our findings are also in continuity with our background chapter (ch. 2), in that: (i) both

---

[138] Thus, the disciples'/believers' cognitive development through the Paraclete's teaching is not only salvific for themselves (see section 4.1, above), but also salvific for the world, in that it prepares the disciples' witness to the world.

[139] Cf. Segovia, *Farewell*, 228-35, 244-45, 278-79.

[140] Cf. Bultmann, *Gospel*, 514-18.

[141] Understanding has, besides a cognitive, also a relational aspect, in that it occurs in relationship with the Father and Son.

depict the concept of the Spirit as the saving power of Wisdom; (ii) both combine the cognitive and relational aspects of salvation; (iii) both portray the Spirit as the agent of salvation, and with respectively Wisdom and Jesus as the source.

We are now finally in a position to assess Loader's position. For Loader the Paraclete is the second revealer envoy (Jesus being the first), who (i) enables greater understanding of Jesus and what he said; (ii) equips the disciples for mission; (iii) secures and assures the ongoing availability and abundance of life/salvation in the community of faith.[142] Loader, allowing for the reality of salvation during Jesus' ministry (see ch. 1), argues that the primary significance of the Paraclete for salvation is that the Paraclete gives greater understanding of and access to the revelation event itself, which deepens the knowledge of faith already in existence.[143] Loader did not explain, however, *how* the Paraclete gives greater understanding and subsequently deepens the knowledge of faith. Moreover, because Loader diminishes the work of the Spirit during Jesus' ministry, he fails to recognize that the work of the Paraclete after Jesus' ministry is essentially a *continuation* of the life-giving cognitive function of the Spirit within Jesus' ministry. Finally, Loader does not seem to give much attention to the Paraclete's soteriological role towards the world.

---

[142] Loader, *Christology*, 86, 105, 126, 210-14, 227.
[143] Loader, *Christology*, 127, 131, 135.

Part III

Conclusions and Recommendations

Chapter 6

Conclusions and Recommendations

1. Conclusions

The aim of this thesis — to elucidate the soteriological function of the Spirit in the Fourth Gospel — has been achieved through an analysis of the nexus Spirit-salvation-W/wisdom (both in John and in sapiential Judaism). We developed a model of John's Pneumatic Wisdom Soteriology that holds together both cognitive and relational aspects, and that depicts the various activities of entering into and remaining in salvation. This model of Johannine soteriology helped us to identify those activities in which the Spirit is involved, and these were consequently examined in more detail.

Our study resulted in the concept of the Spirit as a *life-giving cognitive (and affective) agent* who creates and sustains a life-giving relationship between the believer and the Father and Son (salvation).[1] The Spirit gives or mediates life in his function as provider or facilitator of cognitive perception and understanding, i.e., the Spirit enables a person to come from sensory to cognitive perception and understanding through the mediation of saving wisdom-truth present in Jesus' revelatory life-giving teaching. In this way, the Spirit enables a person to make an adequate belief-response on the basis of this new understanding of the Father and Son in order to enter into a saving relationship with the Father and Son. Moreover, the Spirit sustains the believer's life-giving relationship, in that the Spirit continues to facilitate cognitive perception and (deeper) understanding through further mediation of wisdom.

This Spirit-imbued understanding of God naturally affects the believer's will, attitude and motivation, enables the believer to demonstrate/display discipleship (as a continuous belief-response) and consequently guarantees the Spirit's continuous mediation of the presence of the Father and Son to the believer and the perpetual flow of life. Thus, the life-giving wisdom-truth the Spirit mediates is also expected to influence and transform the person's will, attitude and motivation in order to move him/her, for

---

[1] We have noticed the aspect of 'fellowship' and John's broader soteriological view (cf. ch. 3 section 8 n.181), but this theme was beyond the scope of our study.

example, towards discipleship. Hence, *as a cognitive agent the Spirit will also be an affective agent.*

Our study may affect, for example, our understanding of salvation. Salvation is not simply an intellectual adherence to a particular set of propositions, nor a superficial relationship with Jesus 'with no strings attached'. John advocates a *relational cognitive belief*, i.e., a personal relationship with and allegiance to Jesus (and the Father) based on an adequate understanding of the Father and Son in terms of their identity, mission and relationship. This 'belief' is demonstrated in (continuous) discipleship. Thus, salvation is essentially relational, in that the believer participates in the divine life in relationship with the Father and Son through the Spirit, but this saving relationship has a cognitive foundation, which is provided by the Spirit. Moreover, this relationship is continuously expressed in and as discipleship (as a belief-response). This implies that there is also the possibility of 'losing' salvation, i.e., of breaking off one's relationship with Jesus and defecting, which might reflect the situation the Johannine churches were facing (cf. 1-3 John).[2]

Excursus 3: An Outline of Aspects of the Sitz im Leben *of the Johannine Community*

Tentatively, we will draw the contours of the possible nature of the problems in the Johannine church(es) and John's way of dealing with them.[3] The Fourth Gospel and the Johannine letters seem to reflect problems in the area of christology, soteriology and pneumatology.

A christological problem. The first Johannine letter reveals that in the Johannine church there were apparently defective or inadequate christologies: some seem to deny that Jesus is the Christ (1 Jn 2.22) or to deny Jesus' humanity (1 Jn 4.2-3). John emphasizes that a correct christological confession is provided by the Spirit (of truth) (16.13-15; 1 Jn 4.2-3); the Spirit enables an adequate understanding of Jesus' true identity. Moreover, in his Gospel and letters, the Evangelist presents his audience with a relevant (Wisdom) christology that shows how Jesus is related to both God and humanity. The Fourth Gospel also describes the dispute between Jesus and 'the Jews', which is essentially a christological debate. This conflict between Jesus and the Jewish religious authorities of his time is probably paradigmatic of the conflicts his followers will face in later times — whether Jewish Christians versus synagogue Judaism (16.2) or believers/church versus the world at large (15.18-16.4; 17.14-16). Hence, we need not be

---

[2] It would also be interesting to examine how John's understanding of discipleship as a necessary belief-response relates to Paul's concept of working out one's own salvation (Phil. 2.12).

[3] For similar but more comprehensive theories regarding the Johannine community and its setting/problems, see Hengel, *Question*; Lieu, *Theology*; Stibbe, *Storyteller*, ch. 3; Painter, *Quest*, 75-79; Smalley, *John*, ch. 8; B. Lindars, R.B. Edwards and J.M. Court, *The Johannine Literature: With an Introduction by R. Alan Culpepper* (Sheffield: SAP, 2000).

as specific as Martyn, and John 9.22 and 12.42 may simply reflect the general situation towards the end of the first century.[4]

A soteriological problem. The Fourth Gospel shows the importance of staying with Jesus and the real possibility of apostasy and defection (6.66; 13.27, 30; 17.12).[5] The Johannine church possibly faced the problem of defecting disciples (1 Jn 2.19; 4.1; 2 Jn 7-8).[6] Hence, the Fourth Gospel and the letters emphasize that discipleship is not an option but the *conditio sine qua non* of sustaining salvation. Moreover, our study has argued that for John the Spirit is the primary means to maintain one's salvation.

A pneumatological problem. Some people may have claimed to be prophets empowered by the Spirit of truth, but the author of 1 John reveals that these people are false prophets led by the spirit of error, and emphasizes that true believers have received the Spirit of truth, i.e., the Spirit that professes a correct christology (1 Jn 4.1-6).

Even from this brief excursus it may become evident that John employs, *inter alia*, the concept of the Spirit to address the main problems he faced in his church(es). Perhaps a correct understanding of the Spirit and his activities may also benefit the churches today.

We arrived at our understanding of John's concept of salvation, and the Spirit's role in it, partially on the basis of John's possible background in sapiential Judaism. Rather than speculating on the question of possible literary dependence by John on any of the wisdom writings we investigated, we assert that it is plausible that John knew of these writings and had developed a sapiential worldview. Alternatively, perhaps John simply drew on a common late wisdom tradition, as represented by the wisdom writings we examined. We argued for a strong continuity between the Fourth Gospel and this general sapiential Jewish background. Both in the Jewish wisdom literature and in John the chief end of people is to know God through his Wisdom, and for John Jesus is this Wisdom incarnate. The Spirit functions as the power of saving W/wisdom, in that the Spirit mediates the saving wisdom that is available in (the teaching of) Wisdom (incarnate). Hence, Wisdom (incarnate) is depicted as the source of salvation and the Spirit as the agent of salvation.

Thus, John's concept of the Spirit (as the power of saving W/wisdom) seems especially (but not exclusively) to be developed from, or correspond to, the image of the Spirit as it emerges from the Jewish wisdom traditions. Most, if not all, of the *functions* of the Spirit(-Paraclete) (in relation to Jesus and salvation) in the Fourth Gospel can be seen as rooted in the Jewish sapiential traditions, especially in Wisdom of Solomon and Philo,

---

[4] Cf. Hengel, *Question*, 114-19.

[5] Stibbe interprets the pericope Jn 8.31-59 as a warning against apostasy (see *Gospel*, ch. 5).

[6] Cf. Okure, *Approach*, ch. 7.

and to a lesser extent in Qumran, Sirach and Proverbs.[7] Especially does the intertestamental concept of the Spirit as a cognitive (and affective) agent, facilitating cognitive perception, understanding and life, find a strong continuity in the Fourth Gospel. Hence, this legitimates our decision to elucidate the Jewish sapiential traditions concerning the nexus of Spirit-W/wisdom-salvation, and to use them as a conceptual background to illuminate and illustrate a similar constellation of ideas in John's Gospel. Nevertheless, we still need to assess whether John's concept of salvation is congruous with its background in every aspect. For example, it is rather less clear whether John shares the Jewish sapiential understanding of salvation as an intensification of the Spirit immanent to all human life.

Excursus 4: An Evaluation of the Continuity between Our Models of Salvation in Sapiential Judaism and in the Fourth Gospel

In chapter 2, we suggested that sapiential Judaism understands the Spirit as the principle both of (physical) life and of 'salvation' through a further increase of Spirit. We argued that both concepts of Spirit — the universal gift to all of humanity by virtue of creation and the charismatic gift — are in continuity with one another through that which they provide — life and wisdom. Hence, we may start by asking whether the Fourth Gospel endorses the concept of the Spirit as the principle of (physical) life, which seems so prominent in Judaism. Although the Spirit is explicitly related to ζωή, the divine life (6.63; 7.37-39), the question is whether the Spirit is related in any sense to ψυχή, which for John seems to denote the physical life.

There are reasons to assume that for John, too, the Spirit creates or sustains the physical life. First, in 10.11, 15, 17 and 15.13 Jesus talks about laying down his life (τίθημι τὴν ψυχὴν αὐτοῦ), which, of course, he does at the cross (cf. 12.24-25; 1 Jn 3.16).[8] If, then, Jesus' handing over the Spirit (παραδίδωμι τὸ πνεῦμα) in 19.30 refers to or is an interpretation of τίθημι τὴν ψυχὴν αὐτου (as we have suggested elsewhere), a link between πνεῦμα and ψυχή is strongly suggested: Jesus lays down his life (ψυχή) by handing over his life force (the πνεῦμα).[9] Thus, after having finished (τετέλεσται) his mission, Jesus possibly handed over the divine Spirit that had sustained his physical life as well as empowered his mission.

Second, John possibly relates creation and the new creation via the concept of the Spirit. The new birth/creation in 3.3-8, which is brought about by the Spirit, may evoke the role of the Spirit in creation as described in Genesis 1-2.[10] Moreover, the background to 3.5 (Ezek. 36-37) also links creation and the new creation via the concept of the Spirit. The continuity between creation and new creation is more prominent in 20.22. The allusions in 20.22 to Genesis 2.7 (and Philo's use of it) (πνοή/πνεῦμα ζωῆς), to Ezekiel

---

[7] John's concept of the Spirit also goes beyond the picture of the Spirit in sapiential Judaism: the Spirit-Paraclete has personal traits; the scope of potential recipients of the Spirit is even broader than Wis. and Philo depict; the Spirit-Paraclete empowers the disciples for their universal mission.

[8] Jesus cannot lay down his ζωή but only his ψυχή.

[9] For our interpretation of 19.30, see Bennema, 'Giving', section III.

[10] Gen. 1.2 attributes a creative function to the Spirit, and the creation of man in Gen. 2.7 can (via πνοή) also be attributed to the Spirit (cf. excursus 2, above).

37.1-14 (the life-giving πνεῦμα) and to Wisdom of Solomon 15.11 (πνεῦμα ζωτικόν), and their use of ἐμφυσάω, clearly evoke the role of the Spirit in creation (Gen. and Wis.) and new creation (Ezek.) — his life-giving and life-sustaining role.[11] Thus, by connecting creation and new creation in this way, John perhaps draws attention to the Spirit's continuous function of providing life; the Spirit that sustains one's ψυχή also mediates ζωή.

Nevertheless, the tendency of the Jewish wisdom tradition to present the Spirit as panentheistic (esp. in Wis. and Philo) is not as much endorsed by the author of the Fourth Gospel as perhaps assumed.[12] Perhaps it is more accurate to say that *traces* of the intertestamental concept of the Spirit as the principle of the physical life can still be found in John.

If it is equivocal whether the Johannine Spirit is depicted as the principle of the physical life, i.e., if the foundation for defining salvation in terms of intensification of Spirit appears insecure, then defining John's concept of salvation in these terms becomes also increasingly inappropriate. Does John perhaps support in any other way the idea of degrees of intensity and quality of Spirit? This is ambiguous, but it could be argued that during Jesus' ministry the disciples experienced the Spirit, and that in 20.22 the disciples' relationship with the Spirit was intensified (cf. 7.39).[13] The concept of degrees of intensity and quality of W/wisdom in the Fourth Gospel would be more sustainable: John allows for the possibility that people have various encounters with Jesus in which the Spirit mediates wisdom to people, and that people can consequently make cognitive progression. The Fourth Gospel most clearly upholds the intertestamental concept of the Spirit as the facilitator of cognitive perception, understanding and life.

In the final evaluation, the Fourth Gospel is ambiguous in depicting the Spirit as the principle of the physical life and in indicating degrees of intensity and quality of Spirit. In the Fourth Gospel, the concept of degrees of intensity and quality of wisdom would be more sustainable, and the concept of the Spirit as facilitator of cognitive perception, understanding and life is manifested most obviously. Hence, a soteriological model in terms of degrees of intensity and quality of Spirit and W/wisdom does not seem entirely sustainable on the basis of the Fourth Gospel.

One explanation for this shift could be found in the Gospel's high and radical christological claims: Jesus supersedes Wisdom and all previous wisdom offered; instead saving wisdom is found only in Jesus' radical teaching and mediated to people by the Spirit. Moreover, John stresses that the immanence of the Father and Son (in the Spirit-Paraclete) is in the

---

[11] Cf. Turner (*Spirit*, 90-91) for the evocations of 20.22.

[12] However, the 'silence' of the NT concerning the Spirit in creation and its challenge to pneumatologies that extend God's immanence in the Spirit beyond the church into this world is perhaps not as conspicuous as Chevallier and Turner depict (see M.-A. Chevallier, 'Sur un Silence du Nouveau Testament: l'Esprit de Dieu à l'Oeuvre dans le Cosmos et l'Humanité', *NTS* 33 [1987] 344-69; Turner, *Spirit*, 157-58).

[13] See Bennema, 'Giving', section IV.7. Moreover, an intensification of Spirit, in terms of the Spirit starting a new nexus of activities in relation to people, is also possible; nonetheless, perhaps it is too speculative a point to pursue here.

(community of) believers, i.e., in the church, rather than in the whole of creation. Finally, although John may confirm a continuity between creation and new creation, he indicates, at the same time, a stronger discontinuity. The new creation is not simply an intensification of Spirit, but also connotes, beyond this, a radically new origin (from above), a new father and a new family.

Thus, the single most important continuity between our intertestamental model and John's model of salvation is the concept of the Spirit as an agent of life-bearing wisdom.

2. Recommendations for Further Research

We recommend three areas for further research.

Johannine Soteriology. In chapter 1, we identified the need for a more coherent and complete model of salvation in the Fourth Gospel than Johannine scholarship has produced so far. Consequently, in chapter 3, we sketched the contours of an overall introductory model of Johannine soteriology. However, this model needs to be tested and explored more rigorously than this study has allowed for. For example, an investigation of the various aspects of discipleship as a belief-response, or an inquiry into Johannine spirituality in terms of how the Spirit is experienced within the community of believers (then and now), would involve a thorough examination of Area 2 in our model.[14] The soteriological dimension of the concept of friendship also needs to be more fully elucidated than Ford, Ringe and I have done. Furthermore, it needs to be examined how John's understanding of salvation relates to the covenantal theology of Judaism at large.[15] If the Fourth Gospel depicts the Spirit (rather than Jewish birth and [adherence to] the Torah) as the boundary-marker of the 'in'-group and Jesus as the true 'Israel', does John imply that the Jews were 'out' and needed to get 'back in'? To what extent does the Fourth Gospel portray a 'remnant theology' or 'restoration eschatology'? In what way are the programmes of Torah-intensification, as developed by various groups in Judaism to ensure 'staying in', now replaced or superseded by Jesus' life-giving Spirit-imbued wisdom programme?

---

[14] Burge (*Community*), Barton (*Spirituality*) and Turner ('Churches') have made a start concerning Johannine spirituality. What does it mean, e.g., to worship the Father in Spirit-and-T/truth? What is the ongoing significance of the signs for believers?

[15] For a description of Jewish soteriology, see esp. the categories of Sanders ('covenantal nomism'), Wright ('restoration eschatology') and Elliott ('destruction-preservation soteriology') (cf. ch. 2 section 2 nn.4-5).

The Spirit as an Affective Agent. We argued that in John's understanding, the Spirit is depicted primarily as a life-giving cognitive agent but also as an affective agent. Due to the limitations of this study, it has not been feasible adequately to elucidate the affective dimension of the Spirit. The Spirit sustains people's salvation by enabling people to demonstrate discipleship. The Spirit mediates, for example, the love of the Father and Son to people to enable them to love one another. The Spirit also mediates to the believer the presence of the Father and Son, peace, joy, etc. The Spirit is expected to facilitate/empower worship (Jn 4.23-24). What are the implications of these functions of the Spirit for the believer? How do these activities of the Spirit relate to people's moods, feelings, will, attitudes and motivations? We suggested that the (soteriological) necessity for a continuous demonstration of discipleship is linked with proper attitudes and motivations which are brought about by the Spirit. A Spirit-informed understanding of the Father and Son naturally assumes an understanding of their will, mission, demands, and so on, and hence affects people's will, attitudes and motivations.

Johannine Ethics and Epistemology. Johannine ethics has not received much attention from scholarship,[16] but the Spirit as an affective agent is naturally also related to ethics. In addition, the Spirit as the facilitator of cognitive perception and understanding has direct bearing on one's ethics, for right thinking is inextricably linked to right morality. If we extrapolate the exhortation of Jewish wisdom literature, Christians are to superintend their intellectual life and to cultivate virtue.[17] Moreover, the Spirit as a cognitive agent mediates to people revelatory wisdom which facilitates ongoing cognitive perception and understanding of the Father and Son. In other words, the Spirit creates or provides (the basis for) a new epistemology; an epistemology which is Spirit-driven and Christ-centred. How does this Spirit-informed epistemology affect people's praxis? How do these concepts relate, for example, to the Pauline concept of the renewal of the mind (Rom. 12.2; Eph. 4.23; Col. 3.10), to the Synoptic command to love God with all your mind (Mt. 22.37; Mk 12.30; Lk. 10.27) and to the concept of setting your mind on divine things (Mt. 16.23; Mk 8.33; Col. 3.2)?

---

[16] The most notable exceptions are R.B. Hays, *The Moral Vision of the New Testament: Community, Cross, New Creation: A Contemporary Introduction to New Testament Ethics* (San Francisco: Harper, 1996) 138-57, and J.J. Kanagaraj, 'The Implied Ethics of the Fourth Gospel: A Reinterpretation of the Decalogue', *TynB* 52 (2001) 33-60.

[17] For a recent philosophical defence for and outworking of this imperative, see W.J. Wood's compelling treatise on virtue epistemology (*Epistemology: Becoming Intellectually Virtuous* [Leicester: Apollos, 1998]).

Appendices

Appendix 1

The Soteriological Language of the Johannine Literature: Occurrences

ἀγαπάω Jn 3.16, 19, 35; 8.42; 10.17; 11.5; 12.43; 13.1, 23, 34; 14.15, 21, 23-24, 28, 31; 15.9, 12, 17; 17.23-24, 26; 19.26; 21.7, 15-16, 20
1 Jn 2.10, 15; 3.10-11, 14, 18, 23; 4.7-8, 10-12, 19-21; 5.1-2
2 Jn 1, 5
3 Jn 1

ἀγάπη Jn 5.42; 13.35; 15.9-10, 13; 17.26
1 Jn 2.5, 15; 3.1, 16-17; 4.7-10, 12, 16-18; 5.3
2 Jn 3, 6
3 Jn 6

ἀκολουθέω Jn 1.37-38, 40, 43; 6.2; 8.12; 10.4-5, 27; 11.31; 12.26; 13.36-37; 18.15; 20.6; 21.19-20, 22

ἀκούω Jn 1.37, 40; 3.8, 29, 32; 4.1, 42, 47; 5.24-25, 28, 30, 37; 6.45, 60; 7.32, 40, 51; 8.9, 26, 38, 40, 43, 47; 9.27, 31-32, 35, 40; 10.3, 8, 16, 20, 27; 11.4, 6, 20, 29, 41-42; 12.12, 18, 29, 34, 47; 14.24, 28; 15.15; 16.13; 18.21, 37; 19.8, 13; 21.7
1 Jn 1.1, 3, 5; 2.7, 18, 24; 3.11; 4.3, 5-6; 5.14-15
2 Jn 6
3 Jn 4

ἀλήθεια Jn 1.14, 17; 3.21; 4.23-24; 5.33; 8.32, 40, 44-46; 14.6, 17; 15.26; 16.7, 13; 17.17, 19; 18.37-38
1 Jn 1.6, 8; 2.4, 21; 3.18-19; 4.6; 5.6
2 Jn 1-4
3 Jn 1, 3-4, 8, 12

ἀναβαίνω Jn 1.15; 2.13; 3.13; 5.1; 6.62; 7.8, 10, 14; 10.1; 11.55; 12.20; 20.17; 21.11

ἀναγγέλλω Jn 4.25; 5.15; 16.13-15
1 Jn 5

ἀποστέλλω Jn 1.6, 19, 24; 3.17, 28, 34; 4.38; 5.33, 36, 38; 6.29, 57; 7.29, 32; 8.42; 9.7; 10.36; 11.3, 42; 17.3, 8, 18, 21, 23, 25; 18.24; 20.21
1 Jn 4.9-10, 14

βλέπω Jn 1.29; 5.19; 9.7, 15, 19, 21, 25, 39, 41; 11.9; 13.22; 20.1, 5; 21.9, 20
2 Jn 8

γεννάω Jn 1.13; 3.3-8; 8.41; 9.2, 19-20, 32, 34; 16.21; 18.37
1 Jn 2.29; 3.9; 4.7; 5.1, 4, 18

γινώσκω Jn 1.10, 48; 2.24-25; 3.10; 4.1, 53; 5.6, 42; 6.15, 69; 7.17, 26-27, 49, 51; 8.27-28, 32, 43, 52, 55; 10.6, 14-15, 27, 38; 11.57; 12.9, 16;

	13.7, 12, 28, 35; 14.7, 9, 17, 20, 31; 15.18; 16.3, 19; 17.3, 7-8, 23, 25; 19.4; 21.17
	1 Jn 2.3-5, 13-14, 18, 29; 3.1, 6, 16, 19-20, 24; 4.2, 6-8, 13, 16; 5.2, 20
	2 Jn 1
γνωρίζω	Jn 15.15; 17.26
διδάσκαλος	Jn 1.38; 3.2, 10; 8.4; 11.28; 13.13-14; 20.16
διδάσκω	Jn 6.59; 7.14, 28, 35; 8.2, 20, 28; 9.34; 14.26; 18.20
	1 Jn 2.27
διδαχή	Jn 7.16-17; 18.19
	2 Jn 9-10
δίδωμι	Jn 1.12, 17, 22; 3.16, 27, 34-35; 4.5, 7, 10, 12, 14-15; 5.22, 26-27, 36; 6.27, 31-34, 37, 39, 51-52, 65; 7.19, 22; 9.24; 10.28-29; 11.22, 57; 12.5, 49; 13.3, 15, 26, 29, 34; 14.16, 27; 15.16; 16.23; 17.2, 4, 6-9, 11-12, 14, 22, 24; 18.9, 11, 22; 19.3, 9, 11; 21.13
	1 Jn 3.1, 23-24; 4.13; 5.11, 16, 20
δόξα	Jn 1.14; 2.11; 5.41, 44; 7.18; 8.50, 54; 9.24; 11.4, 40; 12.41, 43; 17.5, 22, 24
δοξάζω	Jn 7.39; 8.54; 11.4; 12.16, 23, 28; 13.31-32; 14.13; 15.8; 16.14; 17.1, 4-5, 10; 21.19
ἕλκω	Jn 6.44; 12.32; 18.10; 21.6, 11
ἐμφανίζω	Jn 14.21-22
ἕν εἶναι	Jn 10.30; 17.11, 21-23
ἐξηγέομαι	Jn 1.18
ἐργάζομαι	Jn 3.21; 5.17; 6.27-28, 30; 9.4
	2 Jn 8
	3 Jn 5
ἔργον	Jn 3.19-21; 4.34; 5.20, 36; 6.28-29; 7.3, 7, 21; 8.39, 41; 9.3-4; 10.25, 32-33, 37-38; 14.10-12; 15.24; 17.4
	1 Jn 3.8, 12, 18
	2 Jn 11
	3 Jn 10
ζάω	Jn 4.10-11, 50-51, 53; 5.25; 6.51, 57-58; 7.38; 11.25-26; 14.19
	1 Jn 4.9
ζωή (αἰώνιος)	Jn 1.4; 3.15-16, 36; 4.14, 36; 5.24, 26, 29, 39-40; 6.27, 33, 35, 40, 47-48, 51, 53-54, 63, 68; 8.12; 10.10, 28; 11.25; 12.25, 50; 14.6; 17.2-3; 20.31
	1 Jn 1.1-2; 2.25; 3.14-15; 5.11-13, 16, 20
ζωοποιέω	Jn 5.21; 6.63
θεάομαι	Jn 1.14, 32, 38; 4.35; 6.5; 11.45
	1 Jn 1.1; 4.12, 14
θεωρέω	Jn 2.23; 4.19; 6.2, 19, 40, 62; 7.3; 8.51; 9.8; 10.12; 12.19, 45; 14.17, 19; 16.10, 16-17, 19; 17.24; 20.6, 12, 14
	1 Jn 3.17
καταβαίνω	Jn 1.32-33, 51; 2.12; 3.13; 4.47, 49, 51; 5.7; 6.16, 33, 38, 41-42, 50-51, 58
κοινωνία	1 Jn 1.3, 6-7
(παρα)λαμβάνω	Jn 1.11-12, 16; 3.11, 27, 32-33; 4.36; 5.34, 41, 43-44; 6.7, 11, 21; 7.23, 39; 10.17-18; 12.3, 13, 48; 13.4, 12, 20, 26, 30; 14.3, 17; 16.14-15, 24; 17.8; 18.3, 31; 19.1, 6, 16, 23, 27, 30, 40; 20.22; 21.13

	1 Jn 2.27; 3.22; 5.9
	2 Jn 4, 10
	3 Jn 7
μαρτυρέω	Jn 1.7-8, 15, 32, 34; 2.25; 3.11, 26, 28, 32; 4.39, 44; 5.31-33, 36-37, 39; 7.7; 8.13-14, 18; 10.25; 12.17; 13.21; 15.26-27; 18.23, 37; 19.35; 21.24
	1 Jn 1.2; 4.14; 5.6-7, 9-10
	3 Jn 3, 6, 12
μαρτυρία	Jn 1.7, 19; 3.11, 32-33; 5.31-32, 34, 36; 8.13-14, 17; 19.35; 21.24
	1 Jn 5.9-11
	3 Jn 12
μένω	Jn 1.32-33, 38-39; 2.12; 3.36; 4.40; 5.38; 6.27, 56; 7.9; 8.31, 35; 9.41; 10.40; 11.6, 54; 12.24, 34, 46; 14.10, 17, 25; 15.4-7, 9-10, 16; 19.31; 21.22-23
	1 Jn 2.6, 10, 14, 17, 19, 24, 27-28; 3.6, 9, 14-15, 17, 24; 4.12-13, 15-16
	2 Jn 2, 9
νοέω	Jn 12.40
ὁδός	Jn 1.23; 14.4-6
οἶδα	Jn 1.26, 31, 33; 2.9; 3.2, 8, 11; 4.10, 22, 25, 32, 42; 5.13, 32; 6.6, 42, 61, 64; 7.15, 27-29; 8.14, 19, 37, 55; 9.12, 20-21, 24-25, 29-31; 10.4-5; 11.22, 24, 42, 49; 12.35, 50; 13.1, 3, 7, 11, 17-18; 14.4-5; 15.15, 21; 16.18, 30; 18.2, 4, 21; 19.10, 28, 35; 20.2, 9, 13-14; 21.4, 12, 15-17, 24
	1 Jn 2.11, 20-21, 29; 3.2, 5, 14-15; 5.13, 15, 18-20
	3 Jn 12
ὁράω	Jn 1.18, 33-34, 39, 46-48, 50-51; 3.3, 11, 32, 36; 4.29, 45, 48; 5.6, 37; 6.14, 22, 24, 26, 30, 36, 46; 7.52; 8.38, 56-57; 9.1, 37; 11.31-34, 40; 12.9, 21, 40-41; 14.7, 9; 15.24; 16.16-17, 19, 22; 18.26; 19.6, 26, 33, 35, 37; 20.8, 18, 20, 25, 27, 29; 21.21
	1 Jn 1.1-3; 3.1-2, 6; 4.20; 5.16
	3 Jn 11, 14
παράκλητος	Jn 14.16, 26; 15.26; 16.7
	1 Jn 2.1
πέμπω	Jn 1.22, 33; 4.34; 5.23-24, 30, 37; 6.38-39, 44; 7.16, 18, 28, 33; 8.16, 18, 26, 29; 9.4; 12.44-45, 49; 13.16, 20; 14.24, 26; 15.21, 26; 16.5, 7; 20.21
πιστεύω	Jn 1.7, 12, 50; 2.11, 22-24; 3.12, 15-16, 18, 36; 4.21, 39, 41-42, 48, 50, 53; 5.24, 38, 44, 46-47; 6.29-30, 35-36, 40, 47, 64, 69; 7.5, 31, 38-39, 48; 8.24, 30-31, 45-46; 9.18, 35-36, 38; 10.25-26, 37-38, 42; 11.15, 25-27, 40, 42, 45, 48; 12.11, 36-39, 42, 44, 46; 13.19; 14.1, 10-12, 29; 16.9, 27, 30-31; 17.8, 20-21; 19.35; 20.8, 25, 29, 31
	1 Jn 3.23; 4.1, 16; 5.1, 5, 10, 13
πνεῦμα	Jn 1.32-33; 3.5-6, 8, 34; 4.23-24; 6.63; 7.39; 11.33; 13.21; 14.17, 26; 15.26; 16.13; 19.30; 20.22
	1 Jn 3.24; 4.1-3, 6, 13; 5.6, 8
σημεῖον	Jn 2.11, 18, 23; 3.2; 4.48, 54; 6.2, 14, 26, 30; 7.31; 9.16; 10.41; 11.47; 12.18, 37; 20.30
σῴζω	Jn 3.17; 5.34; 10.9; 11.12; 12.27, 47
σωτήρ	Jn 4.42

	1 Jn 4.14
σωτηρία	Jn 4.22
ὑπομιμνήσκω	Jn 14.26
	3 Jn 10
ὑψόω	Jn 3.14; 8.28; 12.32, 34
φανερόω	Jn 1.31; 2.11; 3.21; 7.4; 9.3; 17.6; 21.1, 14
	1 Jn 1.2; 2.19, 28; 3.2, 5, 8; 4.9
(φέρω) καρπός	Jn 4.36; 12.24; 15.2, 4-5, 8, 16
φιλέω	Jn 5.20; 11.3, 36; 12.25; 15.19; 16.27; 20.2; 21.15-17
φίλος	Jn 3.29; 11.11; 15.13-15; 19.12
	3 Jn 15

Appendix 2

The Soteriological Language of the Johannine Literature: Statistics

	John's Gospel (878 vss., 15635 words)	1 John (105 vss., 2141 words)	2 John (13 vss., 245 words)	3 John (15 vss., 219 words)	Total (1011 vss., 18240 words)
ἀγαπάω	37	28	2	1	68
ἀγάπη	7	18	2	1	28
ἀκολουθέω	19				19
ἀκούω	59	14	1	1	75
ἀλήθεια	25	9	5	6	45
ἀναβαίνω	16				16
ἀναγγέλλω	5	1			6
ἀποστέλλω	28	3			31
βλέπω	17		1		18
γεννάω	18	10			28
γινώσκω	57	25	1		83
γνωρίζω	3				3
διδάσκαλος	8				8
διδάσκω	10	3			13
διδαχή	3		3		6
δίδωμι	75	7			82
δόξα	19				19
δοξάζω	23				23
ἕλκω	5				5
ἐμφανίζω	2				2
ἕν εἶναι	5				5
ἐξηγέομαι	1				1
ἐργάζομαι	8		1	1	10
ἔργον	27	3	1	1	32
ζάω	17	1			18
ζωή (αἰώνιος)	36	13			49
ζῳοποιέω	3				3
θεάομαι	6	3			9
θεωρέω	24	1			25
καταβαίνω	17				17

	John's Gospel (878 vss., 15635 words)	1 John (105 vss., 2141 words)	2 John (13 vss., 245 words)	3 John (15 vss., 219 words)	Total (1011 vss., 18240 words)
κοινωνία		4			4
(παρα)λαμβάνω	49	3	2	1	55
μαρτυρέω	33	6		4	43
μαρτυρία	14	6		1	21
μένω	40	24	3		67
νοέω	1				1
ὁδός	4				4
οἶδα	84	15		1	100
ὁράω	67	9		2	78
παράκλητος	4	1			5
πέμπω	32				32
πιστεύω	98	9			107
πνεῦμα	24	12			36
σημεῖον	17				17
σῴζω	6				6
σωτήρ	1	1			2
σωτηρία	1				1
ὑπομιμνήσκω	1			1	2
ὑψόω	5				5
φανερόω	9	9			18
(φέρω) καρπός	7				7
φιλέω	13				13
φίλος	6			2	8
Total	1096	238	22	23	1379

Bibliography

This bibliography is not an exhaustive but a select bibliography. It consists mainly of items that are referred to once or more in this work. Only a small number of works are included in the bibliography that have not been formally referenced in the text, but have been influential in my research.

1. Reference Works and Sources

Aland, K., M. Black, C.M. Martini, B.M. Metzger and A. Wikgren (eds.), *Novum Testamentum Graece* (Nestle-Aland; Stuttgart: Deutsche Bibelgesellschaft, 27th edition, 1993).

Bauer, W., *A Greek-English Lexicon of the New Testament and Other Early Christian Literature* (translated and edited by W.F. Arndt, F.W. Gingrich and F.W. Danker; Chicago: University of Chicago Press, 1979[2]).

Belle, G. van (ed.), *Johannine Bibliography 1966-1985: A Cumulative Bibliography on the Fourth Gospel* (BEThL; Leuven: Leuven University Press, 1988).

BibleWorks 4.0 — The Premier Biblical Exegesis and Research Program (Big Fork: Hermeneutika Bible Research Software, 1999).

Burgess, S.M., G.B. McGee and P.H. Alexander (eds.), *Dictionary of Pentecostal and Charismatic Movements* (Grand Rapids: Zondervan, 1988).

Elgvin, T. (ed.) et al., *Qumran Cave 4: Sapiential Texts, Part 1* (DJD 20; Oxford: Clarendon Press, 1997).

Elliger, K. and W. Rudolph (eds.), *Biblia Hebraica Stuttgartensia* (Stuttgart: Deutsche Bibelgesellschaft, 1990[4]).

Funk, R.W., *A Beginning-Intermediate Grammar of Hellenistic Greek* (3 vols.; Missoula: SBL, 1973[2]).

García Martínez, F., *The Dead Sea Scrolls Translated: The Qumran Texts in English* (Leiden: Brill, 1996[2]).

Kittel, G. and G. Friedrich (eds.), *Theological Dictionary of the New Testament* (10 vols.; Transl. G. Bromiley; Grand Rapids: Eerdmans, 1964-76).

Louw, J.P. and E.A. Nida (eds.), *Greek-English Lexicon of the New Testament Based on Semantic Domains* (2 vols.; New York: UBS, 1989[2]).

Philo: Complete Works (10 vols. and 2 supplementary vols.; Transl. F.H. Colson and G.H. Whittaker; Loeb Classical Library; London: Heinemann, 1929-62).

Rahlfs, A. (ed.), *Septuaginta* (2 vols.; Stuttgart: Deutsche Bibelgesellschaft, 1935).

Strugnell, J., D.J. Harrington and T. Elgvin (eds.), *Qumran Cave 4: Sapiential Texts, Part 2* (DJD 34; Oxford: Clarendon Press, 1999).

The Holy Bible. New Revised Standard Version containing the Old and New Testaments with the Apocryphal/Deuterocanonical Books (New York: OUP, 1989).

The Works of Philo: Complete and Unabridged. New Updated Edition (Transl. C.D. Yonge; Peabody: Hendrickson, 1997).

2. Commentaries on the Fourth Gospel

Barrett, C.K., *The Gospel according to St John: An Introduction with Commentary and Notes on the Greek Text* (London: SPCK, 1978²).

Beasley-Murray, G.R., *John* (WBC 36; Milton Keynes: Word, 1991).

Brown, R.E., *The Gospel according to John: Introduction, Translation, and Notes* (AncB 29; 2 vols.; London: Chapman, 1971).

Bruce, F.F., *The Gospel of John: Introduction, Exposition and Notes* (Basingstoke: Pickering & Inglis, 1983).

Bultmann, R., *The Gospel of John: A Commentary* (Transl. G.R. Beasley-Murray; Philadelphia: Westminster Press, 1971).

Carson, D.A., *The Gospel according to John* (Leicester: IVP, 1991).

Haenchen, E., *John: A Commentary on the Gospel of John* (2 vols.; Philadelphia: Fortress Press, 1984).

Hoskyns, E.C., *The Fourth Gospel* (2 vols.; F.N. Davey [ed.]; London: Faber and Faber, 1940).

Howard-Brook, W., *Becoming Children of God: John's Gospel and Radical Discipleship* (Maryknoll: Orbis, 1994).

Lindars, B., *The Gospel of John* (NCeB; London: Oliphants, 1972).

Moloney, F.J., *Belief in the Word — Reading the Fourth Gospel: John 1-4* (Minneapolis: Fortress Press, 1993).

—, *Signs and Shadows: Reading John 5-12* (Minneapolis: Fortress Press, 1996).

Morris, L., *The Gospel according to John* (NIC; Grand Rapids: Eerdmans, 1995 [rev. edn]).

Newman, B.M. and E.A. Nida, *A Translator's Handbook on the Gospel of John* (New York: UBS, 1980).

Ridderbos, H.N., *The Gospel according to John: A Theological Commentary* (Transl. J. Vriend; Grand Rapids: Eerdmans, 1997).

Schnackenburg, R., *The Gospel according to St John* (3 vols.; London: Burns & Oates, 1968-82).

Stibbe, M.W.G., *John* (Sheffield: JSOT Press, 1993).

Witherington III, B., *John's Wisdom: A Commentary on the Fourth Gospel* (Cambridge: Lutterworth Press, 1995).

3. Other Literature

Aalen, S., '"Truth", a Key Word in St. John's Gospel' in F.L. Cross (ed.), *Studia Evangelica Vol. II* (Berlin: Akademie-Verlag, 1964) 3-24.

Aker, B.C., 'John, Gospel of' in S.M. Burgess, G.B. McGee and P.H. Alexander (eds.), *Dictionary of Pentecostal and Charismatic Movements* (Grand Rapids: Zondervan, 1988) 496-507.

Allen, L.C., *Ezekiel 20-48* (WBC 29; Dallas: Word, 1990).

Anderson, A.A., 'The Use of "Ruaḥ" in 1QS, 1QH and 1QM', *JSSt* 7 (1962) 293-303.

Anderson, P.N., *The Christology of the Fourth Gospel: Its Unity and Disunity in the Light of John 6* (WUNT II/78; Tübingen: Mohr Siebeck, 1996).

Appold, M.L., *The Oneness Motif in the Fourth Gospel: Motif Analysis and Exegetical Probe into the Theology of John* (WUNT II/1; Tübingen: Mohr Siebeck, 1976).

Ashton, J., 'The Transformation of Wisdom: A Study of the Prologue of John's Gospel', *NTS* 32 (1986) 161-86.

—, *Understanding the Fourth Gospel* (Oxford: Clarendon Press, 1991).

Aune, D.E., 'Charismatic Exegesis in Early Judaism and Early Christianity' in J.H. Charlesworth and C.A. Evans (eds.), *The Pseudepigrapha and Early Biblical Interpretation* (JSPE.S 14; Sheffield: JSOT Press, 1993) 126-50.

Bammel, E., 'The Farewell Discourse of the Evangelist John and Its Jewish Heritage', *TynB* 44 (1993) 103-16.

Barrett, C.K., 'The Holy Spirit in the Fourth Gospel', *JThS* 1 (1950) 1-15.

Barton, S.C., *The Spirituality of the Gospels* (London: SPCK, 1992).

Bauckham, R., 'For Whom Were Gospels Written?' in R. Bauckham (ed), *The Gospels for All Christians: Rethinking the Gospel Audiences* (Grand Rapids: Eerdmans, 1998) 9-48.

—, *God Crucified: Monotheism and Christology in the New Testament* (Carlisle: Paternoster, 1998).

—, 'Response to Philip Esler', *SJTh* 51 (1998) 249-53.

Baumgärtel, F., 'Πνεῦμα, πνευματικός' in *TDNT*, VI:359-68.

Beasley-Murray, G.R., 'John 3:3, 5: Baptism, Spirit and the Kingdom', *ET* 97 (1985-86) 167-70.

—, *Gospel of Life: Theology in the Fourth Gospel* (Peabody: Hendrickson, 1991).

Beck, D.R., *The Discipleship Paradigm: Readers and Anonymous Characters in the Fourth Gospel* (BIS 27; Leiden: Brill, 1997).

Behm, J., 'Παράκλητος' in *TDNT*, V:800-14.

Belleville, L., '"Born of Water and Spirit:" John 3:5', *TrinJ* 1 (1980) 125-41.

Bennema, C., 'The Strands of Wisdom Tradition in Intertestamental Judaism: Origins, Developments and Characteristics', *TynB* 52 (2001) 61-82.

—, 'The Giving of the Spirit in John's Gospel — A New Proposal?', *EvQ* 74 (forthcoming, 2002).

Berry, D.K., *An Introduction to Wisdom and Poetry of the Old Testament* (Nashville: Broadman & Holman Publishers, 1995).

Betz, O., *Der Paraklet: Fürsprecher im Häretischen Spätjudentum, im Johannes-Evangelium und in neu gefundenen gnostischen Schriften* (Leiden: Brill, 1963).

Beutler, J., *Martyria: Traditionsgeschichtliche Untersuchungen zum Zeugnisthema bei Johannes* (FTS 10; Frankfurt: Knecht, 1972).

Bieder, W., 'Πνεῦμα, πνευματικός' in *TDNT*, VI:368-75.

Billington, A., 'The Paraclete and Mission in the Fourth Gospel' in A. Billington, T. Lane and M.[M.B.] Turner (eds.), *Mission and Meaning: Essays Presented to Peter Cotterell* (Carlisle: Paternoster, 1995) 90-115.

Bittner, W.J., *Jesu Zeichen im Johannesevangelium: Die Messias-Erkenntnis im Johannesevangelium vor ihrem jüdischen Hintergrund* (WUNT II/26; Tübingen: Mohr Siebeck, 1987).

Blenkinsopp, J., 'John vii. 37-9. Another Note on a Notorious Crux', *NTS* 6 (1959-60) 95-98.

Boer, M.C. de, 'Narrative Criticism, Historical Criticism, and the Gospel of John', *JSNT* 45 (1992) 35-48.

—, *Johannine Perspectives on the Death of Jesus* (Kampen: Kok, 1996).

Boers, H., *Neither on This Mountain Nor in Jerusalem: A Study of John 4* (SBL.MS 35; Atlanta: Scholars Press, 1988).

Borgen, P., *Bread From Heaven: An Exegetical Study of the Concept of Manna in the Gospel of John and the Writings of Philo* (NT.S 10; Leiden: Brill, 1965).

—, 'Observations on the Midrashic Character of John 6' in P. Borgen (ed.), *Logos Was the True Light and Other Essays on the Gospel of John* (Trondheim: Tapir Publishers, 1983) 23-31.

—, *Philo, John and Paul: New Perspectives on Judaism and Early Christianity* (Atlanta: Scholars Press, 1987).

—, 'The Gospel of John and Hellenism: Some Observations' in R.A. Culpepper and C.C. Black (eds.), *Exploring the Gospel of John: In Honor of D. Moody Smith* (Louisville: Westminster John Knox Press, 1996) 98-123.

—, 'God's Agent in the Fourth Gospel' in J. Ashton (ed.), *The Interpretation of John* (Edinburgh: T&T Clark, 1997²) 83-95.

—, *Philo of Alexandria — An Exegete for his Time* (NT.S 86; Leiden: Brill, 1997).

Boring, M.E., 'The Influence of Christian Prophecy on the Johannine Portrayal of the Paraclete and Jesus', *NTS* 25 (1979) 113-23.

Bornkamm, G., 'Der Paraklet im Johannes-Evangelium' in G. Bornkamm (ed.), *Geschichte und Glaube I* (Gesammelte Aufsätze Band III; München: Kaiser, 1968) 68-89.

—, 'Zur Interpretation des Johannes-Evangeliums: Eine Auseinandersetzung mit Ernst Käsemanns Schrift "Jesu letzter Wille nach Johannes 17"' in G. Bornkamm (ed.), *Geschichte und Glaube I* [Gesammelte Aufsätze Band III; München: Kaiser, 1968] 104-21.

Botha, J.E., *Jesus and the Samaritan Woman: A Speech Act Reading of John 4:1-42* (NT.S 65; Leiden: Brill, 1991).

Braun, F.-M., *Jean le Théologien* (4 vols.; Paris: Gabalda, 1959-72).

—, 'Saint Jean, la Sagesse et l'histoire' in W.C. van Unnik (ed.), *Neotestamentica et Patristica: Eine Freundesgabe, Herrn Professor Dr. Oscar Cullmann zu seinem 60. Geburtstag überreicht* (NT.S 6; Leiden: Brill, 1962) 123-33.

Breck, J., *Spirit of Truth — The Holy Spirit In Johannine Tradition: Volume 1. The Origins of Johannine Pneumatology* (Crestwood: St Vladimir's Seminary Press, 1991).

Brown, A.R., *The Cross and Human Transformation: Paul's Apocalyptic Word in 1 Corinthians* (Minneapolis: Fortress, 1995).

Brown, R.E., 'The Paraclete in the Fourth Gospel', *NTS* 13 (1966-67) 113-32.

—, 'The Kerygma of the Gospel According to John', *Interp* 21 (1967) 387-400.

—, 'The Qumran Scrolls and the Johannine Gospel and Epistles' in R.E. Brown (ed.), *New Testament Essays* (London: Chapman, 1967) 102-31.

—, 'The "Paraclete" in the Light of Modern Research' in F.L. Cross (ed.), *Studia Evangelica Vol. IV* (Berlin: Akademie-Verlag, 1968) 158-65.

—, *The Community of the Beloved Disciple: The Life, Loves, and Hates of an Individual Church in New Testament Times* (London: Chapman, 1979).

Büchsel, F., 'Ἐλέγχω, κτλ.' in *TDNT*, II:473-76.

Bullock, C.H., 'The Book of Proverbs' in R.B. Zuck (ed.), *Learning from the Sages: Selected Studies on the Book of Proverbs* (Grand Rapids: Baker Books, 1995) 19-33.

Bultmann, R., *Theology of the New Testament* (2 vols.; Transl. K. Grobel; London: SCM Press, 1952, 1955).

—, *Jesus Christ and Mythology* (New York: Scribner's, 1958).

—, 'Γινώσκω, κτλ.' in *TDNT*, I:689-719.

—, 'The History of Religions Background of the Prologue to the Gospel of John' in J. Ashton (ed.), *The Interpretation of John* (Edinburgh: T&T Clark, 1997²) 27-46.

Burge, G.M., *The Anointed Community: The Holy Spirit in the Johannine Tradition* (Grand Rapids: Eerdmans, 1987).

Burkett, D., *The Son of the Man in the Gospel of John* (JSNT.S 56; Sheffield: JSOT Press, 1991).

Burridge, R.A., *What are the Gospels?: A Comparison with Graeco-Roman Biography* (SNTS.MS 70; Cambridge: CUP, 1992).

—, 'About People, by People, for People: Gospel Genre and Audiences' in R. Bauckham (ed.), *The Gospels for All Christians: Rethinking the Gospel Audiences* (Grand Rapids: Eerdmans, 1998) 113-45.

Cadman, W.H., *The Open Heaven: The Revelation of God in the Johannine Sayings of Jesus* (Oxford: Basil Blackwell, 1969).

Carey, G.L., 'The Lamb of God and Atonement Theories', *TynB* 32 (1981) 97-122.

Carson, D.A., 'Predestination and Responsibility: Elements of Tension-Theology in the Fourth Gospel against Jewish Background' (Cambridge: Ph.D. dissertation, 1975).

—, 'The Function of the Paraclete in John 16:7-11', *JBL* 98 (1979) 547-66.

—, *The Farewell Discourse and Final Prayer of Jesus: An Exposition of John 14-17* (Grand Rapids: Baker Book House, 1980).

—, *Divine Sovereignty and Human Responsibility: Biblical perspectives in tension* (London: Marshall, Morgan & Scott, 1981).

—, 'Understanding Misunderstandings in the Fourth Gospel', *TynB* 33 (1982) 59-91.

—, *The Difficult Doctrine of the Love of God* (Leicester: IVP, 2000).

Casey, M., *Is John's Gospel True?* (London: Routledge, 1996).

Charles, J.D., '"Will the Court Please Call in the Prime Witness?": John 1:29-34 and the "Witness"-Motif', *TrinJ* 10 (1989) 71-83.

Chevallier, M.-A., *Souffle de Dieu: Le Saint-Esprit dans le Nouveau Testament* (2 vols.; Paris: Beauchesne, 1978, 1990).

—, 'Sur un Silence du Nouveau Testament: l'Esprit de Dieu à l'Oeuvre dans le Cosmos et l'Humanité', *NTS* 33 (1987) 344-69.

Clark, D.K., 'Signs in Wisdom and John', *CBQ* 45 (1983) 201-209.

Clarke, E.G., *The Wisdom of Solomon* (Cambridge: CUP, 1973).

Clifford, R.J., *The Wisdom Literature* (Nashville: Abingdon Press, 1998).

Collins, J.J., *Between Athens and Jerusalem: Jewish Identity in the Hellenistic Diaspora* (New York: Crossroad, 1983).

—, 'Wisdom, Apocalypticism, and Generic Compatibility' in L.G. Perdue, B.B. Scott and W.J. Wiseman (eds.), *In Search of Wisdom: Essays in Memory of John G. Gammie* (Louisville: Westminster John Knox Press, 1993) 165-85.

—, *Jewish Wisdom in the Hellenistic Age* (Edinburgh: T&T Clark, 1998).

Collins, R.F., *These Things Have Been Written: Studies on the Fourth Gospel* (Louvain: Peeters Press, 1990).

Coloe, M., 'The Structure of the Johannine Prologue and Genesis 1', *Australian Biblical Review* 45 (1997) 40-55.

Colwell, E.C. and E.L. Titus, *The Gospel of the Spirit: A Study in the Fourth Gospel* (New York: Harper & Brothers, 1953).

Congar, Y.M.J., *I Believe in the Holy Spirit. Volume 1: The Holy Spirit in the 'Economy'* (Transl. D. Smith; London: Chapman, 1983).

Cortés, J.B., 'Yet another look at Jn 7,37-38', *CBQ* 29 (1967) 75-86.

Cory, C., 'Wisdom's Rescue: A New Reading of the Tabernacles Discourse (John 7:1-8:59)', *JBL* 116 (1997) 95-116.

Cotterell, F.P., 'The Nicodemus Conversation: A Fresh Appraisal', *ET* 96 (1984-85) 237-42.

Cotterell, [F.]P. and M.[M.B.] Turner, *Linguistics & Biblical Interpretation* (London: SPCK, 1989).

Crenshaw, J.L., 'The Book of Sirach: Introduction, Commentary, and Reflections' in L.E. Keck et. al. (eds.), *The New Interpreter's Bible: Volume V* (Nashville: Abingdon Press, 1997) 601-867.

Crouch, F.L., *Everyone Who Sees the Son: Signs, Faith, Peirce's Semeiothics, and the Gospel of John* (Duke University: Ph.D. dissertation, 1996; Ann Arbor: UMI, 1997).

Cullmann, O., *Early Christian Worship* (Transl. A.S. Todd and J.B. Torrance; London: SCM Press, 1953).

—, *Salvation in History* (London: SCM Press, 1967).

Culpepper, R.A., *Anatomy of the Fourth Gospel: A Study in Literary Design* (Philadelphia: Fortress Press, 1987).

—, 'The Theology of the Gospel of John', *Review and Expositor* 85 (1988) 417-32.

—, 'Reading Johannine Irony' in R.A. Culpepper and C.C. Black (eds.), *Exploring the Gospel of John: In Honor of D. Moody Smith* (Louisville: Westminster John Knox Press, 1996) 193-207.

—, *The Gospel and Letters of John* (Nashville: Abingdon Press, 1998).

Davies, J.G., 'The Primary Meaning of *ΠΑΡΑΚΛΗΤΟΣ*', *JThS* 4 (1953) 35-38.

Davies, M., *Rhetoric and Reference in the Fourth Gospel* (JSNT.S 69; Sheffield: JSOT Press, 1992).

Davis, J.A., *Wisdom and Spirit: An Investigation of 1 Corinthians 1.18-3.20 Against the Background of Jewish Sapiential Traditions in the Greco-Roman Period* (Lanham: University Press of America, 1984).

Davis, J.C., 'The Johannine Concept of Eternal Life as a Present Possession', *Restoration Quarterly* 27 (1984) 161-69.

Dimant, D., 'Qumran Sectarian Literature' in M.E. Stone (ed.), *Jewish Writings of the Second Temple Period: Apocrypha, Pseudepigrapha, Qumran Sectarian Writings, Philo, Josephus* (Assen: Van Gorcum, 1984) 483-550.

Dodd, C.H., *The Interpretation of the Fourth Gospel* (Cambridge: CUP, 1953).

Duke, P.D., *Irony in the Fourth Gospel* (Atlanta: John Knox Press, 1985).

Dunn, J.D.G., *Baptism in the Holy Spirit: A Re-examination of the New Testament Teaching on the Gift of the Spirit in relation to Pentecostalism today* (London: SCM Press, 1970).

—, 'The Washing of the Disciples' Feet in John 13:1-20', *ZNW* 61 (1970) 247-52.

—, 'John vi - A Eucharistic Discourse?', *NTS* 17 (1970-71) 328-38.

—, 'Spirit and Kingdom', *ET* 82 (1970-71) 36-40.

—, *Jesus and the Spirit: A Study of the Religious and Charismatic Experience of Jesus and the First Christians as Reflected in the New Testament* (London: SCM Press, 1975).

—, *Christology in the Making: A New Testament Inquiry into the Origins of the Doctrine of the Incarnation* (London: SCM Press, 1989²).

—, 'Let John be John: A Gospel for Its Time' in P. Stuhlmacher (ed.), *The Gospel and the Gospels* (Grand Rapids: Eerdmans, 1991) 293-322.

—, 'Baptism in the Spirit: A Response to Pentecostal Scholarship on Luke-Acts', *JPT* 3 (1993) 3-27.

Elliott, M.A., *The Survivors of Israel: A Reconsideration of the Theology of Pre-Christian Judaism* (Grand Rapids: Eerdmans, 2000).

Enns, P., *Exodus Retold: Ancient Exegesis of the Departure from Egypt in Wis 10:15-21 and 19:1-9* (Atlanta: Scholars Press, 1997).

Ensor, P.W., *Jesus and His >Works<: The Johannine Sayings in Historical Perspective* (WUNT II/85; Tübingen: Mohr Siebeck, 1996).

Epp, E.J., 'Wisdom, Torah, Word: The Johannine Prologue and the Purpose of the Fourth Gospel' in G.F. Hawthorne (ed.), *Current Issues in Biblical and Patristic Interpretation: Studies in Honor of Merrill C. Tenney Presented by His Former Students* (Grand Rapids: Eerdmans, 1975) 128-46.

Ervin, H.M, *Conversion-Initiation and the Baptism in the Holy Spirit: A critique of James D.G. Dunn, Baptism in the Holy Spirit* (Peabody: Hendrickson, 1984).

Esler, P.F., 'Community and Gospel in Early Christianity: A Response to Richard Bauckham's *Gospels for All Christians*', *SJTh* 51 (1998) 235-48.

Evans, C.A., *Word and Glory: On the Exegetical and Theological Background of John's Prologue* (JSNT.S 89; Sheffield: JSOT Press, 1993).

Fatehi, M., *The Spirit's Relation to the Risen Lord in Paul: An Examination of Its Christological Implications* (WUNT II/128; Tübingen: Mohr Siebeck, 2000).

Ferraro, G., *Lo Spirito e Cristo nel vangelo di Giovanni* (Studi Biblici 70; Brescia: Paideia Editrice, 1984).

Ferreira, J., *Johannine Ecclesiology* (JSNT.S 160; Sheffield: SAP, 1998).

Feuillet, A., 'Participation in the Life of God according to the Fourth Gospel' in A. Feuillet (ed.), *Johannine Studies* (Transl. T.E. Crane; New York: Alba House, 1964) 169-80.

—, 'The Principal Biblical Themes in the Discourse on the Bread of Life' in A. Feuillet (ed.), *Johannine Studies* (Transl. T.E. Crane; New York: Alba House, 1964) 53-128.

—, *Le Prologue du quatrième évangile: Étude de théologie johannique* (Paris: Desclée De Brouwer, 1968).

Fishbane, M., *The Garments of Torah: Essays in Biblical Hermeneutics* (Bloomington: Indiana University Press, 1989).

Foerster, W., 'Der Heilige Geist im Spätjudentum', *NTS* 8 (1961-62) 117-34.

Ford, J.M., *Redeemer — Friend and Mother: Salvation in Antiquity and in the Gospel of John* (Minneapolis: Fortress Press, 1997).

Forestell, J.T., *The Word of the Cross: Salvation as Revelation in the Fourth Gospel* (Rome: Biblical Institute Press, 1974).

—, 'Jesus and the Paraclete in the Gospel of John' in J. Plevnik (ed.), *Word and Spirit: Essays in Honor of David Michael Stanley, S.J. on his 60th Birthday* (Willowdale, Ontario: Regis College Press, 1975) 151-97.

Fortna, R.T., 'Source and Redaction in the Fourth Gospel's Portrayal of Jesus' Signs', *JBL* 89 (1970) 151-66.

—, 'From Christology to Soteriology: A Redaction-Critical Study of Salvation in the Fourth Gospel', *Interp* 27 (1973) 31-47.

—, *The Fourth Gospel and Its Predecessor: From Narrative Source to Present Gospel* (Edinburgh: T&T Clark, 1989).

Franck, E., *Revelation Taught: The Paraclete in the Gospel of John* (Lund: Gleerup, 1985).

Freed, E.D., 'The Manner of Worship in John 4:23f' in J.M. Myers, O. Reimherr and H.N. Bream (eds.), *Search the Scriptures: New Testament Studies in Honor of Raymond T. Stamm* (Leiden: Brill, 1969) 33-48.

—, 'Theological Prelude to the Prologue of John's Gospel', *SJTh* 32 (1979) 257-69.

Frey, J., '"Wie Mose die Schlange in der Wüste erhöht hat..." Zur frühjüdischen Deutung der "ehernen Schlange" und ihrer christologischen Rezeption in Johannes 3,14f.' in M. Hengel and H. Löhr (eds.), *Schriftauslegung im antiken Judentum und im Urchristentum* (WUNT 73; Tübingen, Mohr Siebeck, 1994) 153-205.

—, *Die johanneische Eschatologie II: Das johanneische Zeitverständnis* (WUNT 110; Tübingen: Mohr Siebeck, 1998).

—, *Die johanneische Eschatologie III: Die eschatologische Verkündigung in den johanneischen Texten* (WUNT 117; Tübingen: Mohr Siebeck, 2000).

Friedman, N., *Form and Meaning in Fiction* (Athens: University of Gregoria Press, 1975).

Gammie, J.G., 'Spatial and Ethical Dualism in Jewish Wisdom and Apocalyptic Literature', *JBL* 93 (1974) 356-85.

—, 'The Sage in Sirach' in J.G. Gammie and L.G. Perdue (eds.), *The Sage in Israel and the Ancient Near East* (Winona Lake: Eisenbrauns, 1990) 355-72.

Gaventa, B.R., 'The Archive of Excess: John 21 and the Problem of Narrative Closure' in R.A. Culpepper and C.C. Black (eds.), *Exploring the Gospel of John: In Honor of D. Moody Smith* (Louisville: Westminster John Knox Press, 1996) 240-52.

Gese, H., 'The Prologue to John's Gospel' in H. Gese (ed.), *Essays on Biblical Theology* (Minneapolis: Augsburg, 1981) 167-222.

Geyer, J., *The Wisdom of Solomon: Introduction and Commentary* (London: SCM Press, 1963).

Gilbert, M., 'Wisdom Literature' in M.E. Stone (ed.), *Jewish Writings of the Second Temple Period: Apocrypha, Pseudepigrapha, Qumran Sectarian Writings, Philo, Josephus* (Assen: Van Gorcum, 1984) 283-324.

Goodenough, E.R., *An Introduction to Philo Judaeus* (Oxford: Basil Blackwell, 1962²).

Goppelt, L., '"Ύδωρ' in *TDNT*, VIII:314-33.

Grabbe, L.L., *Wisdom of Solomon* (Sheffield: SAP, 1997).

Grassi, J.A., 'Eating Jesus' Flesh and Drinking His Blood: The Centrality and Meaning of John 6:51-58', *BTB* 17 (1987) 24-30.

Grayston, K., 'The Meaning of PARAKLĒTOS', *JSNT* 13 (1981) 67-82.

Grigsby, B.H., 'The Cross as an Expiatory Sacrifice in the Fourth Gospel', *JSNT* 15 (1982) 51-80.

—, '"If Any Man Thirsts...": Observations on the Rabbinic Background of John 7,37-39', *Bib* 67 (1986) 101-108.

Grundmann, W., *Der Zeuge der Wahrheit: Grundzüge der Christologie des Johannesevangeliums* (Berlin: Evangelische Verlagsanstalt, 1985).

Gundry-Volf, J., 'Spirit, Mercy, and the Other', *Theology Today* 51 (1995) 508-23.

Hamerton-Kelly, R.G., *Pre-existence, Wisdom, and the Son of Man: A Study of the Idea of Pre-existence in the New Testament* (SNTS.MS 21; Cambridge: CUP, 1973).

Hamid-Khani, S., *Revelation and Concealment of Christ: A Theological Inquiry into the Elusive Language of the Fourth Gospel* (WUNT II/120; Tübingen: Mohr Siebeck, 2000).

Harner, P.B., *Relation Analysis of the Fourth Gospel: A Study in Reader-Response Criticism* (New York: Edwin Mellen Press, 1993).

Harrington, D.J., *Wisdom Texts from Qumran* (London: Routledge, 1996).

Harris, E., *Prologue and Gospel: The Theology of the Fourth Evangelist* (JSNT.S 107; Sheffield: SAP, 1994).

Harris, R., *The Origin of the Prologue to St John's Gospel* (Cambridge: CUP, 1917).

Harvey, A.E., *Jesus on Trial: A Study in the Fourth Gospel* (London: SPCK, 1976).

—, 'Christ as Agent' in L.D. Hurst and N.T. Wright (eds.), *The Glory of Christ in the New Testament: Studies in Christology in Memory of George Bradford Caird* (Oxford: Clarendon Press, 1987) 239-50.

Hauck, F., 'Παροιμία' in *TDNT*, V:854-56.

Hays, R.B., *The Moral Vision of the New Testament: Community, Cross, New Creation: A Contemporary Introduction to New Testament Ethics* (San Francisco: Harper, 1996).

Heil, J.P., 'Jesus as the Unique High Priest in the Gospel of John', *CBQ* 57 (1995) 729-45.

Hengel, M., *Judaism and Hellenism: Studies in their Encounter in Palestine during the Early Hellenistic Period* (2 vols.; Transl. J. Bowden; London: SCM Press, 1974).

—, *The Johannine Question* (Transl. J Bowden; London: SCM Press, 1989).

Heron, A.I.C., *The Holy Spirit: The Holy Spirit in the Bible in the History of Christian Thought and in recent Theology* (London: Marshall Morgan & Scott, 1983).

Hildebrandt, W., *An Old Testament Theology of the Spirit of God* (Peabody: Hendrickson, 1995).

Hoegen-Rohls, C., *Der nachösterliche Johannes: Die Abschiedsreden als hermeneutischer Schlüssel zum vierten Evangelium* (WUNT II/84; Tübingen: Mohr Siebeck, 1996).

Hofius, O., 'Das Wunder der Wiedergeburt. Jesus Gespräch mit Nikodemus Joh 3,1-21' in O. Hofius and H.-C. Kammler (eds.), *Johannesstudien: Untersuchungen zur Theologie des vierten Evangeliums* (WUNT 88; Tübingen: Mohr Siebeck, 1996) 33-80.

Holwerda, D.E., *The Holy Spirit and Eschatology in the Gospel of John: A Critique of Rudolf Bultmann's Present Eschatology* (Kampen: Kok, 1959).

Hooke, S.H., 'The Spirit was not yet', *NTS* 9 (1962-63) 372-80.

Horbury, W., 'The Benediction of the *Minim* and Early Jewish-Christian Controversy', *JThS* 33 (1982) 19-61.

Horton, S.M., 'Holy Spirit, Doctrine of the' in S.M. Burgess, G.B. McGee and P.H. Alexander (eds.), *Dictionary of Pentecostal and Charismatic Movements* (Grand Rapids: Zondervan, 1988) 410-17.

Hultgren, A.J., *Christ and His Benefits: Christology and Redemption in the New Testament* (Philadelphia: Fortress Press, 1987).

Ibuki, Y., *Die Wahrheit im Johannesevangelium* (Bonn: Hanstein Verlag, 1972).

—, 'Viele glaubten an ihn — Auseinandersetzung mit dem Glauben im Johannesevangelium —', *Annual of the Japanese Biblical Institute* 9 (1983) 128-83.

Imschoot, P. van, 'L'action de l'Esprit de Jahvé dans l'Ancien Testament', *RSPhTh* 23 (1934) 553-87.

—, 'L'Esprit de Jahvé, source de vie dans l'Ancien Testament', *RB* 44 (1935) 481-501.

—, 'L'Esprit de Jahvé et l'alliance nouvelle dans l'Ancien Testament', *EThL* 13 (1936) 201-20.

—, 'Sagesse et Esprit dans l'Ancien Testament', *RB* 47 (1938) 23-49.

—, 'L'Esprit de Jahvé, principe de la vie morale dans l'Ancien Testament', *EThL* 16 (1939) 457-67.

—, *Theology of the Old Testament. Volume I: God* (Transl. K. Sullivan and F. Buck; New York: Desclée & Co., 1954).

Isaacs, M.E., *The Concept of Spirit: A Study of Pneuma in Hellenistic Judaism and its Bearing on the New Testament* (Heythrop Monographs 1; Huddersfield: Charlesworth, 1976).

—, 'The Prophetic Spirit in the Fourth Gospel', *Heythrop Journal* 24 (1983) 391-407.

Jacob, E., 'Wisdom and Religion in Sirach' in J.G. Gammie, W.A. Brueggemann, W.L. Humphreys and J.M. Ward (eds.), *Israelite Wisdom: Theological and Literary Essays in Honor of Samuel Terrien* (Missoula: Scholars Press, 1978) 247-60.

Johansson, N., *Parakletoi. Vorstellungen von Fürsprechern für die Menschen vor Gott in der alttestamentlichen Religion, im Spätjudentum und Urchristentum* (Lund: Gleerup, 1940).

Johnston, G., *The Spirit-Paraclete in the Gospel of John* (SNTS.MS 12; Cambridge: CUP, 1970).

Jones, L.P., *The Symbol of Water in the Gospel of John* (JSNT.S 145; Sheffield: SAP, 1997).

Jonge, M. de, *Jesus: Stranger from Heaven and Son of God: Jesus Christ and the Christians in Johannine Perspective* (SBL.SBS 11; edited and translated by J.E. Steely; Missoula: Scholars Press, 1977).

Kammler, H.-C., 'Jesus Christus und der Geistparaklet: Eine Studie zur johanneischen Verhältnisbestimmung von Pneumatologie und Christologie' in O. Hofius and H.-C. Kammler (eds.), *Johannesstudien: Untersuchungen zur Theologie des vierten Evangeliums* (WUNT 88; Tübingen: Mohr Siebeck, 1996) 87-190.

Kampen, J.I., 'The Diverse Aspects of Wisdom in the Qumran Texts' in P.W. Flint and J.C. Vanderkam (eds.), *The Dead Sea Scrolls after Fifty Years: A Comprehensive Assessment: Volume One* (Leiden: Brill, 1998) 211-43.

Kanagaraj, J.J., *'Mysticism' in the Gospel of John: An Inquiry into its Background* (JSNT.S 158; Sheffield: SAP, 1998).

—, 'The Implied Ethics of the Fourth Gospel: A Reinterpretation of the Decalogue', *TynB* 52 (2001) 33-60.

Käsemann, E., *The Testament of Jesus: A Study of the Gospel of John in the Light of Chapter 17* (Transl. G. Krodel; London: SCM Press, 1968).

Kasper, W., *Jesus The Christ* (Transl. V. Green; London: Burns & Oates, 1976).

Keener, C.S., 'The Function of Johannine Pneumatology in the Context of Late First Century Judaism' (Duke University: Ph.D. dissertation, 1991; Ann Arbor: UMI, 1992).

—, *The Spirit in the Gospels and Acts: Divine Purity and Power* (Peabody: Hendrickson, 1997).

Kim, D., 'The Church in the Gospel of John' (Cambridge: Ph.D. dissertation, 1999).

Knibb, M.A., *The Qumran Community* (Cambridge: CUP, 1987).

Knöppler, T., *Die theologia crucis des Johannesevangeliums: Das Verständnis des Todes Jesu im Rahmen der johanneischen Inkarnations- und Erhöhungschristologie* (WMANT 69; Neukirchen-Vluyn: Neukirchener Verlag, 1994).

Koester, C.[R.], 'Hearing, Seeing, and Believing in the Gospel of John', *Bib* 70 (1989) 327-48.

—, *Symbolism in the Fourth Gospel: Meaning, Mystery, Community* (Minneapolis: Fortress, 1995).

Kohler, H., *Kreuz und Menschwerdung im Johannesevangelium: Ein exegetisch-hermeneutischer Versuch zur johanneischen Kreuzestheologie* (AThANT 72; Zürich: Theologischer Verlag, 1987).

Koottumkal, S., *Words of Eternal Life: An Exegetical-Theological Study on the Life-giving Dimension of the Word of Jesus in the Fourth Gospel* (Rome: Pontificia Universitas Gregoriana, 1995).

Köstenberger, A.J., *The Missions of Jesus and the Disciples according to the Fourth Gospel: With Implications for the Fourth Gospel's Purpose and the Mission of the Contemporary Church* (Grand Rapids: Eerdmans, 1998).

Köstenberger, A.J. and P.T. O'Brien, *Salvation to the Ends of the Earth: A biblical theology of mission* (NSBT 11; Leicester: Apollos, 2001).

Kügler, J., 'Der König als Brotspender. Religionsgeschichtliche Überlegungen zu JosAs 4,7; 25,5 und Joh 6,15', *ZNW* 89 (1998) 118-24.

Kümmel, W.G., *The Theology of the New Testament: According to Its Major Witnesses Jesus — Paul — John* (Transl. J.E. Steely; London: SCM Press, 1974).

Kvalvaag, R.W., 'The Spirit in Human Beings in Some Qumran Non-Biblical Texts' in
F.H. Cryer and T.L. Thompson (eds.), *Qumran between the Old and New Testaments*
(JSOT.S 290; Sheffield: SAP, 1998) 159-80.

Kysar, R., *The Fourth Evangelist and His Gospel: An examination of contemporary
scholarship* (Minneapolis: Augsburg, 1975).

—, *John the Maverick Gospel* (Louisville: Westminster John Knox Press, 1993 [rev.
edn]).

—, 'The Dismantling of Decisional Faith: A Reading of John 6:25-71' in R.A. Culpepper
(ed.), *Critical Readings of John 6* (BIS 22; Leiden: Brill, 1997) 161-81.

Ladd, G.E., *A Theology of the New Testament* (Cambridge: Lutterworth Press, 1993 [rev.
edn]).

Laurentin, A., 'Le Pneuma dans la Doctrine de Philon', *EThL* 27 (1951) 390-437.

Leaney, A.R.C., 'The Johannine Paraclete and the Qumran Scrolls' in J.H. Charlesworth
(ed.), *John and Qumran* (London: Chapman, 1972) 38-61.

Lee, D.A., *The Symbolic Narratives of the Fourth Gospel: The Interplay of Form and
Meaning* (JSNT.S 95; Sheffield: JSOT Press, 1994).

Léon-Dufour, X., 'Towards a Symbolic Reading of the Fourth Gospel', *NTS* 27 (1981)
439-56.

Levison, J.R., 'Inspiration and the Divine Spirit in the Writings of Philo Judaeus', *JSJ* 26
(1995) 271-323.

—, 'Did the Spirit Withdraw from Israel? An Evaluation of the Earliest Jewish Data',
NTS 43 (1997) 35-57.

—, *The Spirit in First Century Judaism* (Leiden: Brill, 1997).

Liebert, E., 'That You May Believe: The Fourth Gospel and Structural Developmental
Theory', *BTB* 14 (1984) 67-73.

Liesen, J., *Full of Praise: An Exegetical Study of Sir 39,12-35* (JSJ.S 64; Leiden: Brill,
2000).

Lieu, J.M., *The Theology of the Johannine Epistles* (Cambridge: CUP, 1991).

Lincoln, A.T., 'Trials, Plots and the Narrative of the Fourth Gospel', *JSNT* 56 (1994) 3-
30.

—, *Truth on Trial: The Lawsuit Motif in the Fourth Gospel* (Peabody: Hendrickson,
2000).

—, 'The Fourth Gospel as Witness and the Beloved Disciple as Eyewitness',
(unpublished paper given at London Bible College, December 2000) 1-17.

Lindars, B., R.B. Edwards and J.M. Court, *The Johannine Literature: With an
Introduction by R. Alan Culpepper* (Sheffield: SAP, 2000).

Loader, W.R.G., 'The Central Structure of Johannine Christology', *NTS* 30 (1984) 188-
216.

—, *The Christology of the Fourth Gospel: Structure and Issues* (BET 23; Frankfurt:
Verlag Peter Lang, 1989).

Lys, D., *Rûach: Le Souffle dans l'Ancien Testament* (Paris: Presses Universitaires de
France, 1962).

Maier, G., *Mensch und freier Wille: Nach den jüdischen Religionsparteien zwischen Ben
Sira und Paulus* (WUNT 12; Tübingen: Mohr Siebeck, 1971).

Malatesta, E., 'The Spirit/Paraclete in the Fourth Gospel', *Bib* 54 (1973) 539-50.

Mansoor, M., *The Thanksgiving Hymns: Translated and Annotated with an Introduction*
(Leiden: Brill, 1961).

Marböck, J., 'Sir., 38,24 - 39,11: Der schriftgelehrte Weise. Ein Beitrag zu Gestalt und
Werk Ben Siras' in M. Gilbert (ed.), *La Sagesse de l'Ancien Testament* (BEThL 51;
Leuven: Leuven University Press, 1979) 293-316.

Martyn, J.L., *History & Theology in the Fourth Gospel* (Nashville: Abingdon, 1979²).

McGlynn, M., *Divine Judgement and Divine Benevolence in the Book of Wisdom* (WUNT II/139; Tübingen: Mohr Siebeck; 2001).

McKane, W., *Proverbs: A New Approach* (London: SCM Press, 1970).

McKinlay, J.E., *Gendering Wisdom the Host: Biblical Invitations to Eat and Drink* (JSOT.S 216; Sheffield: SAP, 1996).

Meeks, W.A., *The Prophet-King: Moses Traditions and the Johannine Christology* (NT.S 14; Leiden: Brill, 1967).

—, 'The Man from Heaven in Johannine Sectarianism', *JBL* 91 (1972) 44-72.

Menken, M.J.J., 'John 6,51c-58: Eucharist or Christology?', *Bib* 74 (1993) 1-26.

—, 'The Christology of the Fourth Gospel: A Survey of Recent Research' in M.C. De Boer (ed.), *From Jesus to John: Essays on Jesus and New Testament Christology in Honour of Marinus de Jonge* (JSNT.S 84; Sheffield: JSOT Press, 1993) 292-320.

—, 'The Origin of the Old Testament Quotation in John 7:38', *NT* 38 (1996) 160-75.

Menzies, R.P., *Empowered for Witness: The Spirit in Luke-Acts* (JPT.S 6; Sheffield: SAP, 1994).

Metzner, R., *Das Verständnis der Sünde im Johannesevangelium* (WUNT 122; Tübingen: Mohr Siebeck, 2000).

Michaelis, W., 'Zur Herkunft des johanneischen Paraklet-Titels' in A. Fridrichsen (ed.), *Coniectanea Neotestamentica XI* (Lund: Köpenhamn, 1947) 147-62.

Miller, R.J., 'Immortality and Religious Identity in Wisdom 2-5' in E.A. Castelli and H. Taussig (eds.), *Reimagining Christian Origins: A Colloquium Honoring Burton L. Mack* (Valley Forge: Trinity Press Int., 1996) 199-213.

Moeller, H.R., 'Wisdom Motifs and John's Gospel', *BETS* 6 (1963) 92-100.

Moloney, F.J., *The Johannine Son of Man* (Roma: Libreria Ateneo Salesiano, 1976).

—, 'From Cana to Cana (John 2:1-4:54) and the Fourth Evangelist's Concept of Correct (and Incorrect) Faith' in E.A. Livingstone (ed.), *Studia Biblica 1978: II. Papers on The Gospels* (JSNT.S 2; Sheffield: JSOT Press, 1980) 185-213.

Montague, G.T., *The Holy Spirit: Growth of a Biblical Tradition* (Peabody: Hendrickson, 1976).

Morgan-Wynne, J.E., 'References to Baptism in the Fourth Gospel' in S.E. Porter and A.R. Cross (eds.), *Baptism, the New Testament and the Church: Historical and Contemporary Studies in Honour of R.E.O. White* (JSNT.S 171; Sheffield: SAP, 1999) 116-35.

Morris, L., 'The Atonement in John's Gospel', *Criswell Theological Review* 3 (1988) 49-64.

Motyer, S., 'Method in Fourth Gospel Studies: A Way Out of the Impasse?', *JSNT* 66 (1997) 27-44.

—, *Your Father the Devil?: A New Approach to John and 'the Jews'* (Carlisle: Paternoster, 1997).

Moule, C.F.D., 'The Individualism of the Fourth Gospel', *NT* 5 (1962) 171-90.

—, 'The Holy Spirit in the Scriptures', *Church Quarterly* 3 (1970-71) 279-87.

—, *The Origin of Christology* (Cambridge: CUP, 1977).

Mowinckel, S., 'Die Vorstellungen des Spätjudentums vom heiligen Geist als Fürsprecher und der johanneische Paraklet', *ZNW* 32 (1933) 97-130.

Müller, T., *Das Heilsgeschehen im Johannesevangelium: Eine exegetische Studie, zugleich der Versuch einer Antwort an Rudolf Bultmann* (Zürich: Gotthelf-Verlag, 1961).

Müller, U.B., 'Die Parakletenvorstellung im Johannesevangelium', *ZThK* 71 (1974) 31-77.

—, 'Die Bedeutung des Kreuzestodes Jesu im Johannesevangelium: Erwägungen zur Kreuzestheologie im Neuen Testament', *Kerygma und Dogma* 21 (1975) 49-71.

Murphy, R.E., 'Wisdom and Salvation' in D. Durken (ed.), *Sin, Salvation, and the Spirit: Commemorating the Fiftieth Year of The Liturgical Press* (Collegeville: The Liturgical Press, 1979) 177-83.

—, *The Tree of Life: An Exploration of Biblical Wisdom Literature* (Grand Rapids: Eerdmans, 1996²).

—, *Proverbs* (WBC 22; Nashville: Nelson, 1998).

Nereparampil, L., 'Holy Spirit as Living Water', *Bible Bhashyam* 2 (1976) 141-52.

Neusner, J., 'What "the Rabbis" Thought: A Method and a Result. One Statement on Prophecy in Rabbinic Judaism' in J.C. Reeves and J. Kampen (eds.), *Pursuing the Text: Studies in Honor of Ben Zion Wacholder on the Occasion of his Seventieth Birthday* (JSOT.S 184; Sheffield: SAP, 1994) 303-20.

Neve, L., *The Spirit of God in the Old Testament* (Tokyo: Seibunsha, 1972).

Nicholson, G.C., *Death as Departure: The Johannine Descent-Ascent Schema* (SBL.DS 63; Chico: Scholars Press, 1983).

Nicol, W., *The Sēmeia in the Fourth Gospel: Tradition and Redaction* (NT.S 32; Leiden: Brill, 1972).

Nielsen, H.K., 'John's Understanding of the Death of Jesus' in J. Nissen and S. Pedersen (eds.), *New Readings in John: Literary and Theological Perspectives. Essays from the Scandinavian Conference on the Fourth Gospel Århus 1997* (JSNT.S 182; Sheffield: SAP, 1999) 232-54.

O'Day, G.R., *Revelation in the Fourth Gospel: Narrative Mode and Theological Claim* (Philadelphia: Fortress Press, 1986).

Oepke, A., '᾽Εν' in *TDNT*, II:537-43.

Oesterley, W.O.E. and G.H. Box, *The Religion and Worship of The Synagogue: An Introduction to the Study of Judaism from the New Testament Period* (London: Pitman, 1911²).

Okure, T., *The Johannine Approach to Mission: A Contextual Study of John 4:1-42* (WUNT II/31; Tübingen: Mohr Siebeck, 1988).

Osborne, G.R., 'Soteriology in the Gospel of John' in C.H. Pinnock (ed.), *The Grace of God, the Will of Man: A Case for Arminianism* (Michigan: Academic Books, 1989) 243-60.

Painter, J., 'The Farewell Discourses and the History of Johannine Christianity', *NTS* 27 (1981) 525-43.

—, 'Christology and the History of the Johannine Community in the Prologue of the Fourth Gospel', *NTS* 30 (1984) 460-74.

—, 'Tradition and Interpretation in John 6', *NTS* 35 (1989) 421-50.

—, *The Quest for the Messiah: The History, Literature and Theology of the Johannine Community* (Edinburgh: T&T Clark, 1993²).

—, 'Inclined to God: The Quest for Eternal Life — Bultmannian Hermeneutics and the Theology of the Fourth Gospel' in R.A. Culpepper and C.C. Black (eds.), *Exploring the Gospel of John: In Honor of D. Moody Smith* (Louisville: Westminster John Knox Press, 1996) 346-68.

Pascher, J., 'Der Glaube als Mitteilung des Pneumas nach Joh. 6,61-65', *Theologische Quartalschrift* 117 (1936) 301-21.

Pate, C.M., *The Reverse of the Curse: Paul, Wisdom, and the Law* (WUNT II/114; Tübingen: Mohr Siebeck, 2000).

Pazdan, M.M., *Discipleship as the Appropriation of Eschatological Salvation in the Fourth Gospel* (University of St. Michael's College: Ph.D. dissertation, 1982; Ann Arbor: UMI, 1998).

Pedersen, J., 'Wisdom and Immortality' in M. Noth and D.W. Thomas (eds.), *Wisdom in Israel and in the Ancient Near East* (Leiden: Brill, 1960) 238-46.

Perdue, L.G., *Wisdom & Creation: The Theology of Wisdom Literature* (Nashville: Abingdon Press, 1994).

Pillai, C.A.J., 'Advocate — Christ's Name for the Holy Spirit', *Bible Today* 30 (1967) 2078-81.

Pinto, B. de, 'Word and Wisdom in St John', *Scripture* 19 (1967) 19-27.

Pollard, T.E., 'The Father-Son and God-Believer Relationships according to St John: a Brief Study of John's Use of Prepositions' in M. de Jonge (ed.), *L'Évangile de Jean: Sources, rédaction, théologie* (BEThL 44; Leuven: Leuven University Press, 1977) 363-69.

Porsch, F., *Pneuma und Wort: Ein exegetischer Beitrag zur Pneumatologie des Johannesevangeliums* (FTS 16; Frankfurt: Knecht, 1974).

—, *Anwalt der Glaubenden: Das Wirken des Geistes nach dem Zeugnis des Johannesevangeliums* (Stuttgart: Katholisches Bibelwerk, 1978).

Potterie, I. de la, 'L'arrière-fond du thème johannique de vérité' in K. Aland, F.L. Cross, J. Danielou, H. Riesenfeld and W.C. van Unnik (eds.), *Studia Evangelica Vol. I* (Berlin: Akademie-Verlag, 1959) 277-94.

—, 'Οἶδα et γινώσκω: Les deux modes de la connaissance dans le quatrième évangile', *Bib* 40 (1959) 709-25.

—, 'L'Esprit Saint dans l'Evangile de Jean', *NTS* 18 (1971-72) 448-51.

—, 'The Paraclete', *Bible Bhashyam* 2 (1976) 120-40.

—, *La Vérité dans Saint Jean* (2 vols.; Rome: Biblical Institute Press, 1977).

—, 'Parole et Esprit dans S. Jean' in M. de Jonge (ed.), *L'Évangile de Jean: Sources, rédaction, théologie* (BEThL 44; Leuven: Leuven University Press, 1977) 177-201.

—, 'The Truth in Saint John' in J. Ashton (ed.), *The Interpretation of John* (Edinburgh: T&T Clark, 1997²) 67-82.

Potterie, I. de la and S. Lyonnet, *The Christian Lives by the Spirit* (Transl. J. Morriss; New York: Alba House, 1971).

Pratt, M.L., *Towards a speech act theory of literary discourse* (Bloomington: Indiana University Press, 1977).

Pryor, J.W., *John: Evangelist of the Covenant People. The Narrative & Themes of the Fourth Gospel* (Downers Grove: IVP, 1992).

Quast, K., *Peter and the Beloved Disciple: Figures for a Community in Crisis* (JSNT.S 32; Sheffield: JSOT Press, 1989).

Rabens, V., 'The Development of Pauline Pneumatology: A Response to F.W. Horn', *BZ* 43 (1999) 161-79.

Raurell, F., 'The Religious Meaning of "Doxa" in the Book of Wisdom' in M. Gilbert (ed.), *La Sagesse de l'Ancien Testament* (BEThL 51; Leuven: Leuven University Press, 1979) 370-83.

Rea, J., 'The Personal Relationship of Old Testament Believers to the Holy Spirit' in P. Elbert (ed.), *Essays on Apostolic Themes: Studies in Honor of Howard M. Ervin Presented to him by Colleagues and Friends on his Sixty-Fifth Birthday* (Peabody: Hendrickson, 1985) 92-103.

Rengstorf, K.H., 'Διδάσκω, κτλ.' in *TDNT*, II:135-65.

Rensberger, D., *Johannine Faith and Liberating Community* (Philadelphia: Westminster Press, 1988).

Riedl, J., *Das Heilswerk Jesu Nach Johannes* (Freiburg: Herder, 1973).

Ringe, S.H., *Wisdom's Friends: Community and Christology in the Fourth Gospel* (Louisville: Westminster John Knox Press, 1999).

Ringgren, H., *Word and Wisdom: Studies in the Hypostatization of Divine Qualities and Functions in the Ancient Near East* (Lund: Gleerup, 1947).

Robinson, J.A.T., *Redating the New Testament* (London: SCM Press, 1976).

Rowland, C., 'Apocalyptic, Mysticism, and the New Testament' in H. Cancik, H. Lichtenberger and P. Schäfer (eds.), *Geschichte — Tradition — Reflexion: Festschrift für Martin Hengel zum 70. Geburtstag. Band I Judentum* (Tübingen: Mohr Siebeck, 1996) 405-30.

Sanders, E.P., 'The Covenant as a Soteriological Category and the Nature of Salvation in Palestinian and Hellenistic Judaism' in R. Hamerton-Kelly and R. Scroggs (eds.), *Jews, Greeks and Christians: Religious Cultures in Late Antiquity. Essays in Honor of William David Davies* (Leiden: Brill, 1976) 11-44.

—, *Judaism: Practice and Belief, 63 BCE-66 CE* (London: SCM Press, 1992).

Sasse, H., 'Κοσμέω, κτλ.' in *TDNT*, III:867-98.

Schenke, L., 'The Johannine Schism and the "Twelve" (John 6:60-71)' in R.A. Culpepper (ed.), *Critical Readings of John 6* (BIS 22; Leiden: Brill, 1997) 205-19.

Schlier, H., *Besinnung auf das Neue Testament: Exegetische Aufsätze und Vortrage II* (Freiburg: Herder, 1964).

—, 'The Holy Spirit as interpreter according to St. John's Gospel', *Communio International Catholic Review* 1 (1974) 128-41.

Schnabel, E.J., *Law and Wisdom from Ben Sira to Paul: A Tradition Historical Enquiry into the Relation of Law, Wisdom, and Ethics* (WUNT II/16; Tübingen: Mohr Siebeck, 1985).

Schneiders, S.M., 'Born Anew', *Theology Today* 44 (1987) 189-96.

Schnelle, U., 'Johannes als Geisttheologe', *NT* 40 (1998) 17-31.

Schweizer, E., 'Πνεῦμα, πνευματικός' in *TDNT*, VI:389-451.

Scott, M., *Sophia and the Johannine Jesus* (JSNT.S 71; Sheffield: JSOT Press, 1992).

Scott, R.B.Y., *Proverbs-Ecclesiastes: Introduction, Translation, and Notes* (AncB 18; New York: Doubleday, 1979²).

Segovia, F.F., *Love Relationships in the Johannine Tradition: Agap☐/Agapan in 1 John and the Fourth Gospel* (SBL.DS 58; Missoula: Scholars Press, 1982).

—, '"Peace I Leave with You; My Peace I Give to You": Discipleship in the Fourth Gospel' in F.F. Segovia (ed.), *Discipleship in the New Testament* (Philadelphia: Fortress Press, 1985) 76-102.

—, *The Farewell of the Word: The Johannine Call to Abide* (Minneapolis: Fortress Press, 1991).

—, 'The Journey(s) of the Word of God: A Reading of the Plot of the Fourth Gospel', *Semeia* 53 (1991) 23-54.

Sekki, A.E., *The Meaning of Ruah☐at Qumran* (SBL.DS 110; Atlanta: Scholars Press, 1989).

Simon, U.E., 'Eternal Life in the Fourth Gospel' in F.L. Cross (ed.), *Studies in the Fourth Gospel* (London: Mowbray, 1957) 97-109.

Sjöberg, E., 'Πνεῦμα, πνευματικός' in *TDNT*, VI:375-89.

Skehan, P.W., *Studies in Israelite Poetry and Wisdom* (CBQ Monograph Series 1; Worcester, MA: Heffernan Press, 1971).

Skehan, P.W. and A.A. Di Lella, *The Wisdom of Ben Sira: A New Translation with Notes, Introduction and Commentary* (AncB 39; New York: Doubleday, 1987).

Smalley, S., 'Salvation Proclaimed: VIII. John 1²⁹⁻³⁴', *ET* 93 (1981-82) 324-29.

—, '"The Paraclete": Pneumatology in the Johannine Gospel and Apocalypse' in R.A. Culpepper and C.C. Black (eds.), *Exploring the Gospel of John: In Honor of D. Moody Smith* (Louisville: Westminster John Knox Press, 1996) 289-300.

—, *John: Evangelist and Interpreter* (Carlisle: Paternoster, 1998²).

Stadelmann, H., *Ben Sira als Schriftgelehrter. Eine Untersuchung zum Berufsbild des vor-makkabäischen Sōfēr unter Berücksichtigung seines Verhältnisses zu Priester-, Propheten- und Weisheitslehrertum* (WUNT II/6; Tübingen: Mohr Siebeck, 1980).

Staley, J.L., *The Print's First Kiss: A Rhetorical Investigation of the Implied Reader in the Fourth Gospel* (SBL.DS 82; Atlanta: Scholars Press, 1988).

Stanton, G.N., *The Gospels and Jesus* (OBS; Oxford: OUP, 1989).

—, 'The Communities of Matthew', *Interp* 46 (1992) 379-91.

Stenger, W., '"Der Geist ist es, der lebendig macht, das Fleisch nützt nichts" (Jo 6,63)', *Trierer Theologische Zeitschrift* 85 (1976) 116-22.

Stibbe, M.W.G., *John as Storyteller: Narrative criticism and the fourth gospel* (SNTS.MS 73; Cambridge: CUP, 1992).

—, *John's Gospel* (London: Routledge, 1994).

Stuart, S.S., 'A New Testament Perspective on Worship', *EvQ* 68 (1996) 209-21.

Suurmond, J.-J., *The Ethical Influence of the Spirit of God: An Exegetical and Theological Study with Special Reference to 1 Corinthians, Romans 7:14-8:30, and the Johannine Literature* (Fuller Theological Seminary: Ph.D. dissertation, 1983; Ann Arbor: UMI, 1985).

Talbert, C.H., 'The Myth of a Descending-Ascending Redeemer in Mediterranean Antiquity', *NTS* 22 (1976) 418-40.

Thomas, J.C., *Footwashing in John 13 and the Johannine Community* (JSNT.S 61; Sheffield: JSOT Press, 1991).

—, 'Max Turner's *The Holy Spirit and Spiritual Gifts: Then and Now* (Carlisle: Paternoster Press, 1996): An Appreciation and Critique', *JPT* 12 (1998) 3-22.

Thompson, M.M., *The Incarnate Word: Perspectives on Jesus in the Fourth Gospel* (original title *The Humanity of Jesus in the Fourth Gospel* [Philadelphia: Fortress, 1988]; Peabody: Hendrickson, 1988).

—, 'Eternal Life In The Gospel Of John', *Ex Auditu* 5 (1989) 35-55.

—, 'Thinking about God: Wisdom and Theology in John 6' in R.A. Culpepper (ed.), *Critical Readings of John 6* (BIS 22; Leiden: Brill, 1997) 221-46.

Thüsing, W., *Die Erhöhung und Verherrlichung Jesu im Johannesevangelium* (Münster: Verlag Aschendorff, 1970²).

Tobin, T.H., 'The Prologue of John and Hellenistic Jewish Speculation', *CBQ* 52 (1990) 252-69.

Tolmie, D.F., *Jesus' Farewell to the Disciples: John 13:1-17:26 in Narratological Perspective* (BIS 12; Leiden: Brill, 1995).

Tovey, D., *Narrative Art and Act in the Fourth Gospel* (JSNT.S 151; Sheffield: SAP, 1997).

Treves, M., 'The two Spirits of the Rule of the Community', *RdQ* 3 (1961) 449-52.

Trites, A.A., *The New Testament Concept of Witness* (SNTS.MS 31; Cambridge: CUP, 1977).

Trumbower, J.A., *Born from Above: The Anthropology of the Gospel of John* (HUTh 29; Tübingen: Mohr Siebeck, 1992).

Turner, M.M.B., 'The Concept of Receiving the Spirit in John's Gospel', *VoxEv* 10 (1977) 24-42.

—, 'Atonement and the Death of Jesus in John — Some Questions to Bultmann and Forestell', *EvQ* 62 (1990) 99-122.

—, 'The Spirit of Prophecy and the Power of Authoritative Preaching in Luke-Acts: A Question of Origins', *NTS* 38 (1992) 66-88.

—, *Power from on High: The Spirit in Israel's Restoration and Witness in Luke-Acts* (JPT.S 9; Sheffield: SAP, 1996).

—, 'Readings and Paradigms: A Response to John Christopher Thomas', *JPT* 12 (1998) 23-38.

—, *The Holy Spirit and Spiritual Gifts — Then and Now* (Carlisle: Paternoster, 1999 [rev. edn]).

—, 'Historical Criticism and Theological Hermeneutics of the New Testament' in J.B. Green and M.[M.B.] Turner (eds.), *Between Two Horizons: Spanning New Testament Studies and Systematic Theology* (Grand Rapids: Eerdmans, 2000) 44-70.

—, 'The Churches of the Johannine Letters as Communities of "Trinitarian" *Koinōnia*' in W. Ma and R.P. Menzies (eds.), *Spirit and Spirituality: Essays in Honor of Russell P. Spittler* (forthcoming, 2002).

—, 'Spirit in Philo' (unpublished notes), 1-6.

Turner, M.[M.B.] and G.M. Burge, '*The Anointed Community*: A Review and Response', *EvQ* 62 (1990) 253-68.

Twelftree, G.H., *Jesus The Miracle Worker: A Historical & Theological Study* (Downers Grove: IVP, 1999).

Van Leeuwen, R.C., 'Liminality and Worldview in Proverbs 1-9', *Semeia* 50 (1990) 111-44.

Vanhoozer, K.J., *Is there a meaning in this text?: The Bible, the reader and the morality of literary knowledge* (Leicester: Apollos, 1998).

Vawter, B., 'Ezekiel and John', *CBQ* 26 (1964) 450-58.

Verbeke, G., *L'Évolution de la Doctrine du Pneuma du Stoicisme à S. Augustin* (Paris: Desclée De Brouwer, 1945).

Wallace, D.B., *Greek Grammar Beyond the Basics: An Exegetical Syntax of the New Testament* (Grand Rapids: Zondervan, 1996).

Watt, J.G. van der, 'The Use of αἰώνιος in the Concept ζωὴ αἰώνιος in John's Gospel', *NT* 31 (1989) 217-28.

—, *Family of the King: Dynamics of Metaphor in the Gospel according to John* (BIS 47; Leiden: Brill, 2000).

Wedderburn, A.J.M., *Baptism and Resurrection: Studies in Pauline Theology against Its Graeco-Roman Background* (WUNT 44; Tübingen: Mohr Siebeck, 1987).

Wenham, D., 'Spirit and Life: Some Reflections on Johannine Theology', *Themelios* 6 (1980) 4-8.

Wenk, M., *Community-Forming Power: The Socio-Ethical Role of the Spirit in Luke-Acts* (JPT.S 19; Sheffield: SAP, 2000).

Wernberg-Møller, P., 'A Reconsideration of the two Spirits in the Rule of the Community (1Qserek III,13-IV,26)', *RdQ* 3 (1961) 413-41.

Westermann, C., 'Geist im Alten Testament', *Evangelische Theologie* 41 (1981) 223-30.

Whybray, R.N., *Proverbs* (NCeB; Grand Rapids:Eerdmans, 1994).

Wiarda, T., *Peter in the Gospels: Pattern, Personality and Relationship*, (WUNT II/127; Tübingen: Mohr Siebeck, 2000).

Wilckens, U., 'Σοφία κτλ.' in *TDNT*, VII:496-526.

Willett, M.E., *Wisdom Christology in the Fourth Gospel* (San Francisco: Mellen Research University Press, 1992).

Williams, J.T., 'Cultic Elements in the Fourth Gospel' in E.A. Livingstone (ed.), *Studia Biblica 1978: II. Papers on the Gospels* (JSNT.S 2; Sheffield: JSOT Press, 1980) 339-50.

Williamson, R., *Jews in the Hellenistic World: Philo* (Cambridge: CUP, 1989).

Windisch, H., 'Jesus and the Spirit in the Gospel of John' in J. Reumann (ed.), *The Spirit-Paraclete in the Fourth Gospel* (Transl. J.W. Cox; Philadelphia: Fortress, 1968) 27-38.

—, 'The Five Johannine Paraclete Sayings' in J. Reumann (ed), *The Spirit-Paraclete in the Fourth Gospel* (Transl. J.W. Cox; Philadelphia: Fortress, 1968) 1-26.

Winston, D., *The Wisdom of Solomon: A New Translation with Introduction and Commentary* (AncB 43; New York: Doubleday, 1979).

—, 'The Sage as Mystic in the Wisdom of Solomon' in J.G. Gammie and L.G. Perdue (eds.), *The Sage in Israel and the Ancient Near East* (Winona Lake: Eisenbrauns, 1990) 383-98.

—, 'Wisdom in the Wisdom of Solomon' in L.G. Perdue, B.B. Scott and W.J. Wiseman (eds.), *In Search of Wisdom: Essays in Memory of John G. Gammie* (Louisville: Westminster John Knox Press, 1993) 149-64.

—, 'Sage and Super-sage in Philo of Alexandria' in D.P. Wright, D.N. Freedman and A. Hurvitz (eds.), *Pomegranates and Golden Bells: Studies in Biblical, Jewish, and Near Eastern Ritual, Law, and Literature in Honor of Jacob Milgrom* (Winona Lake: Eisenbrauns, 1995) 815-24.

Witherington III, B., *Jesus the Sage: The Pilgrimage of Wisdom* (Minneapolis: Augsburg Fortress, 1994).

Woll, D.B., 'The Departure of "the Way": The First Farewell Discourse in the Gospel of John', *JBL* 99 (1980) 225-39.

Wood, W.J., *Epistemology: Becoming Intellectually Virtuous* (Leicester: Apollos, 1998).

Wright, N.T., *The New Testament and the People of God. Christian Origins and the Question of God Volume One* (London: SPCK, 1992).

—, *Jesus and the Victory of God. Christian Origins and the Question of God Volume Two* (London: SPCK, 1996).

Ziener, G., 'Weisheitsbuch und Johannesevangelium (I)', *Bib* 38 (1957) 396-418.

—, 'Weisheitsbuch und Johannesevangelium (II)', *Bib* 39 (1958) 37-60.

Zuck, R.B., 'A Theology of Proverbs' in R.B. Zuck (ed.), *Learning from the Sages: Selected Studies on the Book of Proverbs* (Grand Rapids: Baker Books, 1995) 99-110.

Index of References

Old Testament

Pseudepigrapha

Qumran

Philo

Rabbinic Literature

New Testament

Index of Authors

Index of Subjects

[Page numbers in *italics* indicate more sustained/important interactions or treatments.]

Index of Greek Words

καρπός
– φέρω καρπός 111, 139
καταβαίνω 111, 113, 175, 176, 198, 202
κοινωνία 111, 135, 223
κόλπος 224
κόσμος 161, 191, 239
κρίνω 240
κρίσις 121
κύριος 113, 115, 191

λαμβάνω/παραλαμβάνω 111, 129, 130,
   175
λόγος 20, 74, 75, 82, 115, 119
– ὁ λόγος σὰρξ ἐγένετο 203

μανθάνω 63
μαρτυρέω 111, 140, 226, 236, 240
μαρτυρία 111, 140
μένω 9, 111, 120, 135, 136, 138, 140,
   163, 191, 201, 222, 242
μέτρον 165
μιμνήσκομαι 133, 144
μνημονεύω 144
μονή
– ποιέω μονή 136

νίπτω
– πόδας νίπτω 243
νοέω 54, 134
νουθετέω 68
νοῦς 63

ὁδηγέω 226, 231
– ὁδηγεῖν ἐν τῇ ἀληθείᾳ 231
ὁδός 111, 113
– ὁδὸς ἀληθείας 113
– ὁδὸς ζωῆς 113
– ὁδὸς σοφίας 113
οἶδα 111, 126, 127, 128, 133, 134, 168,
   175, 191, 206
ὄνομα 107, 109
ὁράω 111, 124, 125, 133, 175
ὀρφανός 234
οὐσία 73

παιδεία 53, 57, 123
παραβολή 230
παραδίδωμι 253
παράκλητος 115, 215, 216, 217, 219, 220,
   228, 236

παροιμία 226, 230
παρρησία 230
πατήρ 224
πείθω 135
πέμπω 111, 112
περιπατέω 121
πηγή 60, 183
πινέτω 192
πιστεύω 8, 11, 12, 23, 24, 37, 107, 108,
   109, 111, 129, 130, 131, 132, 133,
   134, 135, 148, 175, 192, 206, 240
πίστις 37
πνεῦμα 48, 51, 65, 68, 69, 71, 72, 73, 74,
   75, 76, 77, 78, 79, 80, 81, 82, 83, 95,
   96, 97, 98, 161, 169, 170, 171, 172,
   173, 174, 188, 189, 203, 204, 223,
   224, 253, 254
– βαπτίζω ἐν πνεύματι ἁγίῳ 164
– (δίδωμι τὸ πνεῦμα) οὐκ ἐκ μέτρου 165
– ἐν πνεύματι καὶ ἀληθείᾳ 188
– οὔπω γὰρ ἦν πνεῦμα 145, 195
– παραδίδωμι τὸ πνεῦμα 253
– πνεῦμα ζωῆς 253
– πνεῦμα ζωτικόν 68, 254
– πνεῦμα συνέσεως 58
πνοή 73, 97
– πνοὴ ζωῆς 97, 253
πολύφροντις 63
πρότερος 202
προφήτης 115, 191

ῥῆμα 119

σάρξ 3, 6, 174, 203
σημεῖον 111, 146
σκληρός 207
σοφία 48, 54, 57, 63, 74, 75, 82, 94, 113,
   115, 123, 148, 184, 218
σύμβολον 146
– σύμβολον σωτηρίας 146
σύνδικος 216
σύνεσις 57, 58, 94, 198
συνήγορος 216
σῴζω 111, 115
σωτήρ 115, 191
σωτηρία 111, 115, 146

τελειόω 116
τελέω 116, 253
τόπος 188

Printed in Great Britain
by Amazon

57162054R00188